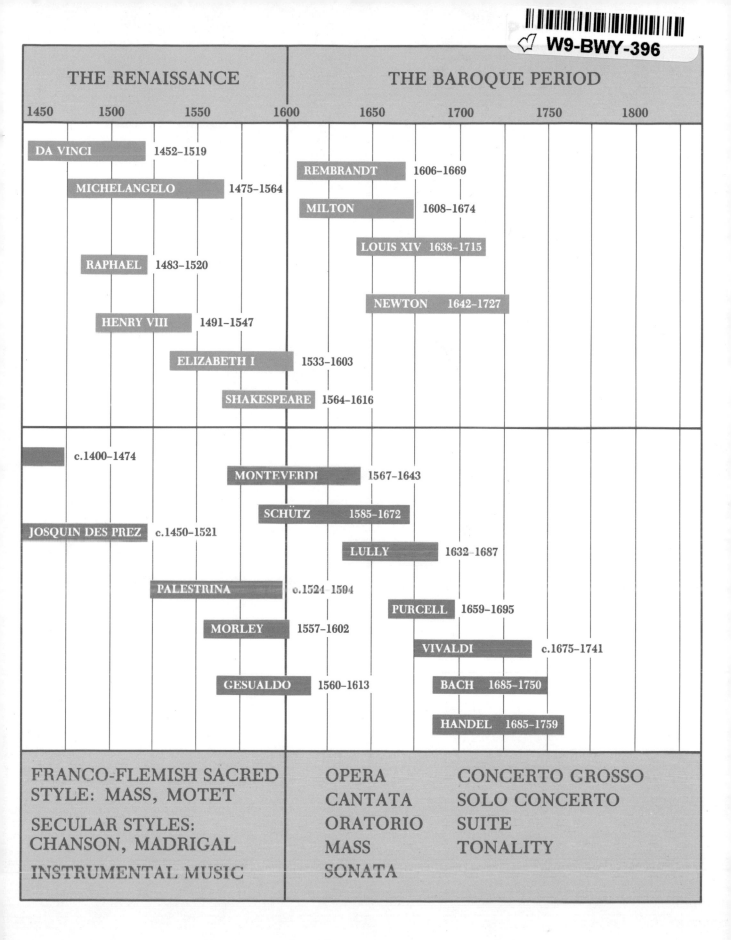

THE RENAISSANCE

THE BAROQUE PERIOD

1450　1500　1550　1600　1650　1700　1750　1800

DA VINCI　1452–1519

MICHELANGELO　1475–1564

REMBRANDT　1606–1669

MILTON　1608–1674

RAPHAEL　1483–1520

LOUIS XIV　1638–1715

NEWTON　1642–1727

HENRY VIII　1491–1547

ELIZABETH I　1533–1603

SHAKESPEARE　1564–1616

c.1400–1474

MONTEVERDI　1567–1643

SCHÜTZ　1585–1672

JOSQUIN DES PREZ　c.1450–1521

LULLY　1632–1687

PALESTRINA　c.1524–1594

PURCELL　1659–1695

MORLEY　1557–1602

VIVALDI　c.1675–1741

GESUALDO　1560–1613

BACH　1685–1750

HANDEL　1685–1759

FRANCO-FLEMISH SACRED
STYLE: MASS, MOTET

SECULAR STYLES:
CHANSON, MADRIGAL

INSTRUMENTAL MUSIC

OPERA　CONCERTO GROSSO
CANTATA　SOLO CONCERTO
ORATORIO　SUITE
MASS　TONALITY
SONATA

EXPERIENCING MUSIC

Richard Wingell

University of Southern California

Alfred

ALFRED PUBLISHING CO., INC.

The cover art is one piece from a suite of five original and embossed lithographs by Alvar entitled *Comenca La Música*. It is used with permission of the publisher, Edward Newman, Incorporated.

Library of Congress Cataloging in Publication Data

Wingell, Richard, 1936–
    Experiencing music

    Includes index.
    1. Music—Analysis, appreciation.   I.   Title
MT6.W565E9   780'.1'5   80-26637

ISBN 0-88284-116-5

Current printing last digit: 10   9   8   7   6   5   4   3   2   1

Music Acknowledgments

Illustration Acknowledgments

Archiv fur Kunst & Geschichte, Berlin: 106, 311.

Artist Consultants, Inc: 436.

Babbitt, Milton: 345, 396.

Bayreuth Press Office: 328.

Bennett, Tony: 448.

Bettmann Archive: 14, 39, 61, 68, 89, 111, 113, 121, 123, 125, 138, 142, 161, 168, 172, 182, 201, 205, 217, 219, 224, 261, 267, 275, 276, 282, 296, 298, 300, 307, 317, 326, 353, 355, 360, 373, 380, 389, 410, 411, 414, 433, 440.

Bildarchiv'd ost. Nationalbibliothek: 226.

Birnau: 116.

Boberg, George: 352.

Brother Publishing Co.: 11.

Bulloz: 304.

California Chamber Symphony: 184.

Leo Castelli: 342.

Chandos Productions: 439.

Culver Pictures: 405, 406, 408, 411, 412, 416, 436, 443.

The Detroit Institute Arts: 166.

Editorial Photo Archives: 38, 155, 180, 254, 274, 290, 319, 334, 371.

French Government Tourist Office: 74, 121.

Giraudon: 257.

Italian Government Tourist Office: 77.

Greek Tourist Office: 177.

Kaufman Eisenberg & Co. Inc.: 451.

The Louvre, Paris: 252, 270, 287, 303.

Lucasfilm, Ltd: 17.

Metropolitan Museum of Art, N.Y.:88, 99.

Museo Teatrale alla Scala: 236.

Museum of Fine Arts, Boston: 244.

Museum of Modern Art, N.Y.: 343.

National Gallery, London: 147.

National Gallery of Art, Washington D.C.: 178.

National Library, France: 82.

N.Y. Metropolitan Opera Assn.: 231, 234, 255, 263, 281, 351, 381.

N.Y. Public Library: 391.

Oxford University Press: 249.

Park Recording Co.: 430.

P.C.P.A.: 417.

Philadelphia Museum of Art: 20, 60.

The Picture Group Inc.: 9, 441.

Popperfoto: 438.

Pryor-Menz-Lee Attractions: 430.

RCA & A&M Associated Labels: 258.

Royal College of Music, London: 164, 279.

Selmer Co., Elkhart, IN.: 26, 27, 28, 30, 31, 32, 34, 35, 36.

Martha Slope: 289.

Stedelijk Museum: XX.

Sutton Artists Corp.:436

Paul Tanner: 431.

UNESCO: 13.

Universitats Bibliothek, Heidelberg: 76.

Viscount L'Isle Collection: 105.

Baron Wolman: 7.

Preface

This book is the result of years of experience teaching music courses to general students, and the conviction that none of the existing texts fully met my needs as a teacher. The goals and overall design of most of the Introduction of Music texts are quite similar, being designed to develop interested, informed listeners. In my judgment, however, two important understandings that are essential to the way these goals are reached are either not pursued in the standard texts, or not utilized fully or consistently. This book was written to create a text that would be designed on teaching approaches that I found successful in the classroom.

First, we must understand that the student in this sort of course is different from the music major. Therefore, a textbook for an Introduction to Music course is neither a music history text nor a theory text. It cannot rely on music notation to explain the music experience, nor can it assume any performing experience on the part of the student. However, the student does enter the course with some background and experience that can be useful in discussing the musical experience, providing that the instructor is sensitive and creative enough to use that background as a constant reference point. Today's undergraduate student grew up surrounded by film, television, and popular music. In addition, he is currently studying literature, writing, political and social history, and many other disciplines. As a result, the teacher of music courses for general students must teach by analogy more than one would in courses for music majors. This book searches constantly for something in the student's experience that will amplify whatever topic is under discussion. Thus the book is designed to lead to the understanding of the musical experience, and to create informed listeners who will be able to make intelligent choices as music consumers in the future.

Second, we must understand that everything in the book is intended to change the way the student listens. All the technical information, or biographical and historical discussion, exists only to improve the listening experience and make it more meaningful. Whatever is discussed in the book should be useful in whatever musical experience the student is involved with in the future.

The emphasis on listening is demonstrated most clearly in the visual listening guides which accompany every extended discussion of a specific musical work. The guides are graphic depictions of the events and structures of the works discussed, and are intended to be used as an aid whenever the student listens to music, in the classroom and in the listening laboratory or in his or her own room. My experience has been that students have a very difficult time making sense of the musical experience on their own. In class, with the instructor's guidance, a work might make sense, and they might be able to follow its development. However, when listening on their own, they often feel completely lost. With these guides, the student's individual listening time will be as efficient and instructive as the time spent listening in class. Since musical notation is a mystery to most general students, and complex orchestral scores are completely confusing, the guides use colors, shapes, verbal clues, and precise timings to make the organization of the musical events clear. Once they get used to the standard devices used in the guides, students will be able to follow the music, aware at all times of where they are in the structure and development of the work. The guides have another useful side effect — comparison of the guides for works from different periods makes the differences between periods visually clear. Compare the guide for the first movement of Haydn's "London" Symphony (p. 199) to the one for the first movement of Beethoven's "Eroica" (p. 272). The obvious differences of proportion and emphasis make a striking visual statement about the contrasting approaches to symphonic form during the Classic and Romantic periods, and make that statement more effectively than several paragraphs describing the ways Romantic composers modified those forms. Note that the guides are keyed precisely to the recording set that accompanies the book; they graphically illustrate any performance of the work, but the timings indicated relate to this specific performance. If a class or individual student uses the recordings provided, and first checks the accuracy of the speed of their turntable, they can rely on the indicated timings. If an instructor chooses to substitute another recorded performance, changes may have to be made in the timings of the guides. My hope is that after a quarter or a semester listening with the aid of instructor and guides, the student will listen to whatever music he or she encounters from then on in a different manner, with greater understanding and critical judgment.

Now, let's look at the organization of the text. The book first introduces the elements of music and follows them with a chronological survey of the history of music. The elements section strives for clarity and brevity, and utilizes analogies from other fields and experiences to explain musical concepts. All necessary technical terms are explained the first time they appear and a glossary is provided. The key chapter of the elements section is Chapter 5, which uses all the information about individual musical elements in a synthetic way. That chapter deals with two widely divergent musical experiences, showing how style is the result of a series of decisions about how each of the elements will be treated. In other words, the elements treated separately in the previous chapters are put back together in the musical experience in Chapter 5.

Chapter 6 begins the chronological survey of music. Each of the historical sections follows a standard pattern. The first chapter is an overview of the history, spirit, and aesthetics of the period, using examples from literature, architecture, and art to illustrate the aesthetic goals pursued by the period's music as well. The second chapter of each section treats the new musical developments of each period, including the changing place of the musician in society. Color and black and white photos and illustrations are profusely used to reinforce the concepts being discussed. The remaining chapters discuss specific musical works, generally as examples of larger trends. In each of these chapters, a brief biography places the composer in his context; a verbal description of the work follows, including single-line musical examples; finally, a visual listening guide is provided.

Note that the sections discussing the later historical periods are longer than the sections on earlier periods, since there are more chapters on individual works. The twentieth century section includes two longer chapters which survey the history of musical theater in America, and the worlds of jazz and popular music; several examples of music in these styles are discussed in detail, and listening guides are provided. More musical works are discussed in the book than can possibly be dealt with in the length of time devoted to most courses of this type; materials and listening guides not used in class can be utilized by the student outside of class. The Instructor's Manual that accompanies the text includes several varied outlines for courses of different durations and emphases, as well as lists of alternate selections. The Study Guide reinforces everything taught in one text with unique as well as traditional activities.

It is my fond hope that this book will prove to be a useful tool for instructors and students in introductory music courses, and that it will be useful in courses of varied focus and emphasis. If this text reaches its goal of helping students understand their own musical experience, and illuminates the fascinating art of music for them, it will not only have served its usefulness for as long as the course lasts, but will also enrich their leisure time for years to come, and involve them more deeply and personally in one of man's sublimest arts.

I am indebted to scores of people not only for their help in the long and involved process of writing and publishing this book, but also for helping to refine and focus the concepts and approaches that underlie it. I am first indebted to generations of students whom I taught in an introductory course; their questions, their discussion, even the outrage of one student who stormed out of class, offended by an example of avant-garde music, have helped form my convictions about how materials should be organized and presented. If the book succeeds in accomplishing its goals, the credit is due in large measure to those students.

I am also indebted to my colleagues in music at the University of Southern California and elsewhere; discussion of the special challenge of teaching music for general students has helped refine my goals and methodology.

Several friends deserve special thanks for their patient tolerance of long discussions of the project's progress and problems; they have provided helpful insights as well as unflagging encouragement. Among this group I would single out especially Robert Elias and Kate Gebr-Franz, who was generous not only with her enthusiastic encouragement, but also with her services as a virtuoso typist.

I also wish to thank the reviewers for their careful reading of the manuscript and their many helpful suggestions and criticisms.

For the actual production of the book, I must of course thank all the people at the Alfred Publishing Company, especially Sandy Feldstein, John O'Reilly, and Joe Cellini. I am especially indebted to Sandy Feldstein for his constant supervision of every phase of the project, and for the hours he spent transforming rough sketches of the listening guides into their precise and beautiful final form.

Finally, I wish to acknowledge the constant support of my family—my wife Jill, and my children, Jessica and Jeffrey. They tolerated abrupt changes in schedules and plans, and remained excited about the book even when I was not. In gratitude I dedicate this book to them.

More About the Listening Guides

The listening guides are visual representations of the musical examples discussed in the text. They are designed to guide the student's listening while reinforcing the understanding of concepts, style, form, and design.

The sample below is the introduction section of the First Movement of Haydn's *Symphony No. 104.* All of the musical happenings are visually represented, related to a time line, so the listener can always be sure of exactly where he or she is in the total structure of the composition. The height of the blocks indicate volume and their width shows duration. The first block is loud, through 19 seconds, followed by a brief pause, indicated by the white space. This is followed by a softer theme which gets louder before the full orchestra enters at 58 seconds. Instrument names are indicated as another guide post for the listener. Keys are indicated to reinforce concepts of form.

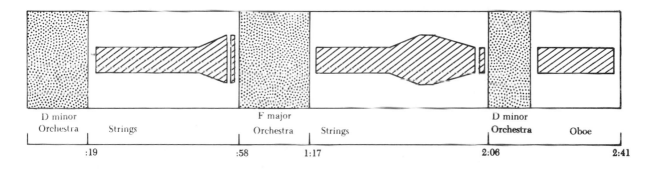

| D minor | | F major | | | D minor | |
| Orchestra | Strings | Orchestra | Strings | | Orchestra | Oboe |

| :19 | :58 | 1:17 | 2:06 | 2:41 |

Color or dot pattern schemes afford instant recognition of different themes and transition material, and overall structure is reinforced by dividing the guides into the appropriate groupings of lines. For example, the first movement of this symphony is in sonata-allegro form. The guide, therefore, is divided to show the Exposition, Development, and Recapitulation sections. (See the complete listening guide on page 199. We feel that these guides will add greatly to your musical understanding and enjoyment.

The original artistic concept for the guides was developed by Frank Nulf and Sandy Feldstein in the mid-1960's as a way to involve audiences in the listening process. These artistic ideas united with Richard Wingell's theoretical and analytical concepts developed into the listening guides as they now appear. Frank Nulf is presently Professor of Art at the University of Regina, Regina Saskatchewan, Canada. His works appear in many of the major galleries of the world.

Contents

PART II   MUSIC IN THE MIDDLE AGES AND RENAISSANCE

PART III   MUSIC IN THE BAROQUE PERIOD

PART **IV**   MUSIC IN THE CLASSICAL ERA

PART VI MUSIC IN THE TWENTIETH CENTURY

PART I

Music and Man

Marc Chagall. *Violinist*, 1912-13 (Stedelijk Museum, Amsterdam).

CHAPTER 1

Music in Man's Experience

The impulse to create music—to sing, to dance, to while away leisure hours experimenting with a musical instrument—is one of the deepest and most universal traits of man. Music has been an important part of every culture, every tribe, and every civilization in the long and involved history of man. All over the world, in huge urban centers and small villages, in areas where tribal cultures still survive the way they were thousands of years ago, as well as in fast-moving cultures like our own, children chant as they play, mothers sing lullabies to their babies, workers hum in rhythm with their tasks, communities have special songs for all their important occasions, and friends gather during leisure time to make music together.

In our own culture, music is pervasive and inescapable. A child watching Saturday morning cartoons, a teenager enjoying a feature film, and an adult viewing a situation comedy all hear music, whether or not they consciously *listen* to it. Tests have shown that school children, who may not be able to name the president of their country or to demonstrate any awareness of current events, can sing commercial jingles, recognize the theme music from hit movies and television shows, and learn almost anything if it is presented to them in the form of a catchy tune.

We should note at the outset that music has a different place in our culture than it did in previous eras of Western civilization. Because we live in a highly technological age, we have available to us a wondrous array of gadgets that did not exist thirty years ago, gadgets that make it very easy for us to experience music. Long-playing records, invented in 1948, give us access to popular hits, classical music from all ages, music of many other cultures, sound track albums from films, and original cast albums from Broadway musicals. Miniaturization of electronic components has made it possible to create inexpensive, easily portable radios, so that one never need be without music. The ubiquitous transistor radio has created a new social problem: one person's right to surround himself

"How would YOU like it if I put Guy Lombardo on full-blast?"

with his favorite music may interfere with another person's right *not* to be subjected to music he does not care for. As a result, people have become very sensitive about what they regard as invasions of their sound environment.

The ease of access to all sorts of music in our culture has two important consequences for us as music consumers. First, we have gradually lost much of our ability to perform. As recently as the 1940's, families frequently owned pianos or other instruments and entertained themselves by playing and singing together. The pervasiveness of television in our country has made it too easy to be a passive consumer of entertainment, rather than a creator of our own amusements. The tendency of our educational system to regard music as a "frill" that can be cut from a budget when money gets tight has encouraged this trend. In some ways, music in our culture is like sports: both have become the exclusive province of a few stars who train in the hope of a career in the field, rather than an activity for all youngsters.

The second consequence of the easy availability of all sorts of music is that the intelligent person has the responsibility of choosing the music he or she will enjoy. Like it or not, we are automatically subjected to an immense amount of music each day of our lives—on television, in the doctor's office and the super-

"Mr. Wallace is on another line. Will you hold, and if so, do you want Bach, rock or dentist-chair pop?"

market, in elevators, and in shops of all kinds. We can drift passively through all of these musical experiences and waste our innate musical ability memorizing advertising jingles, or we can experience various styles of music, try to understand music better, and choose the kinds of musical experiences—the records, the concerts, and the radio stations—that we really like.

Most people go through a series of phases in their growing awareness and appreciation of music. They focus on one style of music as adolescents, move away from that style as young adults, and continue to change their musical tastes throughout their lives. This process of change can be very satisfying so long as one continues to experiment with different styles of music. Because such a wide variety is available to us, the mature approach is to make our own decisions, rather than to accept passively whatever is popular with one's peer group or whatever the record companies are aggressively marketing at any particular moment.

If one is to make individual choices, one needs to be informed and to be receptive to many types of music. That is what this book is about. We will discuss the elements of music, so that you have some information about how music works, information that is useful in understanding and discussing any type of music. We will also discuss Western art music and its development, so that you will understand that particular musical tradition with all of its distinct styles of music. The goal is to help you understand the musical experience so that you can get deeper into any musical experience and make intelligent and satisfying choices for yourself as a listener and as a performer.

THE MEANINGS OF MUSIC

One reason for the pervasiveness of music in human culture and for its powerful appeal to all of us is that it seems to relate closely to some of our deepest instincts. Like poetry, music seems to be able to express powerful feelings that ordinary language is not capable of expressing. Even though our lives and aspirations may be much different from those of the members of other cultures, music speaks to us in much the same way it has always spoken to all human beings. To understand music's appeal and importance to man, it is necessary to look at some of the important facets of human life with which music is associated.

Music and Community

One of our most powerful instincts is the urge to bond together in groups of similar persons with similar dreams and concerns. Nearly all communities, from the local Brownie troop to the counterculture of the sixties, have had their own special music. Music is one of the most powerful ways we express our solidarity with the groups to which we belong. To an extent, we can define ourselves and our place in these groups with a list of songs. Anyone who sang "We Shall Overcome" during the sixties felt the power of the statement that song made. When young people gather at rock festivals, it is the music that binds them together as a group and expresses their unity with each other and their separateness from other groups in their culture.

Religious Music

An easy example of the community aspect of music is its place in religion. Each religious group and congregation has its favorite musical expressions. A group's hymns and songs are a powerful way of expressing group solidarity. Congregations get very upset if the choirmaster changes the musical menu or departs from "traditional" and "appropriate" music. People want to sing familiar music, because of love for the tradition in which they were brought up and unwillingness to tolerate change in what they regard as an island of stability in a world that is changing with frightening speed. There is a thrill in the physical activity of singing with an enthusiastic congregation, a thrill it would be hard to explain in words. The singing seems to express feelings of loyalty and of belonging that are deep and complex.

Patriotic Music

Music is also one of the best ways we express our patriotism, our love for our country. No one knows the words of the second verse of "The Star-Spangled Banner," and few people are comfortable with its wide melodic range. In purely

The Woodstock festival, summer, 1969, unified thousands of young people through music.

musical terms, it is not the world's most successful national anthem. But it still works, and something still stirs in our American hearts when we hear it. Many other patriotic songs have the same effect. "God Bless America," "America the Beautiful," and other songs help us to express our deep feelings about our country. Other countries have their own special songs. "God Save the Queen," "The Marseillaise," and "Oh Canada" have special meaning for citizens of England, France, and Canada.

Music and Ritual

Outside the worship services of organized religions, music is connected with all important rituals. It is hard to imagine a graduation without "Pomp and Circumstance" or some similar solemn piece; it is also difficult to imagine a birthday party without "Happy Birthday to You," or a New Year's Eve celebration without "Auld Lang Syne." That last example is a particularly interesting one, because it is surely not the words that explain the appeal of the song. Sing it to yourself. Do you have any idea what those words mean? Despite the strange Scottish dialect, somehow the song *means* New Year's, and it is always sung just at midnight, to mark the ritual turn of the year. Weddings, funerals, and all important human occasions are marked with music . Music is the way we say the things that are hard to say in words, the way families or groups say the things that mean the most to them, and the way we make a statement together about life's important realities.

Love Songs

Finally, music is the way we communicate perhaps the most important reality of all—love. If we were to excise all the love songs from the world's music, perhaps half of all the music that exists would disappear. Each generation has its own styles of music—the romantic ballads of the forties probably sound dated to you—but each generation has its love songs. Love, requited or unrequited, blissful or painful, happy or full of problems, remains the theme of much of the music in any style you can name—opera, rock, country, or jazz. Whatever is important but difficult to put into words, man has always sung. Music is basic to human life and to our deepest feelings.

TYPES OF MUSICAL EXPERIENCE

It is true that music is a universal experience, an important part of man's culture in all societies and at all times in human history. It is also true that there are different types of music. While all music has melody, rhythm, and harmony, some major types of music are designed, presented, and enjoyed in ways that are different and worth discussing.

Popular Music

By far the most familiar type of music in our culture is popular music. Radios blare it all day long, record stores are filled with the latest pop records, and America now exports its popular culture as successfully as its junk food. Within the general category of "popular" music, there is an almost infinite variety. A scholar interested in classifying varieties of popular music could spend a lifetime listing all of the styles that have appeared on the scene in the past fifty years. Some of these styles have persisted, and some have descended into obscurity as

The Rolling Stones, with lead singer Mick Jagger.

quickly as they have arisen, despite the incredible talent and energy invested in their production and promotion. Popular music of recent vintage includes artists as different as Frank Sinatra and Mick Jagger, or Barbra Streisand and Janis Joplin. The sentimental ballads and jitterbug tunes of the forties, the rock and roll of the fifties, rock, and the disco of the seventies are all popular music. The folk songs of Joan Baez and Joni Mitchell are popular music, and so is all jazz, from early Dixieland to the free and fusion jazz of the seventies. The Beatles, The Who, Kiss, and hundreds of other groups belong in this category, as does the whole world of country music, with all of its varieties and hundreds of performers. Within the world of rock, even a casual observer can see constant style shifts and splinterings, all of which have their notable groups and their loyal fans. Just to name a few, there are such different styles as rock and roll, hard rock, soft rock, bubble-gum rock, jazz rock, heavy metal, punk rock, Latin rock, and New Wave. Any such list is obsolete by the time it appears in print because of rapid change in the pop field.

Why do we classify all of these different types of music under one heading? Or can we even do so? Yes, we can. Although lumping all of these types of music in one category may seem to be an oversimplification, there are some important characteristics that are true of all the diverse styles we group together as popular music. First and most fundamentally, popular music is **performer's music**, not composer's music. In other words, the important person in popular music is the performer. You are not interested in buying a recording of a song you have heard on the radio if it is recorded by someone other than the performers you heard. In record stores, records are classified by the group or singer, not by composer, the way classical records are listed. If you think of three songs you have heard and liked recently, you probably cannot name the composers of these songs. Often the performers of popular music are the composers as well, recording their own material, but that isn't critical and that isn't what the record buyer is concerned about. Whereas the classical record buyer, or the student of classical music, knows names of composers, the popular music world revolves around performers. In the sixties, rock musicians became our cultural heroes, and millions of teenagers dreamed at one time or another of becoming rock stars and achieving the same sort of fame and financial success.

It is true that different versions of the same classical selections differ in subtle ways that real fans or other musicians can spot easily, and some classical music fans restrict their record buying to their favorite performers, conductors, or orchestras. Opera fans are especially notable in this regard, and some purchase their records by singer rather than by work or composer, but that still does not change the fundamental distinction. When you buy the sheet music of a popular song, you get only the skeleton—the basic melody, rhythm, and chord patterns. As you are aware, the sheet music does not include the particular touches, the excitement, the individual genius and sparkle that simply cannot be put on a page. When you buy the score of a classical selection, on the other hand, you have the same score the performer has, with all of the notes that he or she plays. In other words, you get what the composer wrote. Popular music, whether it is country music, jazz, a forties ballad, or a rock tune, is created afresh and spontaneously each time it is performed. As you may realize if you have been disappointed by a live concert of a favorite individual or group, the performance is affected by how the group feels at the time, or how the audience responds. If a group is exhausted or not getting along, or if the audience is restless or unresponsive, somehow the performance doesn't catch fire, despite the talent of the group and the eagerness of the audience. On the other hand, the right night, the right audience, and the right "vibes" between performers can produce a kind of excitement and electricity that is simply not available, at least not in the same way, in other types of music.

The Music Business

There are two other important facts to point out about popular music, at least as it exists in the early eighties. First, it is a world of enormous financial risks, successes, and failures. Popular music is one of the biggest businesses in this country. Each year billions are spent on popular records, a fact that necessarily affects popular music deeply. A group whose records fail to sell is likely to have a difficult time booking a stadium, staying together, or finding work of any kind. It is enormously hard to get to the top of the charts, and the competition is fierce. It is even harder to stay there. You may have been disappointed to hear that a favorite group disbanded, or that a favorite singer has moved into a style that you don't care for. But you and other record buyers hold their fate in your collective hands. If people buy records, the style stays around, and the successful performer, as long as he stays on top, can record anything he wants. But record companies are reluctant to back someone who is slipping and are even more reluctant to take risks for an unknown. Decisions are made at the cash register: the record-buying public controls next year's releases.

The other fact to bear in mind is that new technological advances are enormously important to the present pop world. Synthesizers, **overdubbing**, distortion, and other effects possible only in a well-equipped studio are not just added touches in some popular styles—they are the very essence of the style. The sound you like on records may be impossible to re-create in a live performance. You may have wondered why some groups that you thought consisted of four or five people appear live with an additional five or six backup performers, or why some groups never tour or appear live at all. The answer is that some can't, because their sound depends so much on the studio environment and equipment. This fact may not seem terribly important, but it is, from a historical point of view. We have reached the point where the real test of a group is its recordings. The fans expect that the live performance will match the recording, rather than that the recording will duplicate a live performance. That is a significant change— and a recent one. The long-playing record was not even invented until 1948, and its original purpose was to allow interested persons to hear again at home re-creations of musical experiences they had already enjoyed live, instead of the other way around.

The Beach Boys in their private recording studio.

The present world of popular music is a fascinating one and is still a way for a few very talented musicians to make a fortune overnight. Stay aware of that world and listen critically, applying everything you can learn about music to your enjoyment of it. When you hear something you like, think about why. When you don't like something, try to understand what it is about the music that you don't like before you write it off. As we said before, the intelligent, thinking, open-minded listener is not condemned simply to accept whatever is at the top of the charts at the moment, or whatever outrageous group upsets the adult world, but is receptive to an entire world of musical enjoyment.

Folk Music.

Another type of music always present in man's culture is folk music. The term is somewhat confusing because there is a type of popular music called folk, which includes performers like Joan Baez, Judy Collins, and John Denver (when he isn't performing in country style), and which included a host of popular singers and groups in the sixties. These performers write and sing songs in the folk style, or at least in one folk style we are used to—simple songs whose words tend to be more important than their melodies, with simple accompaniment, usually just one or two acoustic guitars.

Using the term precisely, folk music is music of the people—traditional songs of an ethnic or national group, perhaps of a region, that have been handed down for generations in an oral tradition, and that sprang out of an impulse to celebrate the group's solidarity or history, to make work a little easier, or hard days a bit more pleasant. "American" folk songs are hard to find or discuss because we are not a single folk, but a mixture of many diverse groups. Students of folk music in America are likely to be students of English, American Indian, Mexican, Eastern European, Irish, or some other folk musics that have been imported to this country. Some imported folk traditions have been gradually modified into an identifiably American version. One of the prices we pay for our melting pot culture and the effects of radio and television is that we are losing some of these precious traditions. Fortunately, there now is a wave of interest in preserving these traditions and reviving some of the old ways, including the songs of our member cultures.

In any event, we can identify some of the general characteristics of music we call folk music. It is usually passed on by ear, rather than written down; it is generally performed by amateurs, rather than by professional musicians; it generally has a strong tribal or ethnic significance; and it is one of the ways the group celebrates its separateness from surrounding groups and cultures. Folk music has always existed, and some traditions have remained intact for remarkably long periods of time. The world of folk music, now available, at least to some extent, on authentic recordings, is yet another fascinating musical world for investigation and enjoyment.

The classical combination of North Indian music; tabla, tambura and sitar, the latter played by Ravi Shankar.

Art Musics of Other Cultures

People of the Western cultures sometimes assume naively that the music of all other cultures is a type of folk music, as if only we have a developed tradition of art music, or as if only Western European music were worthy of study or admiration, which simply is not true. In many other cultures, there are long traditions of music of great complexity and subtlety, composed and performed by professional musicians, who have spent a lengthy apprenticeship learning their art. The slightest exposure to these traditions makes clear that this is not music of the common people, learned from one's elders by a careful listening or two, but music that is as technically demanding as anything from our own musical culture. Even if we cannot comprehend the religious or traditional significance of the music, we can admire its beauty, the perfection and skill of the performances, and the new worlds of sound it opens to us. Among the better-known art musics of other cultures are the musics of Asiatic cultures—Java, China, Japan—and the music of India, as performed by virtuosos like Ravi Shankar.

Western Art Music

The art music of our Western culture, what people call somewhat loosely "classical music," resembles in some ways the art musics of other cultures more than it resembles either the popular music or the folk music of our own culture. Music of this type is written and performed by professionals who undergo long

The importance of music in Japanese culture is illustrated by this print of *Geishas with Koto*.

periods of training to develop the required skill. Western art music is *composer's music*. Discussions of great classical music of the past revolve around the names of great composers like Bach, Beethoven, and Stravinsky. Because of the **notation system** developed over the centuries, composers can specify with some precision what they want performers to do in recreating their music—not only the exact notes that are to be played, but also rhythms, tempos, phrasing, and other dimensions of the performance. This **composer control** of the performance is the chief unique characteristic of Western art music. Classical music shares some of the business side that so affects popular music and is likewise affected by the technological revolution in recording. Still, the different roles of performer and composer and the prevalence of **improvisation** in popular music versus composer control in art music make these two musical worlds quite distinct.

The main focus of this book will be on Western art music and its tradition, but it is important to emphasize again that whatever you learn about music is applicable to any form of music. Music is music, no matter how different styles may be. All music is organized sound, with melody, rhythm, harmony, and all of the other characteristics that make sound music. Many performing musicians move with relative ease within several musical worlds, each with its own performing styles and expectations. The studio musicians most in demand among recording companies are people who can play not only rock or classical music, but several styles of popular music, and all types of classical music, from Baroque to the latest experimental styles. Listeners should be equally versatile. Besides their favorite styles of the moment, they should be able to enjoy other types of music and to appreciate the beauty, power, and energy of musical styles beyond their personal favorites.

CHAPTER **2**

The Perception
of Music

The general attitude of our society toward musical taste seems to be "I don't know much about music, but I know what I like." People of all ages tend to cling to their own musical tastes somewhat defensively, as if the only possible reaction to music was an immediate yes-or-no decision: either one likes it or one doesn't; and if one doesn't, there is nothing more to discuss. We argue about books, about films, about television programs, about current events; but we don't seem to want to argue about music. It is true that it is difficult to argue logically about an art that moves us as deeply and instinctively as music does, and perhaps our acceptance of the notion that different people like different music is one response to the incredibly wide choice of music we have available to us. Before we begin discussing how music is put together and how it works, it may help to look at how we perceive music and at how it communicates with us.

LEVELS OF THE MUSICAL EXPERIENCE

As music enters our ears, it acts on us, or can act on us, in ways that create more complex responses than simply "I like that" or "I don't like that." Human beings are multifaceted, and so is the musical experience. We respond to music at several different levels. Our ears take in the sound, and we respond with an immediate feeling of pleasure or displeasure. Our imagination and memories are stimulated by the sounds, and summon feelings and memories associated with the musical sound. Finally, our minds can think about the music and how it is put together. These levels are worth discussing.

The Sensory Level

Music first reaches us through our senses. Obviously, the way it enters our being is through our ears, and there is an immediate response of pleasure or displeasure. Some sounds are nice, or rich, or appealing merely as sounds. But music also appeals to our **kinesthetic sense**, our sense of movement. Disco music, with its throbbing, insistent beat, and Latin dance music, with its complex rhythms, make us want to move. If we are not free to stand up and let the music move us physically around the room, we tap our feet, nod our head, or move our arms in time to its beat.

Cultural Conditioning

The sensory appeal of music, although rooted in human nature and in the senses that we all share, is hard to analyze or measure. While we are born with our senses, our responses to the sensations they detect are conditioned by years of experience or inexperience. The culture of which we are a part influences or conditions our minds to interpret and our bodies to respond to specific incoming sensory messages in a particular way. Think of the sense of taste, for example. If it were entirely innately determined, there would be some precise point beyond which food would be too sweet, too sour, too salty, or too bitter for everyone on the planet; but, as you are well aware, "one man's meat is another man's poison," and food you might find disgusting or painfully spicy is everyday fare to someone somewhere in this world. Parents enjoy some foods that their children find totally unpalatable. And so it is with sounds and music. We dislike what we do not understand or what is unfamiliar. In other words, the mind gets in the way of our senses, and conditions us to like some sounds and rhythms and to dislike others. But certainly, even within those limits, it is easy enough to see that music has sensory appeal.

The Associative Level

Besides appealing to our senses, music speaks very powerfully to our imaginations and memories. It reminds us, in a way beyond words and linear ideas, of past experiences. It summons forgotten feelings from somewhere deep within us when we are not aware we still have those feelings. It can even create strong feelings in people new to the experience. We have already mentioned the universality of music as the way a group expresses and strengthens the bonds that hold it together. National anthems, patriotic marches, and the long tradition of special music in churches of all sorts and in groups of all types testify to this powerful side of music.

Films and Television Shows

In films and television shows, music signals what we should be feeling—terror, sadness, excitement, peace, tenderness. We cry or cringe or smile as much in response to the musical stimuli as to the visual events. We speak of "watching" television and "seeing" movies, but we are also "listening" to television and to films. In fact, it is possible to sit out of visual range of a television show, but within hearing of it, and to follow the whole story. Before television, people listened to dramatic shows on the radio and shivered at the scary ones—"Inner Sanctum," "The Whistler," "The Shadow," and others. They sat around the radio, equally as terrified by the sounds as anyone today is by the sights. If you saw *Jaws*, you remember that the shark's presence was known to the audience before the people in the film realized their beach was under attack. The *music* told us the shark was near, long before its ominous fin pierced the surface of the water. After we have seen a film we like, we can buy a recording of the sound track and recreate the visual and emotional experience by listening to it. Millions of small children ran around in the late seventies humming the theme from *Star Wars* and acting out the events of the film.

Scene from *Star Wars*.

Advertising

The strong associative power that music has is exploited very effectively by the world of advertising. Much attention and creativity are invested in jingles and tunes that will indelibly implant the names of products, or pleasant associations with those products, in our minds. The theory is that, because we remember the tunes, we will select the products associated with them when next we are in the supermarket. The tunes are catchy and hard to forget. Whether they actually make us buy the product or not has not been proven, but the fact that so much time and money is invested in creating the tunes shows that someone believes in the associative power of music.

Sometimes the creators of commercials use familiar music from the Western art music tradition as background for their advertisements, hoping that the prestige associated with great masterpieces will transfer to their products. Thus, it is possible that the music may be better known from the commercial than it is in itself.

Conditioning

Conditioning—what we are used to—affects the associative level of the musical experience even more strongly than the sensory level. The set of responses we have to musical stimuli are taught to us from our very earliest experiences with the outside world. A person of eighteen who has been raised in this culture has spent thousands of hours watching television and movies, and learning the symbolic system of this culture. After certain types of music are connected with certain types of feelings hundreds of times, the response becomes automatic. But there is no guarantee that someone from another culture, without those thousands of hours of conditioning, would respond in the same way. Most musical associations are what anthropologists call "culture-specific," that is, a set of musical associations works only in one culture, and other cultures have different symbolic systems. If you recall the discussion of patriotic tunes earlier, you will remember that they cause patriotic feelings only in certain countries. For example, "The Star-Spangled Banner" does not have the same effect on someone from South Africa or Thailand that it has on an American. Religious music, also, has its powerful associative effect only on those persons who were raised or trained within the tradition of which it is a part.

Personal Symbolism

Some musical associations are even more limited in their application. There is such a thing as individual associative response to music. We are all familiar with jokes about "our song." Because of memorable events in a love affair that were associated with a particular song or theme, that music will remind the couple of those events, even if the song means something entirely different to most people. For example, someone might become sad on hearing a particular song, even if it is a "happy" song, if that person associates the song with the painful breakup of an important relationship. The reverse can also be true. Music intended to convey sad feelings may produce happy feelings in someone who associates it strongly with happy events in an important relationship.

Such individual examples of the strong associative power of music are actually exceptions to the way music generally works, and there is no way such individual reactions can be predicted or programmed by people who write or record music. But the symbolic system of a particular culture like ours can be worked out in great detail. It is thought about very carefully by groups in the business world, and is used very effectively for many purposes, from selling toothpaste to making films more satisfying. People are using or trying to use your responses to music every day of your life. You should become aware of these responses and the ways in which they are used.

The "Musical" or Intellectual Level

There is a third level of human response to music, a level few people reach, at least consciously. This third level is what some authors call the "musical" or intellectual level. Music is a fascinating art to learn more about, to discuss, to try to understand better. Somehow in our society, there seems to be some opposition to speaking of an experience such as the musical one in intellectual terms. This feeling is related to the idea that analysis is the enemy of creativity, that mind is the enemy of soul, and that meaningful experiences are beyond thoughtful analysis. Some authors write their novels and poetry as if careful editing, correct spelling, and clear logic would somehow keep them from "doing their thing" in literary form. In general, although we do not articulate the idea frequently, we seem to value the momentary, intense experience more than the logical, linear one. We somehow suspect that to analyze the momentary experience is to kill it, and that analysis would not yield anything worthwhile anyway, even if we could succeed in somehow fixing the experience within our minds. This idea is false. The mind should be engaged in the musical experience. Thinking can deepen that experience and make it more pleasurable and satisfying.

Pablo Picasso. *Three Musicians*, 1921. (Philadelphia Museum of Art)

Program Music

Related to the different levels of perception of music is the classification of music as either program music or absolute music. **Program music** is designed to appeal to the associative level, our memories and imaginations. It is music that refers to ideas, stories, or pictures from outside the musical world, music with a title that refers to a story or feeling. The familiar background music from television and movies is, of course, program music. Many of the compositions from the world of art music are also. If a work has a title like "Night on Bald Mountain" or "Romeo and Juliet," we may be sure that it is program music. The fact that a literary or pictorial title is affixed to the work means that the composer was thinking of the story or picture as he wrote the music, and he intends for us to be thinking of it also as we listen to his music. Program music is no problem for us; we are very much used to it from the music we experience constantly in this culture. Whether we know it or not, we have a fairly sophisticated set of emotional responses to specific musical stimuli.

Absolute Music

We are less familiar with what is called **absolute music,** music that has no specific literary or pictorial reference. At certain times in history and in certain styles, musical works tend to have titles such as Ninth Symphony or Fifth Concerto. These and similar titles are generic names of the form rather than specific references to a story or picture. Such **abstract music,** as it is also called, may very well not sound abstract to us, and may remind us of stories, pictures, or moods; but the composer did not have a specific picture, story, or mood in mind as the inspiration for his work, or, if he did, he did not want to advertise the fact. Abstract music, like abstract art, is more about art than it is about other topics or ideas. Sometimes composers and artists want to play with their materials or to experiment with new structures or means of organization, or with new sounds or combinations, rather than to tell a story or to depict a specific idea or mood. Some people think all abstract art is a put-on, and that all art should "look like something." Those same people probably expect all music to create a mood or tell a story. But we know now that painting can do things other than imitate photography, and we know that music can do things other than convey a mood or tell a story. Abstract art and abstract music are very much the fashion in our own day. Current experiments in new sounds and new structures are fascinating, once the listener accepts what the composer is trying to do.

In this book, you will be introduced to music you may not like immediately, or at all. But music you find sensually unappealing or not very meaningful in the associative realm may be fascinating from the intellectual point of view. Not every artistic experiment succeeds, but we can admire the artist who is bold enough to experiment in new ways as much as we admire the scientist who invests his life in breaking new ground. The study of the arts should be approached the way thoughtful people approach their dealings with other people. In any group of people you encounter, there will be some people you are naturally attracted to and feel comfortable with, some people you will feel neutral about, and some you take an immediate dislike to. As you get to know and understand people better, your immediate feelings may or may not change. Some people you did not like at first you may come to respect, even if you still are not inclined to choose them as your friends. You may find out that there are perfectly good reasons for your immediate feeling of dislike—different values, opposed ideas, or something similar. You may also find that, among the group of people toward which you initially feel not much of anything, are persons you come to value and respect as friends. In any event, we regard the combination of understanding and feelings as more mature than feelings alone. The same should be true of your study of music. Even with unfamiliar styles, or styles that put you off at first, you should try to understand why the composer or performer works in that particular way and what he or she is trying to say. If you approach the world of music with an open mind, you will better appreciate an art form that is universally appealing and may discover new worlds that you will enjoy exploring further.

SUMMARY

Music is experienced on three levels: the sensory level, the associative level, and the intellectual level. Our responses to music on any level are influenced, or conditioned, by the culture of which we are a part and by our previous experience or inexperience. We tend to feel comfortable with the familiar and to dislike what we have not heard before or do not understand. The creators of musical jingles for commercials and of musical themes for films and television shows use our culturally conditioned responses to music to sell products and to evoke moods.

Music can be classified as either **program music** or **absolute music**. **Program music** paints a picture or tells a story and is designed to appeal to our memories and our imaginations. **Absolute music** explores the art of music creation and is designed to appeal to our intellect. An open mind will make possible more complete enjoyment of music on all three levels.

CHAPTER **3**

The Surface
Elements of Music

To understand the musical experience better, we need to break that experience down into its elements. Any musical experience—background music in a film, a rock recording, or a concert performance—is an arrangement of sounds in certain patterns. Each individual note has certain acoustic characteristics that give it its individual identity. These characteristics include **pitch, timbre** or tone quality, **and duration.** They can be measured scientifically and differ from note to note. The individual notes are combined to form melodies, chords, and combinations of sound. And all of these effects take place in a time arrangement, producing what we call rhythm. The components of musical sounds we will now discuss are the same in any musical experience. Music comes out different in its meaning and effect because of the decisions made by composer and performer about how these various elements will be arranged in an individual composition.

We have divided the discussion of the elements of music into two large sections, somewhat arbitrarily. In the first section, we will discuss what can be called the **surface elements**, characteristics of musical sound that are immediately apparent on first hearing, even of just a few notes. The surface elements give us an immediate impression of the music and tell us whether we wish to listen further, change the station, put on another recording, or try to ignore the music. The next chapter deals with the underlying elements of music, characteristics we might instinctively sense immediately, but which may take repeated or more careful listening to understand or discuss intelligently. Among those underlying elements are texture—the relationship between the several voices or lines of a musical composition— harmony or chord patterns, and musical structure. The surface elements treated in this chapter include **instrumental color** or **timbre, melody, rhythm, and dynamics.**

INSTRUMENTAL COLOR

Probably the first thing we sense in hearing even a short bit of a musical performance or recording is the **timbre** or quality of the sound. We immediately recognize the sound of a favorite singer or group, the familiar combined sound of a particular band, an instrumental color we either like or do not like. Barbra Streisand does not sound like Roberta Flack or Dolly Parton. Each voice has a particular sonic profile that distinguishes it from all other voices.

The unique sonic profile of individual voices and instruments results from an acoustic phenomenon called the **harmonic series**. Each musical note is a complex combination of frequencies. In addition to the note we hear, there are less prominent frequencies that modify and enrich it. This phenomenon is easiest to understand in a vibrating string. The sound we hear is produced by the full length of the vibrating string; but the string also vibrates in fractional lengths, producing less prominent sounds, called **overtones**. The following diagram illustrates the way a string vibrates (Figure 3-1).

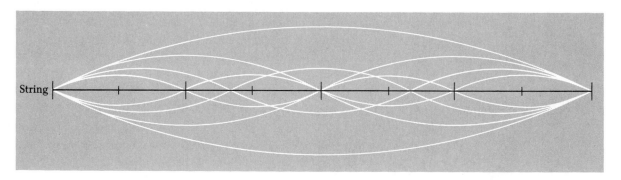

Figure 3-1. Diagram of vibrating string.

Another illustration of the harmonic series may help us to understand how it works. If you hit a low *C* on a piano, that is the note you will hear. Involved in that sound, however, are all the following higher notes, which help to color and enrich the basic sound (Figure 3-2).

Figure 3-2. Diagram of harmonic series of low *C*.

The color of the sound elicits an immediate response—positive or negative—from us, and causes us to like the sounds of some voices and of some instruments or groups better than others.

It is important to remember that these immediate responses are conditioned. There seems to be no scientific way to measure or depict which sounds will be pleasant or unpleasant. Nowadays, because we enjoy music through the medium of recordings more than by attending live performances, the acoustic qualities we enjoy may be modified, enhanced, or even produced entirely by electronic means. Voices can be enhanced greatly or even transformed by echo chambers, as well as by devices which boost the bass or treble ends of the sound. Instrumental sounds can be fuzzed, changed, boosted, or modified electronically to produce the sound we are trained to like. Whereas recording engineers once worked hard to avoid and eliminate **distortion**, it has now become an important effect.

Besides helping us to identify our favorite performers, timbre is one way musical associations are produced by composers and arrangers. Particular instruments have come to be associated with particular moods and ideas, so that it makes an enormous difference in the effectiveness of background music which instrument the arranger chooses to spotlight at a particular moment. A solo trumpet usually accompanies a shot of deserted city streets; oboes and English horns sound pastoral; French horns create a feeling of spacious open country; flutes in the low register sound breathy and yearning; large string sections are used for love themes; exotic percussion instruments remind us of foreign lands. The process of arranging something for a symphony orchestra, a studio orchestra, or any group is called **orchestration** and it is an art separate from composition, or creating musical ideas. The orchestrator must know the capabilities of each individual instrument at his command and which instruments will work together in a harmonious blend. He also must sense the particular qualities and associations that sounds produce in people in this culture, so that he can match the sound as closely as possible with the mood he is trying to create.

MUSICAL INSTRUMENTS

Musical instruments are usually classified into four basic groups; **woodwinds**, **brasses**, **strings**, and **percussion instruments**. We will also discuss keyboard instruments and the electronic instruments that have become important in recent years.

The Woodwinds

Woodwind is a general term for several types of instruments that produce sound by setting a column of air vibrating. Holes, with or without keys, allow the player to make the column longer or shorter, thus producing lower or higher notes. Woodwinds are among the oldest and most universal types of instruments: flutes of some sort are found in all cultures. In earlier times, woodwinds were hollow tubes of wood or some other material. Modern instruments are often made of some metal alloy and have complicated key mechanisms to allow the player to cover holes in the tube more easily than he could using only his fingers. The woodwinds break down further into three categories, depending on the mechanism for setting the column of air vibrating. Some instruments work from a carefully directed stream of air; others have a **reed**; and still others have two reeds. Because each of these types is further broken down into different sizes of the same instrument, these three basic types include a large number of instruments.

The first category of woodwinds is the **flutes**, which produce their sound by a stream of air angled in such a way that it sets the air inside the instrument vibrating. Modern flutes have a **mouthpiece** that helps direct the air correctly, but older flutes and most flutes in other cultures merely have a hole near one end of the instrument, across which the player blows. The principle is exactly the same as blowing across the neck of a bottle to produce a sound: if the air stream is directed just right, a clear tone results.

The Flute

The modern flute is held sideways. Keys controlled by both of the player's hands allow the sound to be made higher or lower. The flute, like most woodwinds, is a very agile instrument, capable of playing rapid scales and decorative figures. It is used both as a solo instrument in the orchestra and as one of the top voices in the instrumental ensemble. Its lower range is breathy and sweet, a favorite sound for lyric solos.

Flutes come in various sizes. Besides the basic size, the half-size flute, called the **piccolo**, is a standard orchestral instrument. Because pitch is relative to size, the piccolo, half the length of the flute, plays considerably higher than the flute. The sound from such a tiny instrument is remarkably piercing, and can be heard through a large band or orchestra. It is often used for special effects, such as storm scenes. Perhaps the most famous piccolo solo appears in John Philip Sousa's march, "Stars and Stripes Forever."

Other sizes of flute exist and are used occasionally in standard classical literature and more frequently in popular arrangements. The **alto flute** is longer than the standard flute, and thus extends downward the special sound of the low register. There is even a **bass flute**, eight notes lower than the standard flute. Because it is much longer than the regular flute, the player may have problems reaching the holes and keys. For this reason, bass flutes are made with a loop near the mouthpiece, so that the distance between mouthpiece and holes is shortened. It is important to realize that bending a tube or winding it in coils does not change its acoustic properties. Pitch results from the length of the vibrating air column, and the shape of that column has no effect on it.

The second category of woodwinds is the **single reeds**. The reed is a carefully cut and shaped piece of cane, which is attached to a mouthpiece. Blowing into

Flute.

the mouthpiece sets the reed vibrating, which activates the vibrating column of air inside the body of the instrument.

The most important single reed instrument is the clarinet, a versatile, agile instrument, much used in both orchestras and bands. It is also a standard solo instrument in Dixieland jazz.

The Clarinet

The **clarinet** is usually made of wood and comes in several sizes. The standard version is the B flat or A clarinet. A smaller version, in E flat, has a more piercing sound and is used for special effects in twentieth-century music. A larger version, the **bass clarinet**, is often used in nineteenth-century orchestral music for its rich, low sounds. Modern music for bands includes other sizes of clarinet, the **alto clarinet** and the **contrabass clarinet**.

The Saxophone

Related to the clarinets is the **saxophone**, a single-reed instrument whose body is made of metal. While saxophones in various sizes are used occasionally in symphony orchestras, especially to create a jazz or cabaret sound, they are found

Clarinet.

Saxophone.

Oboe.

much more frequently in jazz and popular music. Many of the great jazz soloists, such as Charlie Parker, Lester Young, and Paul Desmond, were saxophonists.

The third category of woodwinds consists of the **double reeds**, so called because the air column is set in motion by the vibrations of two reeds, attached back to back at the upper end of the instrument, without a mouthpiece. The double reeds are difficult to play. A small amount of air under considerable pressure is needed to make the instrument sound, so that breath control and the workings of lips and muscles around the mouth (called the **embouchure**) are critical to playing these instruments.

The Oboe

The smallest of the double reeds is the **oboe**, which looks something like a clarinet at a distance, but is somewhat shorter and thinner. The oboe has a reedy, nasal sound, which is unique and striking. It is capable of playing long, melodic lines and rapid passages. It is used both for solo melodies and as one of the high voices of the wind section of the orchestra.

The English Horn

The **English horn** is neither English nor a horn. It is actually a larger, therefore lower, version of the oboe, usually played as an alternate instrument by someone in the oboe section. It was a favorite solo instrument of nineteenth-century composers, who often utilized its sound to depict peaceful pastoral scenes. It has a sound that is mellower than that of the oboe, but possesses the same nasal quality.

The Bassoon

The lowest double reed is the **bassoon**, which looks like a cylinder of wood with an air pipe coming from its side. The bassoon is an instrument of enormous range, and each of its registers has a distinctive sound. Like the higher woodwinds, it is agile and capable of very fast playing, which makes it a favorite instrument for comic effects. In its low range, it can sound full and mellow, or dry and comical; in its extreme upper range, the sound is thin and haunting. The

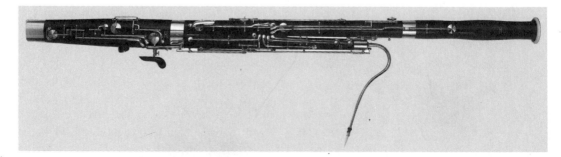

Bassoon.

most famous example of a solo in the high range is the opening of Stravinsky's "Rite of Spring," where the bassoon, in its extreme upper range, creates the eerie feeling of a deserted landscape.

The lower version of the bassoon, the **contrabassoon**, is the lowest instrument in the orchestra. It is rarely used as a solo instrument, because the sound it makes is ponderous and not very pleasant. It is usually used as the lowest voice of a full wind section, but is occasionally played by itself to create weird effects.

The Brasses

The **brasses** are the next family of orchestral instruments. They are, perhaps, more familiar to us than the woodwinds, because brass instruments are used in marching bands and other types of familiar ensembles, as well as in jazz and popular music. The basic principle of brass instruments is different from that of the woodwinds. While the sounds of brass instruments are also made by the vibrating column of air inside them, the air column is set in motion in a different way. Brass instruments have a cup-shaped mouthpiece. The player buzzes his lips into the mouthpiece, and varies the pitch of the sound with his lip tension, as well as with the three or four **valves**, or the slide in the case of the trombone, at his disposal.

Older versions of the brass instruments had no valves; players could sound only the notes of the harmonic series. If you have heard **bugle calls**, such as "Reveille" or "Taps," you have probably noticed that they consist of only three or four notes. When valves were added to brass instruments in the nineteenth century, the effect was to join four or five horns of different lengths in one instrument. When the player depresses a valve, the air inside the horn is routed through an additional section of tubing, making it possible for him to play all the notes of the harmonic series on a different length horn.

The physical aspects of sound production become somewhat complicated; however, it is important to realize that valves on a brass instrument are different from the keys on a woodwind. Each key on a woodwind lengthens the air column, making available one more note. On a brass instrument, each length of tubing makes available seven or eight additional notes, and it is by lip pressure that the player selects the note he wants from those available in each valve position. The brass instruments did not reach their present state of development until the nineteenth century, and it was at this time that composers began to exploit the possibilities of the brass choir as a separate family, equal in importance to the strings and the woodwinds.

The Trumpet

The **trumpet** is familiar from jazz bands and marching bands. The highest brass instrument, it has always been associated with fanfares, military marches, and princely processions. It has a bright, piercing sound that can cut through a full

Trumpet.

orchestra. Played with less force, it is capable of a softer, darker, more lyric sound. Like the other brasses, the trumpet comes equipped with several **mutes**, devices made of metal or other materials, which are inserted in the bell of the instrument to modify the sound in various ways.

The **cornet** is a slightly smaller version of the trumpet, used nowadays mostly in military bands. The **flugelhorn** is an alto version of the trumpet, used mostly in marching bands. It is also a favorite instrument of some jazz and pop players, such as Shorty Rogers and Chuck Mangione.

French Horn

The **French horn** is not used as frequently in popular music as the trumpet, although it is used occasionally in large-scale arrangements of popular music for its unique sound. It is the descendent of the hunting horn and still retains its coiled shape. It has a very wide range. The mouthpiece is quite small relative to the length of the tubing, which makes playing high notes easier. The sound is darker and more mellow than that of the trumpet, and the horn as a solo instrument paints a very effective picture of nature, wide open spaces, or heroic dreams. The French horn is the most versatile of the brasses. It can blend effectively with a small string section, and customarily takes its place in a wind quintet, along with a flute, a clarinet, an oboe, and a bassoon. The French horn is played with the player's right hand in the bell of the instrument, and the player can create special colors and muting effects by the way he places his hand in the bell. The sound of a large horn section was a favorite with nineteenth-century composers, and a well-known horn solo appears at the beginning of "Till Eulenspiegel's Merry Pranks," a symphonic poem by Richard Strauss.

Trombone

The **trombone**, like the trumpet, is familiar in appearance and sound from our knowledge of jazz and popular music and is used in bands of all types. It produces a large, dark sound, often associated in Western culture with the underworld and with supernatural menace. Modern trombones are equipped with a

French Horn.

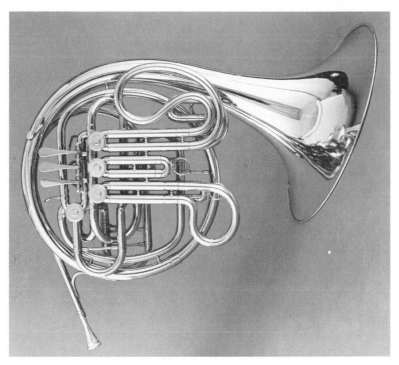

slide mechanism, rather than valves, to lengthen the tubing and make other notes available. Because of its unique construction, the trombone is the only wind instrument that can slide easily from note to note, and this sliding effect, called **glissando**, is sometimes exploited by composers for either comic or sinister effect. Trombones come in two main sizes now, the tenor and bass. Some nineteenth-century composers wrote for other sizes of trombone. Nowadays, these parts are played on one of the two standard-sized instruments.

Trombone.

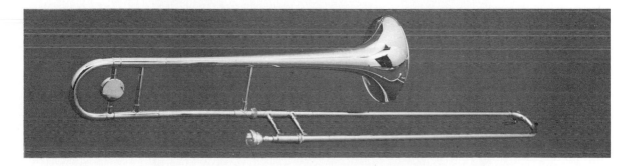

Tuba

The bass instrument of the brass section is the **tuba**, which produces a sound lower, darker, and fuller than that of the trombone. It is generally used as the strong bass voice of either the brass choir or the whole orchestra. Good players

Tuba.

Sousaphone, fiberglass
model for lightness.

can manage to play this unwieldy instrument with remarkable speed and lightness; and, especially in the twentieth century, composers have written solo music for the tuba and for groups of them. Occasionally, composers write comical passages for tuba; there is something intrinsically funny about an instrument of that size and pitch playing light, fast lines. Tubas come in various sizes and shapes. The marching band instrument, with the tubing coiled around the player and the large bell facing forward, is technically called a **sousaphone**, named after John Philip Sousa, the great American bandmaster who modified the tuba in that way to facilitate its use in marching bands.

The Strings

The family of instruments that is closest to the human voice in tone quality and expressiveness is the **strings**, consisting of the **violin**, **viola**, **cello**, and **double bass**. As you know from watching orchestras in action, by far the largest group of instruments is the string family. A large number of first and second violins, and proportional numbers of lower strings are necessary to balance the normal woodwind and brass sections. The strings are capable of very quiet sounds, a rich full sound, and very rapid playing. The sound of the string instruments is made by the vibrating strings. The strings are set in motion either by a bow or by plucking. Their sound is amplified by the sound box or body of the instrument. All of the string instruments except the double bass are equipped with **mutes**, wooden devices that fit over the instrument's bridge and dampen some of the vibrations, to produce a covered, darker, and quieter sound. Many works have been written for orchestras consisting only of strings; and the string quartet—two violins, a viola, and a cello—has always been one of the most popular chamber music ensembles.

The Violin

The highest of the string instruments is the **violin**, popular as a solo instrument and as the soprano voice of the orchestra. The violin is descended from older string instruments imported to the West from the Arab countries during the Middle Ages. The instrument as we now know it goes back to the sixteenth century, and was perfected around 1700 by the great Italian violin makers, such as Stradivarius, Amati, and Guarneri. Their innovations made the sound more brilliant, gave it more power, and made the instrument capable of the high playing and rapid virtuoso work that we now associate with it. The violin has a large, expressive range and a warm, appealing sound.

The Viola

The alto voice of the string ensemble is the **viola**, which is larger than the violin and, therefore lower in sound. It is played in the same position as the violin. Although there is a considerable body of solo music for viola, its usual role is to

Violin.

play the inner voices in the string ensemble. It has never been as popular as a solo instrument as either the violin or the cello. Its sound is not only lower than the violin's, but also darker and less penetrating.

The Cello

The **cello** (more formally, the **violoncello**) is the tenor of the string family, played in an upright position by a seated player. Its strings are tuned an octave lower than those of the viola, and an octave and a half lower than those of the violin. It is a very expressive instrument that has appealed to composers as a solo instrument since the Baroque period. Like the violin, it has always been treated as a virtuoso instrument. In fact, in Baroque times, cellists took pride in being able to play violin pieces an octave lower. It became quite popular in the Romantic period because of its full, intense sound in the higher registers. In Romantic symphonies, the cellos are often assigned the lyric second theme, or other expressive melodies.

The Double Bass

The strong bass voice of the string section is the **double bass**, the largest string instrument. Like the basses of the woodwind and brass families, the string bass does not often play solo lines, and it sounds ungainly when it does. Generally, it plays the bass part of a larger ensemble sound, but occasionally it has to move around with great agility when a passage comes swooping down from the higher instruments and continues among the basses. The bass, usually plucked with the fingers of the right hand rather than bowed, is also an important part of any jazz ensemble. Some jazz groups and nearly all rock groups use the **electric bass**. This instrument is much smaller than the acoustic version because the function of the large sound box is taken over by the amplifier. The electric bass looks like a

Cello, Double Bass.

guitar and is played in the same position as the guitar. In fact, it is sometimes called a **bass guitar**, although it is an electric version of the double bass, with the same four strings, tuned to the same pitches.

Other String Instruments

Another string instrument added to the orchestra by many composers of the Romantic era is the **harp**, which is used for the ethereal atmosphere it creates. It is a complicated instrument to learn and has a limited but important role in the orchestra.

There is a huge array of string instruments in the world of popular music, dominated by the omnipresent **electric guitar**, the staple instrument of rock music. Others include the **acoustic guitar**, the **banjo**, and the **mandolin**. Some of these popular instruments occasionally find their way into the symphony orchestra for special effects, or to make reference to a certain people or country.

Percussion Instruments

The last major orchestra family is the **percussion instruments**. The name means instruments that are struck rather than bowed or blown into, and the category includes a limitless array of instruments, from the familiar tympani, snare drum, and cymbal to the brake drums, prayer stones, gongs, and flower-pots sometimes called for by twentieth-century composers. Percussion instruments in the orchestra are usually used either for punctuation and excitement in louder passages or for special, colorful effects. For example, the xylophone often is used to portray skeletons or the dance of death, gongs evoke the exotic East, castanets remind us of Spain, and so forth. We cannot possibly discuss all of the percussion instruments that exist. In general, they are divided into instruments of definite pitch—**tympani, xylophone, marimba, vibraphone**, and so forth—and instruments without definite pitch—**bass drum, snare drum, gongs** and **cymbals, castanets, triangle,** and the like. Not only is the percussion section exciting to the ear; it is also fun to watch a busy percussion section in action.

Keyboard Instruments

Although they are not usually members of the standard symphony orchestra, we should say a word about the **keyboard instruments**, which have been and remain extremely important to the history of music, both as solo instruments and as members of smaller ensembles of all kinds.

Percussion Instruments.

Piano.

The Piano

There is certainly no need to introduce you to the **piano**, which you have seen and heard all your life and which some of you may play. The piano appeared in the eighteenth century, although the pianos of Mozart's day were somewhat different from the modern instrument. Late in the eighteenth century, the piano became a popular solo instrument, a ubiquitous home instrument, and the vehicle with which touring virtuosos dazzled adoring audiences—a function it still retains. It was also a mainstay of jazz groups, the big bands of the swing era, and all styles of popular music, until rock pushed it aside in favor of the electric guitar. Many rock groups use the **electric piano**, although it is not as important in rock as it is in other forms of jazz and popular music.

The Organ

The **pipe organ** became an important keyboard instrument in the Baroque era and has, of course, always been an important instrument in church music. Much music has been written, and continues to be written, for this instrument, which is capable of an enormous variety of sound and whose effect is more like that of an orchestra than of a piano.

The pipe organ is basically a large number of sets of pipes, all controlled by two, three or four keyboards and a bank of **stops**, devices by which the organist selects the sets of pipes that will play at any time. A recent invention, the **electronic organ** is designed to produce electronically a variety of sounds similar to the sounds several sets of pipes can produce, but without the bulk and in far less space than would be needed for thousands of pipes. There is some question as to whether or not that goal can be achieved, but the electronic organ has become popular both as a home instrument and as a portable instrument for jazz and rock bands.

Harpsichord.

The Harpsichord

The **harpsichord** is another keyboard instrument of great importance to the history of music. It is mechanically quite distinct from both piano and organ: it has strings like a piano, but the strings are plucked rather than struck, as piano strings are; and the sound dies out quickly, like the sound of the plucked classical guitar. Playing the harpsichord is different from playing the piano: the player cannot change the sound by changing the weight of his touch. Once the string is plucked, it sounds more or less the same whether the player has hit the key with great force or gently. The only way the player can increase the amount of sound is by playing more notes.

The harpsichord was the standard keyboard instrument for much of the late seventeenth century and most of the eighteenth century. It was eclipsed in the nineteenth century by the piano, but has returned to some popularity in the twentieth, both because of renewed interest in authentic playing of earlier music and because new music has been written for the instrument in this century.

The Synthesizer

A recent development, related in some ways to the electronic organ, is the invention of the keyboard version of the **synthesizer**. When interest first arose in composing electronic music in the 1940's, the available equipment was very cumbersome. Individual sounds had to be produced one at a time and then mixed together. There was no possibility of a live performance of this music; the only way to hear it was by means of laboriously produced recordings. Miniaturization of electronic components made possible the synthesizer, the keyboard electronic

Synthesizer.

instrument on which electronic music could be composed and performed live. Synthesizer technology, like all electronic technology, has advanced rapidly in recent years, and several companies now manufacture large electronic instruments that are capable of producing an enormous variety of sounds and are playable as part of a live ensemble. Most rock bands regularly use synthesizers, and it is entirely possible that the synthesizer will become the home keyboard instrument of the future.

One final word on instruments. Several recordings designed to acquaint listeners with the sounds of the various instruments are available. Some of them go through the instrument families, illustrating the sound each instrument makes and then offering typical examples of the way in which various instrument families are used. All include examples of the full orchestra, so that the listener can focus on the interaction of the various families of instruments in a typical orchestral work.

Benjamin Britten, a twentieth-century English composer, wrote a work called "The Young Person's Guide to the Orchestra," which is a set of variations on a theme by Henry Purcell, a British composer of the seventeenth century. Each variation features a different section of the orchestra, both as a series of solo voices and as a section. The work is worth listening to not only for the demonstrations of various instrument sounds and sections but also because it is a well-crafted, coherent piece of music.

MELODY

The term **melody** refers to a series of individual notes heard as a coherent unit. We tend to think of melody as the most prominent dimension of music. If we wish to identify a song for a friend, we say, "It goes like this," and then we hum an approximation of the tune or melody. Actually, the melodies we remember in our heads and hum or sing are much more than series of pitch levels. They also have a specific rhythmic shape. The same series of pitches in two different rhythmic arrangements would sound like totally different melodies to us. The musical examples in Figure 3-3 illustrate this point. The first example is the beginning of the familiar melody of the song, "The Sound of Music." The second example, as you can see, consists of exactly the same notes, but in a different rhythmic arrangement, that is, the length of the notes is different from the familiar arrangement, and different notes fall on the various beats of the measure. Play or sing the second tune, or get someone to play it for you. It sounds like a completely different melody from the one you are used to.

Figure 3-3.   "Sound of Music" opening phrase as is, then rearranged rhythmically.

When we sing or hum a melody, or just think of it in our heads, we also hear in our heads the **chords**, or combinations of notes, that usually accompany the melody as we have heard it. If you have ever tried to find the right chords on a guitar to accompany a melody you like, you remember that the melody doesn't "come out right" with the wrong chords. In other words, melodies seldom exist by themselves. In Western music, they appear in a context of rhythm and chords.

To speak of melody as a coherent series of notes is to isolate artificially the element of pitch series from the other musical elements with which it is usually associated. We do this sort of artificial isolation in trying to analyze any artistic experience. For example, when analyzing a film, we can discuss plot, acting, camera angles, lighting, and several other elements of film technique, although they always appear together, not in isolation. Still, it helps our understanding of music to think about melody by itself.

There are large bodies of music in our Western art tradition, as well as in other types of music, that consist of melody alone. In fact, the history of Western art music begins with the chants of the medieval Christian church, which consist of melodies alone, without instruments or accompaniment of any sort. The concept of melody—what note should come next, what series of notes will be satisfying—is as old as music itself, and is a basic element of any sort of music.

It is possible to classify some types of melody. Some are easy to remember and relatively easy to sing, such as the hit tunes from successful musical shows like *South Pacific* and *Annie*. These tunes seem to have a "singability" about them: they are designed somehow to be easily remembered and sung. Other melodies defy repetition. Usually they are designed for an instrument, not for the voice, and often they are marked by large jumps or other characteristics that make them difficult to remember or sing. Singable melodies usually move by **step**, are made up of symmetrical **phrases** or musical ideas that fit together logically, and are easy to reproduce. An example of a singable, stepwise melody is the Beatles' song, "Yesterday" (see Figure 3-4). Its melody moves almost entirely by step and, as you can see by looking at the **melodic curve** of this song (Figure 3-5), starts low, ascends to a high climax, and then descends again to a low cadence, or stopping place.

Figure 3-4.   The Beatles' "Yesterday", an example of a singable stepwise melody.

Another example of a melody that moves by step, but has a different type of organization and melodic curve, is "The Sound of Music" (see Figures 3-6 and 3-7). Note that the melodic curve for this song consists of segments with some repetition rather than of the single, long curve we saw in "Yesterday." The opening idea descends and is followed by more descent. The next segment is exactly like the opening idea, but at a lower pitch, and this time is followed by an ascending segment. In this small section of one melody, we can see several ways melodies are organized into a logical pattern and, therefore, are more easily sung and remembered. One way is repetition at a different pitch level, a technique we call **sequence**. Another is the relationship among subsequent sections of melody, something like clauses in a compound sentence.

One final idea about melody. We should not dismiss a musical experience because it does not contain tunes we can remember or lyric melodies that stand out, please us, and make us want to sing. The composer can choose not to spotlight a nice melody or not to write singable tunes at all. He may wish, instead, to put all of his emphasis on rhythm or on the interplay of several melodic lines, so that we cannot pick out one prominent tune. Sometimes music is filled

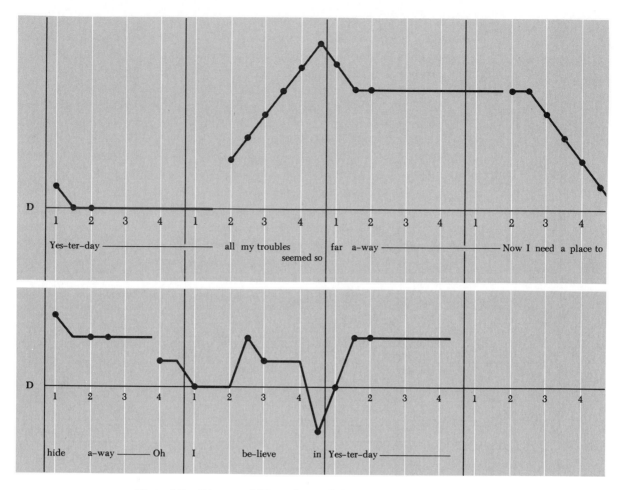

Figure 3-5. Diagram of "Yesterday" melodic curve.

Figure 3-6. Musical notation of "The Sound of Music" opening melody.

with wondrous melody; sometimes it is not. We need to have several different criteria by which to judge musical experiences, just as we have several by which we judge any other sort of experience.

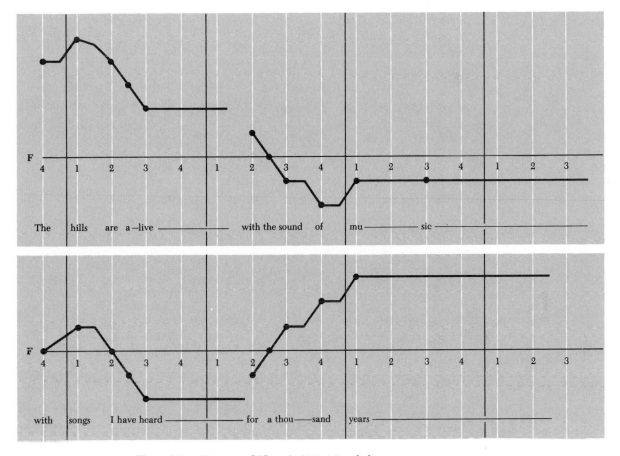

Figure 3-7.   Diagram of "Sound of Music" melodic curve.

RHYTHM

Rhythm is a general term for the way musical events are arranged in time. Because music deals in time the same way the visual arts deal in space, rhythm is obviously a crucial and fundamental dimension of music. It is also, according to psychologists, the basic way in which music relates to other facets of human life, and thus the source of much of music's appeal. Rapid, busy rhythm sounds exciting or tense to us, whereas slower rhythms sound tranquil and peaceful, because of the analog with our body rhythms. Tension and excitement make our hearts and pulse rates speed up; these same body rhythms slow down when we are at rest or asleep. Rhythm is a general concept, which encompasses several types of time arrangement, including **meter** and **tempo**.

Meter

As we listen to a musical selection, we hear a series of **pulses** or **beats**, some of them major ones, some less strong. These pulses are arranged into sets of two, three, or four, and sometimes in larger sets in complex rhythm patterns.

Whether or not we allude consciously to these sets of pulses, we feel them. The term for the arrangement of accented and unaccented pulses is **meter**. The songs we discussed in the melody section are all in **4/4 time**, the most common meter in Western art music and in popular styles as well. The meter of "The Sound of Music" is diagramed in Figure 3-8. Count the beats as you say the words in the metrical arrangement of the song. The important accented pulses are those on the first beat of each unit or measure. There is a secondary accent on the third beat of each measure, so that 4/4 time is really a type of **duple meter**, with each metrical unit consisting of two pulses. In the diagram, primary accents are marked with two underlines; secondary accents, with one.

Meter:	1	2	3	4
The	hills	are a ————	live ————	
	—————————	with the	sound	of
	mu ————————		sic ————	
				with
	songs	I have	heard ————	
	—————————	for a	thou ————	sand
	years ————			

Figure 3-8. Metrical diagram of "The Sound of Music."

Note that the syllable "The" comes before the first major accent of the first measure. Such an introductory pulsation is called an **upbeat**, **pickup**, or **anacrusis**. Note also that the pattern of a 4/4 tune can be varied considerably within the same metrical scheme. Each beat can divide into unequal parts, as in most jazz styles and some popular styles, or into exactly equal parts, as in most rock styles. Beats 2 and 4 can be accented more, as in the so-called **back beat** that is an important feature of rock rhythm. Precise tests of rhythmic exactitude have shown that, even when the meter seems quite consistent and regular, there are minute anticipations of some beats or slight delays in others, so that meter is never really as regular as it seems in many styles.

The other common meter in Western art music is **triple meter**, in which the pulses or beats are arranged in sets of three, with the major pulse on the first beat of each set of three. The **waltz** is a familiar example of triple meter. Popular songs and show tunes are sometimes written in triple meter; familiar examples are "Matchmaker" and "Sunrise, Sunset," from *Fiddler on the Roof*. Compound meters are more complex arrangements of pulses, in which a basic duple or triple meter is subdivided into smaller duple or triple units. For example, **6/8 time** is a compound meter in which each **measure** is divided into two units, each of which is further divided into three beats. Latin rhythms are even more complex. In the **bolero**, for example, each measure is divided into three units, each unit is further divided into two, and each of these two units is divided into three again. Figure 3-9 illustrates the organization of bolero meter.

Basic triple meter:	1		2		3	
Duple subdivision	Tum	tum	Tum	tum	Tum	tum
Triple subdivision	Tum	ta—ta—ta	Tum	ta—ta—ta	Ta—ta—ta	ta—ta—ta

Figure 3-9.   Bolero meter.

A composer can also choose to write without regular meter, as happens in what is called **recitative style**, when voices or instruments are allowed to proceed in a conversational, nonmetrical way, as in natural everyday speech.

Tempo

Different pieces of music in exactly the same meter may sound entirely different and produce an entirely different rhythmic effect. One of the important variables between pieces in the same meter is **tempo**, which means how fast or slow a piece is to be played. For example, 6/8 meter sounds like a peaceful river or a sea voyage when it is played in a slow tempo; when played fast, it is the meter of a jig. In general, tempo in art music is determined beforehand by the composer. In the Romantic era, composers got quite specific about the tempo they wished. They even listed **metronome** settings and indicated how many notes of a certain value should be played each minute. In popular music, tempo indications are quite general, and performers experiment to find the exact tempo at which the piece "feels right."

In Classical scores, general tempo terms are usually in Italian. The following terms, arranged from slow to fast, are commonly used:

Lento: Very slow   Moderato: Moderately
Adagio: Slow, or leisurely   Allegro: Fast
Andante: Slow (literally, "walking")   Presto: Very fast

Romantic composers modified these markings further by adding such descriptive qualifiers as "appassionato" and "religioso."

The approach to tempo may be strict or more fluid. The latter is quite necessary in some styles of music, which would not sound right if played in strict time. The standard term for the shifting, give-and-take approach to tempo is **rubato**, an Italian term meaning "robbed": the fluid effect is created by "robbing" one note of some of its value and adding it to another. Some other styles of music, particularly dance music of any type, are more likely to require a very strict approach to tempo. Disco music, for example, consists almost entirely of a prominent, subdivided beat. Not only is the tempo emphasized and maintained quite strictly, but most tunes in that style are played at almost the same tempo so that, from one song to the next, the tempo never varies.

As is true of any of these musical elements, composers may choose to emphasize one or more of them and make others less prominent. There is a large amount of music in styles that place more importance on rhythm than on singable melody. Other styles have as their most prominent element color, rather than either melody or rhythm. Rhythm, meter, and tempo will always be important parts of our discussion of musical selections and are critical to understanding any musical experience.

DYNAMICS

One last surface element of music, immediately apparent on first listening, is **dynamics**. This term refers to the volume level of music and to changes in that level. This level is specified by the composer in Western art music but is left to the performing group in popular styles. In some styles of art music, the volume level is relatively constant for long periods and then changes suddenly as the instrumental group changes or moves from one major section or movement to another. In other styles, particularly in nineteenth-century music, changes in volume are worked out very carefully, specified in the score, and coordinated among all the players. A gradual increase in volume is called a **crescendo** (Italian for "growing"), and a decrease is called a **decrescendo**. Examples of long, dramatic crescendos may be found at the end of Mahler's Eighth Symphony and at the end of Stravinsky's *Firebird* Suite.

In specifying dynamics, eighteenth-century composers simply wrote **forte** for "loud," and **piano** for "soft." Nineteenth-century composers were more specific, and developed a standard set of markings to indicate various dynamic levels and changes in those levels. The following table lists some of the standard dynamic markings:

ppp :extremely soft	*f* :forte (loud)
pp :pianissimo (very soft)	*ff* :fortissimo (very loud)
p :piano (soft)	*fff* :extremely loud
mp :mezzo-piano (medium soft)	< :crescendo (gradually growing louder)
mf :mezzo-forte (medium loud)	> :decrescendo (gradually softening)

In employing dynamics to create dramatic effects, composers often work counter to our expectations and to what would naturally happen. For example, they build a long orchestral crescendo and then hit the climax softly, rather than making it the loudest moment of all. Dynamics have much to do with the emotional power of music. We can be moved by a single, soft voice or a solo flute playing quietly, and we are thrilled by the overwhelming sound of a rock group or a full orchestra playing as loudly as it can.

SUMMARY

The **surface elements** of music include **instrumental color** or **timbre, melody, rhythm,** and **dynamics. Timbre** is the quality of the sound. It is created by a combination of the basic tone and its **overtones** as determined by the **harmonic series.** Timbre enables us to identify individual performers and is one means by which composers and arrangers produce musical associations. Each musical instrument has its own distinctive timbre.

Musical instruments are usually divided into four basic groups: **woodwinds, brasses, strings,** and **percussion instruments.**

Woodwinds are instruments in which sound is produced by causing a column of air to vibrate. Instruments in this group may be classified as **flutes (flute, piccolo, alto flute, bass flute), single reeds (clarinet, saxophone),** or **double reeds (oboe, English horn, bassoon, contrabassoon).**

In **brasses,** the sound is also produced by causing a column of air to vibrate, but the method for setting the air in motion is different. Among the brass instruments are the **trumpet,** the **French horn,** the **trombone,** and the **tuba.**

Strings are the instruments closest to the human voice in tone quality and expressiveness. The string family consists of the **violin,** the **viola,** the **cello,** and the **double bass.** Other string instruments include the **harp,** the **electric guitar,** the **acoustic guitar,** the **banjo,** and the **mandolin.**

Percussion instruments are struck rather than bowed or blown into. They are divided into two groups, those with definite pitch and those without.

While not usually members of the standard symphony orchestra, **keyboard instruments** are extremely important as solo instruments and in smaller ensembles. They include the **piano,** the **pipe organ,** the **electronic organ,** the **harpsichord,** and the **synthesizer.**

Another surface element of music is **melody.** Melody refers to a series of individual notes heard as a coherent unit and may be depicted by a **melodic curve.** Some melodies are easy to remember and sing while others defy repetition. "Singable" melodies usually move by **step** and are made up of symmetrical **phrases.**

Rhythm is the general term for the way musical events are arranged in time. It encompasses several types of time arrangement, including **meter** and **tempo.** Meter refers to the arrangement of accented and unaccented **beats,** or **pulses. Tempo** refers to how fast or slow a piece is to be played. The performer's approach to tempo may be strict or more fluid.

The last surface element of music is **dynamics.** This term refers to the volume level of music and to changes in that level, which are specified by the composer in Western art music but left to the performing group in popular styles. Dynamics have much to do with the emotional power of music.

CHAPTER 4

Underlying Elements of Music

The concern of this chapter is those elements of music that are not as immediately perceptible or obvious as the ones discussed in Chapter 3. These less obvious elements are present in any musical style, just as the surface elements are, and you have considerable experience with them already, just as you have with the others. These **underlying elements** of music are **texture**, **harmony**, and **structure**.

TEXTURE

The word **texture** is used to classify music on the basis of the way in which different musical lines occurring at the same time relate to one another. The word itself, of course, is an analogous one, borrowed from the world of touch sensations. Musical textures may be **monophonic** ("one voice" in Greek), **homophonic** ("same voice"), or **polyphonic** ("many voices").

Monophonic Texture

Music is called **monophonic** when it consists of one unaccompanied line. As we already mentioned, medieval chants were monophonic, and so are several types of folk music, from Western peoples and others. Even in orchestral music or popular music, there are occasionally passages when a solo voice, a solo instrument, or a group of instruments playing in **unison** (all playing the same thing) set out a monophonic line. This effect is often used for contrast, for an eerie introduction (as in the opening of Stravinsky's *The Rite of Spring*), or for some pictorial or storytelling effect.

Homophonic Texture

The term **homophonic** is used for texture in two different senses. Some authors restrict its use to describing music written in a **block chord** style, where every voice moves at the same time, the way most hymns are written. Most authors, however, use it in a more general sense, to describe a texture that has one prominent melody, against which all the other voices play subsidiary, accompanying parts. In this broader sense, much of the music of the Western tradition and nearly all popular music can be called homophonic, because we are used to the texture of melody plus accompaniment. It is easy to identify this texture by looking at a score, even if one does not read music very well, because the difference between the melody line and the accompaniment figures is very clear. In piano music of this sort, one hand plays the melody, while the other hand plays chord patterns or **arpeggios** (chords played in broken patterns), which could conceivably fit with a number of melodies.

Polyphonic Texture

The last kind of texture is called **polyphonic** or contrapuntal (the adjective from the word **counterpoint**), and consists of a number of melodic voices, all working together to produce the ensemble sound. In some periods and some styles of music, the polyphonic texture is the standard one. For example, it predominates in Baroque music and in most kinds of jazz, in which the soloists' improvisations are nearly always accompanied not only by chords from the rhythm section, but also by **counter-melodies** from other soloists. Polyphonic texture is readily apparent from a glance at the score: all of the parts are playing melodic lines, and the chords or arpeggios of homophonic style are nowhere to be seen.

Perhaps the clearest way to explain the three basic textures is by means of diagrams and musical examples. Monophonic texture consists of one single melodic line. The diagram in Figure 4-1 illustrates this simple texture. Kyrie XI from the repertory of Gregorian chant (Figure 4-2) is an example of monophonic texture.

Homophonic texture usually consists of a melody accompanied by supporting chords. The diagram in Figure 4-3 and the musical example in Figure 4-4 illustrate this common texture.

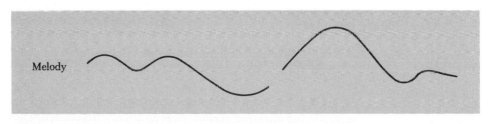

Melody

Figure 4-1. Graphic representation of monophony.

Figure 4-2.   Kyrie XI (Gregorian Chant).

Figure 4-3.   Graphic representation of homophony.

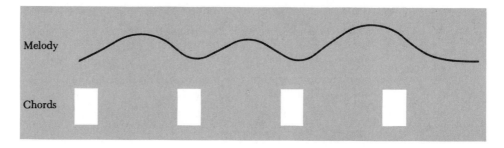

Figure 4-4.   Mazurka in C-sharp minor, by Chopin.

Note that the accompanying chords in this example are divided into an "oom-pah-pah" waltz pattern, with a bass note on the first beat of each measure and chords on the second and third beats. This arrangement gives rhythmic interest to the accompaniment, but it still consists of chords in support of the prominent melody.

Polyphonic texture—several melodies interacting—is most apparent in the **fugues** of the Baroque period. Figure 4-5 is a diagram of the way polyphonic texture works, and Figure 4-6 is a musical example. Note that in this example, one single melody is used against itself, a type of polyphony called **imitation**, in

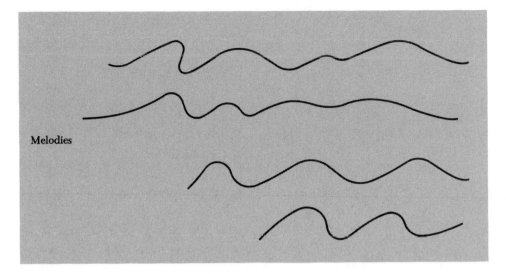

Melodies

Figure 4-5.   Diagram of polyphonic texture.

Figure 4-6.   Fugue in *C* major, WTC I, by Bach.

which all of the voices are versions of one melodic idea. Polyphonic texture may also be constructed from the interaction of several distinct melodies sounding at once.

Textures are never totally exclusive. Counter-melodies appear even in homophonic style, and passages that might be construed as melody-plus-accompaniment appear even in largely polyphonic music. It is all a matter of the composer's choice. If he wants to spotlight a lyric melody, the best way to do so is to set it off against a background of accompaniment. On the other hand, if he wants to increase the tension in a largely homophonic movement, he may write a section in polyphonic texture.

HARMONY

One of the more complex areas of musical study is what we refer to as **harmony**, which means the proper progression of chords. **Chords** are groups of notes, usually used as accompaniment to a melody in homophonic style. The standard Western chords are three-note groups called **triads**. Triads consist of the first, third, and fifth notes of the scale. Figure 4-7 shows you how to find a *C* chord on a piano keyboard. It is important to realize that any chord can be arranged in many different ways, with one or more of the three notes doubled, and in entirely different spacings. As long as the three notes sounding are *C*, *E*, and *G*, we will hear the combination of notes as a *C* major chord. Figure 4-8 shows some of the ways a *C* major chord can be written for the piano. As you can imagine, a symphony orchestra can play a *C* major chord in an almost infinite variety of ways.

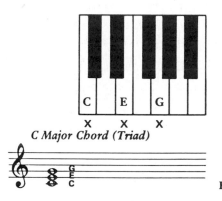

C Major Chord (Triad)

Figure 4-7.   *C* major chord with keyboard diagram.

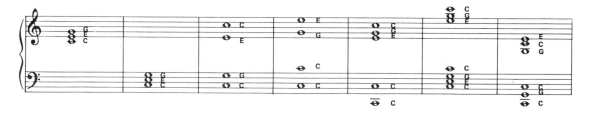

Figure 4-8.   Musical example showing different spacings of a *C* major chord.

Chords arranged in logical series form harmony. You are familiar with harmony if you have tried to learn some chords on a guitar to accompany your own or someone else's singing. If you don't hit the right chord, something sounds terribly wrong. We have an intuitive sense of harmonic rules even if we have not studied music. There is nothing more annoying and frustrating than trying to pick out a favorite song on the piano and finding that your harmonic vocabulary does not include the chords you know you need.

In our Western harmonic system, certain chords set up an expectation in us that they will lead to certain other chords. We feel a sense of tension until the proper, final chord is sounded. This tension is similar to what we experience when we watch a precariously balanced weight, knowing that it will fall, and are not able to relax until it does. The final chord is also like the last page of a mystery novel: it is absolutely necessary to balance the tension set up by all of the previous suspense, and the whole book is unsatisfying if the ending somehow doesn't work, if it doesn't grow from the previous chapters in a logical way.

It is important to realize at the outset that the harmonic system we will discuss briefly is not some sort of natural or acoustic phenomenon common to all cultures or all times. The Western harmonic system came into being around 1700 and remained in use until about 1900 in art music. Before that time, and in our own century, composers used different systems to organize music and to combine sound. That same harmonic system is still in use in our own day in most popular music, as well as in film music, musical comedy, and other musical contexts. But it is not, as some writers of the last century thought, based on natural phenomena. We can change the system any time we want. We are now aware that early music, twentieth-century art music, and musics of others cultures, which do not use our system, are equally as valid as ours. Although our system feels natural to us, it is as arbitrary as any other.

Scales and Steps

Our Western harmonic system starts with a seven-note **scale**, the *do-re-mi-fa-sol-la-ti-do* scale we learned as children. What gives this scale its particular shape is the arrangement of steps within the scale. Basically, we recognize two kinds of steps, half steps and whole steps. The **interval** between any note and the nearest possible note is called a **half step**. The interval between any note and the one two half steps away is called a **whole step.** In our **major scale**, there are **half steps** between the third and fourth notes and between the seventh and eighth notes, between *mi* and *fa*, and between *ti* and *do*.

Figure 4-9 is a diagram of part of a piano keyboard. Note that there are black keys between *C* and *D*, *D* and *E*, *F* and *G*, *G* and *A*, and *A* and *B*.. There are no

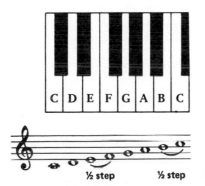

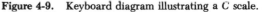

Figure 4-9.   Keyboard diagram illustrating a *C* scale.

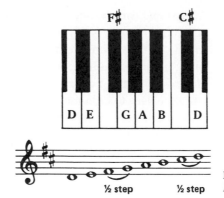

Figure 4-10. Keyboard diagram illustrating a *D* major scale.

black keys between *E* and *F*, or *B* and *C*; therefore, those intervals are half steps, whereas the others are whole steps. The same intervals can be illustrated easily on a guitar. Half steps are found between any note and the note one fret away; whole steps are two frets away.

The way our system works, a **major scale** like the white key *C* scale can be constructed starting on any note. All we have to do is utilize whatever black keys are necessary to keep the half steps and whole steps in their proper places. The diagram in Figure 4-10 illustrates the location of a *D* major scale on the piano keyboard. The same process can be used to construct a major scale on any note, using black keys when necessary to keep the half and whole steps in their proper position.

We also use another scale, called the **minor scale**, in our Western music. Actually, there are three different minor scales, with half steps in different places; but all take their character from the fact that the third note of the scale is flat, that is, there is a half step between the second and third notes, not between the third and fourth. The diagrams in Figure 4-11 illustrate the the three different types of minor scales.

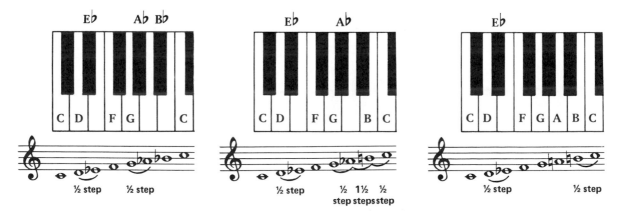

Figure 4-11. Three different types of minor scale, natural minor, harmonic minor, melodic minor. The descending melodic minor scale is the same as the natural minor.

Now that we know something about chords and scales, we can discuss our Western system of harmony. We have seen that a scale, major or minor, can be constructed on any note; that is, we can place *do* wherever we want, or wherever it is convenient for the voices or instruments one is writing for. *Do*, wherever we place it, becomes the main note of the piece, the place where the work probably begins, and certainly ends. If we write something using C as *do*, for example, the C is the **tonal center** around which the work revolves, and it is said to be "in the key of C." The term **key** is used to indicate where *do* is, or which note is the tonal center.

The most important chord in any key, then, is the triad based on *do*, or the first note of the scale. The two next important chords are the triads built on the fourth and fifth notes of the scale, *fa* and *sol*. If you play triads using the C major scale—the white notes of the piano—you will notice that they do not all sound the same, because of the placement of half steps. The only **major triads** in the major scale appear on notes one, four, and five, the important chords in our harmonic system. Figure 4-12 illustrates the I, IV and V chords of the key of C major.

Figure 4-12. The I, IV, and V chord of the key of C major.

The importance of these three chords in our harmonic system is clear in many styles of popular music. Rock and roll tunes of the fifties, many songs in blues style, and other types of popular music use these three chords almost exclusively. If you learn these three chords in a few keys on the guitar, you can accompany a remarkable number of popular and folk songs. Naturally, other pop songs, and most classical pieces extend this basic harmonic system considerably, so that people learning music are constantly expanding their harmonic vocabularies, or their knowledge of standard harmonic patterns.

Cadence

Another fundamental idea in our harmonic system is the notion of **cadence**. Cadence (from the Latin word "to fall") means a stopping place. Cadences can be **melodic, rhythmic, harmonic,** or all three. A cadence provides a resting place for a section of a piece, or for the whole piece. At a cadence, the chord progression must go from tension to calm, from expectation to arrival. There are many cadences within any piece of music; the composer and performer must be careful to write and play the series of cadences at the ends of sections in such a way that they do not create the impression of total relaxation and arrival, which should, of course, be reserved for the final cadence. **Internal cadences** are something like the stopping places every fifteen minutes or so in a television drama. To provide time for commericals, the drama must reach a temporary stopping place without totally resolving the tension and suspense of the story. A particular climactic point is arrived at, or an incident ends, without ending the drama. One reason theatrical films are not entirely satisfactory on television is that the film's internal "cadences" do not come at the right times for commericals, because the films were not designed for television. Without the proper internal "cadences," the breaks for commercials seem abrupt and jagged, and badly interrupt the flow of the film.

Composers have at their disposal several ways to avoid stopping completely before the work is finished. For example, they can write internal cadences on notes other than the home key (*do*) of the piece. They can create a temporary resting place by turning another note of the scale, usually the fifth degree, into a temporary *do*. After a slight rest, the piece then must continue until the real *do* is arrived at in a satisfactory way. Cadences can be avoided also by being set up and then resolved in a way we do not expect. Many nineteenth-century composers sustained the tension and movement of their long orchestral works by means of a string of **evaded cadences**.

Consonance and Dissonance

The last concept basic to our notion of harmony is the idea of **consonance** and **dissonance**. Conditioned by our experience and what we are used to hearing, we hear some sounds as restful and pleasant, and others as unpleasant or grating. We expect the dissonant (tension-filled) chords to resolve to consonant ones, and if we sense that we are hearing nothing but dissonance, we find the music unsatisfactory and frustrating. The spectrum of consonance and dissonance changes from style to style and from period to period. Without consciously realizing it, we sense that jazz harmony and rock harmonic progressions are different from the systems of classical music. Jazz progressions sound out of place in symphonic music, and different rock groups use different levels of harmonic sophistication. Early rock-and-roll groups and some present-day ones manage on a diet of three or four chords, while other groups are much more harmonically adventurous and exciting. The listener's sense is the result of conditioning. The intelligent listener constantly expands his harmonic sense and is open to the attempts of modern composers to create new harmonic systems and new principles of organization, even if they are, at first, unfamiliar and strange.

STRUCTURE

The final element that needs to be discussed is the element of structure. Structure in music is somewhat difficult to discuss, because people usually do not think of music in this way. We have a tendency in this century to think that analysis of an experience kills its spontaneity and excitement, and many people think of music as an emotional outlet, removed from the world of thought and logical structure. But music of any style has a logical pattern and structure that we sense, at least instinctively, and our discussion is aimed only at making that sense more conscious.

The first point to realize about musical structure is that we expect music to be logical. If you listen to people's complaints about unfamiliar music, you will notice that the music they find strange and senseless is music whose patterns they cannot discern. Just as we have a conditioned sense of harmony—of what is "right" and "wrong" in the harmonic sphere—we have a sense of musical logic and structure as well. Just as music that defeats our harmonic expectations seems random or perverse to us, music that seems to have no logical beginning and end frustrates us as well. Our sense of structure is based on our sense of all the other elements. We know a musical piece is coming to an end because the melody is winding down to a conclusion, the harmony is reaching the home key in a final way, and the rhythmic tension is beginning to release and come to rest. An easy way to verify our structural sense is to stop a recording two or three notes before the end. We feel we have been left hanging, as if a detective novel was missing the final pages, and the book ended just as the detective was gathering all the suspects in the room and saying, "One of the people in this room is the murderer."

In this chapter we will talk about some of the basic ways musical structures are defined and conveyed to the listener. We must remember that music takes place in time, not space, and through the ears, not the eyes. We cannot go back and "reread" a musical movement as we can a chapter in a novel, or stare at the music until it starts to make sense, the way we can with a great painting or a great cathedral. Composer and performer must make the point clear at a single hearing. Themes must be memorable, and repeated and spotlighted sufficiently so that we can recognize them when they return.

The basic principle of coherent structure in music is the same as it is in any other art form. There must be unity and variety; the work must be coherent enough to be heard as a satisfying unit, making a single statement, but we do not want to hear the same ideas over and over again. The composer must, therefore, delight and surprise us with enough new twists and turns and changes to keep our interest; but he can't keep jumping from one idea to another, or the sense of unity and coherence is lost. The artistry of the composer, then, is spinning out a few musical ideas in such a way that we sense their relationship, follow the structure, at least in its main outlines, and stay interested; therefore, for every adventure into new and exciting areas of surprise, there must be a balancing return to the familiar—the home key, the **refrain**, the first theme, or other familiar ideas. Repetition of earlier material is a crucial part of musical logic and form, much more so than in drama, literature, or the visual arts. The sense of finality, or arrival, or wrapping up the whole experience in a satisfying conclusion depends on repetition of some familiar elements. If you stop to think about it, you will realize that repetition and return to the familiar are very important elements in your enjoyment of music, both in classical and popular styles. Let's look now at some standard musical forms and how they are organized.

Popular Music

The structures in popular songs are easy enough to hear, and you are used to them, even if you have not thought about this element of the music you listen to. Popular songs may have several verses sung to the same music, or a series of verses each followed by a **refrain**, which has music different from the verses. Within each verse, the tune may divide into similar halves, each with a different ending, or into four segments, two or three of which may be similar, and one or two different. In any event, they are usually symmetrical, which helps us remember them. It may be helpful for you to listen to some favorite popular songs, paying particular attention to structures; but you must bear in mind that structures in classical music consist of longer units and more complex patterns.

Theme and Variations

One of the simplest ways to achieve the unity and variety we expect in music is the **theme and variations** pattern: an idea or musical unit is set forth in recognizable fashion first and then presented in different guises and treatments, so that the listener can feel at home in the familiar material and still appreciate the artistry involved in each new version of the material. This structural pattern is a basic one, not only in classical music, but in several popular styles as well. In most styles of jazz, for example, theme and variations is the standard pattern. The tune is laid out first in an ensemble version, arranged beforehand, then the soloists each take their turn improvising new versions of it while the rhythm section continues to play support behind the melody instruments. Usually at the end there is a final ensemble chorus to wrap things up. Many rock bands work the same way: the tune is laid out first, then the soloists do their personal versions of it, and the final chorus is an arranged ensemble version.

Strophic Songs

A similar structure is present in many settings of vocal music. The melody is the same for all the verses, which provides the unity. The variety comes from different words in each verse, plus slightly different treatment, or an arrangement that builds and links the successive verses to a climactic point near the end.

Sometimes songs, classical or popular, are linked by a recurring refrain, which provides the unity and ties the whole song into a single experience.

A-B-A Form

Another way to provide unity and variety is to have the music divided into three sections: an A section, which lays out the basic materials; followed by a contrasting B section, which is different in rhythm, key, melody, orchestration, or a combination of several of these elements; and a return of the A section, with the opening material presented again, in the home key, but probably with some new twists and variation, to keep up the listener's interest. The number of musical pieces written in this pattern is enormous. Music as varied as Gregorian chant Kyries, arias of Baroque operas, symphonic movements of the eighteenth and nineteenth centuries, and three-quarters of the popular standards from the thirties, forties, and fifties are all written in this form. Evidently, it is a natural way to write and hear music, at least in the West. The pattern of statement-digression-return neatly satisfies our desire for unity and variety in the same musical work. Popular songs of the thirties and forties are often in a slightly different version of the A-B-A pattern, which we might call A-A-B-A. The standard tune from that period is thirty-two measures long, divided into four units of eight measures each. The first eight bars is one melodic idea, which repeats for another eight bars; then there is a contrasting section, the "bridge," which is eight bars long, and leads into one last eight-bar statement of the main idea. Hundreds of songs were written in that pattern; some of them are still heard, especially in the acts of night club and lounge singers, and at piano bars that cater to crowds who like these older songs.

Rondo Forms

Much music of the late eighteenth century was written in an extension of the basic A-B-A form, which lengthens that basic pattern to include several more digressions and returns. Usually, the digressions differ from each other, as well as from the A section, so that the resulting patterns fall into schemes we could describe as A-B-A-C-A or A-B-A-C-A-D-A patterns. Occasionally, in seven-section rondo forms, the first digression returns also, so that the pattern becomes A-B-A-C-A-B-A. We can also hear that pattern as a three-part, A-B-A pattern, with each A section subdivided into three subsections.

We should point out that here we are discussing only some basic ideas about form in music. In the late eighteenth and early nineteenth century, when form was a primary element in the composer's effort, great attention was paid to balance and symmetry of form. In the late nineteenth century, when lyric expression and serious philosophical statement was the top priority, form was pushed into the background: the standard Classical forms were stretched almost beyond recognition to accommodate what the composer wanted to say. In our own century, composers are as adventurous in inventing new approaches to form as they are in creating new harmonic systems, and the old standard forms may be hard to find. We should also point out that musical form is a technical and difficult subject. Working out the details of a formal structure may take considerable study, and nearly always we must resort to study of the score, where measures can be compared visually. Musicians argue about exactly where one section stops and another begins, where they overlap, and so forth. That level of detail does not concern us, but any intelligent listener should be able to hear the basic formal outlines of a work, know what forms to expect, and be able to ap-

Marcel Duchamp's *Nude Descending a Staircase, No. 2*, 1912 (Philadelphia Museum of Art) illustrates new approaches to form in twentieth-century art.

preciate the individual variants and twists composers introduce into the inherited formal patterns. We will deal with some of the standard forms, especially first movement symphonic form, when they come up in the historical survey.

SUMMARY

The **underlying elements** of music include **texture, harmony,** and **structure**.

Borrowed from the world of touch sensations, the term **texture** in music refers to the way in which different musical lines occurring at the same time relate to one another. Musical textures may be predominantly **monophonic** ("one voice"), **homophonic** ("same voice"), or **polyphonic** ("many voices") but are rarely exclusively of one type.

Harmony means the proper progression of chords. Fundamental to our Western harmonic system are **scales** and **steps**, **cadence**, and **consonance** and **dissonance**. Our harmonic system starts with a seven-note scale, which is given its particular shape and sound by the arrangement of **half steps** and **whole steps** within it. In our **major scale**, there are half steps between the third and fourth notes and between the seventh and eighth notes. We also use another scale, called the **minor scale**, in which the third note of the scale is flat, that is, there is a half step between the second and third notes, rather than between the third and fourth.

Cadence (from the Latin word "to fall") means a stopping place. In music, a cadence is the place where the tension is relaxed and the music pauses or concludes. Cadences can be **melodic, rhythmic, harmonic**, or all three. Based on our experience we hear some sounds as unpleasant or grating. These create tension and are termed **dissonant**. We hear other sounds as restful and pleasant. These ease or relax tension and are termed **consonant.** We expect dissonant chords to resolve into consonant ones and find music in which this resolution does not take place unsatisfactory and frustrating.

The basic principle of coherent **structure** in music is the same as it is in any other art form: there must be unity and variety. Innovative themes must be balanced by returns to familiar refrains. Devices and forms used to achieve this "diversified unity" include **verses** and **refrain**, **theme** and **variations**, **strophic songs**, **A-B-A form**, and **rondo form**.

Jackson Pollock's *Greyed Rainbow* shows a new approach to structure in art.

CHAPTER **5**

The Musical Experience

At the close of this section on elements, and before we begin a historical survey of Western art music, it is important to take one more step: we need to see how these elements work together in music of contrasting styles. As we have pointed out, melody, harmony, rhythm, and all of the other elements do not appear in the abstract, separately, or removed from a total musical experience. Because we cannot think about all of that new information in a block, we have to move analytically through a discussion of several aspects of music separately, but that is not the way they appear. Your mind is now filled with many new terms and ideas, and we need time to work with these terms in thinking about and discussing musical experiences before we complicate the picture further with historical information and new variables.

In this chapter, we will listen to and discuss two contrasting musical examples. What we discover in these examples will help us in all of our future listening and discussion. All musical styles are made up of the same elements—melody of some kind, rhythm, harmony, color, and structure—but these elements are handled in widely varying ways. All composers and performers work with the same basic materials, but they deal with them differently, and that is what makes different styles of music in all their endless variety. A composer may choose to put his emphasis entirely on one element—rhythm, for example. To do so, he must subordinate all the other elements to his main purpose. The questions to ask in understanding a musical experience are basically two: Which elements are the foreground elements, the elements that are emphasized as the important elements in this experience? How does the composer or performer treat each of the elements, both the ones that are the important ones in his style and those that are not? To illustrate how these questions may be answered, we will analyze two contrasting musical experiences, one from the world of popular music and one from the art music tradition. We do not mean to imply that either is typical of its own class of music, or to imply by comparing them that one is "good" music and one is not. What we are trying to understand is why they differ, how they differ, and how each deals differently with the same musical elements.

"LET IT BE" BY THE BEATLES

Our example from the world of popular music is a Beatles tune from the sixties, a song that enjoyed considerable popularity. The recorded performance is from *Beatlemania*, a hit show of the late seventies that recreated the music, spirit, and history of the Beatles through live performance and photographic projections from the various periods of their popularity. The performances were remarkably faithful duplications of the Beatles' own performances; still, it would be interesting to compare the Beatles' recordings with the later recreations, to see how some of the details vary. We will consider each of the elements of musical style in the *Beatlemania* recording to see how they work together to create the style.

Color is a prominent element in this music. The lead singer in this number strives to duplicate the high, clear voice of Paul McCartney. The drums are used imaginatively, entering during the second verse and gradually becoming more prominent. The piano is the most consistent accompaniment instrument, playing chords and an important bass line. The most striking color is the sound of the lead guitar, which substitutes for the voice in the third verse of the song. Its color is the standard lead guitar sound of sixties rock—loud, dramatic, and modified by electronic effects. Much of the structure of the piece is based on the addition of colors gradually to the simple voice and piano which open the song.

Melody is another important element, as we would expect in a popular song. The basic melody is simple and folklike, easily memorable, and hard to get out of one's head. Both the voice and the lead guitar improvise on the melody, adding ornaments, different turns of phrase, and new melodic shape.

Rhythm is another important element. Although the slow 4/4 meter is consistent throughout the song, there are subtle rhythmic changes. Sometimes the four beats are divided into two equal halves, creating the standard "split four" rhythm of rock. At other times the drums double the rhythm, subdividing the eight beats into sixteen. Listen for that effect in the fourth verse; the doubling of the pulse adds drive and urgency to the rhythmic feeling.

Dynamics are important also. Like many popular songs, this song begins softly and gradually builds to a loud climax in the third verse. The refrain is also generally louder than the verses. Dynamic changes play a great part in making one long structure out of the several similar verses.

The texture is basically melody and accompaniment, with occasional counter-melodies. The harmony is simple and regular, centering on I-IV-V chord patterns prominent in many rock styles.

The structure is a kind of theme and variations, based on varied repeats of a simple, twelve-measure pattern, consisting of two lines of text followed by a refrain, the "Let It Be" section. The first and third choruses end with one appearance of the refrain; the second and fourth choruses repeat the refrain, making those units longer than the others. Further structure is created by an interlude after the second chorus, which divides the whole song into two halves. The interlude consists of descending chords, which echo the descending chords which are prominent in the piano accompaniment for each chorus. The descen-

FIGURE 5-1. LISTENING GUIDE

"LET IT BE," BY THE BEATLES

INTRODUCTION

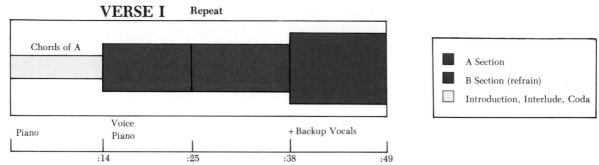

VERSE II

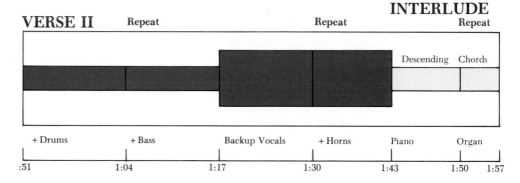

VERSE III

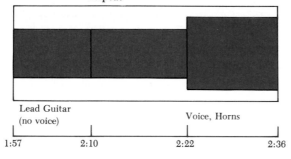

VERSE IV

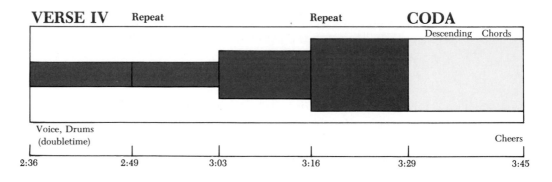

ding chords appear twice after the second verse, played the first time by the piano, and the second time by an electronic organ. At the end of the song, the descending chords are played once more as a coda to the whole song.

The clearest way to see how the various elements combine to form a musical experience is to follow the listening guide (Figure 5-1) as you listen to the recording. In this case, as well as in any musical experience, style is created by the way the various component elements are treated.

PRELUDE TO *TRISTAN UND ISOLDE* BY WAGNER

The second musical example is quite different from the Beatles tune, although there are some intriguing similarities. Richard Wagner, the composer of this example, is a complex and fascinating man, whose life and work are discussed in Chapter 37. Here our concern is the style of this one isolated orchestral work. The Prelude serves as an overture or introduction to *Tristan und Isolde*, a German Romantic opera, first performed in 1859. Wagner's operas are heavily symbolic and philosophical, concerned not so much with the actions of real people as with feelings, ideas, and myth. This particular opera, based on a medieval tale, concerns the struggle between love and duty. The hero and heroine love one another intensely, but their love is doomed. In the opera, they meet only at night, in darkness. Daylight represents the real world, where their love is impossible because of his knightly vows and her betrothal to another. Both die at the end, he from poison drunk willingly, she from love. The Prelude sets the tone and mood for the opera, and is filled with yearning. It is gorgeous music, both intensely pleasureable and very tragic. Wagner uses each of the musical elements very skillfully to depict this mood of yearning and tragedy.

Color is a critical element in this work. The composer had at his disposal the huge Romantic orchestra, with all of its varied and colorful sounds. We hear cellos in the intense high register, the heroic sound of the horn, harps, violins, and the special sounds of the solo woodwinds, such as the bass clarinet and English horn. Wagner chooses his colors and balances them with extreme care and skill.

Melody is important also. Wagner uses specific melodic figures in his operas to depict specific characters or ideas. This entire prelude is made up of three or four melodies, which are repeated, transformed, combined, and layered to make a long, unified musical statement. Rhythm is not so important, at least not as a foreground element. As you listen, you will note that the rhythm seems organic and shifting, rather than mechanically regular. All of the pauses and delicate variations of tempo are carefully specified in the score. Dynamics are as critical to this piece as to the Beatles tune. Much of the overall shape of the Prelude results from the carefully controlled buildup to an intense climax late in the piece. We hear it as one long crescendo, until the accumulated tension explodes in a stunning climax and then quickly subsides into almost nothing.

The element of texture is a complex one. Although the basic Romantic texture is melody and accompaniment, here there is so much going on and so much layering of the basic melodies that the texture is sometimes more polyphonic than homophonic. The harmony is fascinating and complex, and critically important to the overall effect. A device Wagner uses constantly is to set up clear harmonic progressions and then to turn them in surprising directions, avoiding the expected cadence. This constant deflection of the harmonic motion works in conjunction with the controlled dynamics to create the effect of a huge wave, gathering force, but not breaking until it finally crashes on the shore with all its accumulated force. The avoided cadences are also a very effective way to depict the frustration and longing that are the theme of the opera. Wagner's harmony is complicated. This particular work has kept many generations of music students up late trying to work out a logical harmonic analysis. While the details are not our concern here, certainly you can hear that the harmony is rich and complex. A particularly striking example of an evaded cadence is the one that follows the repeated statements of the opening idea.

As we have indicated, the structure results from the coalescence of the other elements, rather than being a primary element in itself, as it would be in a Mozart symphony. We hear the work, as we have said, as one long crescendo, made up of thicker and thicker layers of familiar melodic ideas, growing ever more intense until the grand climax. In Figure 5-2 you can see the main melodic ideas of the work, each of which reappears constantly.

The following diagram in Figure 5-3 attempts to outline the structure of the Prelude. In this instance, different colors represent different melodic ideas, and the various families of instruments are noted in the diagram. To help you orient yourself to the musical sounds, a time line indicates the elapsed time in minutes.

Figure 5-2. Main melodic ideas of the Prelude to *Tristan und Isolde* by Wagner.

FIGURE 5-3. LISTENING GUIDE

PRELUDE TO *TRISTAN UND ISOLDE*, BY WAGNER

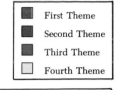

■ First Theme
■ Second Theme
■ Third Theme
□ Fourth Theme

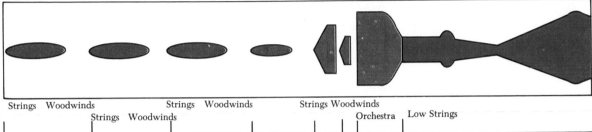

Strings Woodwinds   Strings Woodwinds   Strings Woodwinds
    Strings Woodwinds   Orchestra   Low Strings

:25   :48   1:12   1:24 1:32 1:36   1:48

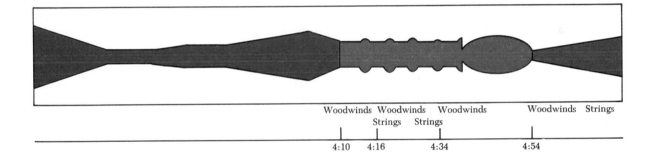

Woodwinds Woodwinds   Woodwinds   Woodwinds Strings
   Strings   Strings

4:10   4:16   4:34   4:54

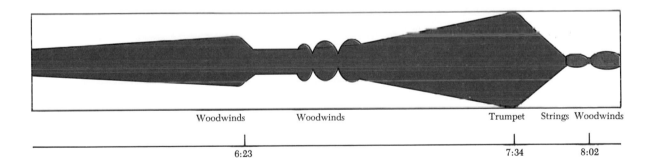

Woodwinds   Woodwinds   Trumpet   Strings Woodwinds

6:23   7:34   8:02

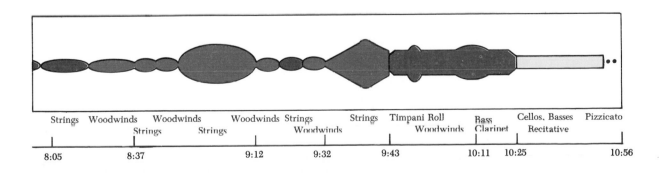

Strings Woodwinds   Woodwinds   Woodwinds Strings   Strings Timpani Roll   Bass   Cellos, Basses   Pizzicato
   Strings   Strings   Woodwinds   Woodwinds   Clarinet Recitative

8:05   8:37   9:12   9:32   9:43   10:11 10:25   10:56

Sandro Botticelli. *Birth of Venus*, c. 1480.

PART II

Music in the Middle Ages and Renaissance

CHAPTER 6

Social and Cultural Background

The modern concertgoer does not often encounter music from before the Baroque period. Occasionally, however, it does turn up in our musical world. The sacred choral music of the Renaissance is often performed by church choirs and community choruses. School choral groups of all levels perform sacred and secular music of the Renaissance. Renaissance instrumental music is programmed by classical music stations. Occasionally, films or television programs create the atmosphere of this period by using authentic Renaissance music as background music. The Zeffirelli film *Romeo and Juliet*, for example, and the Masterpiece Theater presentation of *The Six Wives of Henry the Eighth* both utilized music of the Renaissance period. The sound track recordings from these presentations brought people who would never have attended live concerts of this music into contact with it. The music is interesting and rewarding to listen to. Beyond that, the musical developments of the Middle Ages and Renaissance shaped later culture in fundamental ways. Assumptions were worked out and premises were established that affected all later music. We cannot understand the way we think about or listen to music without understanding the important developments of these earlier ages.

THE MIDDLE AGES

The Middle Ages are a period quite remote from our own in the way people thought about man and his world. Because of that remoteness, later ages tend to take extreme views of medieval culture. The Renaissance, convinced of its own greatness, coined the term "Middle Ages" as a derogatory term for what it regarded as a cultural backwater between the high points of Greco-Roman culture and its own flowering. Some people use the term "Dark Ages" for the long period between Rome and the Renaissance, as if the entire age wallowed in ignorance and savagery. Others use "medieval" as an insulting term for what they regard as backward or cruel societies, or cultures that value religious ideas more than individual freedoms. At the other extreme, the Romantics of the nineteenth century glamorized the Middle Ages beyond recognition. Reading some of the literature of that period, one gets the impression that the only people alive for a thousand years were pure-hearted knights, damsels in distress, wise kings, and black-hearted villains. King Arthur, Sir Lancelot, Merlin, Robin Hood, and other such figures are part of our culture and mythology, but are not to be taken as historical figures representative of an age.

Actually, the Middle Ages comprised a long period of such profound social change that it is nearly impossible to generalize about it; however, a few basic ideas were quite persistent. It was a hierarchical age. In the view of the time, all society was organized into interacting levels, and everyone had his or her place within these tightly organized strata. It is hard for us to imagine why the age looked so unfavorably on scientific discoveries and adventurous thinkers. Even Thomas Aquinas, regarded now as a bulwark of conservative Catholic thought, saw his works condemned for their originality. Anything that threatened the tidy world-view in any aspect threatened all of society. Church and state were one. The king's role was to keep civil order, but even the king could be excommunicated by the church, which meant then that a person was excluded from all social life and became a nonperson.

Our purpose here, of course, is not to discourse on this remote and fascinating age, but to trace some important developments in Western music. To that end, we are particularly interested in those cultural situations and fertile times when music flourished, along with the other arts.

Cultural Centers

Monasteries

The first important cultural center was the monastery, where Christian culture was preserved and enlarged, particularly in those times when the cities were overrun by barbarian hordes. The monasteries were microcosms of medieval society, with a complex organization that used the talents of each member for the good of the community. Some monks farmed, cooked, and built and maintained the buildings; others copied manuscripts, taught, worked as musical soloists and composers, or wrote histories and treatises on various subjects. In this stable atmosphere grew the first and largest body of medieval music, the chants of the Mass and Office.

Government Centers

At other times, centers of government became important cultural centers. One particularly fertile cultural center was the duchy of Aquitaine, now Southern France. In the eleventh and twelfth centuries, this society was greatly influenced by close contacts with the cultures of the Middle East. Secular song, in the form of troubadour poetry and melody, flourished in Aquitaine, as did early experiments in polyphony. The same important contact with the East resulted, of course, from the Crusades, which failed to accomplish their stated goal of liberating Jerusalem from "the infidel," but established important contacts between East and West.

Universities and Cathedrals

Another crucial development for culture was the rise of the universities and the scholastic movement. In some ways, this development signaled the end of medieval culture, because the emphasis was shifted from the authority of the church to the questing of man's mind. The University of Paris became the world capital of theological and philosophical studies. Giants like Abelard and Aquinas attacked all possible questions, armed with reliable Latin translations of Plato and Aristotle, which had come from the great Arab centers of thought. Connected with the rich intellectual life of Paris was the musical culture that revolved around the Cathedral of Notre Dame, an important center for the composition of polyphony.

Transitional Period

The following centuries witnessed a gradual breakdown of the unified medieval world. This transitional period can be viewed as "the waning of the Middle Ages," in one author's term, or the first stirrings of the new thought of the Renaissance. Dante's *Divine Comedy*, for example, is one of the masterpieces of Western literature, a work that exhibits characteristics of both the Middle Ages and the Renaissance. During the same period, Petrarch was writing Italian love poetry that is completely Renaissance in outlook. In England, Chaucer was a pioneer of literary English; in some ways, he too, belongs to the Renaissance more than to the Middle Ages. In France, Guillaume de Machaut (c. 1300-1377) is regarded both as the greatest medieval composer and as a poet of the early Renaissance. The fourteenth century saw a total breakdown of the medieval system, with three simultaneous claimants to the papal throne and a turbulent rearrangement of the entire society caused by the ravages of the Black Plague, which killed a third of the people of Europe. A history of this "disastrous" century, *A Distant Mirror* by Barbara Tuchman, which was a best seller in the late 1970s, paints a detailed and fascinating picture of these turbulent times, which Tuchman views as similar to our own century.

Aesthetic

The aesthetic of the Middle Ages was theocentric—centered on God and on the teachings of the church. Medieval art depicts saints in symbolic fashion: anatomy and perspective do not matter, and art is two-dimensional. Its purpose is to present the saints as didactic models, holding symbolic buildings, books, or instruments of martyrdom so that we know who they are. The visual creativity of the time was devoted to illuminating manuscripts and decorating churches; creativity and technique were in the service of God. The "serious" music of the time was church music. Secular music was a parallel but completely subsidiary development.

The choir and altar of Chartres Cathedral. This French church drew many religious visitors in the Middle Ages and still does today.

THE RENAISSANCE

The Renaissance, on the other hand, is an anthropocentric (man-centered) culture, proud and adventurous. Our country was discovered during the Renaissance as an accidental by-product of one of the great foolhardy adventures of all time. Scientific discoveries, instead of being greeted with suspicion and fear, were now welcomed and highly regarded. The centers of culture shifted from churches to the magnificent courts of the ruling families of European city-states and countries. Advances in the arts were welcomed, and the great painters, sculptors, and musicians of the time were eagerly sought after to ornament the surroundings and the life of the great courts. In many ways, the Renaissance is the first modern age, guided by ideas and principles that we still subscribe to and totally different in outlook from the unfamiliar Middle Ages. Like all subsequent periods of Western culture, the Renaissance looked back to the golden age of Greece and Rome as its model, and valued the arts for their intrinsic delights, not for their didactic effectiveness. When we read a novel like *The Agony and the Ecstasy*, a fictional treatment of the life of Michelangelo, we can identify with the artist's struggle to satisfy all of his competing patrons and still do what he felt he should do. The Renaissance is alive still in a city like Florence, where today's citizens are surrounded by the magnificent works of art sponsored by the Medici dynasty during that time.

If one were to choose a figure typical of the Renaissance and its spirit, most people's choice would be Lorenzo de' Medici, known in his time as "Lorenzo the Magnificent." Soldier, statesman, patron of the arts, and avid collector of great masterpieces, he is the very model of a Renaissance prince. One of the typical books of the time is Machiavelli's *Il Principe* ("The Prince") which discusses how princes and those around them should act.

The Medici court was not the only center of the arts. The D'Este family in Ferrara, the Gonzagas in Mantua, the Sforzas in Milan, and other ruling families in the city-states of North Italy all had magnificent courts and commissioned a steady stream of works from the finest painters, sculptors, and musicians they could find. The great courts sent ministers to scout for new talent to employ in the rich life of their courts. The Pope in Rome and the King in France also kept magnificent courts that strove to rival the Medici in splendor.

The Renaissance begins, at least as music historians view history, with the court of Philip the Good in the duchy of Burgundy, in the middle of the fifteenth century. The period ends, by music history reckoning, around 1600, during the reign of Elizabeth in England. One can argue that there has never been an English cultural period to rival the Elizabethan period, when Shakespeare, Marlowe, Dowland, and a host of other composers and poets were turning out their masterpieces, and Sir Francis Drake extended English sway over the seas. The Elizabethan period extended beyond 1600; the primary reason for using the turn of the century as the dividing line is the development of opera around 1600 in Florence.

Marriages

The courts competed fiercely in cultural splendor, and supported armies of artists of all types. The most splendid occasions of all were the royal marriages, when two families managed to work out a union between the daughter of one and the son of another. These unions, which had important military and diplomatic implications, were carefully arranged for years in advance and celebrated with weeks of feasting and lavish entertainment. We still have records of menus and accounts of entertainments from some of these occasions, and the details are staggering. Countries were nearly bankrupted to pay for these celebrations, and hundreds of artists and artisans of all sorts were paid to supply the requisite lavish settings, food, art, and music.

Music

The fact that so much music of the Renaissance is sacred music should not imply to us that composers worked for the church. They wrote for court **chapels**, groups of singers and instrumentalists who were employed by the great courts so that their celebrations of worship would be as lavish and up-to-date as every other aspect of their lives. The extravagant courts of the Renaissance may shock

Famous *Minnesinger* Heinrich von Meissen playing a fiddle, while fellow-musicians hold bagpipes, psaltery and shawn.

Michelangelo Buonarotti
David, 1501-04.
Approx. 18 ft. high.

our egalitarian sensibilities, but we certainly are in their cultural debt. All of the great masterpieces of this age were produced so that some court could "keep up with the Medici" and vie with other courts in magnificence.

Aesthetic

The Renaissance aesthetic was totally different from that of the Middle Ages, as we have noted. It was an age of great painting. Raphael, Michaelangelo, Leonardo da Vinci, and Botticelli, to name a few, were Renaissance masters. Their paintings are immediately recognized as different in style from earlier medieval works. Suddenly the people look like people, backgrounds are in perspective, and details of anatomy become important. The human figure is dealt with as a magnificent structure of muscle, sinew, and bone, not as a frame for vestments, as in medieval works. The human form is almost worshiped. The magnificence of Michelangelo's *David*, for example, is godlike. The anatomy is correct, but few of us have ever seen a human being that splendid in form and proportion. Sculptors revived the reverence for the human form exhibited by the great sculptors of classical Greece, although the Renaissance depictions of the human form in stone may be more dramatic than their classical models. The subject of Renaissance art is *man*—perhaps man glorified, with no limitations or imperfections, and perhaps under the guise of mythological themes—but still man. The twin achievements of the Renaissance visual arts—making a two-dimensional canvas appear to have depth and making stone appear to live and breathe—are among the towering achievements of all Western culture. They are still models for aspiring artists and are still revered as treasures by anyone who appreciates our Western cultural heritage.

SUMMARY

Western music had its roots in developments that took place during the **Middle Ages** and during the **Renaissance**.

People in the **Middle Ages** subscribed to a hierarchical world-view. All society was rigidly stratified beneath God and king. Seeking to preserve the status quo, this age looked unfavorably upon disturbing thought and scientific discovery. The aesthetic of the Middle Ages was theocentric. The primary purpose of the arts was to promote the worship of God and to promulgate the teachings of the church.

During this time, first monasteries, then government centers, and finally cathedrals became the centers of cultural achievement.

The rise of the great universities signaled, in some ways, a shift in emphasis from the unquestioned authority of the church to the questing of man's mind and an end to theocentric medieval culture.

The **Renaissance** was an anthropocentric age, proud and adventurous. It was an age of exploration and one in which scientific discoveries were welcomed and scientists were highly regarded. The magnificent courts maintained by the ruling families of Europe replaced the churches as centers of culture. Works of art were valued for their intrinsic delights, not for their didactic effectiveness, and much of the sacred music composed during this time was written for court **chapels**, groups of singers and instrumentalists employed by the great courts to make their celebrations of worship as lavish as every other aspect of their lives.

CHAPTER 7

Musical Developments

THE MUSICIAN AND SOCIETY

It is important for us to realize that our notion of the artist as a free spirit, able to do what he wills and create when he wills, is a very recent idea. In previous ages, the lives and careers of musicians, even the greatest among them, were vastly different from the life of a talented musician today.

During the Middle Ages

In the Middle Ages, the typical composer was an anonymous monk, who composed chants as needed for new feasts in his monastery's liturgy. He also sang in the choir, served as one of the soloists, or functioned on a rotating basis as **precentor**, or director of music for worship. A tremendous repertory of chants was written by a long series of such men. Another group of medieval musicians were the *jongleurs*, or **minstrels**, who traveled from place to place performing troubadour songs for aristocrats; they were the forerunners of later musicians who found court positions in the Renaissance and in the Baroque and Classical periods. Another important group wrote treatises about music, and an endless series of discussions about the purpose and basic ideas of music poured from these men. Best known among them was Guido of Arezzo, an eleventh-century theorist who is credited with developing clear staff notation and a practical system of designating specific pitches by pointing to certain areas of the hand.

The best-known medieval composer is Guillaume de Machaut, whom we have already mentioned as an important French poet. Machaut lived in the fourteenth century, during the breakdown of the medieval world, and his life is more typical of a Renaissance artist than of a medieval one. He was a cleric who served as secretary and scribe to a Bohemian nobleman. He traveled widely and achieved unusual fame for a medieval composer.

During the Renaissance

The life of a typical Renaissance composer, as we have already indicated, was quite different. Most of them began as choirboys in the chapel of a great court, that is, in the group of singers and instrumentalists hired to perform church and secular music for the court. The choirboys sang the soprano and alto parts in the church music—women did not perform publicly at this time—and received education in music and other subjects. Their apprenticeship ended when their voices changed in adolescence. The more talented boys were kept for further training and eventually sang the tenor and bass lines. The better musicians among the adult singers received training in composition, and the best individual of all was selected to be **maestro di capella**, or music director and composer for the court. Once a man made his name in that capacity, he could start looking around for better positions at competing courts. The best composers worked for as wide a variety of noble patrons as did their painting and sculpting colleagues. The highest mark of recognition was to be singled out to write music for the royal weddings described in Chapter 6. Naturally, the patrons wanted the composer with the highest possible reputation for that special task.

One interesting sidelight of the musical situation at the North Italian courts was that it was fashionable to have an *ultramontano*, a Northerner, from Flanders or the Low Countries, as *maestro di capella*. Northerners were much in demand, and there must have been some talented Italian composers who were passed over in the rush to compete with other courts. Later in the Renaissance, when specifically Italian forms such as the madrigal developed, Italian composers could make their name in that repertory and then move on to fame as composers of sacred music. One of the greatest composers of the late Renaissance and early Baroque period, Claudio Monteverdi, wrote music in many styles and moved as easily from court position to court position as his northern predecessors. We will deal with the life of the greatest northern composer, Josquin des Prez, in Chapter 9.

THE MEDIEVAL PERIOD

Notation

As we already mentioned, some of the most significant developments of the medieval period did not concern composition, but other disciplines connected with music. One of the most significant developments was the gradual evolution of **notation**. The notion of representing musical events in visual form is one of the most fundamental premises of Western music. An accurate system of musical notation, able to specify pitch, duration, rhythmic patterns, and subtle details of articulation, dynamics, and shifts of tempo is peculiar to Western art music. As you know, in the realm of popular music in our own culture and in the folk and art musics of other cultures, notation systems, when they exist, make no attempt at the completeness of the notation system used in Western art music.

Pitch-Specific Notation

Notation was not an overnight invention. Some of the earlier systems are difficult to decipher, and the world's scholars are still not completely sure how to interpret some of the systems developed in the medieval period. The first notation we know of appeared about A.D. 900 and was used in liturgical books. This

St. Gall notation, c. 900.

early notation was not pitch-specific, that is, one could not sight-read it with any accuracy at all. It simply indicated on which syllables the cluster of notes appeared and what types of **neumes**, or clusters of notes, were included. Every note of the chant melody is depicted, but one is not made aware what note to start on, how wide the intervals are, or what any particular note is. This notation was intended as a memory aid for singers who had already learned the melodies by rote.

It was a short and logical step from this early notation to **pitch-specific notation**, using something like a modern staff, or, in the absence of staff lines, writing high notes higher and low notes lower in the space available between the lines of text.

Polyphonic Notation

When *polyphony* began to appear around the year 1000, the question of notation became enormously more complicated. If two or more voices are to be coordinated and synchronized, the notation must indicate not only pitch, but also rhythm and alignment of the various voices. By about 1300, a system was established which was very much like our own, with different shapes and colors of notes indicating different time values.

Landini Manuscript, 14th century.

We cannot overestimate the importance of this achievement. Polyphonic Western music could not exist if the composer did not have available to him a universal way of making his intentions and wishes known. Without accurate notation, the composer would have to rely on performers to interpret his less-than-specific instructions, and works would vary widely from performance to performance and from group to group. Composer control, the fundamental premise of Western art music, would not be possible.

Music Theory

Music theory was another important development of the Middle Ages, occupying a large number of the great musical minds of the period. The questions discussed by musical writers of the time are both philosophical and practical. Among the philosophical concerns are the definition and purpose of music, its place in the medieval scheme of reality, and the music of the spheres. Among the practical concerns are scales, modes, interval sizes, notation, and ways to construct polyphonic textures.

Vocal Music

Monophony

The most extensive and important body of music composed in the Middle Ages was the huge repertory of **chants** for the communal worship of the monasteries and major churches. Thousands of individual chant selections were composed over the course of at least a thousand years, and the resulting body of music exhibits considerable variety of structure and organization. Most of the chant repertory exists only in manuscript form. Until recently, the only chants published were those that were part of the standardized worship of the worldwide Catholic church. We will look at one example of the chant repertory in Chapter 8.

Another body of monophonic music is the **secular song** of the period. This is a much smaller repertory, but also a significant one. As early as the Middle Ages, the Western tendency to set to music poetry depicting love, grief, longing, and heroic deeds found creative expression.

Polyphony

The discovery of polyphony is another crucial medieval innovation. Polyphony was first developed in liturgical music as a way to add extra solemnity to major feasts like Christmas and Easter. The first polyphony was additive, constructed by adding another voice or voices to a preexisting melody. It is important to note that the process of adding chords to a melody, a process we think of as quite natural, was a much later development. Melody and accompaniment texture, the pattern we regard as standard, appeared long after the development of contrapuntal writing.

By the end of the Middle Ages, the techniques developed for liturgical polyphony had been transferred to the realm of secular music. A standard type of late medieval polyphony is the three-voiced **motet**, with a preexisting melody as the lower voice and two new upper voices added. It is also standard in these late medieval motets to have two or three texts sung simultaneously, perhaps even in different languages, a practice we find difficult to understand.

Those who are interested in investigating this development may readily find discussions of medieval music in standard music history textbooks. Recordings are also available. The music sounds angular and somewhat harsh to our ears: notions of smooth harmony did not develop until the Renaissance. We must remember that the notion of logical sequences of chords, which we take for granted, had not been thought of at this time. As usually happens in the arts, the creators of music experiment at and beyond the frontiers of their supporting systematic thought.

Instrumental Music

One last area deserves mention. Although most medieval music is vocal, and very little music was written specifically for instruments, instruments were used, especially in secular music. The visual art of the time always depicts troubadours and ministrels accompanying their vocal performances with bowed string instruments, which we know were imported from the Arab lands. We also know that harps, plucked strings, and various wind instruments, including a small organ, existed. Late in the period, some dance music, written specifically for instruments, appeared. Instruments usually were used to double vocal lines in the polyphonic secular music of the period. Percussion instruments—bells and small drums—were used for rhythmic punctuation.

The musical history of the Middle Ages is a long and complex story. The significant fact from our vantage point is that Western music began with improvised solo sacred music and ended with a workable concept of polyphonic writing, a notation system, and some concepts about the way voices should sound together. On those bases, each worked out laboriously over hundreds of years, Western art music developed in its own directions, distinct from all the musics of the rest of the world.

THE RENAISSANCE

The music of the Renaissance sounds much less foreign to us than the music of the Middle Ages. That fact, of course, is a result of a different approach to certain elements of musical style. The chief reason that Renaissance music sounds less "angular" and more pleasant to us than late medieval polyphony is a new way of thinking about harmony and texture.

Harmony

One school of fifteenth-century English composition, led by composers like John Dunstable, drew international attention because of the sweetness of its sound. English composers favored a smooth sound based on triads as the usual combined sound of the three voices. This **"English sweetness,"** as it was called, was adopted by the continental composers of the **Burgundian school** and became the standard sound of Renaissance choral music. The voices still moved in linear fashion, but the medieval concern for linear motion in each voice was now balanced by a concern for chords of a smooth and pleasing nature.

Texture

The standard late medieval texture, adopted in Burgundy as well, is three voices, with the preexisting voice or "tenor" at the bottom and two newly composed voices added on top. The standard Renaissance texture is four voices, with the tenor second from the bottom and three added voices. This change may seem unimportant, but it facilitated "harmonic" thinking because the bottom voice could now function any way the composer liked, including as a harmonic bass line. The resulting four-voice texture remains the standard layout of a chorus, and our names for the four voices are derived from the Renaissance terms.

Soprano: Superius (high voice)

Alto: Contratenor altus (high contratenor)

Tenor: Tenor

Bass: Contratenor bassus (low contratenor)

Choral Music

Sacred Choral Style

Another fundamental innovation was the creation of a standardized international style: the sacred choral style. This style was consciously employed by all Renaissance composers who worked in the field of sacred music. Although there are subtle differences among the styles of individual composers, the overall characteristics of the sacred style are found in all sacred works. The style, which flourished in the first half of the Renaissance, was revived and codified by

Palestrina and others late in the Renaissance. Thus, it became the first truly international style and the first one reduced to a system of compositional rules. Today, students of composition are still taught to write in an approximation of the Renaissance style to learn control of polyphonic writing.

The sacred style included performance specifications as well. The music was written for four voices, the soprano and alto parts to be performed by boys, and the tenor and bass parts by men. Although instruments were used occasionally to reinforce some of the lines, it is still fundamentally a vocal style.

The music written in this style consists of Masses and motets. By **Mass** we now mean a unified setting of the sung parts of the Ordinary of the Mass. A Mass, therefore, includes related settings of the Kyrie, Gloria, Sanctus, and Agnus Dei. The various selections may be unified by making use of the same preexisting material, or in other ways. The various parts of a Mass setting are so closely related that they should be performed in those units, rather than as individual selections. In Chapter 9, we will look at Renaissance Mass composition in more detail.

Written in somewhat the same style are **motets**, which during the Renaissance meant sacred choral pieces, usually settings of one of the sung parts of the Proper of the Mass. They often utilize as the material for all four voices the successive phrases of the chant setting of the same text. Longer motets are customarily written in A-B-A form, with a contrasting section, usually in lighter three-voice texture, in the center.

The Renaissance sacred style sounds quite "churchy" to us, because it is a style of great restraint, control, and care. Seldom is there much attention paid to the depiction of emotion, or to the expressive possibilities of various words or texts. In fact, one reason the style was revived late in the period was that the Council of Trent (1545-1563) had outlawed operatic display in church music, and musicians were casting about for a fitting style of polyphony. Church documents on sacred music exalt the Renaissance style as proper and fitting for church music and put it on a par with chant as a prototype of what church music should be.

Secular Music

As you can imagine, no period or composer would be satisfied by the creation of just one style, particularly when that style is as restrained and systematic as the Renaissance sacred style. Almost by necessity, the evolution of the international sacred style was accompanied by the creation of more expressive and impulsive national styles of secular music. In France, the **chanson** developed. It consisted of rhythmically active tunes, set usually in three voices, sounding like a melody and two accompaniment voices. In Italy, composers wrote in a similar chordal and dance-like style, called the **frottola.** Out of the frottola grew the most important secular form of the period, the Italian **madrigal.**

The madrigal went through a long evolution. At its height, it combined polyphonic and chordal sections in a five-voice texture. Its chief characteristic was the attention paid to depiction of feeling. The texts, usually about the pain of love, were filled with interjections of grief and reference to weeping, sighing, and dying. Composers developed standard ways of depicting each of these emotions in music. Although madrigals are often performed nowadays by choruses, they were written for a different sort of performance. They were intended to be sung by chamber vocal groups, one singer to a part, using women for the soprano and alto lines. They were performed for a sophisticated court audience, who could appreciate the apt depictions of feeling. The whole point was a series of dramatic musical climaxes at each emotional high point of the text. Madrigals were often performed between the acts of dramatic presentations at court. The connection between madrigal and later opera, therefore, becomes clear: opera was written originally for the same setting and audience, and simply extended to the solo voice the expressive dramatic possibilities developed for the vocal group in the madrigal. The Italian madrigal style was copied in Elizabethan England. Chapter 10 looks at an English madrigal.

The polarity between the sacred and secular styles of the Renaissance reflects a fundamental polarity in subsequent Western art music, the polarity between strict, four-voice, "classical" style, and more expressive, impulsive styles.

Instrumental Music

A last important area of Renaissance music is music for instruments. The great courts had groups of instrumental players, including indoor and outdoor groups. Instruments were classified as "loud" or "soft" and grouped in standard ensembles. The idiomatic possibilities of certain instruments were also greatly exploited.

Instrumental Idiom

In music, **idiom** means the particular styles of melodic and chordal writing that are easily performed on a particular instrument. Consciousness of specific instrumental idiom leads a composer to write differently for a lute, for example, than he would for a keyboard instrument, and differently for a flute than he would for a trumpet. The discovery of the capabilities of the various instruments was a very important development and led to the awareness we still have of what sounds best on each instrument.

The Lute

The clearest example of the growing consciousness of idiom is writing for the lute, an instrument much like the modern classical guitar in tuning and playing technique. Because the strings of the lute are plucked, either with a quill held in the right hand, or with the player's fingernails, the sound "decays" (fades) quickly. Because the player has only the four fingers of his left hand to stop the strings, and therefore to change the pitch, it is hard for a lute to play a four-voice,

This German woodcut by Hans Burgkmair shows a shop for the manufacture of musical instruments, including organ, harp, drums, viol, recorders, lute, cromorne and trumscheit.

polyphonic texture. One or two voices are fairly easy; and chordal accompaniments, such as a modern folksinger would play to accompany his tune, are easily produced by strumming. We can see how aware Renaissance composers and "arrangers" were of the potential and the limitations of the lute by studying their arrangements of four-voice vocal pieces for solo voice and lute accompaniment. Usually the composer wrote a combination of countermelodies in one or two voices and occasional six-string chords.

The Keyboard Instruments

The next class of instruments for which composers developed specific idioms were the keyboard instruments. Like the lute, the harpsichord (or its smaller version, the **virginals**) cannot sustain a tone for very long. The sound is produced by plucking, and the player has no way of sustaining or increasing the sound once the string is plucked. But the player is able to do several specific things that fit

Double spinet or virginal. The left side can be moved for outdoor use. This one was made by the famous Rucker family of Antwerp.

easily under the fingers, like rapid scale passages, trills, and ornamental patterns using nearby notes. Rolling the chords (playing them as successive notes rather than as a single sound) makes them stand out more clearly and ring longer. The player can also play as many as ten notes at once, provided they are written to fit within the span of his two hands. Harpsichord music of the late Renaissance, particularly of Elizabethan England, shows a clear awareness of these techniques.

The organ, unlike the other keyboards, has the power to sustain any note as long as the player holds down the key and the person pumping the bellows maintains constant wind pressure. Late Renaissance music for organ is distinct at a glance from music for other keyboards because of the combination of rapid passage work, which is easy on any keyboard, and sustained long notes, possible only on the organ.

Music for the other instruments was not so specific as to idiom. Much of the wind music of the Renaissance works as well on flutes or recorders as it does on other types of winds. It remained for the Baroque period to extend the idea of instrumental idiom, particularly regarding the special potential of the new violin family and the high register of the trumpet.

The Consort

Our twentieth-century ears are used to listening to instruments combined in standard groups, such as the symphony orchestra, wind band, woodwind quintet, and other mixed chamber groups. The Renaissance idea was generally to use instruments in **consorts**, groups of like instruments in different sizes, such as recorders or flutes in soprano, alto, tenor, and bass sizes. Composers also wrote for *mixed consorts*, groups made up of instruments compatible in color and dynamic range, but rarely for all instruments at once. The only remnants of the consort idea in music after the Baroque period are the string quartet, made up of different members of the violin family, and occasional pieces for groups of like instruments, which are used more as teaching pieces in music schools than as a regular part of our concert and recital programs.

The Instruments

As we mentioned, some Renaissance instruments are familiar to us through their modern analogs, and some are not. Whether or not the instruments still exist in modern versions, the sound and color of the modern versions are so changed that we may not immediately associate them with their Renaissance counterparts.

Keyboards

We have already mentioned the harpsichord, virginals, and organ of the Renaissance. Like the modern piano, which used to be standard equipment in many middle-class parlors, the virginals and harpsichord developed as household instruments for the amateur soloist. Renaissance instruments of this type were simpler than the large, multiple-strung harpsichords of the Baroque period and were not designed as virtuoso instruments, or instruments for public solo performance. Organs also were simpler than their Baroque counterparts and lacked the pedal keyboard. They were found in churches, like their modern counterparts, and were used to play incidental music in services.

The Strings

The lute, already discussed, was the most popular instrument, both for home amateur playing and for accompanying solo songs. It was tuned much like the modern guitar, played with the fingernails of the right hand or with a quill plectrum, and usually strung with **courses** of double strings. Its construction was significantly different from that of the guitar, however, because the **sound box** was shaped like half a melon, and the **fingerboard** usually angled sharply back toward the pegs.

The bowed string instrument popular at the time was the **viol**, which is a different family from the later violins. The viols have sloping shoulders, a body of different shape from that of the violin, frets on the fingerboard, and a softer, darker sound than the violin family. The most common viol was the *viola da gamba*, or "leg viol," which was held vertically in front of the player, on the lap or between the knees, like a modern cello. The other type was the *viola da brac-*

cia, or "arm viol," held like a modern violin. **Gambas** (a common shorter term for *viola da gamba*) were made in soprano, alto, tenor, and bass sizes and often played as a consort. The viola family persisted into Baroque times, but was eventually superseded by the new violins, particularly after new developments in violin making and composition turned the violin into a brilliant solo instrument.

Winds

Renaissance winds come in a bewildering variety of types and sizes. The **recorder**, a wooden flute with a mouthpiece designed like a whistle, was very popular and was made in many sizes. **Transverse flutes** appeared also, that is, wooden flutes held sideways, with a hole to blow across rather than a mouthpiece. Recorder and flute are related instruments, but the sound is somewhat different.

Several types of double reeds were used. The **krummhorn**, with a capped double reed, has no modern analog. Its sound is nasal and buzzing, and quite distinctive. Exposed double reeds, older versions of the modern oboe and bassoon, also existed. The **shawm** is the ancestor of the oboe, and the **dulcian** is the mellower version of the modern bassoon. Other double reeds include the startingly loud **rauschpfeife** and the **racket**.

Brass

Brass instruments in use at the time include the **sackbut**, the ancestor of the trombone, which has a smaller bell and bore than the modern version and, consequently, a softer sound. They, too, were made in various sizes and played in consorts. Natural trumpets existed also, but did not really come into their own until the Baroque period. An instrument peculiar to the Renaissance is the **cornetto**, which has a cupped mouthpiece like a trumpet but holes in its body like a woodwind. The body is made of wood and covered with leather, and the sound is something like a soft trumpet.

Some Renaissance instrumental music consists of adaptations of vocal models, such as the motet or chanson. A large amount of *dance music* exists also, written specifically for particular instrumental groups. Chapter 11 looks at an example of dance music for instruments. Our own day has seen a revival of interest in Renaissance instruments and their special sound. Fortunately, performances and recordings of authentic Renaissance instrumental music are much more available now than they were ten or twenty years ago.

Renaissance music is, in many ways, the first stage of "modern" music, accessible and enjoyable to us without our having to spend time educating our tastes. The sacred music sounds ethereal and otherworldly to us, as it was supposed to, and the secular and dance music still has an immediate appeal. Although you will seldom hear much of it in a concert hall, except at choral concerts, it is well worth experiencing.

SUMMARY

During the Middle Ages, the typical composer was an anonymous monk who sang in the monastery choir and wrote **chants** for new feasts. Other musicians were **minstrels** or **troubadours**.

In contrast, the typical Renaissance composer began as a choirboy in the **chapel** of a great court and aspired to become **maestro di capella**, music director and composer of a court chapel.

One important musical development of the medieval period was **pitch-specific notation**, which made possible the accurate representation of **polyphony** and the composer control characteristic of later Western art music.

Among the vocal music forms developed during the medieval period were **monophonic chants** and **secular songs** and **polyphonic** liturgical and secular works.

Although most medieval music is vocal, **troubadours** and **minstrels** often accompanied their vocal performances on bowed string instruments. Late in the period, dance music written exclusively for instruments appeared. Bells and small drums were used for rhythmic punctuation.

Renaissance music was, in many ways, the first stage of modern music. It was characterized by a different approach to **harmony** and **texture**. The standard Renaissance texture is four voices, with the **tenor** voice second from the bottom and three added voices: **soprano**, **alto**, and **bass**. This period also witnessed the development of the **sacred choral style** and of national styles of secular music.

The instrumental music written during the Renaissance consisted primarily of dance music and adaptations of vocal models. It was based on an awareness of **idiom**. Among the instruments commonly used, singly or in **consorts**, were the **lute**, **harpsichord**, **virginals**, organ, strings, **recorder**, **transverse flute**, and members of the double reed and brass families.

CHAPTER 8

Chant: Offertory, "Jubilate Deo"

As we already mentioned, the huge repertory of Latin chant constitutes the only sizable body of monophonic music within the Western art music tradition. Secular song of the Middle Ages is another monophonic style; but at the time, secular song was regarded not as art music but as popular music.

CHANT

Composition

Chant, the first body of music in our Western art music tradition, is an enormously complex and varied body of music. We are not really sure how it was composed in the first few centuries of the Church's existence. In fact, it was probably not "composed" at all, but improvised by singers who had the texts in front of them and were able to improvise in whatever mode they chose. Remember that notation did not appear until the ninth century, so that our notions of the early history of chant are necessarily conjectural. We know that the Christian liturgy was designed after the model of the Hebrew liturgy and that there are great similarities between Hebrew and Christian chant. We therefore assume that Western chant began like its Hebraic model. Singers knew an assortment of standard **lesson tones**—ways of chanting a passage of Scripture—and an assortment of phrases in each **mode** that could be strung together to improvise a musical piece. What is fascinating about the long history of chant is that, after it started from these improvisatory Hebrew or Middle Eastern roots, it became Westernized. We know that, in the ninth and tenth centuries, new chants were composed in our sense, that is, a musician sat down with the text in front of him and *wrote* out a melody to which the text would be sung. In these later chants, we can observe Western compositional principles at work, principles such as symmetry, logical structure, even word-painting. The total body of chant, then, is a hybrid group of musical settings, some quite improvisatory in style, some logically and symmetrically constructed, some Eastern in flavor, and some Western.

Form or Type

Chant was, of course, music for a specific purpose, and we must understand something of its context in order to understand the music. We mentioned the organization of a medieval monastery in an earlier chapter. Monks committed themselves for life to a particular monastery and were assigned tasks that would fit their talents and training and would serve the greater good of the community. Whatever work the monks did, they all spent three or four hours a day in communal prayer, most of which was sung. Some chant was sung by the congregation; some was sung by a choir of monks; and some was sung by soloists. Congregational chants are usually **syllabic**—that is, there is one note per syllable of text. The chants for choir and soloists are **neumatic**, with small clusters of notes on each syllable, or **melismatic**, with long, florid passages or **melismas** on each syllable of text. The style results from the liturgical function of a particular chant. The principal purpose of some chants is the declamation of the text, whereas the primary purpose of others is to provide a pause for contemplation.

The simplest form of chant is the **Psalm tone**, which is used for the singing of psalms in the Divine Office, those prayer services that are celebrated throughout the day. A Psalm tone consists of a reciting note on which most of the verse is sung, an opening formula of a few notes, and interior and final cadential formulas. The Psalm tones, borrowed from the Hebrew liturgy, provide a flexible way of singing the Psalms or other Scriptural passages in natural speech rhythm, to a simple melody easy to memorize. Because the monks chanted the entire book of Psalms—all 150 of them—each week in the Office, they needed an easy way to set these texts.

Rhythmic Practice

Despite the fact that we know a lot about chant and how it was performed, there are some important things that we do not know. One nagging question concerns rhythmic practice. When you hear chant performed, the performers usually sing all of the notes in equal duration; but there is evidence that, at least at one period, chant was performed in a way that made some notes longer and some shorter, a practice which was lost around the year 1000. Some contemporary commentators complain that "no one knows how to sing chant correctly any more." It is frustrating to know so much about the authentic melodies and about how they should be sung, and still to be ignorant about a question as fundamental as rhythm. In any event, the present system, although not satisfying to scholars, certainly makes a satisfying performance and allows us to appreciate the beauty and artistic quality of this large body of music.

"JUBILATE DEO OMNIS TERRA"

The one chant selection we will look at in detail is an Offertory chant. The Offertory is one of the **Proper chants**, that is, one of the texts that changes for each Sunday or feast, as opposed to the **Ordinary texts**, which are the same in each celebration of the Eucharist. The Offertory serves as background music for the preparations for the sacrifice part of the Mass, after the readings. Therefore, it is not concerned chiefly with declamation of text, but has a more contemplative function.

This particular chant is proper to the Mass of the Second Sunday after Epiphany, during a contemplative season of the church year, between the drama of Christmas and the following cycle of Lent and Holy Week. The text, taken from one of the Psalms, follows, in Latin and English.

> *Jubilate Deo universa terra,* (repeated)
> *psalmum dicite nomini ejus.*
> *Venite et audite, omnes qui timetis Deum,*
> *quanta fecit Dominus animae meae, alleluia.*

> Shout out with joy to the Lord, all the earth,
> sing praise to his name.
> Hear now, all you who revere God,
> what great things the Lord has done for my soul, Alleluia.

One striking thing about this particular chant selection is the repetition of the first line, a very rare occurrence in the chant repertoire. The "composer"—more likely, the long line of singers who improvised a melody in the first mode for this text—considered the first line deserving of additional musical treatment. As you look at the outline of the musical setting in Figure 8-1, note that the syllable "-la" of the second "jubilate" is set to a very long group of notes, or melisma. Not only is the melisma long, but it snakes its way up beyond the normal range of the first mode to the highest point of the entire melody. This unusual treatment singles out the verb for "praise" for unique and effective musical treatment. Note also that, like most chant melodies, this tune moves in very controlled fashion,

FIGURE 8-1. LISTENING GUIDE

"JUBILATE DEO OMNIS TERRA"

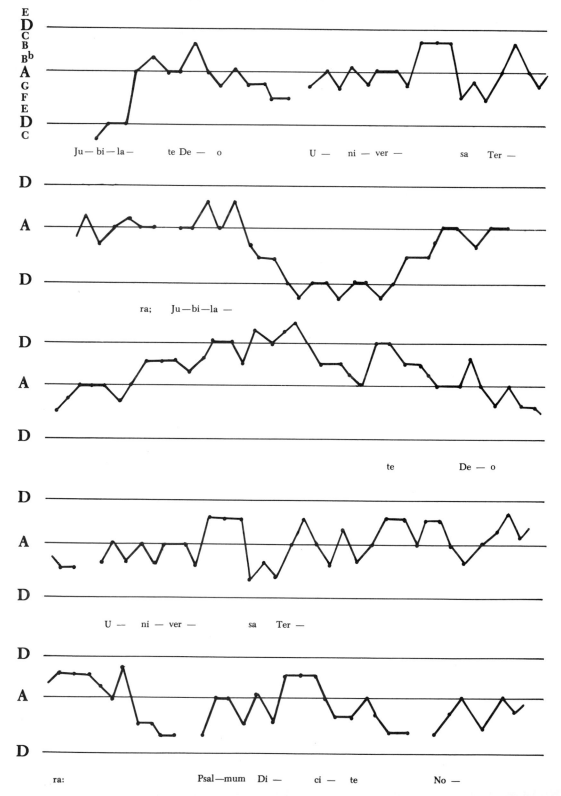

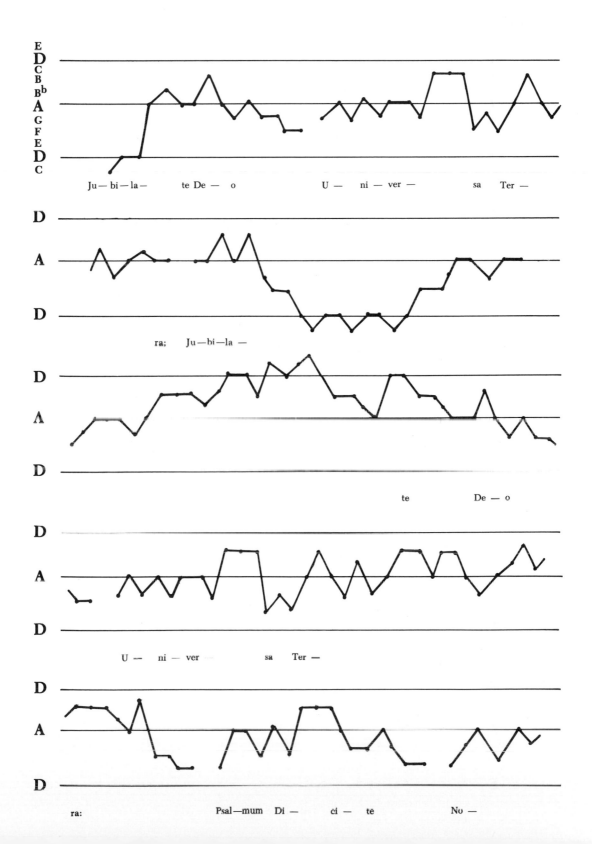

generally by step rather than by leap, and constantly doubles back on itself to create a gently moving, ethereal effect. What we hear is a long ribbon of sound, rising and falling in gentle waves, with balanced phrases, momentary pauses, and a slow, sinuous descent back to the **final** or key note of the mode at the end. This is effective worship music, used for centuries as the ideal music to express the Church's faith.

The listening guide for this selection (Figure 8-1) is somewhat different from the other guides in this book. There is no time line here; instead, the melodic contour is diagrammed on the vertical scale marked at the left of each segment. The most important notes of the mode—D and A—are marked so that you can see the basic motion from one main note to the other, and the way the melody tends to swirl around these main structural notes. The horizontal distance is the same for each note, following the rhythmic theories by which chant is usually performed today. Repeated notes are extended one space, and pauses between phrases are marked by an interruption of one space between the segments of the melody. The text is included as a point of reference.

As you listen to this religious piece, note how effective monophony can be. After the year 1000 or so, we seldom hear unaccompanied melody in the West. Our ears are used to polyphony, choruses, and orchestras, but we can sense from this one example how effective a single melody can be to express human feelings and aspirations. We can also appreciate why monophony is such a common texture in the folk musics and art musics of other cultures.

SUMMARY

Chant, the first body of music in our Western art music tradition, is enormously complex and varied. It is both improvisatory and logically constructed in style, both Eastern and Western in flavor.

Early Western chant was probably not "composed" but, like its Hebraic model, improvised by singers familiar with standard melodic formulas.

An integral part of religious services, chant was music for a specific purpose. It declaimed the text or provided pauses within the service for contemplation. **Syllabic chant** was written in simple form to be sung by the congregation. More complicated **neumatic** and **melismatic chants** were written to be sung by choirs of monks and by soloists. The simplest form of chant is the **Psalm tone.**

While we know a great deal about how chant was performed, we know little about the rhythms that were used.

CHAPTER 9

Josquin Des Prez "Kyrie" from Missa Pange Lingua

JOSQUIN DES PREZ

As we mentioned in Chapter 7, it was fashionable in the great courts of the Renaissance to have a Northerner, a musician from the region that now comprises France and the Low Countries, as *maestro di capella*, music director and chief court composer. Among the greatest of these Franco-Flemish composers was Josquin Des Prez, who lived from about 1440 until 1521.

Josquin's Life

Josquin's life is typical of the way a musician made his way in Renaissance society. He was born in the province of Hainaut, which is near the present border of France and Belgium. From court records and documents, we can piece together the outlines of his career. He first surfaced as a member of the chapel, or musical entourage, of the Sforza family in Milan, where he spent about ten years. After that, he is mentioned in connection with the Papal Chapel in Rome and the court of Louis XII of France. After a year as *maestro di capella* at the court of Ferrara in North Italy, he returned to France. He spent the last years of his life in retirement in the region of his birth. He was very highly regarded by his contemporaries. One writer of the time says he occupies the same position in music that Michelangelo occupies in the visual arts. Others called him "the Father of Musicians," and "the best composer of our times." Modern research has provided us with reliable editions of his works, and the present consensus among scholars is that he is certainly one of the greatest composers of the Franco-Flemish style.

Josquin's Works

Like most of the composers of the time, Josquin was versatile and wrote in a number of distinct styles. He is best known for his sacred choral works, which include about eighteen Masses and one hundred motets. He also wrote about seventy secular works we know of, including chansons and several instrumental pieces. One of his most famous works is a touching *"Deploration,"* or elegy, to the recently deceased Ockeghem, an earlier composer who had been the teacher of Josquin and of many other Franco-Flemish composers.

Masses

Among his Masses are examples of all of the standard ways of organizing coherent settings of the Ordinary of the Mass then in practice. All are based on preexisting material, which explains the subtitle affixed to the title of each Mass, for example, *Missa L'Homme Armé Sexti Toni* ("Sixth Tone Mass on 'L'Homme Armé' ") and *Missa Malheur me bat*. The preexisting material could have been a secular tune used in the tenor of the Mass, a polyphonic chanson which was the model for the new polyphony, or a monophonic chant tune which was used as the material for all four voices.

Motets

This last technique—having all four voices sing the same borrowed material—is the basis for Josquin's chief contribution, the motet. He perfected **four-voice imitation**, utilizing the same borrowed material, as the basic organizing principle of sacred polyphony. In this style, each of the voices enters, singing a modified version of the first phrase of the preexisting chant melody in imitation. After all voices have entered, there is a free section in which the texture and rhythm become more complicated; the effect is to increase the tension and activity before a cadence. The cadence resolves that tension. Generally, three voices sing the last note of the cadence while the fourth begins the next section of polyphonic entries, based on the second phrase of the chant melody. That kind of cadence is called an **overlapped cadence**. Each of the imitative sections, then, uses a different segment of the preexisting melody. This same technique is utilized by

Bach, when he writes choral movements based on four-voice imitation of successive phrases of Lutheran hymn tunes. The development and perfecting of **motet style**, as this technique is called, is regarded as the chief contribution of Josquin to the development of Renaissance sacred style.

Another frequent characteristic of his style is called **paired imitation**, and consists of varying the four-voice texture by sometimes disposing the voices in pairs. Varying the pairings changes the color of the sound and sets up subsections within each imitative segment. The sound of paired imitation, his mastery of all imitative techniques, his clear phrase structure, and his relatively lively approach to rhythm make Josquin's personal style recognizable to a trained ear. Like many great composers in the history of Western art music, he appeared when a style was fairly settled, well past its experimental phase, and brought the innovations of others and his own contributions into an integrated, sophisticated style.

"KYRIE" FROM *MISSA PANGE LINGUA*

The *Missa Pange Lingua* is one of the more famous of Josquin's Masses and is regarded as one of his masterpieces. It is written in what is called **paraphrase style**. Actually, the Mass is written in motet style, with the material for all four voices based on the preexisting monophonic chant tune. This distinction is important. In a **cantus firmus Mass**, the preexisting melody is laid out in the tenor voice in various ways and then three freely written voices are added to it. In motet or paraphrase style, the borrowed melody becomes the material for all the voices. As an example of how the chant melodies are adopted as imitative ideas, compare the first line of the chant with the opening imitative idea of the "Kyrie" setting in Figure 9-1.

Figure 9-1. Musical example of chant and polyphonic idea.

FIGURE 9-2. LISTENING GUIDE

"KYRIE" FROM *MISSA PANGE LINGUA,* BY JOSQUIN

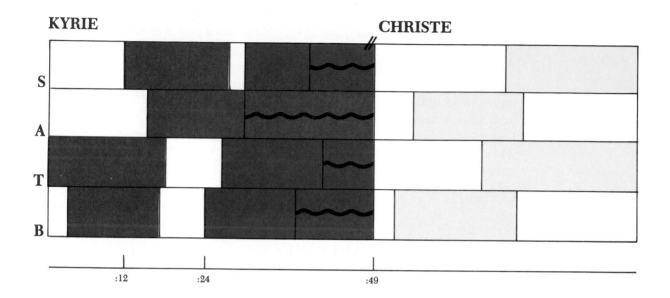

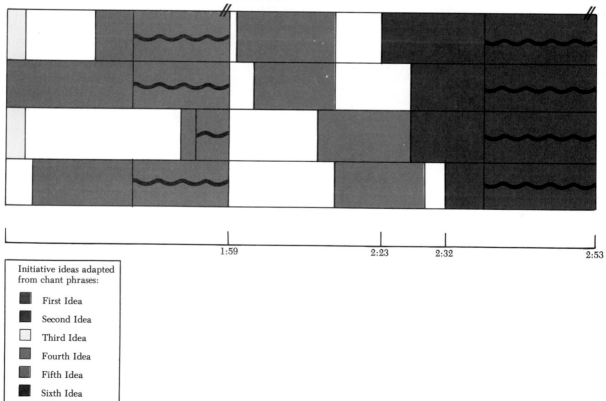

The chant melody, which is a hymn written to accompany the Eucharistic procession on the feast of Corpus Christi, is divided into six phrases. Josquin fits the six phrases symmetrically into the three sections of the Kyrie. The first two chant phrases become the imitative material for the "Kyrie" section, the next two for the "Christe" section, and the final two for the closing "Kyrie" section. Overlapped cadences, often preceded by busy precadential writing, separate the sections based on different phrases of the chant. The same kind of process is used in the later movements, the "Gloria," "Sanctus," and "Agnus Dei." Each movement begins with a version of the first phrase of the chant melody, which gives unity to the Mass setting.

As is true of many compositional processes, the method of adapting a chant melody to become a series of polyphonic sections is easier to hear or depict graphically than to describe. The listening guide in Figure 9-2 outlines the organization of the music. The pattern of entries in each section is laid out graphically. Different colors represent different segments of the chant melody, and the wavy lines represent free, precadential material. The usual time line provides a point of reference as you listen to the recording. With the aid of the guide, you should be able to hear how the work is organized and to appreciate the composer's skill in creating a new work from existing material.

SUMMARY

Josquin Des Prez (*c.* 1440-1521) was among the greatest of the Franco-Flemish composers. He was likened to Michelangelo and termed by some "the Father of Musicians" and "the best composer of our times."

He is best known for his sacred choral works. He combined **four-voice imitation** and **overlapped cadence** in a technique called **motet style,** regarded as his chief contribution to the development of Renaissance sacred music. Among his works are *Missa L'Homme Armé Sexti Toni* and *Missa Pange Lingua*, and about one hundred motets.

CHAPTER **10**

Renaissance Secular Vocal Music: Thomas Morley

NATIONAL VOCAL STYLES

In Chapter 7, we pointed out that the evolution of the international sacred style of Renaissance choral music was accompanied, as if by necessity, by the parallel development of distinct national styles. Examples of national vocal styles include the **chanson** in France, the **villancico** in Spain, and the **frottola** and **madrigal** in Italy. The madrigal was the most important of these forms. It underwent a long development, involving many of the most creative and original composers in Italy. The madrigal gave musical expression to feelings of longing and grief, particularly the pain of frustrated love. In many ways, the madrigal was the predecessor of **opera**, which extended to the solo voice the expressive potential developed for a small group of singers in madrigal literature.

The examples of Renaissance secular music we will listen to are from Elizabethan England. English composers adopted the Italian madrigal style in some of their own compositions and also developed a native English style in what they called the **ballett**, a homophonic, strongly rhythmic style, marked by refrains on the syllables "fa-la-la."

ELIZABETHAN ENGLAND

If anyone actually manages to invent the time machine, one of the first periods I would wish to visit would be Elizabethan England. As we have often pointed out, culture flourishes in stable, strong regimes, especially when the person in power values the arts and takes pride in the achievements of the region's literary, visual, and musical artists. The reign of Elizabeth of England, from 1558 to 1603, was one of the best examples of such a regime. The defeat of the Spanish Armada in 1588 consolidated England's dominion over the seas, and her power was unchallenged. The long rule of the queen, who was greatly interested in supporting English arts, made possible one of the great cultural flowerings in English history.

Musical Styles

It is intriguing that England seems to become an important center in the history of music during periods of transition elsewhere in Europe. The first great period of English music is in the early fifteenth century, when medieval music on the Continent had settled into an overly intellectual, mannered phase. The fifteenth-century English style, adopted on the Continent, became the basis of the new Renaissance style. The music of Elizabethan England utilizes all of the exciting innovations of late Renaissance European music and adds some native English touches to create a style that fits midway between late Renaissance style and the new ideas of the Baroque.

This painting depicts Elizabeth taking part in an energetic court dance.

Elizabethan composers produced music in a wide variety of styles. During Catholic reigns, like that of Mary Queen of Scots, they wrote skillful Latin Masses and motets, in a revival of Franco-Flemish sacred style. When Protestant kings were in power, they invented new types of service music for the Anglican Mass, with English texts. They produced a large amount of instrumental music, especially for the lute and virginals. The latter was a small, tabletop harpsichord, which became the most popular instrument for amateurs to play at home. They also wrote for viol consorts. The prevalent forms in the instrumental repertory they developed were variations and dance forms.

In their secular vocal music, they adapted the techniques of the Italian madrigal, writing complex and expressive pieces for four or five voices. They even devised new stylized names for the ladies to which the pieces were addressed—names like "Belinda"—so that the names of the love objects in the poetry would have the standard rhythmic patterns of Italian names. Even the Queen was honored and addressed under invented names of Italian flavor, names like "Oriana" and "Parthenia."

Thus, while Shakespeare, Jonson, and Marlowe were producing the masterpieces still regarded as crowning achievements of English literature and drama, equally great composers, like William Byrd, John Dowland, Thomas Campion, and Thomas Morley, were producing musical works that are still regarded as one of the high points in the history of music in England. Among the forward-looking works of this period are very expressive and harmonically adventurous solo songs with lute accompaniment. These works belong more to the Baroque period than to the Renaissance, because of their innovative exploitation of the expressive power of the solo voice. Modern British composers, like Benjamin Britten, have written many works based on these Elizabethan songs by composers whom the moderns regard as their direct ancestors.

This Gobelins tapestry depicts a Renaissance musician at an organ (Cluny Museum, Paris).

Thomas Morley

Thomas Morley, the composer of the examples of Elizabethan music we will study, lived from about 1557 until 1603. His lifetime thus coincided almost exactly with the reign of Elizabeth. Like most English composers of the period, he began his career as an organist, at St. Paul's in London. He wrote a famous treatise, *A Plaine and Easie Introduction to Practical Musicke*, which condenses the standard European treatises of the Renaissance into practical rules for composition, written in the form of a dialogue between two questioning students and a learned master. In the early 1590s, he was made a Gentleman of the Chapel Royal, a position that provided him the leisure and royal sponsorship for publishing music. He published nine books of vocal and instrumental music, some of which were reprinted in Italian and German editions.

We will listen to two short pieces by Morley, one a madrigal in the Italian style, and the other a jolly ballett, replete with the usual fa-la-las.

"In Dew of Roses"

The madrigal is from the first book of *Madrigalls in Foure Voyces*, published in 1594, the year of the premiere of Shakespeare's *Romeo and Juliet*. The fact that the Elizabethans called these Italian-style works "madrigals" indicates that they acknowledged their debt to the important Italian genre. Like an Italian madrigal, this work is **through-composed**; that is, it is not made up of repeating sections, but written as a continuous series of new musical ideas. The text is an English version of a typical Italian madrigal text, which focuses on the bitter pain of unrequited love and is filled with tears and sighs. The names of the lovers—Lycoris and Dorus—have the classical Greek flavor typical of Italian poetry of the time, with its sophisticated humanist and classical interest. The poetry is stylized and filled with plays on words and ideas, like the clever treatment of the idea of "kill" or "slay" in the last few lines. The text follows:

> In dew of roses steeping
> her lovely cheeks, Lycoris thus sat weeping:
> "Ah, Dorus false, that hast my heart bereft me,
> And now unkind hast left me.
> Hear me, alas! Cannot my beauty move thee?
> Pity me then, because I love thee.
> Thou scorn'st the more I pray thee.
> And this thou dost to slay me.
> Ah, then kill me and vaunt thee.
> Yet my ghost still shall haunt thee."

The music greatly resembles Italian settings of similar texts. Complex polyphonic patterns are established, setting up a layered texture. The interjections of grief are set to **sighing figures** borrowed from the Italian repertory. The standard musical depiction of a sigh is a two-note, descending figure (see Figure 10-1). The overall feeling is quietly sad. Some words and phrases are repeated, along with their musical settings, for emphasis, another trait borrowed from the

Figure 10-1.   Musical example of sighing figures in a Morley Madrigal.

Italian models. The resulting combination of text and music is a dramatic, expressive depiction of strong human feeling, designed to bring out effectively the successive ideas of the poetic text.

"Now Is The Month of Maying"

The next piece is a **ballett**, a term used by Elizabethan composers to denote a strongly rhythmic type of vocal music related to instrumental dance music. The text is happy rather than sad, and speaks of a May dance. Like many Elizabethan poetic texts, it urges the hearer to join in the merriment.

The musical setting is quite distinct from the style of the madrigal just described. Instead of a through-composed work, we now have two repeating ideas, to which the entire text is set. Instead of the sighing languor of the madrigal, we now have toe-tapping dance rhythms. Instead of polyphonic texture, we have a basically chordal texture, varied by the more polyphonic fa-la-las that follow every couplet. The listening guide (Figure 10-3) gives the texts and marks the repeats of each couplet. The letters A and B indicate the two musical ideas that alternate throughout the text. Each couplet ends with a string of fa-la-las, and then repeats, so that the overall form can be described as follows: A-A-B-B-A-A-B-B-A-A-B-B.

Figure 10-2.   Musical example of A and B ideas in the Morley ballett.

These contrasting examples of secular vocal music from the Elizabethan period illustrate England's awareness of Continental styles, and her own native style. They also illustrate the variety of music produced in this fertile period and give us an idea of the music that was being written at the same time as the monuments of English literature and drama.

SUMMARY

The evolution during the Renaissance of an international sacred style of choral music was accompanied by the development of distinct national styles of secular vocal music. Among these styles were the **chanson** in France, the **villancico** in Spain, the **frottola** and **madrigal** in Italy, and the **ballett** in England.

The long and stable rule of Elizabeth I (1533-1603), who encouraged and supported achievements in literature and in the visual and performing arts, made possible a cultural flowering, of which composers William Byrd, John Dowland, Thomas Campion, and Thomas Morley were a part.

Thomas Morley (1557-1603) wrote a famous treatise, *A Plaine and Easie Introduction to Practical Musicke*, and published nine books of vocal and instrumental music. Among his works are a **through-composed** madrigal entitled "In Dew of Roses," with its **sighing figures**, and a ballett entitled "Now Is the Month of Maying," with its fa-la-las.

FIGURE 10-3. LISTENING GUIDE

"NOW IS THE MONTH OF MAYING," BY MORLEY

A   Now is the month of maying.
          When merry lads are playing, fa la la . . . *

B   Each with his bonny lass,
          Upon the greeny grass, fa la la . . .

A   The Spring, clad all in gladness,
          doth laugh at Winter's sadness, fa la la . . .

B   And to the bagpipe's sound
          The nymphs tread out their ground, fa la la . . .

A   Fie then! why sit we musing,
          Youth's sweet delight refusing? fa la la . . .

B   Say, dainty nymphs, and speak,
          Shall we play barley-break? fa la la . . .

          *Each verse is repeated

Renaissance Instrumental Music A Sixteenth Century Dance Suite

One of the most significant musical developments in the late Renaissance was the rise of instrumental music, as a separate type. Before the late Renaissance, instruments were used to double voice parts in polyphonic music, both sacred and secular, but very little music was written specifically for instruments, or in a style that took into account the individual capabilities and limitations of specific instruments. In the late Renaissance, all over Europe, composers began to write music for specific instruments and for instruments alone, functioning not as accompaniment for voices, but as a new and exciting resource of varied color. Composers gradually developed some important assumptions about how to write for instruments and what types of music were appropriate for specific instruments and instrumental combinations.

HOME, "INDOOR," AND "OUTDOOR" INSTRUMENTS

As we already indicated, not all instruments were regarded as equals, or used for the same functions. Organs were used, as they still are, largely for church music; harpsichords and lutes were home instruments; and the lute also was used as the chief accompanying instrument for solo singing.

The winds were used for different functions also. The higher class winds were the **indoor instruments**, also called the "soft" and "low" instruments. Included in this group were the recorder, flute, krummhorn, viol, sackbut, and sometimes the lute, which might also function as a member of the indoor mixed consort. Lower on the social scale, and less well paid, were the **outdoor instruments**, the trumpets, cornetts, and double reeds. Both groups were necessary for the lavish

B. van der Helst, *The Musician* (Metropolitan Museum of Art).

life of a great court, but the outdoor instruments had a less noble history, evolving from the town trumpeters and groups that accompanied armies on the march.

It is interesting that Renaissance instruments of whatever type are generally softer and more nasal in quality than modern instruments. Obviously, the Renaissance notion of an ideal instrumental sound was different from later notions. But the sound has a unique and pleasing quality, and our own century has seen a revival of interest in these instruments. Several professional groups specialize in concerts of Renaissance music, and recordings made on these instruments are readily available.

A SIXTEENTH CENTURY SUITE OF DANCES

Instrumental music in the late Renaissance served a variety of functions. Instruments added pomp and splendor to royal processions and ceremonies of all types, added to the solemnity of church services for special occasions, and served a variety of other functions. One of the most important purposes for instrumental music was to accompany dancing.

Music written for dancing necessarily takes on a number of characteristics. The meter must be strongly emphasized, the tempo must be quite regular and strictly maintained, and phrase structures are usually regular and symmetrical. The dances popular in the late Renaissance were not solo performances, but stylized group dances, performed by members of the court. Dance manuals of the time still survive, so that it is possible for us to reconstruct the actual movements and steps done to the music.

There was a large assortment of standard dances; the names and details of the music for each do not concern us here. The significant fact is that there were standard types, each calling for music in a certain meter and tempo, with other standard characteristics as well. Long after the dances had fallen out of fashion, composers continued to write instrumental music in these dance forms. Baroque composers wrote large amounts of dance suites—sets of dance movements—no longer intended to accompany dancing. One standard dance group in the late Renaissance was the *Pavane and Galliard*. The **pavane** was a dignified dance in 4/4 meter and a moderate tempo; the **galliard** was a rapid leaping dance in 3/4 meter. The contrasting meters and tempos appealed to composers who wrote many pairs of these movements using the same melodic and harmonic material in both movements.

The example we will hear is a reconstruction of a dance suite from the sixteenth century. The performing group—in this case the Ancient Instrument Ensemble of Zurich—decides which instruments to use, whether or not to add percussion, which composers of the time did not bother to write in the score, and how much to ornament the melodic line. The situation for the performers is very much like what we now find in music for Irish jigs and reels, or other bodies of folk dance music. If the music is written down at all, only the outlines are noted. Performers decide who will play what, and how free the ornamentation will be, based on a tradition of performance passed down through generations of players. Even the structure of the piece may be left to the players; often there are two or three melodic ideas, which are repeated and grouped into a larger structure at the discretion of the players. All those practices are involved in this performance.

The suite consists of five dances. The first is a pavane, in 4/4 meter at moderate tempo. In keeping with the tempo and the dignified character of the dance, the players play long legato lines. This group chooses a recorder consort to play the first dance, accompanied by a bass viol on the lowest line, and adds a tambourin, a Renaissance drum, to underline the meter. There are three separate ideas in the music; each consists of two eight-measure phrases, and each is repeated. The structure therefore might be designated as A-A-B-B-C-C.

A meeting of musicians in Old England. Instrumental music was often moved outdoors especially as the popularity of dancing increased.

The second dance contrasts with the first in every possible way. It is a **bergerette**, a brisk dance in fast triple meter. The group varies the instrumentation to add to the contrast. Here we have a Baroque oboe on the melodic line; the rest of the parts are played by recorders, and the viol and tambourin play the same role as in the pavane. Each cadence is marked by **hemiola,** a rhythmic device which breaks up two 3/4 measures into three sets of two beats. This device is standard in triple meter; it must have added considerable interest to the dance rhythm. The structure is slightly different in this dance; the first melodic idea is twice as long as the second, and consists of two similar phrases with different cadences. Since the first idea returns and is repeated after the contrasting middle section, there is considerably more repetition of similar material in this dance than in the first. The structure may be designated A-A-B-B-A-A, bearing in mind that the A sections are twice as long as the B's.

The third dance is a **galliard**, in fast 3/4 meter, played staccato. The oboe continues to play the top line, accompanied by recorders. The structure, like the pavane, is A-A-B-B-C-C.

Placing the galliard after the bergerette runs the risk of insufficient contrast; the group compensates by slightly different instrumentation. In the galliard the viol and tambourin do not play.

The fourth dance is called **ronde**, and has the 4/4 meter, slower tempo, and sustained articulation of the opening pavane. It is played by the recorder consort with the bass viol. Again the structure is A-A-B-B-C-C; the C section repeats the last ending phrase, played more softly, each time.

The last dance is called **Ballo Milanese**, which means "Dance from Milan," and, as we would expect, is in quick triple time. Actually, the meter is interesting, since frequent hemiolas, including the opening idea, make the meter sound like alternating 4/4 and 3/4 meter. This dance is also played in this arrangement by recorders and viol, and the structure is A-A-B-B-A-A-B-B.

The following listening guide (Figure 11-1) summarizes the style of each dance in this performance, so that you can follow the progress of the set of five.

It is important to emphasize again how much of this performance depends on decisions by the performers. Another group could play the same dances and produce quite a different effect, using different instruments, exercising more freedom of ornamentation, and perhaps even choosing different patterns of repetition, thus producing different structures.

The revival of interest among musicians in Renaissance music has brought it to life again. It is catchy, easy to understand, and appealing in its strong rhythmic drive and clear symmetrical structures. We are fortunate to live in an age when recordings of this music played on authentic instruments are available, so that we can enjoy the music that enlivened the social life of Renaissance courts.

SUMMARY

One of the most significant musical developments in the late Renaissance was the rise of instrumental music as a separate form. At this time, composers began to write music for specific instruments and for instruments alone, rather than as an accompaniment to choral music and solo singing. Instruments were thought of as **church** and **home instruments**. Winds were classed as **indoor** or **outdoor instruments**. Also, instruments were combined into **loud** and **soft consorts**, which were seldom called upon to play together.

Of the many functions of instrumental music of this period, group dancing was one of the most important. There were standard types of dancing, each calling for a certain meter and tempo. Some of these were the **pavane**, **galliard**, **bergerette**, **ronde**, and **Ballo Milanese**.

FIGURE 11-1. LISTENING GUIDE

SIXTEENTH CENTURY SUITE OF DANCES

I. Pavane

Time:1:32
Meter: 4/4
Tempo: moderate
Instruments: Recorder consort, viol, tambourin
Structure: A A B B C C

II. Bergerette

Time: 1:24
Meter: 3/4, with hemiola at all cadences
Tempo: fast
Instruments: Oboe, recorders, viol, tambourin
Structure: A A B B A A

III. Galliarde

Time: :38
Meter: 3/4
Tempo: fast
Instruments: oboe, recorders
Structure: A A B B C C

IV. Rondo

Time: :50
Meter: 4/4
Tempo: moderate
Instruments: recorder consort, viol
Structure: A A B B C C

V. Ballo Milanese

Time: 1:00
Meter: 3/4, with frequent hemiola
Tempo: fast
Instruments: recorder consort, viol
Structure: A A B B A A B B

This Baroque organ was the summit of the instrument maker's art and matched the mighty compositions for it by Bach and his contemporaries.

PART III

Music in the Baroque Period

CHAPTER 12

Social and Cultural Background

Like all the terms applied to periods in the history of Western music, baroque is a term borrowed from the visual arts and one that is used in many different senses. We may read of a baroque film, a baroque style of writing in a contemporary novel, or a baroque quality in some work of modern art or architecture. Used in this general sense, the term often implies a grandiose spirit, or a fussy, decorative style. In the historical sense, the term refers to a period in Western cultural history.

THE BAROQUE AGE

Historians of music usually apply the term **Baroque** to the years between 1600 and 1750, the time of Bach and Handel, Vivaldi and Telemann, and a host of other great musicians. The customary boundary dates were chosen not only because they are such convenient round numbers, but because, in those particular years, events took place which signaled the end of one era and the beginning of another. The year 1600 saw the rise of opera in Florence. Opera is such a typically Baroque invention that its beginning is a handy starting date for the entire period. In 1750, Johann Sebastian Bach died. Although he was very conservative for his time, his works are a culmination of all the preceding Baroque styles, so that the year of his death makes another fitting boundary line.

Science and Thought

The age enclosed by these boundaries was fascinating and complex. It was an age of magnificence, of discovery, of great confidence. All knowledge seemed within man's grasp, and discoveries were made in the sciences during this period that remained unchallenged until our own century. Galileo and Kepler laid the foundations for astronomy, and Harvey discovered the circulation of blood. Newton formulated the laws that became the basis of modern physics, which were not challenged until Einstein and Heisenberg questioned them in the twentieth century.

The world was expanding during the Baroque age. The great courts of Europe paid for their lavish standard of living partly through riches brought back from the recently colonized New World. In our own country, Jamestown was founded in 1607, the year the first successful opera, *Orfeo* by Monteverdi, was presented at the court of Mantua in North Italy. It was an age of limitless possibility, when man truly seemed the master of an expanding universe.

Monarchs and Politics

Politically, it was an age of magnificent absolute monarchs, none more magnificent that Louis XIV of France, the "Sun King," who ruled from 1643 until 1713. This monarch, whose life-style is incredible to our more democratic age, could say in all seriousness *"L'etat c'est moi,"* "I am the state." His palace at Versailles, outside Paris, still stands as a monument to the Baroque idea of a king. The magnificent sprawl of the architecture, the ornate splendor of the Hall of Mirrors, and the stately gardens with their carefully arranged paths and vistas—all testify to the limitless grandeur and power of the absolute monarch.

There were other monarchs elsewhere in Europe, such as George I of England, but none so grand as Louis XIV. Other sections of Europe did not follow the monarchical pattern. Germany remained a group of independent states, each ruled by Electors. The first grand monarch in German territory was Frederick the Great of Prussia, who came to power in the 1740s, near the end of the period we are discussing. The territory we now call Italy was not a nation, but a group of independent city-states and some regions that were under the control of other powers, such as the Austro-Hungarian Empire. England at this time was unstable, politically and religiously. During part of this period, the royal family was banished and the Commonwealth established in its place. Gone were the stability and cultural flowering of the Elizabethan Age. Very little opera was written in England at this time, because opera was regarded as a decadent extravagance of royalty.

Regional Style and National Pride

Finally, the age was a time of great national awareness and pride, a time of struggle to create a national culture or a regional style that would match or surpass the cultural models produced elsewhere. French culture was uniquely and proudly French, even if that French quality could be found only in the

(Left) Francois Girardon. *Portrait of Louis XIV* (The Louvre, Paris).

(Above) The palace of Louis XIV at Versailles.

avoidance of the characteristics of competing Italian models. Each nation took fierce pride in the qualities of its own language, and rapidly strove to create a body of great literature in that language. Milton and Donne in England, Racine and Molière in France, and Cervantes in Spain produced works that still stand as pioneer works of great literature.

THE BAROQUE AESTHETIC

Naturally, the excitement and magnificence of the Baroque age is mirrored in its arts. The grandeur of kings, the focus on man the master of the universe, and the high drama of the age are reflected in its architecture, sculpture, and paintings.

In Architecture

We have seen how the architecture of Versailles mirrored the Baroque notion of the monarch. Another well-known example of Baroque architecture shows the same magnificence applied to a different purpose. St. Peter's in Rome, the mother church of Roman Catholics, was designed by Michelangelo during the Renaissance as a much simpler building than it eventually became. By the time the church was actually built, ideas of architecture were different, and Michaelangelo's design was modified in grandiose ways. The original

Renaissance design was made much larger and more ornate to fit the new aesthetic. The elaborate facade, the sweeping colonnades enclosing the huge square, and the Bernini altar with its twisting columns were Baroque additions, designed to awe and overwhelm the individual. If you visit Rome, you can see how successfully the edifice accomplishes these aims. The sheer mass and scale of the church are incredibly effective. All of the details work together to convey the notion that the king dealt with here is mightier even than the world's most powerful monarchs.

In Sculpture and Painting

Another key element in the Baroque aesthetic, besides mass and grandeur, is drama. The Baroque arts leave behind the classic serenity of Renaissance art in favor of dramatic intensity. Figures in Baroque sculpture and painting are never still: they are twisted, moving, struggling, and dramatically lighted. If the figure itself is still, the draperies or decorations seem to be in motion. The emphasis on motion is what makes Baroque art sometimes appear so busy and fussy. The late sculptures of Michelangelo are quite different from his earlier, typically Renaissance works. The earlier works have a classical repose about them, whereas the late works, such as the series of unfinished prisoners, straining to escape from the surrounding stone, are contorted, moving, and struggling.

Baroque painting reflects the same change in emphasis. Instead of restful Renaissance madonnas, serene in their repose, Baroque painting tends to focus on dramatic subjects and to experiment with dramatic lighting, in the technique known as **chiaroscuro**, "light and dark." The dramatically lighted paintings of Caravaggio and Rembrandt are the best-known examples of this new approach to painting.

Related to the focus on drama is the Baroque concern with human emotions and their depiction in art. It is interesting to compare several treatments of the same subject by Michelangelo. He sculpted three Pietàs, at different times in his life. The first and most famous, the one presently in St. Peter's in Rome, is calm and tragic, timeless in its resignation. Mary looks like a young girl and certainly does not appear grief-stricken. In the last version Michelangelo made of this same subject, the effect and feeling of the work are totally different. Here we can see the emotions, and the proportions are changed to give emphasis to the feeling of movement and drama. The Baroque age is concerned with feelings, the stronger the better.

In Church Structure

All of these themes are visible at once in a Baroque church. The proportions are grandiose, designed to impress and awe the observer. Ceilings are painted in dramatic versions of religious scenes. Everywhere there is decoration, gold, rich textures and surfaces. The eye is forced to move about the whole interior. The effect is not one of serenity, but one of drama and excitement.

Michelangelo. Unfinished *Pietà* with self portrait of the artist.

In Music

As we shall see, all of these themes and concerns are clear in the music of the Baroque period. The magnificence of the king is audible in the ceremonial court music composed for great occasions. The concern for drama is evident in the invention of the exciting new form, opera, and in the use of operatic techniques in dramatic music for the church. Finally, the concern for human feeling and passion is clear in the constant attempt to codify human emotions and devise specific musical means to depict them. The Baroque period is a heroic, exciting age, and its music not only reflects that excitement but also continues to delight us hundreds of years later, in a totally different society.

CHAPTER 13
Important Musical Developments

The music of the Baroque era reflects the spirit of the age, with its interest in drama, human emotions, and grandeur. In this chapter, we will focus on the general characteristics of Baroque musical style.

THE MUSICIAN IN THE BAROQUE ERA

Kapellmeister

The first question to consider is the place of the musician in Baroque society. In general, the situation was much the same as it had been in the Renaissance. Musicians were not known only as composers: they competed first for positions as performers at the great courts and churches and then worked their way up to positions at the head of the musical programs of the churches and courts. The most successful musicians were the composer-performers who somehow, through a combination of talent and diplomacy, achieved the position of *Kapellmeister*, or music director at one of the great courts. These few musicians—Lully in the court of Louis XIV, Handel at the court of George I of England, and Quantz at the court of Frederick the Great—had enormous power. They were responsible for all of the music at the court, and the music they composed was guaranteed performance. But even their positions were insecure. These musicians had to stay in the good graces of their patrons and had to scramble for position when there was a change in the political situation. Most composers were always on the lookout for new opportunities and continually sent new compositions to courts were they thought there might be better employment.

This engraving shows a cantata performance in the Baroque period.

Church Musicians and Performers

On a level below that of the elite who held the top court positions, there were a number of fine church musicians, like J. S. Bach, who ran the music programs of large churches and composed vast quantities of music for the worship services. At still another level were well-known singers and instrumentalists, who were performers, not composers. Like the composers, performers also changed positions frequently and were constantly on the lookout for better situations. The most successful representatives of this group were the **castrati**, adult male singers who underwent surgery in adolescence to prevent their voices from changing. This bizarre custom produced an elite corps of adult male sopranos and altos, who were the superstars of the Baroque Italian opera world. The best among them were extremely wealthy and successful.

Virtuoso instrumentalists were in demand as well: some of them became famous and had their choice of court positions. The music of the time was generally written for a small group of virtuoso singers and instrumentalists, accompanied by a larger chorus and an orchestra of journeyman players. Good solo players and singers were, therefore, in demand; and composers wrote to show off the particular abilities of their soloists. Music was written for specific occasions, and performed immediately after its composition.

Performers' Responsibilities

The responsibilities of the singer or instrumentalist during this period were different from those of musicians in later ages. Because of the tremendous demand for new music, music was written at a furious pace hard to imagine today. Bach, for example, was responsible for a cantata a week while he was music director at Leipzig. The **cantata** was a work for soloists, chorus, and orchestra, twenty minutes to a half hour long. He had to write a new work each week, or find an appropriate one in his files, and rehearse the performers so that a polished performance could be presented each Sunday. Working under this kind of pressure, composers wrote in a form of shorthand, relying on performers to fill in the details. Melodies, for example, were often set down in outline form. The basic contours were specified, and the bass line was written with numbers indicating the chord progressions. Performers would then ornament the melodic line in well-known, standard ways; and keyboard players would improvise a two-handed part based on the bass line and chord symbols. Baroque music is, therefore, like jazz, in which soloists play their own versions of a basic melody, and the rhythm section improvises, based on a chord pattern, so that no two performances are exactly the same. As is true in jazz, the smaller the group, the more freedom to improvise.

Revivals of Baroque Music

The nineteenth-century musical world loved the grandiose side of Baroque music, but tended to modify Baroque style to fit its own aesthetics. In the twentieth century, there has been a great revival of interest in authentic Baroque performance. A new generation of performers has arisen, capable of playing early instruments or modern copies of them and able to improvise ornamentation and play from shorthand outlines of Baroque music in authentic Baroque style. Modern recordings have made available to all listeners performances that duplicate as closely as possible the sound of Baroque music as it was played in the great courts and churches.

BAROQUE STYLE

Baroque music sounds different from music of other periods. This difference of sound results, of course, from particular ways of dealing with the basic elements of music. Although Baroque music exists in great profusion and in a wide variety of styles, there are some generalizations we can make.

Color

Color is a prominent element in Baroque style. Baroque composers were very conscious of the individual capabilities of various instruments and types of voices, and wrote in different styles or idioms for different voices and instruments. Often a prominent element is the contrast of colors. In the concerto grosso, for example, one of the basic principles of organization is the contrast between a small group of soloists, often playing instruments of distinct colors, and the larger orchestral group. The concerto grosso is discussed in more detail in Chapter 15.

The most prominent instrumental family of the period is the string family. The violin came into prominence during this period. Its expressive quality, similar to that of the human voice, was greatly exploited. The agility of the various woodwind instruments, which at the time were really "woodwinds," made of wood, was also much prized. One characteristic Baroque sound is the high trumpet register, written for virtuoso players of the valveless natural trumpets of the time, which could play scale passages only in the upper reaches of their range. Keyboard instruments underwent great development during this time, also. The harpsichord became a solo virtuoso instrument as well as a member of the orchestra. Advances in organ building made the pipe organ a virtuoso instrument as well, for which an enormous amount of great solo literature was written.

Dynamics

The use of dynamics during the Baroque period is a function of the capabilities of Baroque instruments, and is quite different from the dynamics of later periods. Baroque instruments did not have a great dynamic range, so that the gradual crescendos of Classical and Romantic style are simply not possible. In the

Baroque period, changing dynamics means changing color, because the only way to get louder is to increase the number of instruments playing. Dynamic changes are sudden, not gradual, and form part of the contrast among various groups, each instrument playing at a more or less constant dynamic level. The composers of this time usually did not specify dynamics in their scores, but simply wrote "loud" or "soft."

Rhythm and Texture

The most noticeable and prominent elements in Baroque music are rhythm and texture. In a Baroque fast movement, one generally gets the feeling of tremendous rhythmic drive. Tempos are constant throughout entire movements, without the subtle speeding up and slowing down that is an important characteristic of some later music. The texture is quite busy. The prevailing texture in Baroque music is polyphonic, combining several melodic lines. Even when textures are less dense, as in slow movements, there is at least the combination of a prominent melody and bass line; and, in some fast movements, there are four or more melodic lines going at once. The combination of the busy texture and the motoric rhythm produces a feeling of drive and intensity that makes Baroque music fun to listen to and even more fun to play: nobody is reduced to playing dull accompaniment patterns.

Melody

The element that is less prominent in Baroque music than in more recent and familiar music is melody. The gorgeous lyric melodies that are so much a part of later styles are absent in Baroque music, except in slow movements. We find it difficult to hum Baroque fast movements. The effect is in the dense texture, not in one memorable melody. As we have seen so often, all of the musical elements cannot be equally prominent: a composer cannot spotlight an important tune unless he reduces the other instruments to background accompaniment. We might not even *want* to hum the melodies of Baroque fast movements. Instead of carefully wrought tunes, they are more likely to be simple ideas, with strong rhythmic shape and clear harmonic implications, designed not to exist alone, but to work well as contrapuntal motives. Most Bach fugue subjects are simple combinations of chord outlines and scale passages, recognizable when they recur in the texture, but not the sort of thing one leaves the hall humming.

Harmony and Tonality

One extremely important Baroque innovation is the gradual rise of tonality, the major-minor system that remained the basic harmonic framework of our art music until the twentieth century. As the Baroque period began, composers still accepted the harmonic premises of the Renaissance period. Music was organized on the modal system, but unusual chord progressions were allowed for expressive purposes. By 1700, however, the eight modes were reduced to the two we are familiar with—major and minor—and chord progressions began to move in ways that still feel "right" and "natural" to us today. The situation in music parallels events in the scientific realm. Newton's laws stood unchallenged until the twentieth century, just as the tonal system lasted through the Classic and Romantic periods, until composers of twentieth-century art music replaced it with new systems in which there is more than one tonal center (**polytonality**) or in which there is none at all (**atonality** or **pantonality**).

Bach's harmonies are always completely clear and logical, within the tonal system we are familiar with, and we feel the rightness and logic of the chord progressions, even if our attention is more often focused on his mastery of polyphony. Within the same tonal system, Baroque harmony is different from Classic or Romantic harmony. Chords change more often, and tonal areas do not have the structural impact that they do in the Classic style. In Baroque music, we are more likely to hear cycles of harmonies and rapid changes, but the tonic is still the tonic, and cadences are clear and satisfying.

Idiom and National Style

Another important development was the consciousness of idiom and national style. In the late Renaissance, composers began to write specifically for some instruments, but most Renaissance music is playable by whatever forces happen to be available. In the Baroque period, composers wrote music for violin that was quite different from that written for trumpet, for example, and parts cannot be interchanged among instruments. Organ music is quite distinct from music for harpsichord, and vocal style is different from instrumental style. The clear sense of idiom was balanced by a tendency to mix idioms, that is, to write passages in instrumental style for voices, and vice versa. For this reason, Baroque vocal music includes passages that are awkward for the voice—long melismas on one syllable and wide skips. These are examples of the conscious transfer of instrumental idiom into vocal writing. The slow movements of instrumental pieces, on the other hand, are generally in vocal style, and sound like arias.

By the late Baroque period, national styles were clearly established also, and composers could write in any of them. Handel, for example, made his reputation writing very successful Italian operas. He also wrote court music in the French style. Most of Bach's music is in the long tradition of German religious music, but he also wrote concertos in the Italian style and suites in French and English style. Henry Purcell, a great English composer, wrote *Dido and Aeneas*, an English chamber opera, which has a French overture, arias in Italian style, and choruses in Elizabethan madrigal style. The composers and performers of the period were masters of all national styles. Modern performers who specialize in Baroque music must understand all of these national styles also, and must be able to switch styles, from Italian to French to German, as readily as performers did two hundred years ago.

Popularity

One last comment should be made about Baroque music. The music of this period is much more frequently performed now than it was before about 1950. Many modern performers have discovered the delights of playing this music, and have trained themselves to play in authentic Baroque style. Listeners have become very fond of Baroque music also; the large number of Baroque recordings available testifies to this interest. Attempts have been made to perform Baroque music in some popular styles. The Swingle Singers vocalize on Baroque pieces, adding a jazz bass and drums to produce an interesting combination style that works and "swings" as jazz should. "Cool" jazz groups of the late fifties, like the Dave Brubeck Quartet and the Modern Jazz Quartet, often quoted Baroque phrases in the arranged introductions to their jazz improvisations and often used Baroque polyphonic techniques in constructing their original music. In the early seventies, one of the biggest sellers among classical albums was *Switched-On Bach*, a recording of well-known Bach works played on the Moog synthesizer by Walter Carlos. Finally, the works of P. D. Q. Bach, allegedly a long-lost son of the German master, have been performed and recorded. Like most parodies, the P. D. Q. Bach recordings and concerts are more enjoyable the more one knows about Baroque music. In whatever guise, Baroque music is certainly alive and well in the late twentieth century.

BAROQUE FORMS

Vocal Forms

Opera

As we have already mentioned, **opera** was one of the most important developments in the Baroque era. The discovery of the expressive power of the solo voice and the drama and pageantry possible in this new genre are two of the most significant innovations in the entire history of Western art music. Opera began in Florence around 1600. Later centers of Italian Baroque opera were Rome and Venice. Italian Baroque opera is seldom performed nowadays. It was a highly conventionalized form, featuring *castrato* male roles, mythological stories, and long strings of florid arias. The emphasis was on technical display by star singers. Occasionally, a Baroque opera is revived. The New York City Opera Company revived Handel's *Giulio Cesare* in the 1960s. The music can be enjoyed on recordings, where it is possible to use female singers for the *castrato* roles.

Lully developed a French style of opera at the court of Louis XIV. French Baroque opera featured more emphasis on the orchestra and chorus, and less on the solo stars. The French regarded the florid Italian aria style as an aberration and preferred a more natural singing line, which would allow the text to be heard and would do less violence to their language. England produced a few operas, although the unstable political situation was not favorable for this costly, extravagant medium. Henry Purcell wrote several English operas, of which *Dido and Aeneas* is the most famous and the most frequently performed.

Cantata

The techniques of exploiting the dramatic possibilities of the solo voice were extended from the world of opera into church music as well. The term **cantata** denoted any sort of dramatic religious vocal music featuring soloists, chorus, or both. Eventually, in North Germany, it denoted a specific form, used in the Lutheran Sunday service, written for soloists, chorus, and orchestra. In Chapter 14, we will look at one of Bach's cantatas in detail.

Oratorio

Another Baroque form, midway between cantata and opera, is the **oratorio**, written first in Latin, but much more famous as an English form, developed by Handel. The standard Handel oratorio is a large work for soloists, chorus, and orchestra, sung in concert format, without costumes or staging, in a concert hall rather than as part of a church service. Handel wrote a large number of these works, the most famous being *Messiah* (see Chapter 16). Oratorios have remained quite popular and are frequently performed.

Instrumental Forms

A large amount of chamber music was written in the Baroque period for various combinations of instruments. One popular form for solo keyboard, either harpsichord or organ, is the **prelude and fugue**, or **toccata and fugue**. The first movement of these sets is improvisatory in style, filled with passage work, chromatically bold chords, and dramatic effects. The second, the fugue, is more "learned" in style, consistently four-voice, and regular in structure. Fugue form is discussed later in this chapter.

A favorite form of chamber music for more than one player is the **trio sonata**, usually for two violins and **basso continuo**, a standard term for the Baroque "rhythm section," made up of a bass string instrument and a harpsichord or organ to fill in the chords. Therefore, a trio sonata is for four, not three, players, because "basso continuo" implies two players. Late in the Baroque period, two types of sonatas emerged: the **sonata da chiesa** or "church sonata," in four movements, slow-fast-slow-fast, and the **sonata da camera**, or "chamber sonata," consisting of several dance movements in binary form.

Prominent among larger instrumental forms are the concerto grosso and the suite. The **concerto grosso** is often in three movements, fast-slow-fast, and pits a small group of soloists against the larger string ensemble. One of Bach's concerto grosso works is discussed in detail in Chapter 15. The **suite** is a less formal structure, consisting, like the sonata da camera, of several binary dance movements. The sonata da camera and the suite are lighter and less serious than the sonata da chiesa and concerto grosso. The same distinction between two levels of instrumental music persists in the Classical period between the tightly organized symphony and the less formal **divertimento**, also a collection of dance movements.

FUGUE

The term "fugue," from *fuga*, Latin for "flight" or "chase," denotes a standard Baroque compositional process, which may appear in any of the forms mentioned above. It is derived from the Renaissance motet and **ricercar**, but is much more strict in its organization than those earlier forms. It is called a **monothematic** ("one-theme") form, because in a fugue there is one main melodic idea, called the **subject**, out of which the entire composition is constructed. Fugues are usually written for four voices, although they may be written for any number. A fugue begins with the subject being presented in each of the voices in turn. The subject must be designed so that it works harmonically against itself, and the **countersubject** (what the first voice plays after it presents the subject) must be carefully designed to complement the subject, harmonically and rhythmically. Generally, the countersubject is rhythmically active when the subject has longer notes, and vice versa. The opening section of a fugue, made up of successive entries of the subject, is called the **exposition**. After all voices have entered with the subject, a contrasting section follows, called the **episode**. Episodes are usually lighter in texture than the expositions; one or more voices may rest during episodes. They are also lighter thematically, usually made up of sequential repetitions of short motives, which are sometimes related to the subject. Expositions and episodes alternate throughout the fugue. During the last expository section, tension is usually increased by shortening the time interval between successive entries of the subject, so that entries are rapidly layered upon one another. This technique is called **stretto**. After the stretto, a fugue usually concludes quickly, perhaps extending the final cadence through a short concluding musical passage called a **coda** or **codetta**. A well-written fugue is a joy to listen to: the expositions are easy enough to hear; the layered busyness of the texture and the driving rhythm create a cumulative sense of tension; and the final cadence arrives with a fine sense of inevitability.

The fugue is a perfect example of the Baroque approach to composition. The materials are laid out in the first entry, and the pleasure for the listener is not in finely crafted tunes, but in the endless invention and creativity with which the materials are spun out. As you can imagine, fugues are easy enough for four instruments to play, but quite a challenge for a single keyboard player, who must shape each appearance of the subject in such a way that the listener is aware that it is happening. Playing four independent melodic lines with two hands, or two hands and two feet, is quite a task. One of the most satisfying musical experiences I know is arriving successfully and cleanly at the final cadence of one of the big organ fugues of J. S. Bach.

Verbal descriptions of musical forms are not always helpful. The best way to understand how the form works is to see a diagram of it and to hear it in action. We turn now to a diagram of a fugue, the "Little" G minor Fugue by J. S. Bach, written for the organ. The listening guide (Figure 13-3) makes a clear distinction between exposition and episode, and attempts to separate the strands for the four voices, marked S for soprano, A for alto, T for tenor, and B for bass. The time line should help you keep your place and follow the structure as it develops. The subject is simplicity itself, with a contour that is instantly recognizable when it recurs, and a very clear harmonic underpinning. Note in Figure 13-1 that the first three notes outline the tonic chord of G minor, and the first phrase ends by outlining the dominant chord, D major.

Figure 13-1.   Subject of the "Little" G minor fugue.

After the fourth voice has entered with the subject, the first episode (See Figure 13-2) is standard Baroque filler, a sequential pattern between the top two voices, over running sixteenth notes in a third voice.

Figure 13-2.   "Little" G minor fugue, episode one.

Subsequent episodes also appear in thinner textures of two or three voices. Several entries of the subject appear in B-flat major, the relative major of the main key. The last entry of the subject is in the bass, in the home key of G minor. The piece ends, as most minor-key Baroque works do, with a *major* chord in the home key. This phenomenon is often referred to as a **Picardy third**; but, no matter what term we use for it, the final major chord is the usual practice, giving a greater sense of finality to the final cadence.

The fugue is a very common Baroque form. Fugal procedure—contrapuntal writing of this type—is also very common in works in other forms. The undisputed master of fugal technique is Bach, who wrote a collection of pieces, *The Art of the Fugue*, which illustrates fugal and canonic procedures in a sort of technical manual of fugal writing. Another collection that copiously illustrates his mastery is *The Well-Tempered Clavier*, a set of preludes and fugues for keyboard in all possible keys. There are forty-eight fugues of various types in this collection, which constitutes an endless resource for students of Baroque compositional technique.

SUMMARY

The music of the Baroque era reflects the interest of that period in grandeur, drama, motion, and emotion.

Composers competed for positions as musical directors at the great courts or large churches. Conscious of **idiom**, they wrote in distinct national styles for specific instruments.

Vocal and instrumental performers changed positions frequently. Among this group were the *castrati*, an elite corps of adult male singers who, because of surgery in adolescence to prevent their voices from changing, were able to sing soprano and alto roles in Italian operas.

Baroque music sounds different from music of other periods largely because of the way Baroque composers treated the basic elements of music—color, dynamics, rhythm and texture, melody, and harmony and tonality.

The strings constitute the most prominent instrumental family of this period, which also relied for **color** on the woodwinds and trumpet but saw great development in the keyboard instruments as well.

Because Baroque instruments did not have great dynamic range, changing **dynamics** meant changing color, increasing or decreasing the number of instruments playing.

Rhythm and **texture** are the most prominent elements in Baroque music. The texture is characteristically polyphonic and busy, and the rhythm is motoric. **Melody** is less prominent.

The Baroque period gave rise to **tonality**, the major-minor system that remained the basic harmonic framework of Western art music until the twentieth century.

The **opera**, **cantata**, and **oratorio** were important vocal forms developed during this period. Important instrumental forms of the period include the **trio sonata, sonata da chiesa, sonata da camera, concerto grosso, suite,** and **fugue.**

The **fugue**, a perfect example of the Baroque approach to composition, is based on one melodic idea, called the subject, and consists of a succession of alternating expositions and episodes.

FIGURE 13-3. LISTENING GUIDE

"LITTLE" ORGAN FUGUE IN G MINOR, BY BACH

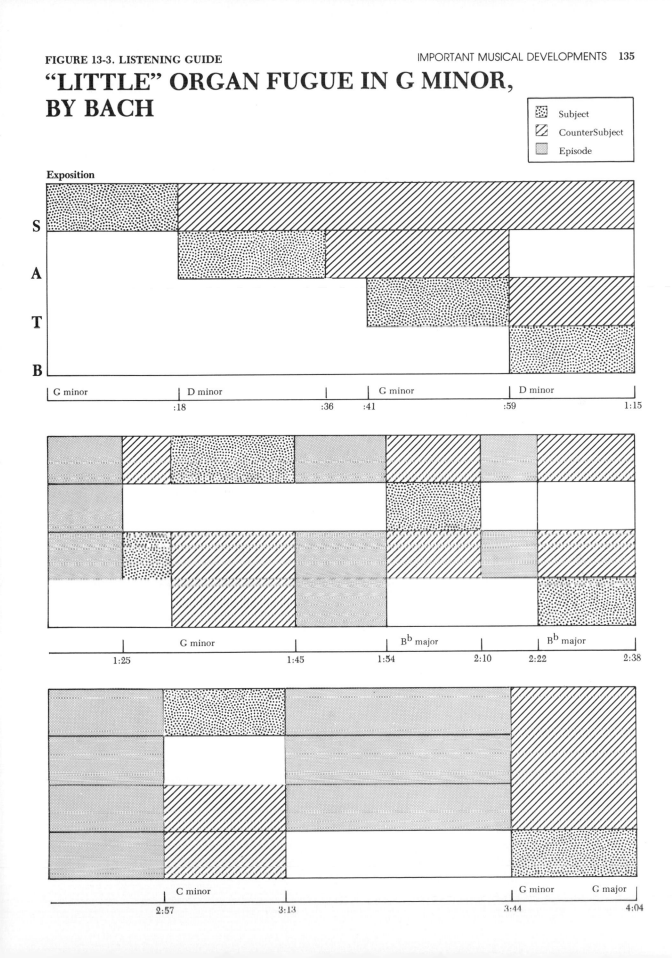

CHAPTER 14

Johann Sebastian Bach, Cantata No. 140

THE LIFE OF BACH

Johann Sebastian Bach (1685-1750) is a giant of Western art. His music constitutes one of the great artistic achievements in the history of Western man and is an endless topic of study and source of pleasure for all musicians and listeners. He came along late in the Baroque age and consolidated and perfected all of the various Baroque musical forms. Particularly treasured is the huge legacy of religious music he left, music whose sincerity and honest human emotion speaks eloquently to any listener, regardless of his or her religious background or commitment.

Bach is one of the towering geniuses of our culture. In a science fiction scenario, if our society were about to be destroyed and only a few remnants of our culture could be saved, Bach's works, along with those of Mozart and Beethoven, would be the first works people would try to save.

Bach was not an international celebrity like the great court composers. He was born into a family of church musicians and always thought of himself in that light. Few of his works were published: they were written for one performance and then filed away carelessly, so that scholars have had to work hard to reconstruct the body of his work.

Bach was born at Eisenach in North Germany on March 21, 1685, and raised by an older brother after being orphaned. He was trained for the family profession—church organist—and moved into his first professional post as a church organist at Arnstadt at the age of eighteen. The authorities of the church seem to have been displeased by some of the bold harmonies he introduced in his playing.

At the age of twenty-three, he moved to a more important post at Weimar, where he served as court organist and concertmaster for the Duke's chapel. He remained in that post for nine years, during which he composed a large number of organ works and some church cantatas. In 1717, Bach accepted a post as music director at the court of Cöthen, where the prince had a great interest in instrumental music and kept a small orchestra. His six years at this court saw the composition of most of his instrumental music, notably the famous Brandenburg Concertos (see Chapter 15).

Bach's most important position began in 1723 and lasted until his death on January 28, 1750. That post was "Cantor" at the Church of St. Thomas in Leipzig, a post in which he was responsible for composing and directing all of the music for the church services and also for supervising the education of the choirboys. During this period, he wrote many of the great religious masterpieces that are his most famous works and continued to write for the organ and other keyboard instruments.

Attempts have been made to glamorize Bach's life, but without much success. He was a simple, pious man, devoted to his family and to his art, which he viewed as a way to give glory to God. Bad jokes have been made about his twenty children, many of whom died in infancy. He trained his sons to continue in the family tradition of church music, but most of his musician sons—Wilhelm Friedemann, Carl Philip Emmanuel, Johann Christoph—moved in different directions, caught up in the new styles that were then developing. Bach's fame never extended very far, although he was known in Germany as a church musician and organist, and as a composer of first-rate contrapuntal music. He wrote huge quantities of glorious music, content to fulfill the duties of his post.

THE MUSIC OF BACH

Bach's output is so vast and so varied—the only major form he did not attempt was opera—that we can only outline the main types of music he wrote and mention a few of his better-known compositions in each genre.

Instrumental Music

Bach's own performing medium was the keyboard instruments; and, as we would expect, many of his greatest achievements as a composer are in that area. He wrote sonatas, suites, and concertos for clavier, by which he meant harpsichord. The collection of preludes and fugues known as *The Well-Tempered*

J. S. Bach's autograph manuscript, Fugue No. 2 in *C* Minor.

Clavier has already been mentioned. It explores contrapuntal techniques, as well as the technical possibilities of the instrument. The *Goldberg Variations* is another collection of keyboard music, sometimes performed at one sitting as a recital tour de force by present-day keyboard players.

For Organ

Bach's contributions to the literature for the organ are among his most important music. He wrote a great number of paired preludes and fugues (or toccatas and fugues) for organ, which are as fundamental a part of the organist's repertoire as the Beethoven sonatas are for the pianist. Organ recitals nearly always include some of the larger Bach works. The Toccata and Fugue in *D* Minor is perhaps the best known of these works. A Romantic arrangement for orchestra by Stokowski even found its way into Disney's film, *Fantasia*. The chorale preludes constitute another important class of Bach's works for the organ. They are keyboard settings of the Lutheran hymn tunes that were an important part of the Lutheran liturgy, associated closely with the various Sundays of the church year. Bach's treatment of these preexisting tunes is varied and interesting. Sometimes he uses them as fugue subjects; sometimes as ornamented solo melodies, almost like opera arias; and sometimes he sets up a complex contrapuntal texture in several voices, over which the hymn tune rides in slower notes. These chorale preludes are very effective incidental organ music for the church service, because they utilize the familiar tunes that will appear elsewhere in the same service. Thus, they give unity to the service, but allow the organ to do completely idiomatic things with the familiar tune.

For Strings

We should also mention Bach's solo string music. Along with sonatas and concertos for various instruments, he wrote suites for unaccompanied violin and cello, using the four strings of each instrument to build up complex contrapuntal textures. These works, as you can imagine, pose a tremendous technical challenge, extending the natural abilities of the instrument into new realms. The Suite for Unaccompanied Violin in *D* Minor is performed from time to time on violin recitals.

For Orchestra

Bach's music for orchestra, most of which was written in the Cöthen period, includes several suites and several examples of the concerto grosso. Among the latter are the Brandenburg Concertos (see Chapter 15).

Vocal Music

Cantatas

Most numerous among Bach's vocal works are the cantatas, written in the Weimar period, and especially in his first few years at Leipzig. We know of over two hundred cantatas he wrote, and others may have been lost. They are written in a wide variety of styles, some including arias and duets in operatic style, some using a chorale in every movement, some more freely composed. There are even a few secular cantatas, although they are more of a curiosity now than an important facet of Bach's musical output.

Larger Choral Works

Late in his Leipzig days, Bach turned to larger choral works, which stand as his greatest masterpieces. He wrote two settings of the Passion, according to St. Matthew and St. John. These huge works are frequently performed, both as religious music in church and also as concert works. They are written for a narrator, who sings the German text of the Gospel accounts of Christ's Passion; soloists, who represent Christ and other characters in the narrative; and a chorus, who represents both the crowds in the story and the congregation's reaction to the events described. A small orchestra, including important solo parts for various wind instruments, completes the musical forces. In the Passions, one has a clear idea of the type of piety that inspired Bach. The grief and exultation he depicts are completely human feelings, easy for anyone to identify with, in either a church or concert setting.

During the Leipzig years, he also wrote the *B Minor Mass*, a huge setting of the Latin Mass. We do not know whether he ever heard this work performed. Although much too long to serve as liturgical music, the Mass is an incredible masterpiece.

Didactic Collections

A last group of works are the didactic collections, written to illustrate some facet of compositional technique. Included in this group are the *Musical Offering*, a collection of settings of a single theme, sent to the court of Frederick the Great, and *The Art of the Fugue*, a compendium of fugal techniques, written for no specific instrument or group, and left unfinished at Bach's death.

So vast is Bach's output and so careless were people of that time about cataloging or even saving musical scores, that the work of assembling and publishing authentic versions of all of Bach's compositions is still going on. One edition of his collected works was published in the nineteenth century. A second version of his complete works is still under way, based on discoveries and research that have made the first collection unreliable in some of its details. The simple church musician of North Germany would probably be amazed at the position he occupies in today's musical world: his works are frequently performed; endlessly recorded; studied by historians, composers, and performers; and beloved by the entire musical world.

CANTATA NO. 140, "WACHET AUF, RUFT UNS DIE STIMME"

As we mentioned earlier, Bach wrote several yearly cycles of cantatas, most dating from his early years at the Church of St. Thomas in Leipzig. The cantata was a fairly free form. There are solo cantatas, with no chorus, secular cantatas not intended for religious use, and cantatas of various other types and patterns; but by far the most common pattern is a multimovement form, based on one of the Lutheran chorales, involving soloists, chorus, and a small instrumental ensemble.

The cantatas were part of a long Sunday service, and occupied much the same position that a choral anthem now occupies in church services. They are longer than most choral selections now performed in church, because the service was proportionately longer.

It is important to appreciate the role chorales played in the worship of the Lutheran church of this period. We are used to hearing the great chorales, such as "A Mighty Fortress is Our God," "O Sacred Head Surrounded," and "Now Thank We All Our God," performed in their four-voice settings, often the Bach versions of the harmony. But the melodies were much older than the Bach versions. When the Lutheran church was formed early in the sixteenth century, one of its central reforms was the insistence on congregational singing in the language of the people. A collection of hymns was rapidly assembled; some of them were newly written, some adapted from Latin hymns or chants, some adapted from folk melodies. They had been in use for two hundred years before Bach's time and were known by heart by the congregations for which he wrote. The chorale cantatas are therefore artistic elaborations of hymns the congregation knew well. These cantatas always end with the last verse of the chorale sung in its four-part harmonized version, so that the form is like variations followed by the theme. We can also view it as an exploration of the musical and dramatic possibilities inherent in the preexisting text and music, followed by the chorale in straightforward form, as a summary of all the ideas presented in the cantata. They must have been very effective as religious expressions, and they still work quite effectively, both as religious music and in concert performances.

The high point of most chorale cantatas is the opening chorus, which is usually the longest movement of the work and is a choral treatment of the chorale tune set either fugally or in *cantus firmus* style—that is, set in long notes, against a complex polyphonic texture in the other voices. The second climactic point is the homophonic final verse, in which the chorus, orchestra, and congregation join in the harmonized setting of the tune. In between, there are, generally, another chorus and some solo recitatives and arias. We can see, therefore, that many musical elements are involved in the cantata—the preexisting hymn tune, the contrapuntal techniques with which the tune is elaborated in the large choruses, solo operatic style in the recitatives and arias, and the solo and ensemble playing of the small orchestra. The dramatic and musical means that Bach perfected in the many cantatas he wrote are the same means used in his larger religious works; we can view the Passions and the *B* Minor Mass as large-scale cantatas.

Cantata no. 140, "Wachet auf," is an excellent example of the chorale cantata form. It was written for one of the final Sundays after Trinity, late in the Church year, when the readings and prayers of the day focus on the end of time and the Second Coming of the Messiah. The central image of the day's Gospel is the Bridegroom, representing Christ, appearing unannounced for the wedding feast, and the necessity to be prepared for this moment. The way Bach deals with

Baroque nave and ceiling in the Wieskirche.

this idea gives us an insight into his type of piety. The picture he paints is not at all like the frightening idea of the Last Judgement we see in Michelangelo's famous mural in the Sistine Chapel. Instead, Bach looks forward eagerly and longingly to this moment as an encounter with the loving Redeemer. In between the choruses, which are built on the chorale tune, he inserts love duets between a soprano, representing the soul, and a bass, representing Christ. While this imagery may not represent our modern feelings about religion, we can certainly appreciate Bach's obvious sincerity. It is almost as if he is weary of the demands of his busy life and longs for the repose and peace that will greet him at death or the end of time.

On the following pages are the German text of the cantata and an English translation. Note that this particular layout makes the form look like a seven-part structure. If we consider the short recitatives as introductions to the duets that follow them, we can view the work as a five-part structure.

I Chorus
II Recitative and Duet—Soloists
III Chorus
IV Recitative and Duet—Soloists
V Chorale—Chorus and Congregation

Figure 14-1.   The choral melody.

We should also look at the preexisting musical material before we discuss the organization of each movement. Like many chorales, this tune is a sturdy, solemn melody, particularly notable for its extremely clear harmonic implications and also for the two climactic points on the high *G*s in each half (see Figure 14-1). The small orchestra includes two oboes, an English horn, a solo **violino piccolo** (an obsolete, slightly smaller form of the standard violin), a string section, and continuo, played in this instance by a bass string instrument and organ.

I. Opening Chorus

The first verse of the chorale is set for chorus and orchestra. Actually, there are three distinct groups, each with its own material. The orchestra plays either dotted rhythms or sixteenth-note scale passages. The dotted rhythms suggest marching feet, proceeding forth to meet the bridegroom. The chorus is divided: the sopranos, reinforced by a horn, sing the chorale in long notes, while the other three voices sing short motives, set contrapuntally. The effect of this setting is to extend the hymn's first verse considerably. A listening guide (Figure 14-3) for this first movement is added at the end of this description, so that you can follow the somewhat complex organization.

II. First Recitative

The short recitative for tenor solo, in *C* minor, the relative minor, is in the narrative style of the Evangelist sections of the Passions, or the narrator sections of oratorios. It is accompanied by the continuo instruments.

CANTATA NO. 140, "WACHET AUF," BY BACH

Music Sections	German Text	English Translation
		I
I. Chorus— Chorale Fantasia	Wachet auf, ruft uns die Stimme der Wächter sehr hoch auf der Zinne, wach auf, du Stadt Jerusalem!	"Awake," the voice of watchmen calls us from high on the tower, "Awake, you city of Jerusalem!"
	Mitternacht heisst diese Stunde; sie rufen uns mit hellem Munde: wo seid ihr klugen Jungfrauen?	Midnight is this very hour; they call to us with bright voices: "Where are you, wise virgins?"
	Wohl auf, der Bräut'gam kömmt, steht auf, die Lampen nehmt! Alleluja! Macht euch bereit zu der Hochzeit, ihr müsset ihm entgegen gehn.	Take cheer, the Bridegroom comes, arise, take up your lamps! Hallelujah! Prepare yourselves for the weddings, you must go forth to meet him.
		II
II. Solo— Tenor Recitative	Er kommt, er kommt, der Bräut'gam kommt! Ihr Töchter Zions, kommt heraus, sein Ausgang eilet aus der Höhe in euer Mutter Haus.	He comes, he comes, the Bridegroom comes! Daughters of Zion, come forth, he is hurrying from on high into your mother's house.
	Der Bräut'gam kommt, der einem Rehe und jungem Hirsche gleich auf denen Hügeln springt und euch das Mahl der Hochzeit bringt.	The Bridegroom comes, who like a roe and a young hart leaping upon the hills brings you the wedding meal.
	Wacht auf, ermuntert euch! den Bräut'gam zu empfangen; dort, sehet, kommt er hergegangen.	Wake up, bestir yourselves to receive the Bridegroom; there, look, he come along.
		III
III. Duet— Soprano And Bass	Wann kommst du, mein Heil? Ich komme, dein Teil. Ich warte mit brennendem Öle; Eröffne den Saal zum himmlischen Mahl. Ich öffne den Saal zum himmlischen Mahl. Komm Jesu! komm, liebliche Seele!	Soul: When will you come, my salvation? Jesus: I am coming, your own. Soul: I am waiting with burning oil. Throw open the hall to the heavenly banquet! Jesus: I open the hall to the heavenly banquet Soul: Come, Jesus! Jesus: Come, lovely Soul!
		IV
IV. Chorus— Tenors Sing Chorale	Zion hört die Wächter singen, das Herz tut ihr vor Freuden springen, sie wachet und steht eilend auf. Ihr Freund kommt von Himmel prächtig,	Zion hears the watchmen singing, for joy her very heart is springing, she wakes and rises hastily. From heaven comes her friend resplendent.

von Gnaden stark, von Wahrheit mächtig,	sturdy in grace, mighty in truth
Ihr Licht wird hell, ihr Stern geht auf.	her light shines bright, her star ascends.

Nun komm, du werte Kron,	Now come, you worthy crown.
Herr Jesu Gottes Sohn.	Lord Jesus, God's own Son.
Hosianna!	Hosanna!
Wir folgen all'	We all follow
zum Freudensaal	to the joyful hall
und halten mit das Abendmahl.	and share the Lord's Supper.

V

V. Solo—
Bass
Recitative

So geh herein zu mir,	Come enter in with me,
du mir erwählte Braut!	my chosen bride!
Ich habe mich mit dir	I have pledged my troth
in Ewigkeit vertraut.	to you in eternity!
Dich will ich auf mein Herz,	I will set you as a seal upon my heart.
auf meinen Arm	and as a seal upon my arm
gleich wie ein Siegel setzen,	and restore delight to your sorrowful eye.
und dein betrübtes Aug' ergötzen.	Forget now, o soul,
Vergiss, o Seele,	the anguish, the pain.
non die Angst, den Schmerz,	which you had to suffer;
den du erdulden müssen;	on my left you shall rest,
auf meiner Linken sollst du ruh'n,	and my right shall kiss you.
und meine Rechte soll dich küssen.	

VI

VI. Duet—
Soprano
And
Bass

Mein Freund ist mein!	Soul: My friend is mine!
Und ich bin dein!	Jesus: and I am his!
Die Liebe soll nichts scheiden.	Both: Love shall separate nothing!
Ich will mit dir in Himmels Rosen weiden,	Soul: I will feed with you among heaven's roses,
Du sollst mit mir in Himmels Rosen weiden,	Jesus: You shall feed with me among heaven's roses.
da Freunde die Fülle, da Wonne wird sein!	Both: There fullness of joy, there rapture shall be!

VII

VII. Chorus—
Harmonized
Chorale

Gloria sei dir gesungen	Gloria be sung to you
mit Menschen-und englischen Zungen,	with men's and angels' tongues,
mit Harfen und mit Cymbeln schon.	with harps and beautiful cymbals.

Von zwölf Perlen sind die Pforten	Of twelve pearls are the gates
an deiner Stadt; wir sind Konsorten	at your city; we are consorts
der Engel hoch um deinen Thron.	of the angels high about your throne.

Kein Ang' hat je gespürt,	No eye has ever sensed.
kein Ohr hat je gehört	no ear has ever heard
solche Freude.	such a delight.
Des sind wir froh,	Of this we rejoice.
io, io!	io, io,
ewig in dulci jubilo.	forever in dulci jubilo.

III. First Duet

The first duet is also in *C* minor and is sung by a soprano representing the soul and a bass representing Christ. As we mentioned earlier, love duets between the soul and Christ may be somewhat foreign to our notions of religious feeling, but the movement is lyric and beautiful. It features a rapidly moving obligato part for the solo violino piccolo. As is usual with Baroque arias or duets, the introduction for violino and continuo is repeated at the end of the piece. The vocal parts feature expressive **appoggiaturas**, a Baroque ornamental device that consists of emphasizing the upper neighboring note at the end of a melodic phrase, so that there is a crunching dissonance on the strong beat and resolution on the following weak beat (see Figure 14-2).

Figure 14-2.   Appoggiaturas in Cantata No. 140.

IV. Chorus

The middle piece of the cantata, where we expect a second chorus, is a section for tenors alone. The strings play a unison melody over a marching bass played by the continuo instruments. Against this two-voice texture, the tenors of the chorus sing the second verse of the hymn to a slightly adapted version of the hymn tune.

V. Second Recitative

The second recitative, in *B*-flat, the dominant, is for a bass, representing Christ. It is accompanied by the continuo instruments, augmented by the string section, whose sustained chords form a halo of sound around the words of Christ. The same device is used in the Passions for expressive and dramatic effect.

VI. Second Duet

The second duet for soprano and bass is also in *B*-flat and is a joyful, fast-moving love duet. This duet is accompanied by continuo and a solo oboe obligato. Like most Baroque opera arias, it is in **da capo form**, that is, it consists of an initial section, followed by a contrasting section, and a repeat of the first section. The sections are begun and ended with short instrumental **ritornellos**.

VII. Final Chorale

As we have said already, the final section of a chorale cantata consists of a four-part setting of the chorale tune, which is always in the soprano voice. The congregation joins the sopranos on the melody, and the instruments double the voices on all four parts. This homophonic final statement announces the familiar material on which the preceding sections were based and summarizes all of the musical and textual ideas that have preceded it. In this particular cantata, the final chorus has as its text the third verse of the preexisting chorale. The choral sections use the preexisting words; the words for the intervening recitatives and duets are new, and we do not know who wrote them. They may have been written by Bach himself.

This cantata, at once an effective communal expression of the congregation's feelings, a dramatic exploration of the ideas of the Sunday Gospel and the chorale of the day, and an intensely personal statement of the composer's own religious feeling, is a fine example of the cantata genre. The more than two hundred surviving cantatas by Bach are a fascinating study for students of religious music, a large body of beautiful music that still communicates effectively with modern audiences, and a witness to the strong faith and endless creativity of this incredible composer.

Rembrandt van Rijn, *An Old Man Seated*, 1652 (The National Gallery, London).

FIGURE 14-2. LISTENING GUIDE

OPENING CHORUS, CANTATA NO. 140, BY BACH

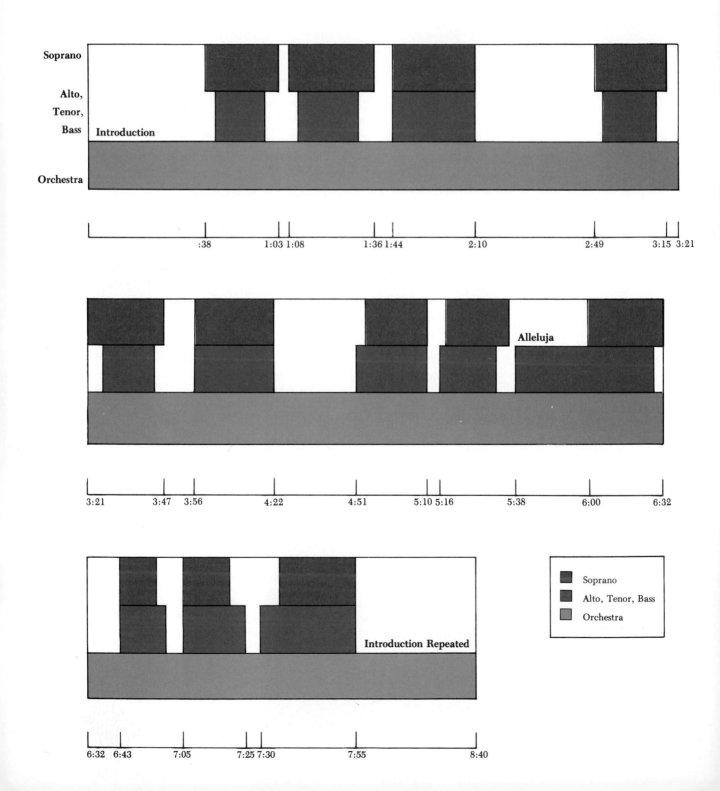

CHAPTER 15

Johann Sebastian Bach, Brandenburg Concerto No. 5

As we mentioned earlier in discussing Bach's life, he wrote most of his secular music while serving at the court of Cöthen. Among the works of that period were six concertos he wrote for the Margrave of Brandenburg. Composers in both the Baroque and Classic periods usually wrote sonatas and concertos in groups of six; it was also a standard custom to offer musical works to princes. When Bach had visited the Brandenburg court, the Margrave had requested some music. Bach sent the music, along with the usual fawning dedication. (He was probably thinking of the possibility of a better position at that court.) The Margrave never even opened the package, which was discovered among his papers after his death. The Margrave's lack of interest, however, is not the tragedy it might seem. In typical Baroque fashion, Bach wrote the works for a double purpose. He also needed music for the orchestra at Cöthen, and scholars are sure that these six concertos were played there. Bach wrote the extraordinary harpsichord part in the Fifth Concerto for himself. His princely patron had recently acquired a new instrument, and this concerto was written to show off the new acquisition. Baroque composers often wrote with these double purposes in mind. In the works of Handel, for instance, we can see that he used his better tunes in all sorts of different ways. The same melody may show up as an opera aria, a slow movement in a solo sonata, and perhaps also in a suite or concerto grosso.

CONCERTO GROSSO FORM

The Brandenburg concertos are examples of a Baroque form known as the **concerto grosso**, which is based on the principle of contrast between two groups, or sounds of different colors and dynamic levels. It was not a strict form but, rather, a principle of organization.

The two groups that alternate in a concerto grosso are a small group of soloists of virtuoso level and a larger group of journeyman orchestral players. Thus, the form, like the cantata, is written for the forces available at the better courts and churches.

Composers wrote the solo parts for the small group, often called the **concertino**, with particular players in mind. Because the solo players were salaried professionals, their wages appear in the account books of courts and churches, and we have a fairly clear picture of the forces available in specific places at specific times. The unusual instruments in the solo groups of the six concertos match the forces we know were available at Cöthen. For this reason, scholars conclude that these concertos were played at Cöthen.

SOLO INSTRUMENTS

The choice of the solo instruments is, of course, a crucial one. By this time composers were well aware of the possibilities and limitations of each instrument. In the Second Brandenburg, for example, the solo group consists of a trumpet, oboe, flute, and violin, a group of varied color.

Harpsichord

The solo group of the Fifth Brandenburg Concerto is unusual, also. It consists of a flute, violin, and harpsichord. This is a rare instance of such use of the harpsichord, which was generally relegated to service as the continuo keyboard instrument. As we know, Bach wrote solo concertos for harpsichord and orchestra, but it was seldom used as one member of the solo group in a concerto grosso. We have already explained the special purpose for this use. In fact, in this work the harpsichord tends to dominate. At times, the work sounds like a solo concerto for harpsichord, rather than a concerto grosso.

Baroque composer, Michel de la Barre, and the performers for his trio sonata.

Violin

The other solo instruments deserve some discussion, also. It was usual to use a violin as one member of the solo group, because every orchestra had an able violin soloist in the **concertmaster**, or first-chair violin, position. The chief violinist was rewarded for leading the string section by being given these solo opportunities. Besides, the Baroque period was very aware of the technical and expressive possibilities of the string instruments. The Baroque violin, however, was not exactly like the modern violin. Gut strings were used, not the wound strings used today, and the string tension was looser. The sound was more mellow and less brilliant in the upper registers than that of a modern violin.

Flute

The flute was different also. Baroque flutes were made of wood, with a few holes for the fingers and none of the keys of the modern instrument. The sound was softer, more mellow, and less brilliant than that of the modern metal flute. As you can imagine, the way to appreciate this music best is to hear it on old instruments or modern reproductions of old instruments. Changing one or two of the solo instruments throws off the balances and colors. Fortunately, many players own and play reproductions of old instruments, and recordings made on old instruments are available, so that we can hear these works more or less as the people of the time heard them and as the composers expected them to sound.

"Orchestra" of Strings

Alternating with the solo group of violin, flute, and harpsichord was an "orchestra" of strings. Actually, this group was quite small—probably more than one person to a part but not more than ten or twelve players in all. When the harpsichord functions as the continuo instrument of the orchestra, its part consists of the usual bass line and figures indicating chord progressions. When this instrument is featured as one of the soloists, every note intended for the right hand is fully written out.

MOVEMENTS

The usual structure of the concerto grosso was three movements, fast-slow-fast. The first movement was generally the one in which the contrast between the small group and the orchestra was the clearest. The second movement, as we would expect, was lyric, often more vocal than instrumental in style. It was usually scored for the small group and continuo, without the orchestra. The last movement was fast, usually brilliant, and often one of the common dance forms, such as a gigue.

BRANDENBURG CONCERTO NO. 5, IN *D* MAJOR

All of the generalizations we just listed are true of this work. It is in three movements, fast-slow-fast.

First Movement

The first movement is in **ritornello form**, with the solo group and the orchestra playing distinct material. The movement begins with the orchestra playing the entire **ritornello** in the home key of *D* major. The ritornello, an Italian word derived from *ritornare*, "to return," functions as a unifying element, providing repose and a sense of return of the familiar between the solo passages. The ritornello, in its various appearances, can be compared to the piers of a bridge, providing stability for the arching solo flights in between. It is interesting to note the ways in which this ritornello returns. If it came back in its entirety each time or always in the home key of *D* major, it would provide too much repose, and the forward drive of the movement would sag. Therefore, it comes back in sections and in different keys. The only time the entire ritornello reappears in *D* major is at the very end of the movement, providing it a sense of finality and rest.

The ritornello is made up of three basic ideas, all "instrumental" in nature, that is, they are not memorable or lyric ideas, but simple patterns that fit well on an instrument. The first segment of the ritornello (see Figure 15-1) consists of an ascending *D* major chord, followed by a descending scale and another ascending chord. The chord outlines employ repeated sixteenth-notes to increase the rhythmic activity and drive of this simple tune. The second segment (see Figure 15-2) is made up of repeated notes which outline large skips, easy to play on an instrument but difficult for a singer—another example of specifically instrumental style. The final segment is a routine cadential melody.

Figure 15-1.   Ritornello, segment 1.

Figure 15-2.   Ritornello, segment 2.

The material for the soloists is not especially "melodic" in a Classic or Romantic sense either. Their first idea is a four-note descending scale passage, treated contrapuntally (see Figure 15-3). A second solo motive (see Figure 15-4) is an ornamented ascending scale passage; we could easily view it as being the same as motive 1, here turned upside down and decorated with ornamental triplet turns. Motive 3 (see Figure 15-5) of the solo material is a different version of an idea from the second segment of the ritornello.

Figure 15-3.   Motive 1 of solo material.

Figure 15-4.   Motive 2 of solo material.

Figure 15-5.   Motive 3 of solo material.

The entire movement is made up of these simple materials. None of the musical ideas could be seriously called a "theme" and compared to the themes of, for example, a Beethoven symphony. There is no development in our later sense either: the materials are not broken down and recombined the way Mozart or Beethoven would work with them. Instead, the movement is a sort of luxuriant growth, in which the combining and varying of these materials is the main business, along with the rhythmic drive, the constantly varied texture, and the changing instrumental colors.

One unique feature of this movement is the long harpsichord cadenza Bach wrote for himself, which has been the delight of generations of harpsichord players. It begins with motive 1 of the solo material of the movement, the descending scale passages, but soon moves into completely free material, designed to show off player and instrument. Scales, runs, and sequential passages eventually give way to a dominant pedal, and we think the cadenza is coming to an end. But a deceptive cadence, defeating the expectations Bach has carefully set up, extends the cadenza for five more measures. Finally the harpsichord cadences triumphantly in *D* major, and the orchestra repeats the entire ritornello in the home key. The movement is exciting and delightful.

FIGURE 15-6. LISTENING GUIDE

FIRST MOVEMENT, BRANDENBURG CONCERTO NO. 5, BY BACH

	Soloist		Orchestra
First Theme	■		■
Second Theme	■		■
Transition Materials	■	Third Theme	☐

Note: This graph shows the main sections of the work. The orchestra does play accompaniment parts under the soloists at various points in the movement.

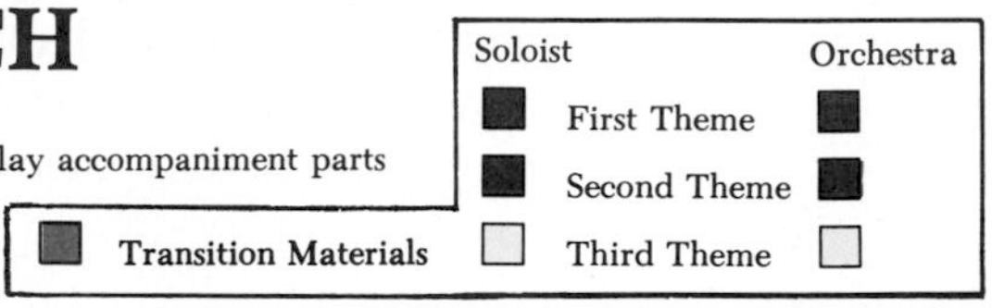

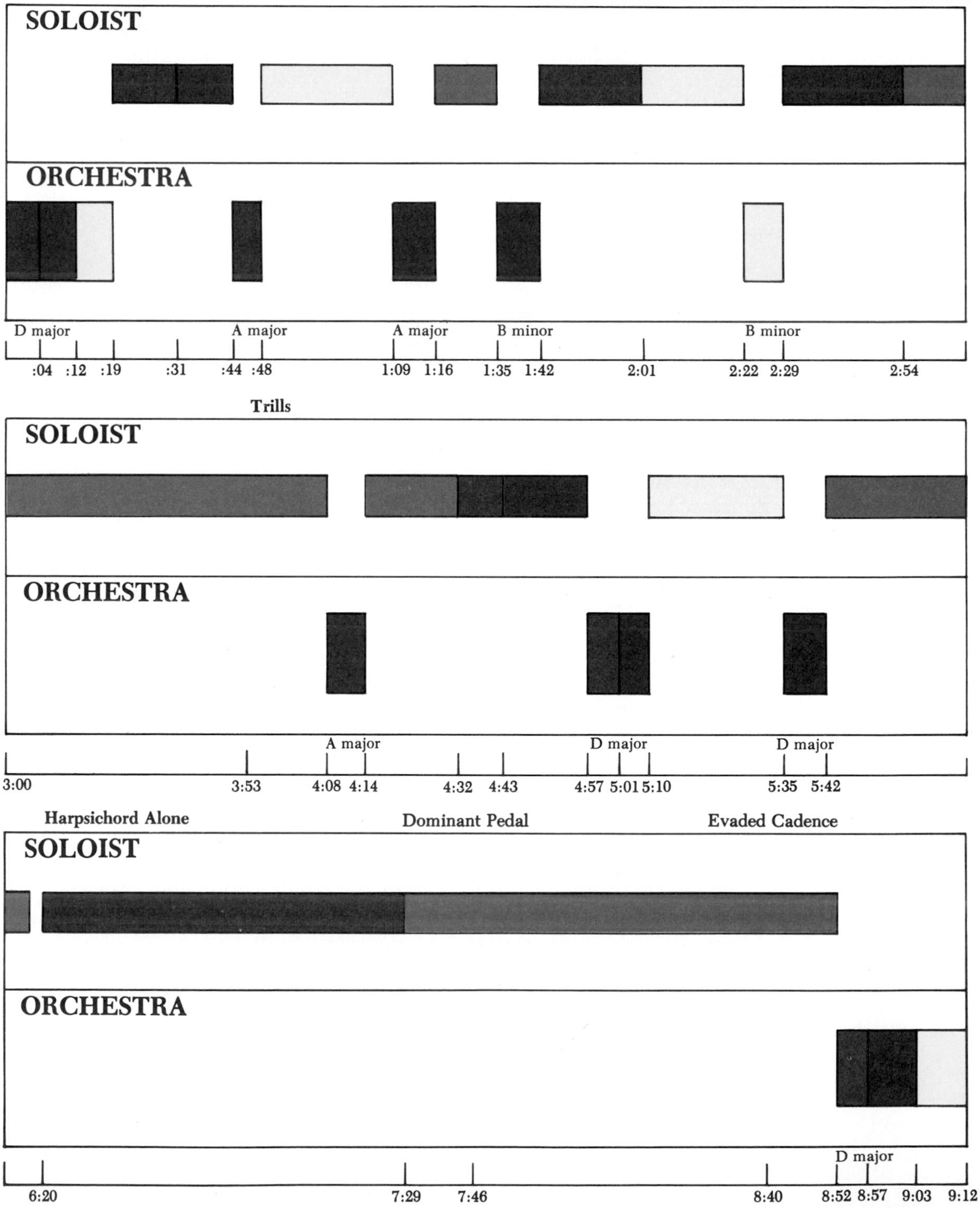

Second Movement

The second movement is for soloists and continuo, without the string orchestra, and is a lyric movement in *B* minor, the relative minor of the home key. Like many Baroque slow movements, it is built on the opposition between a steadily "walking" bass part and a dotted melody that reminds one of a tragic aria.

Third Movement

The third movement involves both soloists and orchestra, and is a headlong gigue in the key of *D* major, in fast 6/8 rhythm. It includes very rapid passages for the soloists, providing one last opportunity for virtuoso display and bringing the whole work to a brilliant conclusion.

The listening guide (see Figure 15-6) outlines the major musical events of the first movement, listing when and in what form the ritornello returns, and in what key. Note as you glance at the guide that the occurrences of the ritornello get further and further apart as the movement progresses. We might say that the solo flights get more and more adventurous and lead us further and further from familiar ground. The cadenza is the longest flight of all and builds suspense, which is satisfied by its eventual cadence in the home key and the return of the ritornello.

Jan Breughel (the Elder). *The Sense of Hearing.* (The Prado, Madrid)

CHAPTER 16

George Friederich Handel
"For Unto Us A Child is Born" from Messiah

George Friederich Handel (1685-1759) is the "other" Baroque composer, Bach's best-known contemporary. Much has been written about the contrasts between these two great masters. Although they lived at about the same time, their personalities were entirely different, and their careers went in entirely different directions. Handel was a man of huge ego and fiery temperament, who moved easily through the great courts of Europe, specialized in instrumental music and opera, and developed the English oratorio, creating one of the most popular choral forms in the history of music.

HANDEL'S LIFE

Unlike Bach, Handel was not born into a musical family. His father was a middle-class barber who wanted his son to train for a law career. Handel also received musical training and was a virtuoso player of the violin, oboe, and harpsichord. When his father died, Handel wasted no time abandoning his law career and turning to a full-time career in music. He began as a violinist in the opera orchestra at the court of Hamburg and composed a few works that were performed at court. He also rose to the much more important position of harpsichordist, which at the time included the functions of conductor. In 1706, he journeyed to Italy where he stayed for three important years. There he came into contact with the Italian operatic world and met two composers important to his later output: Alessandro Scarlatti, a master of Italian opera, and Giacomo Carissimi, a composer of Latin oratorios.

His next position was music director at the court of George, the Elector of Hanover. In 1710 he journeyed to England, a trip that was a turning point in his life. Italian opera was immensely popular in London, and the opportunities for a composer like Handel were very attractive. He returned to Hanover, but in 1712 journeyed to London again and stayed there for the rest of his life. Two years later, by a strange quirk of fate, the Elector whose service he had left without permission became King George I of England. It is a sign of Handel's nerve and reputation that the King forgave the composer the unpardonable crime of having walked out on him and appointed Handel court composer. For a while, Handel was music director to the Duke of Chandos, where he wrote some frequently performed choral pieces, the so-called Chandos Anthems.

In 1719, a group of aristocrats formed the Royal Academy of Music, an organization devoted to furthering Italian opera in London. Handel wrote a large number of very successful operas for this organization. The success of the Royal Academy's presentations was threatened and finally eclipsed by two developments. First, a rival opera company was formed, with Nicola Porpora, an Italian composer, as its chief composer. Its supporters were members of a political circle opposed to the Royal Academy. Second, *The Beggar's Opera* by Gay and Pepusch, a satirical musical comedy in English, with music compiled from popular tunes of the day, became enormously popular. *The Beggar's Opera* is a riotous work concerning a Cockney family. The running joke of the story is that Polly, the daughter, wants to marry an upper-class young man. The family is shocked and disappointed in her: no one in their family has ever been married, let alone to an aristocrat. Political ideas were obviously involved in this success also: the work pokes fun at the upper classes and takes an egalitarian, anti-royalist stance. It was also in English. No one could listen to Italian opera in quite the same way after *The Beggar's Opera*. A popular musical comedy of our own day makes a useful comparison. *My Fair Lady*, with its contrast between the stilted artificiality of the upper classes and the exuberant vitality of Doolittle and his friends from the lower classes makes much the same point that *The Beggar's Opera* did.

Casting about for another genre to replace the now out of fashion (and no longer lucrative) Italian opera, Handel hit upon an English adaptation of the earlier **oratorio**, originally a concert setting of a biblical story in Latin. Handel modified the form considerably, using Old Testament stories in English and dramatic music, including operatic solo sections and grand choruses. Something in the Handel version of the form caught the national taste of England, and his oratorios have been successful there and elsewhere ever since. The oratorios ran for months, and a steady stream of new compositions made Handel increasingly more wealthy and famous. In 1753, he lost his sight, but remained a celebrity in London. When Handel died in 1759, this transplanted German was honored as a national hero of England and buried ceremoniously in Westminster Abbey with England's great poets and artists.

HANDEL'S MUSIC

Handel was one of the most prolific and successful composers of his own time, or any period in the history of music. He produced a considerable body of music in many different forms.

Instrumental Music

Handel's instrumental music includes a large body of solo sonatas, concerti grossi—usually for strings—and ceremonial music for the English court. Two examples of his court music are especially famous: the "Water Music," so called because it was written for the King's orchestra to play as they traveled the Thames on a barge, accompanying the King's boat; and the "Royal Fireworks Music," written for a large wind ensemble, to be played at a lavish outdoor gala which featured fireworks. The latter occasion was a disaster. People in the crowd were burned when some of the more elaborate fireworks collapsed, and the person in charge of the pyrotechnics killed himself over the fiasco. The "Fireworks Music" is seldom performed—it is not easy to assemble the large groups of wind instruments called for—but the "Water Music" appears frequently on orchestra programs. Handel also wrote concertos for organ and orchestra which are still performed.

Vocal Works

Operas

Handel's vocal works include nearly forty Italian operas, of which *Rinaldo* and *Giulio Cesare* are the best known. The latter was revived by the New York City Opera Company in the early 1970s. The conventions of Italian Baroque opera make it difficult to present. These operas were based on the solo singers, who perform long strings of recitatives and arias, designed to spotlight their virtuoso abilities. There is very little for the chorus or orchestra to do, and dramatic sense is subordinated to the need to string together long series of arias. Because the leading male roles were written for castrati, a modern company must either transpose the parts for tenors and basses or record the operas with females singing the castrato roles. The music is gorgeous, but the drama and staging do not fit modern tastes.

Oratorios

Much more successful, more frequently performed, and better known are the oratorios, of which Handel wrote about twenty-five. The oratorios were not written to be staged, and the balance of the various elements is much more pleasing to modern tastes than it is in the operas. Soloists are used, and vocal display is occasionally called for, but the soloists are balanced by the chorus, which is often the most prominent element. Like the chorus of a cantata or Passion, the chorus of an oratorio represents both historical groups and the feelings of the audience. The prominence of the "people" appealed to the middle-class audience of the time with its growing anti-royalist sentiments. The English texts helped their popularity also. Although the plots are Old Testament stories, they are skillfully chosen for their timeliness. They are usually stories of liberation by a great hero who alleviates the suffering of his people. The obvious analogy to any great kings who happened to be in the audience was not lost on George and his successors. The purpose of the oratorios is not directly religious: they are concert pieces, based on stories of strong feelings, deliverance from tyrants, and heroic efforts to establish and preserve freedom. Among the well-known oratorios are *Solomon*, *Judas Maccabeus*, *Saul*, *Samson*, and *Israel in Egypt*. Handel's best-known and most frequently performed oratorio is *Messiah*, whose "Hallelujah Chorus" from the end of one section is perhaps the best-known piece of Baroque music. It appears in commercials and cartoons whenever a stock effect of triumph is needed.

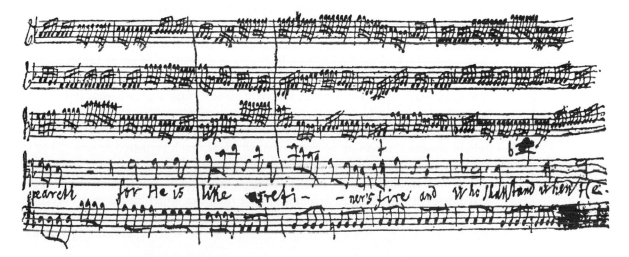

Handel's manuscript of *Messiah*.

MESSIAH

Messiah is not a typical oratorio, because it is longer than most and is contemplative rather than dramatic in nature. Whereas most of the others deal with an Old Testament hero acting in God's name to save his people, *Messiah* deals with the promise of Christ's coming, his nativity, and his suffering and death. The text is compiled from short biblical quotations.

"For Unto Us A Child Is Born"

This chorus, from the nativity section of the *Messiah*, is a splendid example of Handel's choral style, the element that makes the oratorios so popular. Handel's way of dealing with a chorus is different from Bach's in several respects. First, Bach wrote for a relatively small group of boys and men, whereas Handel is fond of grandiose effects, such as double choruses and opposed masses of sound. Second, Bach wrote in polyphonic style for his chorus. Handel developed an effective way of alternating fugal writing and homophonic, block-chord settings within the same choral piece. He was capable of writing a complete fugue, but instead interspersed the homophonic sections in his choruses for the sake of the text, which naturally is declaimed more effectively in homophonic style than in fugal style. He also depended on the cumulative effect of repetition rather than on the endless development and variety that was Bach's specialty. A note of caution should be introduced here. This sort of comparison between composers' styles always runs the risk of making one composer sound "better" than another. The Bach-Handel comparisons always tend to make Bach sound sincere and Handel cynical and "commercial," exploiting simple devices for maximum effect. That impression is not fair. These two composers, both geniuses, wrote with different purposes, for totally different circumstances, and chose the best means to accomplish their goals. Bach's choruses were written to be sung in church, as part of the Sunday service, whereas Handel's had to impress a concert audience who had paid admission to hear a presentation of much larger dimensions than a cantata. Handel came from the world of opera, master of all the standard ways to depict feelings and paint ideas musically, whereas Bach came from the long tradition of German religious music.

Analysis of this one chorus will help us understand how Handel worked. The whole chorus is made up of three musical ideas, each repeated several times in various keys and slightly different treatments. The first idea is developed polyphonically (see Figure 16-1). A striking example of the transfer of idiomatic writing from one medium to another is the melisma which serves as countersubject to idea A. On the syllable "born" is a long chain of sixteenth notes in instrumental idiom, not especially graceful for the voice, particularly on that vowel (see Figure 16-2).

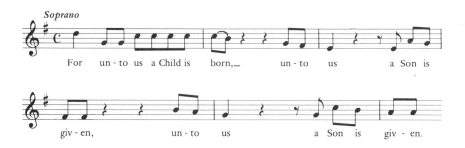

Soprano

For un-to us a Child is born,__ un-to us a Son is

giv-en, un-to us a Son is giv-en.

Figure 16-1. Idea A.

Soprano

born

Figure 16-2. Melisma from A.

Sandro Botticelli. *The Adoration of the Magi.*

The second idea, which we will call B, is a distinct, dotted ascending line, also treated contrapuntally (see Figure 16-3).

Figure 16-3.   Idea B.

Figure 16-4.   Idea C, soprano line of the homophonic section.

The third idea is the setting of the words, "Wonderful, Counselor, the Mighty God, the Everlasting Father, the Prince of Peace" (see Figure 16-4). Here the style changes radically: the chorus sings in block chords, leaving to the orchestra the responsibility of maintaining the rhythmic vitality. The style change is startling, and the words hit us much more powerfully than they would in a contrapuntal setting. Note that Handel has followed the natural rhythm of the English words, as you can sense if you recite the text in the rhythm he chose. It is surprising that Handel, a transplanted German who never learned to speak English without an accent, was one of the most successful composers in setting English texts. As the cadential chord of this block-chord section sounds, the altos have already begun to repeat idea A, setting off another series of fugal entries, this time in a different key.

The rest of the piece simply repeats these three ideas in order, with some changes made for the sake of variety and smooth transitions from key to key. The listening guide (Figure 16-5) outlines the relatively simple structure of the piece. Note that the final repetitions of A and B are much thicker in texture than the earlier contrapuntal sections. The materials are the same, but the thicker texture creates a tension that leads to the climactic repetition of the C section. The three ideas are quite distinct and are always kept separate, never combined. Out of this simple, repetitive structure comes a satisfying effect: the listener feels the triumph and joy of the text and is able to follow the materials easily. The piece does not feel artifically extended, but seems to be the right length to express adequately the wonder of the Incarnation. From this one chorus we can understand the long English oratorio tradition: the music is easy to understand and magnificent to sing.

FIGURE 16-5. LISTENING GUIDE

"FOR UNTO US A CHILD IS BORN" FROM *MESSIAH* BY HANDEL

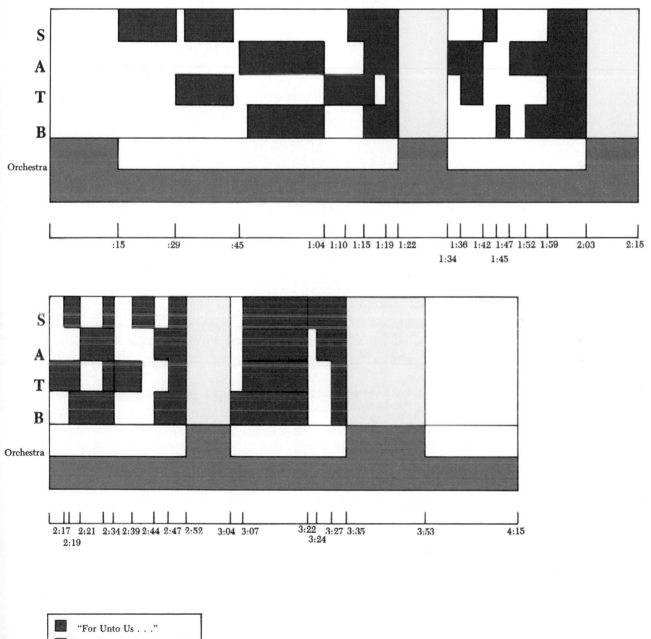

CHAPTER 17

Antonio Vivaldi "Spring" from The Four Seasons

Although Bach and Handel are the best-known Baroque composers, they are not the only great composers of the period. We now turn to another master, Antonio Vivaldi. Not only is his style different from those of Bach and Handel, but his works are representative of the important Italian school of string music. Bach was influenced by Vivaldi's works, and transcribed several of them for keyboard instruments. Vivaldi has been rediscovered in the twentieth century. A reliable edition of his complete works is in progress, and many of his instrumental pieces have been recorded and appear on concert programs.

VIVALDI'S LIFE

Vivaldi was born in 1678. His father was a violinist at the important church of St. Mark's in Venice. He was educated for both the priesthood and a musical career. He served only one year as a priest and was excused from those duties because of ill health. For thirty-six years, from 1704 until 1740, he was music director at the Ospitale della Pietà. This institution was not a hospital, but a convent school for girls, nominally "foundlings," but more commonly the illegitimate daughters of the aristocracy. In such institutions, girls could receive the education and social graces they needed to be accepted in the upper classes, and music was one of the chief subjects.

Vivaldi thus had a unique situation, because he worked with a steady stream of musicians who were full-time students. With his all-girl orchestra, he put on concerts that were very popular. He left this post only to conduct opera in other Italian cities. He wrote a great amount of music for the Pietà concerts, and produced many solo concertos for unusual solo instruments, the kinds of instruments that would not be available in the standard court or church group. Thus, he wrote concertos not only for violin and the standard winds—oboe, flute, bassoon—but also for unusual instruments such as the piccolo, mandolin, and guitar.

VIVALDI'S MUSIC

Vocal Works

Vivaldi was famous in his day as an opera composer. At the time Venice was a center of opera, with six permanent opera companies and several other organizations that produced operas. Like Handel's operas, Vivaldi's were written according to the conventions of the time and are little known and never performed today. He also wrote choral music for church use. Some of those works, such as the "Gloria," are frequently performed today.

Instrumental Works

We know Vivaldi chiefly for his instrumental works, the style of which is not as dated as his operatic style. Besides the solo concertos already mentioned, he wrote numerous solo sonatas and concerti grossi. He grew up within the Italian Baroque tradition of string writing. Composers like Legrenzi, his teacher, and Albinoni, Torelli, Corelli, and Geminiani had produced an impressive collection of idiomatic music for strings. Vivaldi, therefore, handles the strings exceptionally well, using the register shifts, arpeggios, passage work, and new bowing techniques that were part of that Italian tradition. The small group in most of the concerti grossi consists of three solo violins, with many sections that feature one solo violin, so that they sound like combinations of concertos for solo violin and concerti grossi.

Form and Style

In the matter of form and style, Vivaldi developed some standard ways of writing concertos that were followed by others. He usually used the three-movement, fast-slow-fast pattern that Bach adopted. This pattern became the standard format for the Classical concerto as well. Unlike Corelli and others of his predecessors, Vivaldi usually made a distinction between the material played by the orchestra and the material of the small group, a pattern we saw utilized by Bach in the concerto grosso (see Chapter 15).

Texture

In the matter of texture, Vivaldi shows the influence of the new stylistic ideas that were circulating in the first half of the eighteenth century. Instead of the consistently polyphonic texture we see in Bach, Vivaldi uses a texture that is predominantly homophonic, with a prominent melodic line supported by a slower bass line and accompaniment patterns in the inner voices. There are, of course, many passages in polyphonic style, but the melody-and-accompaniment texture is prevalent in much of his music. Thus, he was more up-to-date than Bach stylistically. His works give clear evidence of the approaching shift away from contrapuntal texture.

Canaletto. *The Piazza of St. Mark, Venice.* (The Detroit Institute of Arts)

THE FOUR SEASONS

Perhaps the best-known work by Antonio Vivaldi is *The Four Seasons*, a set of four programmatic concerti grossi which depict nature in each of the seasons of the year. All four concertos are quite brief and naive in their literal depiction of natural effects. In this particular instance, we are certain that the programmatic intent was the composer's, rather than the result of the imagination of some later commentator. Besides the title of the set and the titles of each concerto, early editions of these works include the texts of four sonnets on which the concertos are based. Not only is the sonnet describing each season printed at the beginning of each concerto, but the individual lines are printed right in the music, at the places where the music is supposed to depict the ideas of that particular line.

These works are a combination of both the solo concerto and the concerto grosso. The only player consistently designated as a soloist is a solo violin; however, the first-chair players of the first and second violin sections of the orchestra function as soloists also, so that, in this instance, the contrast is between the string orchestra and either a single soloist or three solo violins. Because both the large group and the three soloists consist of string instruments, this work lacks the color contrasts between the individual members of the small group and between the small group and the orchestra that we heard in the Brandenburg concerto. However, we do hear one contrast that resembles Bach, the contrast between the solo material and the orchestra material. In this particular concerto, the distinction between solo material and orchestra material is blurred somewhat, because the orchestra gets involved in some of the dramatic pictorial effects and because the solo violin also functions as the first violin of the orchestral sections. Still, there are clear sections of distinctly orchestral material.

"SPRING"

Text

The *"Sonetto Dimostrativo"* or "explanatory sonnet" that accompanies the "Spring" concerto, the first of the set, is given below, first in Italian and then in a free English translation.

> Giunt' e' la Primavera e festosetti
> La salutan gl'Augei con lieto canto
> E i fonti allo apirar de' Zeffiretti
> Con dolce mormorio scorrono intanto.
> Vengon' coprendo l'aer di nero amanto
> E lampi, e tuoni ad annuntiarla eletti
> Indi tacendo questi gl'Augelletti
> Tornan' di nuovo allor canoro incanto.
> E quindi sul fierito ameno prato

Al caro mormorio di fronde e piante
Dorme'l caprar col fido can'a lato.
Di pastoral Zampogna al suon festante
Danzan Ninfe e Pastor nel tetto amato
Di Primavera all'apparir brillante.

Joyously Spring comes,
And the birds greet it with happy song.
The Zephyr's breezes play upon the fountains
Which respond with sweet murmurs.
Suddenly the sky turns black,
And thunder and lightning, Spring's heralds, come,
But soon they fall silent and the birds
Return and sing their songs again.
On the verdant meadow,
While the leaves sigh and murmur,
The goatherd sleeps, with his faithful dog at
his side.
To the festive sounds of country pipes
Nymphs and shepherds dance
Shining in the brilliance of spring.

The Guardi family, Piazetta San Marco and the Palazzo, seen from the canal.

First Movement

The first two four-line stanzas of the poem are the material for the first of the concerto's three movements. The orchestra begins with a ritornello (see Figure 17-1) that depicts a generalized happy feeling. The first solo section consists of birdcalls for the three solo violins, followed by a brief return of the second phrase of the ritornello. Next, the orchestra and the solo violin play the murmuring zephyr sounds, in a section of great charm and beauty. Another short segment of the ritornello leads to the storm sounds, consisting of tremolos (rapid bow strokes on one note) and ascending scales played in unison by the orchestra. Another short section of ritornello leads to the return of the bird calls for the three soloists. The second phrase of the ritornello, now in E major again, brings the movement to a happy ending.

Violin

Figure 17-1. Ritornello theme.

Second Movement

The second movement is based on the next three lines of the poem, depicting the sleeping shepherd. It is a brief, serene movement, featuring a lyric melody in C-sharp minor for the solo violin over dotted accompaniment figures in the first and second violins and repeated notes in the violas, which are supposed to represent the faithful dog. The melody begins as shown in figure 17-2.

Solo Violin
Largo

Figure 17-2. Theme, second movement.

Note as you listen to the second movement that the cello and continuo are silent: the lowest line is the repeated note figure for the violas. Not only does this orchestration provide color contrast, utilizing only the higher end of the orchestra, but it also creates a texture of melody and accompaniment, rather than the more polyphonic texture of the other movements. This texture change happens frequently in the late Baroque period, foreshadowing the melody-and-accompaniment texture that would prevail in the Classic and Romantic periods.

FIGURE 17-4. LISTENING GUIDE
FIRST MOVEMENT, "SPRING" FROM *THE FOUR SEASONS,* BY VIVALDI

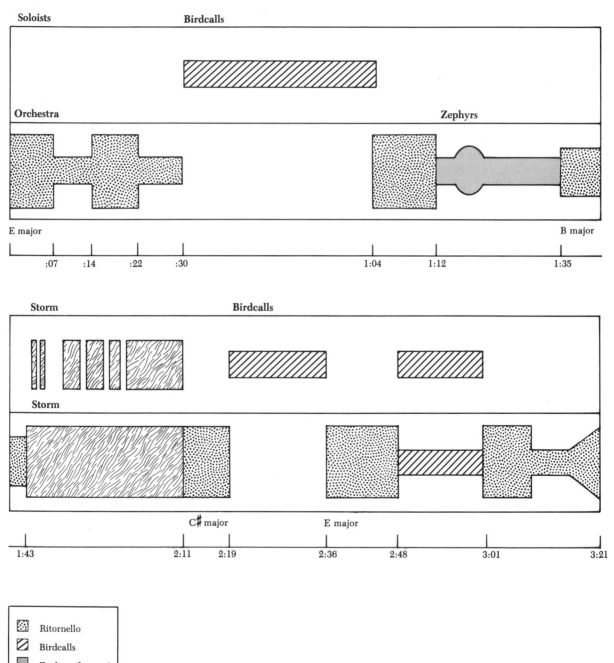

Soloists

Birdcalls

Orchestra

Zephyrs

E major

B major

:07 :14 :22 :30 1:04 1:12 1:35

Storm

Birdcalls

Storm

C♯ major

E major

1:43 2:11 2:19 2:36 2:48 3:01 3:21

Ritornello
Birdcalls
Zephyrs (breezes)
Storm

Last Movement

The last three lines of the poem provide the idea for the last movement of the concerto, a happy dance in 12/8 meter. In this movement, the sections for the solo violin and the three solo violins do not depict nature scenes and sound effects. Rather, they are ornamental virtuoso passages that provide contrast with the dance tune played repeatedly by the orchestra. The main melody of the dance is illustrated in Figure 17-3.

Figure 17-3. Melody, third movement.

The listening guide (Figure 17-4) outlines the musical events of the first movement. The pictorial ideas of the poem are noted in the diagram where they occur in the score. Actually, these notations are not necessary: we would clearly sense the succession of pictures—birds, soft breezes, a storm, the return of the birds—from the obvious sounds of the music.

This concerto and its companions in the set of four are works of great charm, with a surface appeal and facility that may, at first, seem opposed to the seriousness of much Baroque music. This spirit of childlike playfulness was another important facet of Baroque style. It is easy to see why Vivaldi's music has been played and recorded so frequently in recent years.

Frederick the Great playing the flute at Sans Souci.

PART IV

Music in the Classical Era

CHAPTER 18

Social and Cultural Background

CLASSIC AND CLASSICAL

The words "classic" and "classical" are used in a bewildering variety of ways, which can cause confusion and misunderstanding. We speak, for example, of "classic" films or "classic" examples of early rock and roll. The term used in this way implies that the object described is a model to be followed, a perfect example of its type, or an early milestone in the evolution of a particular art form. We also use "classical" in the realm of music to describe art music as opposed to folk or popular music, so that one could call most of the musical works discussed in this book "classical." In a historical context, "classic" or "classical" often refers to the civilizations of Greece and Rome, which later perioes have viewed as models of Western institutions and culture. Thus, "classical" or "neoclassical" implies a return to what we consider to be Greek or Roman ideals, or a return to reason and logic as guiding forces in art. In this sense, "classic" and "romantic" designate two poles or tendencies in the arts, always in tension, one or the other seeming dominant at any particular historical point, but both always present to some extent. Thus, the Baroque era can be described as more "romantic" than "classic," and the twentieth century, as more "classic" than "romantic." Like all generalizations, this one is slippery and misleading. One gets the impression from reading some texts that Classical music is entirely without emotion or drama, and that Romantic music is entirely devoid of logic, reason, or balanced organization. Obviously this artificial distinction misrepresents both musical styles. No music can be entirely devoid of form and balance, or totally lacking in emotional content. The terms and the generalizations they imply are useful and instructive, as long as we use them with some caution.

CLASSIC PERIOD

Here we are using the term "Classic" to denote a specific era, a period of time in which certain common elements of style and intent can be applied to all of the arts. Historians of music generally define the Classic period as extending from around 1750 until about 1825. The year 1750 makes a handy boundary, not only because it is a nice round number, but also because it is the year in which Bach died. As we have already noted, however, Bach was out of touch with his time. Classical style features and ideas appeared long before his death; and in some ways, 1720 or 1725 makes a better starting date for the new era. Bach's own sons were pioneers in the development of a style much different from their father's. They were at work in this new atmosphere and style long before his death.

Whatever dates we use as the outer limits, some general social and aesthetic tendencies can be observed in the middle and late 1700s. These tendencies created a new context for the arts and a different atmosphere in which fresh styles in literature, architecture, the visual arts, and music could flourish.

French Revolution

It is difficult to generalize about the politics of this period. Some absolute monarchs remained, like the Empress Maria Theresa of Austria, Frederick the Great in Prussia, and Louis XV of France, successor to Louis XIV. But while Louis XV reigned, the world was changing fundamentally. The French Revolution overturned his reign, consigning the King and many of his aristocrats to death by the guillotine and forbidding any trappings of class distinction or aristocracy. The leaders of the Revolution even passed laws changing the French language. Like all Romance languages, French has two forms of the second person: a familiar form, to be used when addressing family members and close friends, and a "formal" or honorary form, to be used when speaking to superiors or strangers. The revolutionaries outlawed the formal second person, thus legislating equality among all citizens, at least in their speech. Titles like *Monsieur*, now translated as "Mister" but originally meaning "My Lord," were outlawed also; and strangers were ordered to address each other as "Citizen." The revolutionary government in Paris established boards of censorship which passed judgment on all the arts. Artists and composers who were flexible enough to work within the new legal limits were highly successful, supplying the new arts required by the new state.

America

The United States of America was formed in this period, and its fundamental documents—the Declaration of Independence and the Constitution—are magnificent expressions of the ideas of this new era. Both are quite reasonable

The Acropolis, the site of the ruins of several ancient Greek temples, still stands above the city of Athens.

and logical. From the basic premise that all men are created equal flow consequences, such as republican political organization, inalienable rights for all citizens, and a fine system of government based on checks and balances, preventing a king or dictator from taking over the political system. The new nation was not perfect at the outset. The founding fathers kept slaves, for example, and restricted the vote to educated property holders. Still, they built a fine system of government on logic, reason, convictions about equality, and the bitter lessons they had learned from autocratic political systems in Europe. No king or state religion was going to impede the freedom of Americans; and a new culture, not dominated by king or church, was created. The group established as the basis of the new country was the middle class, educated and moneyed families who had achieved their position, accumulated their wealth, and acquired their power, not from accidents of birth or social class, but from business sense and good management. Naturally, this transition from a class-conscious society to a nation of equals was not a process accomplished overnight or, perhaps, ever fully achieved. But these noble ideas were widely discussed in the Classic period, and nations like the United States of America were set on their way by the careful drafting of a system of government designed to deal with all men as equals.

Industrial Revolution

Many new developments and discoveries provided the context in which the old class system could be replaced by a new type of society. The Industrial Revolution, made possible by such discoveries and inventions as electricity, the steam engine, and the spinning jenny, created a new class of economically powerful families. Thinkers like Adam Smith and Emmanuel Kant developed revolutionary ideas about the ways in which man, history, and society are organized. Reason was exalted, and all knowledge was rethought and reorganized. The French Encyclopedists sought to gather all knowledge in every discipline between the covers of one large collection. Clear prose and scientific investigation were valued above the excesses of poetic fancy and submission to authority. A new age of independence was born.

THE CLASSICAL AESTHETIC

Architecture

As we would expect, the new ideas of reason, the dignity of the individual, and a return to Greek ideals of democracy were reflected in the arts of the time. The clearest examples of Classical ideas embodied in architecture are the government buildings in Washington, D.C., which are built in Greek revival style, in imitation of Greek temples. The Capitol, The Lincoln Memorial, and Jefferson's estate at Monticello are excellent examples of our homage to Greek artistic ideals.

Literature

In some literature of the period, we can see the same sort of homage to the Greeks. Poets such as Alexander Pope revived the meters and didactic style of Greek poetry; expository prose was favored over sentimental poetry. The middle class became the subject of novels by Fielding, and middle-class sentiments appeared in the poetry of Cowper and others.

Visual Arts

The visual arts showed the same Greek influence. Greek and Roman themes began to appear in paintings, and the religious themes and dramatic lighting of a painter like Caravaggio were replaced by calm still lifes and serene portraits.

Giovanni Paolo Panini *Interior of the Pantheon, Rome.*

Romantic Influences

But to reduce the Classical spirit entirely to reason and logic is to miss the point of much of the art of the period. In many senses, the Classical and subsequent Romantic periods are one: the basic premises remain the same, while the emphasis shifts from Classical form and balance to Romantic expression and drama. Although the Classical period began as a reaction against the political system and aesthetics of the Baroque age, it never was as completely rational and unemotional as we might suppose. In the 1770's, a literary movement arose in Germany called *Sturm und Drang* ("Storm and Stress"), epitomized in Goethe's novel, *The Sorrows of Young Werther*. Some commentators see this movement as a foretaste of Romanticism in the Classical age. It makes more sense to realize that drama and emotion were never really absent from the Classical aesthetic. Along with the elevation of reason and the rejection of Baroque "excess," the Classical aesthetic always included drama and emotion. The transition from Classic to Romantic is not a revolution, but a gradual shift of emphasis, an elevating of individual expression.

A. Watteau. *Amore in Campagna.* (Charlottenburg)

Music

Understanding the dualism inherent in the Classical aesthetic is essential if we are to understand the music of the period. It is easy to dismiss Classical music as elegant background music for aristocratic courts. The Classical interest in balanced forms inclines some listeners to regard the music of the period as formula hack work, obviously less meaningful and valuable than the personal outpourings of the Romantics. To adopt this stance is to misunderstand the whole focus of Classical music. It is true that the composers of the period were interested in balanced structures and symmetrical melodies and that most of them worked under the old patronage system, in court or church; but drama and personal innovation were important also. The gorgeous lyricism of Classical slow movements, the towering drama of some Mozart operas, the sudden dynamic shifts and surprises of many Classical works—all belie the exaggerated image of Classical music as controlled, impersonal, and formulaic. There is Romantic individualism and lyricism in Classical music, just as there is classical logic and balance underlying most Romantic music.

CHAPTER **19**

New Musical Developments

Although the music of the Classical period changed considerably from that of the Baroque era, the situation in which composers and performers worked did not change all that much. Most musicians continued to work under the patronage system, for the courts of kings and princes or for the church. In those contexts, they were bound by contract to produce music for particular occasions. Some were obliged in still other ways. Haydn, who worked at the Esterhazy court outside Vienna, was responsible for the uniforms and wigs of the orchestra, as well as for procuring and caring for the instruments. There were also public concert halls and opera houses in large cities, and composers could negotiate to have their works performed there. The new middle class, with time and money to support leisure pursuits, began to form a new audience, providing composers with outlets other than church and court.

INSTRUMENTS

Piano

One of the important new instruments in the Classic period was the piano. The full name of the new instrument was **fortepiano** or **pianoforte**. The name points out its main advantage over the earlier keyboard instruments: its sound can be both loud (*forte*) and soft (*piano*). A change in the way a key is struck can change not only the dynamic level, but even the color of the sound to some extent. The piano is also capable of a more sustained tone than the harpsichord, which makes it suitable for legato, lyric melodies.

18th century clavichord with decorative painting, and one of the earliest fortepianos built by Cristofori in 1720. Note that the first pianos resembled harpsichords in appearance, but the action is different. The appearance of the piano changed gradually.

The first pianos appeared around 1710—J. S. Bach apparently once accepted a position demonstrating the new instruments—but the piano replaced the harpsichord only gradually. The harpsichord continued to be used for harmonic filler in many of Haydn's symphonies until new ways of writing for the orchestra made its support role unnecessary. The piano became a favorite instrument for solo music, and the standard accompaniment instrument for other solo instruments. It also became a favorite solo instrument with orchestra, in the concerto form.

Woodwinds

Members of the woodwind family of instruments took on new importance during this period, both as solo instruments and within the larger orchestra. Solo woodwinds and brasses were a prominent feature of the better Baroque ensembles, but the basic orchestral family was the strings, who had their greatest period of development in Baroque times. An important new instrument was added to the woodwind family. The clarinet, which during Classic times was constructed in such a way that it could play in tune throughout its wide range, appeared as a solo instrument and as a member of the woodwind section of the orchestra. The standard wind section included two flutes, two oboes, two clarinets, two bassoons, and a pair of French horns. The horns were the only regular members of the brass family: the high trumpet parts of the Baroque period were no longer in fashion. Occasionally, a pair of trumpets were added for military effects, usually along with additional percussion.

ORCHESTRAS

Classical Orchestra

The standard Classical orchestra consisted of the expanded wind choir, a string section, and a set of two tympani. The wind choir was capable of playing alone as a unit, contrasting with the string choir. Sometimes the winds sustained and reinforced the harmonies, and sometimes they played as an independent group. It is interesting to listen, for example, to a Mozart piano concerto from the point of view of orchestral color. Because the piano is capable of functioning as a third independent unit, great variety is possible in the disposition of the various elements of the texture. The piano can play the melody, with string accompaniment; the winds can play accompaniment to the piano melody; either winds or strings can play the main lines with piano accompaniment; or all three groups can play together to reinforce the texture.

The addition of winds was not the only basic change in the orchestra. Baroque orchestral and choral works were written for the two levels of performers generally available in the standard court or church: a few professional soloists and a larger group of journeyman choristers or players. The Classic orchestra was different. The new way of writing for the orchestra required virtuoso players in every chair. Performing standards rose dramatically, and good orchestras became internationally famous for their clean attacks, their discipline, and their ability to achieve dramatic dynamic effects. One such world-renowned orchestra early in the Classic period was at Mannheim, in Germany. The Mannheim orchestra was known all over Europe for its fine wind players and the high performance level of the entire group. In his letters, Mozart reports having heard the Mannheim orchestra and having been amazed at their skill. Because the Classical style became an international style, performance levels were raised all over Europe.

Conductors

The change in the quality of orchestral playing led to another significant change. As orchestral music became more demanding and as composers and audiences came to expect precision and well-done dramatic effects, conductors became more important. Baroque orchestras were likely to include the composer, playing basso continuo at the harpsichord and leading the other players. The Classic period conductor did not play, but directed the other players.

A final word about the Classical orchestra. These groups consisted of twenty-five or thirty players. We now realize that the Romantic size orchestras of our large cities, consisting of ninety or a hundred players, are not the best groups to play the Classical orchestral literature, at least as the composers intended. When large orchestras do play Classical orchestral literature, many players leave the stage, and the group is reduced to an approximation of a Classical orchestra.

Chamber Orchestra

Smaller chamber orchestras have also been organized. Their programs consist of Baroque and Classical works and twentieth-century literature, which is usually written for smaller ensembles. The only works a chamber orchestra cannot play are the large works of the late Romantic period and of the early twentieth century. It is much easier for a group of thirty virtuoso players to achieve the lightness and elegance characteristic of Classical orchestral style than it is for a group of eighty or ninety.

The California Chamber Symphony, under the direction of Henri Temianka, is a modern ensemble of the size for which Haydn and Mozart wrote their symphonies during the Classical Era.

ELEMENTS OF CLASSICAL STYLE

Texture

The most radical change from the preceding Baroque style in the Classic period is in texture and approach to melody. As you recall, Baroque music is generally contrapuntal in texture. It is impossible to hum a Bach fugue, because the point of the music is not the fugue subject, but the complex texture formed when the melody is used against itself. Classic composers rejected contrapuntal texture, at least as the prevailing texture. They continued to use contrapuntal writing, generally in development sections, as a device for building dramatic tension. The last movement of Mozart's "Jupiter" Symphony is a rare example of an extended fugal section in a Classical orchestral work. The use of contrapuntal writing as a dramatic device in developmental sections continued in Romantic compositions. The rejection of polyphony as a standard texture is part of the Classical rejection of the grandeur and "exaggeration" that characterized the Baroque arts, at least in the view of Classical aestheticians. Jean Jacques Rousseau, the French philosopher, who also was a musician, rejected polyphony as unnatural. He said that it made no more sense to juxtapose four melodic lines, all going on at the same time, than it would to listen to four speakers lecturing on different topics simultaneously. In place of the complex polyphonic texture of the Baroque period, Classical composers established melody and accompaniment, sometimes called homophonic texture, as the basic, prevailing texture. This change is extremely important. Melody and accompaniment became the basic texture, not only of music of the Classic period, but of the ensuing Romantic period as well, and of most forms of popular music in the West: jazz, musical comedy, pop, and rock. The typical Classical texture spotlights an appealing melodic line over background harmonies. Some instruments play sustained chords, and others play more active alternating figures or arpeggios to give the accompaniment some rhythmic life. Over and over in Classic period music we can hear the same basic disposition of the orchestral forces: the melody in the first violins or perhaps high winds, second violins and violas playing rocking accompaniment figures, winds and low strings playing sustained chords.

Melody

The shift from polyphonic texture to melody-and-accompaniment texture naturally puts great emphasis on the single prominent melody, which automatically becomes a foreground element. The Classical melodies thus brought into prominence naturally needed to be considerably different from Baroque melodies. Classical melodies are free to take any shape they want and can make use of expressive notes outside the harmonies. Classical melodies are individual and memorable—aggressive, dramatic, folk-like, or lyric.

The kinds of melodies we find in the high Classical style of Haydn and Mozart did not spring up suddenly. In the styles of those two masters, we have come to expect elegantly balanced melodies, symmetrical in shape, that divide and subdivide into antecedent-consequent, question-and-answer pairs. An example of a symmetrical Mozart melody is the first theme of the *G* minor Symphony, K. 550 (see Figure 19-1). (The "K" numbers after Mozart titles refer to a chronological index of Mozart's works published by Köchel, an amateur Mozart scholar, and since updated by several scholars.)

Figure 19-1. Main theme, *G* minor Symphony.

These phrases are paired in several ways. First, the second phrase is obviously a sequential variant of the first, that is, the shape of the melody is the same, but the second phrase starts on a pitch different from the first and, thus, moves the melody down a whole step. The harmonies are symmetrically paired also: the first phrase begins in *G* minor, the tonic key of the movement, and moves to another harmony; the second phrase begins on this second chord and ends back in the tonic. The departure of the first phrase is balanced by the return of the second. Note that both phrases have a balanced internal shape as well: the first half of each consists of the two-note figure, repeated three times, followed by a leap of a sixth; the leap is answered by step-wise motion downwards in the second half. These few measures can be subdivided even further, into small units called **motives**, that are used as distinct brief ideas later in the development section.

Rhythm

Some other elements of Classical style deserve mention. Rhythm is generally quite regular, with a single tempo maintained for entire movements. Because of the simpler texture, Classical rhythm does not have the inexorable drive that Baroque rhythm does, and Classical fast movements generally should feel relaxed and comfortable. Sometimes performers and conductors try to infuse Romantic drama into a Classic movement by playing at a breakneck tempo, but this expedient always seems artificial and foreign to Classical style.

Dynamics

Classical dynamics are different from Baroque dynamics. In the Baroque orchestra, dynamic contrast came from the alternation between large and small groups, each playing at a more or less consistent level of volume. In the Classic orchestra, gradual crescendos were expected from the whole orchestra, gradual shadings of volume were carefully accomplished by adding or subtracting instruments, and composers were more specific about dynamic instructions in their scores. We already mentioned that orchestras became famous for their ability to play dramatic crescendos as a unit, and dynamics became an important element for the composer to specify and for the performer to accomplish.

Harmony

One last area is important: the classical approach to harmony. Generally, Classical harmonies are simple and clear. Key areas are used as structural devices, as we shall see in our discussion of sonata-allegro form. Prominent areas are the **tonic** (I) and **dominant** (V) keys, and the move from one area to the other in the exposition section is made quite clear by emphatic cadences. In **development** sections, many more keys are introduced to create tension. The return to the tonic at the beginning of the **recapitulation** is made quite clear, and has the dramatic effect of coming home to the awaited tonic. In other words, harmony is controlled and used logically and structurally.

CLASSICAL FORMS

Classical composers continued to write choral music for church use, such as Masses, and other large choral forms. Haydn's oratorio, *The Creation*, is a masterpiece in this genre. But most of the innovation and creativity of the period was unleashed in instrumental forms. Most of the instrumental music is absolute rather than program music. Works have generic titles and numbers rather than picturesque titles. The picturesque titles we do have—the *Jupiter* symphony, the *Emperor* quartet—are descriptive or convenient nicknames added by later commentators, not subtitles intended by the composers.

THE SYMPHONY

By far the most important innovation of the Classic period was the development of standard symphonic form. This development was not, of course, an overnight occurrence; and calling Haydn "the Father of the Symphony," the way some older books used to, does not do justice to the historical facts. Beginning around 1720, thirty years before the death of J. S. Bach, composers in centers like Venice and Mannheim began to experiment with orchestral works in a new, melody-and-accompaniment texture, in a style different from Baroque orchestral works. Some of the early works sound experimental: the tunes are mosaics of unrelated, assymetrical fragments, and the forms are not clear. From those experiments eventually came a clear idea of the symphonic model, based on a combination of Baroque forms, the Italian opera overture, and new orchestral techniques. The symphony, as we have mentioned, is so pliable and basic a structure that it remained a viable form for Romantic and some twentieth-century composers. Like the Elizabethan drama or the nineteenth-century novel, it became a standard form, open to the creativity and innovation of the individual composer, but one of the basic structural contributions of Western culture.

As it evolved in the high Classical style of Haydn and Mozart, the symphony is a four-movement form. The first movement is in sonata-allegro form, one of the most fascinating of musical structures. The second is generally simpler and more lyric, often in an A-B-A form. The third movement in the Classical model is a **minuet and trio**, in compound **ternary form**. It is the most repetitive and least dramatic of the movements, and the only remnant of the stylized dance forms so prevalent in Baroque orchestral music. The last movement matches the first in intensity and is generally fast, in either **rondo** or sonata-allegro form. The entire four-movement structure is balanced and satisfying. An interesting question to bear in mind is the relationship among movements of a particular symphony. Constructed as independent, separate movements, they nevertheless hold together in a satisfying way that is hard to describe but easy to sense. Two symphonies from the Classical period are described in detail in Chapters 20 and 22.

Sonata-Allegro Form

The most complicated and interesting structure of the several involved in four-movement symphonic form is **sonata-allegro form**, sometimes also called first-movement form or simply **sonata form**. Like the larger four-movement symphony structure, it is one of the great achievements of the Classic period specifically and of Western music in general. It results in a coherent, audible structure that keeps the listener's interest, but provides endless opportunity for innovation, originality, and even surprise.

Exposition

The standard model for sonata form goes as follows. The first section, called the **exposition**, presents two themes or groups of melodic ideas. Often the first is strong and aggressive and the second, more lyric, although that contrast is not necessarily present in all first movements. More basic is the question of keys. The first theme or group is always presented in the tonic key and the second, in a contrasting key, usually the dominant if the tonic key is major and the relative major if the tonic is minor. Whether or not we hear clearly contrasting themes in the two sections, we certainly hear the move, usually in a transition section, to the second key area. A closing section usually rounds out the exposition, which should always be repeated in a Classic first movement.

Development

After a strong cadence in the second key (usually the dominant), the **development section** begins. Generally, the development presents no new material. It consists of manipulations of materials we have already heard and usually includes excursions, sometimes very brief, into remote key areas. The melodic material usually consists of motives from earlier themes, often the first theme and the closing theme (if there is one), because they tend to be more suitable for motivic treatment than the more lyric second theme. Whatever the developmental process in a particular movement, developments are always heard as dramatic flights, away from familiar key areas and simple melodies into remote keys and intense, perhaps contrapuntal motivic layers. Developments often end with a **dominant pedal**—a sustained sounding of the dominant or fifth degree of the tonic key—which prepares for the return of the tonic key and the first theme.

Recapitulation

The final section of the form is called the **recapitulation**. The moment when the development ends and the recapitulation begins is the dramatic climax of the structure and a favorite place for witty innovations. Sometimes composers write **false recapitulations**, deliberately deceptive references to the first theme before the proper harmony has returned, or **covered recapitulation**, when the first theme actually begins before the harmony is "right." The recapitulation brings back both theme groups from the exposition, but both in the tonic, without the move to the dominant (or relative major). The transition in the exposition, therefore, which moves from one key to the other, has to be omitted or modified in the recapitulation. The recapitulation ends with some sort of closing section, often the one from the exposition, transposed to the tonic key, and may also include an additional section, called the **coda**, which serves to wrap up the movement and reassert the tonic key.

OTHER ORCHESTRAL FORMS

Concerto

Besides the symphony, a favorite Classical orchestral form was the solo concerto. Many concertos were written for the piano and the violin; important concertos were also written for other instruments, such as the French horn and clarinet.

Concerto form is different from symphony form in two respects. First, there are generally three movements: the minuet and trio does not appear in the concerto. Second, sonata-allegro form is modified because of the soloist. There are usually two expositions, one for the orchestra and one for the soloist, and space is created for **cadenzas**, improvised solo passages inserted before final cadences. We will look at one of Mozart's piano concertos in more detail in Chapter 24.

Divertimento or Serenade

Another type of lighter instrumental music was written in this period. Composers wrote loosely structured groups of several movements, sometimes for string orchestra, sometimes for winds alone, and sometimes for full orchestra. Although these lighter pieces make use of standard structures, like rondo and sonata-allegro, they are obviously lighter in mood and intent than the symphony and are generally given the generic title of **divertimento** ("entertainment") or **serenade**. A famous example is Mozart's *Eine Kleine Nachtmusik* ("A Little Night-Music") for string orchestra. We will discuss one of his wind serenades in Chapter 23.

Chamber Music

Sonata

An enormous amount of music was written for solo instruments and small groups during this period. The **sonata** for piano solo, or for a solo instrument with piano accompaniment, became a favorite form. A solo sonata, like the concerto, usually consists of three movements: a fast first movement in sonata-allegro form; a slow, lyric second movement; and a final fast movement in either sonata-allegro, rondo, or theme-and-variation form.

String Quartet

The favorite chamber genre was the string quartet, written for a group consisting of two violins, viola, and cello. Quartets are usually in four-movement form, like the symphony, and are mini-symphonies not only in form, but in complexity and seriousness. The orchestration problems in the Classical quartet are fascinating. Composers have to be very creative to provide a variety of texture and color with a small group of similar instruments. All of the instruments play the prominent melody at some times and accompaniment at others. Textures tend to be more frequently polyphonic than they do in the symphony. The string quartet in general and one specific example by Haydn are the subject of Chapter 21.

This long description, sprinkled with "perhaps," "often," and alternate possibilities, may seem confusing. We therefore add at this point a graph (Figure 19-2) of a typical sonata-allegro movement from the Classic period, with the warning that there are many alternate possibilities, as we shall see in our study of specific symphonies. The graph is a composite of the main outlines of most sonata-allegro movements and may help us understand the basic outlines of the structure. Bear in mind, however, that it is not an automatic system—pour in two melodies and out comes a movement—but a flexible framework that many composers found workable and satisfying as a vehicle for their creative expression.

EXPOSITION

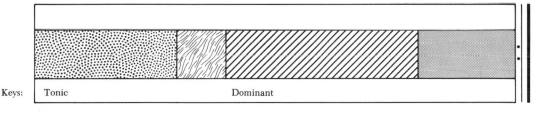

Keys: Tonic   Dominant

DEVELOPMENT*

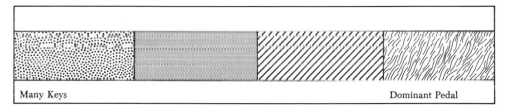

Many Keys   Dominant Pedal

RECAPITULATION

Or Coda

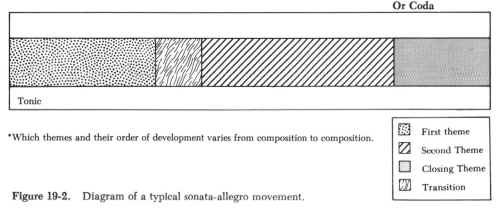

Tonic

*Which themes and their order of development varies from composition to composition.

Figure 19-2.   Diagram of a typical sonata-allegro movement.

OPERA IN THE CLASSIC PERIOD

During the Classic period, composers continued to write opera in the forms inherited from the Baroque period. The important continuing forms were **opera seria**, which had plots based on mythology, arias that provided opportunity for vocal display, and male roles written for **castrati**; and **opera buffa**, with comic plots, stock characters such as the comic servant, and happy endings marked by long ensemble finales.

But there was also a strong current of reaction against Italian opera from the Baroque era. The excesses of vocal display, the mythological subjects, and the stock characters were viewed as artificial, tired clichés that desperately needed reform. Christoph Gluck, an important reform composer, argued for musical unity, valid motivation for the characters, and restriction of vocal display for its own sake. *Orfeo* is one of his reform operas, written in the new style. New types of opera developed, notably the German *Singspiel*, a sort of musical comedy, with realistic characters and spoken dialogue rather than recitative.

The undisputed master of Classic opera is Mozart, whose works still remain staples of the opera repertory. Not only was he a master of all of the standard types of opera—*buffa* (*The Marriage of Figaro*), *seria* (*Idomeneo* and *La Clemenza di Tito*), *Singspiel* (*The Abduction from the Seraglio*)—but he also invented new types of opera, not readily classified as any of the standard types. Among these new types are *The Magic Flute*, technically a *Singspiel* but really a unique work of astonishing depth and symbolism, and *Don Giovanni*, which he called a *drama giocosa* ("comic drama"), neither an *opera buffa* nor a standard *opera seria*, and one of the operatic masterpieces of all time. Mozart is a master of musical drama. The audience is drawn into the plot, whether the work in question is a comedy or a serious drama. Mozart's characters sing in styles suited to their role and social station. Even in the ensembles, each maintains his own style, and Mozart often pokes fun at class distinctions by opposing musical styles or by parodying typical aristocratic styles. His masterpiece, *Don Giovanni*, is discussed in more detail in Chapter 25.

In short, then, the Classical period was a time when the basic assumptions of much later music were worked out, when the forms, textures, and harmonic language basic to subsequent Western music were developed. It might be called the beginning of the modern era in music. Although much of its music was written for social situations and occasions far removed from present life and society, the music of this period is still a staple of our concert programs and listening.

CHAPTER **20**

Joseph Haydn
Symphony No. 104

THE LIFE OF HAYDN

Joseph Haydn, the composer in whose hands the symphony reached its definitive Classical form, was born in 1732 in Rohrau, a small village in Lower Austria. As a child, he studied voice, violin, and keyboard instruments. His talent as a singer led to his appointment as a choirboy in the Cathedral of St. Stephen in Vienna, a post he held for nine years, until his voice broke in adolescence. After his dismissal from choir service, Haydn stayed on in Vienna, supporting himself as a freelance musician and often playing the violin in the evening serenades popular in the city at that time. During this period, he also studied music on his own, especially the sonatas of Karl Philip Emmanuel Bach, one of the forward-looking sons of J. S. Bach, and the *Gradus ad Parnassum* by Johann Fux. This work was a systematic course in counterpoint, a basic text for composers all through the Classic period and into the nineteenth century. After a short stint as music director at a minor court in what is now Czechoslovakia, Haydn was engaged as the vice music director at the Esterhazy court at Eisenstadt, outside Vienna. In 1766, he was appointed *Kapellmeister*, or music director, a position which put him in total charge of the fine court orchestra, a small private opera company, and a marionette theater. His arrangement obligated him to compose any music the Prince needed, and to rehearse and conduct the performances as well.

Haydn's relationship with his two princely patrons is always cited as one of the most satisfactory and productive patronage arrangements in history. Although Haydn occasionally chafed at the isolation of Eisenstadt, it was a fruitful arrangement for him. He wrote music at a tremendous pace, because courts of that time wanted to listen only to new music. His symphonies were published and performed in Paris, London, and even as far away as New York City, where sections of some of his works were performed at a benefit concert in 1782.

When the second of his patrons, Prince Nicholas, died in 1790, Haydn was invited to London to appear at a series of concerts arranged by Johann Salomon, a string player and impresario. Haydn made two very successful trips to London, in 1790 and 1794. He was highly respected in England, was given an honorary degree by Oxford University, and was revered as a great genius by the London audiences. He retired to Vienna, where he was an honored celebrity until his death in 1809.

Haydn's career is a striking example of a long and fruitful patronage arrangement. His princely employers appreciated his talent and gave that talent free rein to create. Haydn, for his part, seems to have been a modest man; he thought of himself as a musical craftsman, using a God-given talent to bring pleasure and beauty to others. Late in his life, he lamented that he was just beginning to understand how to write for the wind instruments, and it was too late to do much about it. This calm, professional attitude is a bit hard for us to understand. We have come to accept the much more glamorous Romantic notion of the artist or composer as a mystical genius who pursues his artistic ideal in a lonely, personal struggle. Haydn is probably more the norm than the exception, and more typical of the Classical composer than is Mozart. Haydn's unpretentious personality and approach to his art combined with one of the greatest creative musical minds in the history of Western music to produce works that are frequently played and studied as landmarks in the evolution of the Classic style.

HAYDN'S MUSIC

During his long and successful career, Haydn wrote a tremendous amount of music. As we mentioned, audiences of the period listened to nothing but new music. Eighteenth- and nineteenth-century audiences were used to listening to a steady diet of world premieres, or at least to the local premieres of works recently composed. Haydn wrote in a wide variety of media, including opera, large choral works, and instrumental works. He even composed a large number of works for the **baryton**, an obscure string instrument of the viol family. As you might have guessed, the baryton was a favorite instrument of Prince Nicholas, his patron, and it was always important to keep the patron happy and provide music he could play.

Many of Haydn's works are not performed much in our own day. His operas are known only to scholars. Unlike the operas of Mozart, they were written specifically for the aristocratic audience and lack the universal appeal of Mozart's works. They have never found their way into the standard repertory. Haydn wrote fourteen settings of the Mass for soloists and chorus. These works are still performed today, usually in a concert setting rather than in worship services, like most Masses from the Classic period. Two of Haydn's oratorios are still performed. They are *The Creation* and *The Seasons*. *The Creation* was a great favorite in England, which has always been fond of the oratorio genre. Haydn also wrote many piano sonatas.

The works that are frequently performed and on which Haydn's fame rests are his symphonies and string quartets. We will look at examples of his works in both of these forms in this chapter and the next. While Haydn wrote more than one hundred symphonies, his later works, such as the twelve symphonies composed for his visits to London, are the most frequently performed. In his long lifetime of symphonic writing, he worked with the symphonic ideas that had been developing since about 1720 and gradually perfected symphonic form. He had a gift for delightful melody and an endlessly fertile talent for variety and surprise within the standard form.

Haydn wrote about eighty string quartets, and those works show the same gradual development as his symphonies. The early quartets resemble sonatas for the first violin, with the other three instruments relegated to accompaniment patterns. Gradually, all of the parts became more important, and he developed a great variety of texture and disposition of voices. The quartets are as fundamental a part of the string quartet literature as the symphonies are of the orchestral repertory.

SYMPHONY NO. 104, *LONDON*

Haydn wrote Symphony No. 104 as the last of the two sets of six symphonies he composed for his trips to London, hence the nickname. Classic composers, like their Baroque predecessors, often presented or published their sonatas and symphonies in sets of six. The *London* Symphony is the last symphony Haydn wrote, and it is a fine example of the flexibility of the form. We will describe all four movements briefly, concentrating on the first. A listening guide (Figure 20-8) is provided only for the first movement, although all four movements should be heard as a unit.

First Movement

Introduction

The first movement begins with a solemn introductory section in *D* minor. The introduction opens with a strong unison idea, consisting of *D* (the tonic) and *A* (the dominant) in a dotted rhythm (see Figure 20-1). It provides a dramatic beginning for the movement and for the whole symphony. The opening idea appears three times in the introduction, the second time in *F* major, the relative major of *D* minor. In between these appearances are quieter sections in the same dotted rhythm.

Figure 20-1. Opening figure.

Exposition

The exposition begins with the first theme, quietly presented in the strings. The section marked X in Figure 20-2 is a motive used extensively in the later development section. Louder material in the first group leads to the modulation into *A* major for the second group. The second section begins, not with a new theme, but with the first theme transposed into *A* major. Among the other materials in the second key area is another theme (see Figure 20-3)—we might classify it as the closing theme—which also appears later in the development. The exposition concludes, as we expect, with a strong cadence in the key of *A* major, the dominant. The exposition is then repeated.

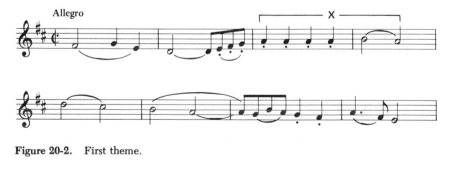

Figure 20-2. First theme.

Figure 20-3. Theme from the second group.

Development

The development section begins with motive X from the first theme, presented in various keys and treated in canonic form. The theme from the second group appears in various keys also. The development concludes with a loud dominant seventh chord and a pause.

Recapitulation

The recapitulation begins with the first theme, in the tonic key. After its literal return, it is presented again, this time with a counter-melody in the winds. Classical composers were fond of varying returning material and often used the winds in this fashion to provide the variety. After the presentation of the first group, a short reference is made to the motive from the first theme, in developmental fashion, and then the materials from the second group return, in the tonic. A very short coda, emphasizing the tonic harmony, brings the movement to a loud conclusion.

Second Movement

The second movement is a lovely slow movement in the key of *G* major, contrasting with the key and spirit of the first movement. The structure feels like a combination of A-B-A form and theme and variations: the middle section explores the keys of *G* minor and its relative major, *B*-flat. The gentle first theme of the second movement is shown in Figure 20-4.

Figure 20-4.   First theme of the second movement.

Third Movement

The third movement is a minuet and trio in the usual compound ternary form. The theme of the minuet is a robust melody in *D* major (see Figure 20-5). The minuet and trio found its way into symphony structure as the least dramatic and most repetitive of the forms, between the drama of the first and last movements and the lyric intensity of the slow second movement. This particular third movement follows the typical structure. Its sections, repeats, and key areas are outlined in Figure 20-6. But Haydn fills even this most regular of movements with surprises, in the form of evaded cadences, cross rhythms, and pauses at unexpected places.

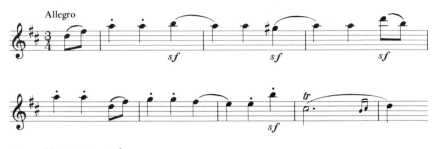

Figure 20-5. Minuet theme.

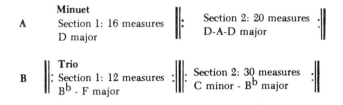

Figure 20-6. Outline of the third movement, the minuet and trio, from Symphony No. 104, *London*, by Haydn.

Final Movement

The final movement is a sonata-allegro structure, lighter in feeling than the first movement. The main theme (see Figure 20-7) seems to be derived from folk materials, and the whole movement dances along merrily.

Figure 20-7. Main theme, last movement.

As we mentioned earlier, one should really hear the entire four-movement structure as a unit. It is always interesting to raise the question of how the four separate movements fit together as a satisfying musical unity. Are they really independent units? Could they be shuffled and reassembled with parts of other symphonies and work just as well, or do they really belong together? In any event, this work is one of Haydn's masterpieces of symphonic writing, filled with delightful melodies and color effects, and peppered with just enough witty surprises to amuse and delight the listener.

FIGURE 20-8. LISTENING GUIDE

FIRST MOVEMENT, SYMPHONY NO. 104, *LONDON*, BY HAYDN

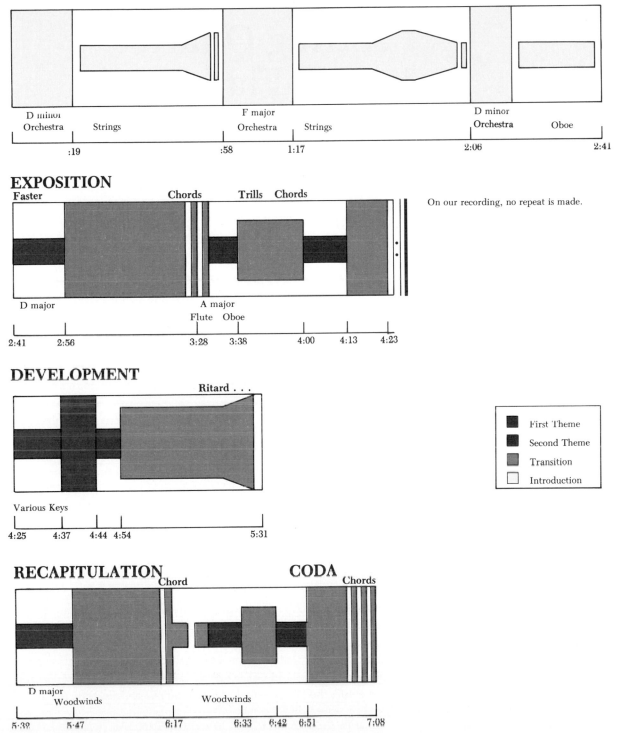

INTRODUCTION

D minor
Orchestra   Strings

F major
Orchestra   Strings

D minor
Orchestra   Oboe

:19   :58   1:17   2:06   2:41

EXPOSITION

Faster   Chords   Trills   Chords

On our recording, no repeat is made.

D major
A major
Flute   Oboe

2:41   2:56   3:28   3:38   4:00   4:13   4:23

DEVELOPMENT

Ritard . . .

Various Keys

4:25   4:37   4:44   4:54   5:31

■ First Theme
■ Second Theme
■ Transition
□ Introduction

RECAPITULATION   CODA

Chord   Chords

D major
Woodwinds   Woodwinds

5:39   5:47   6:17   6:33   6:42   6:51   7:08

CHAPTER 21

Joseph Haydn String Quartet in E-Flat, Opus 71, No. 3

CHAMBER MUSIC: STRING QUARTET

In Chapter 19, we mentioned that a huge amount of chamber music was written in the Classic period, to be played by amateurs as well as professional musicians. One of the standard chamber music groups was the string quartet: two violins, viola and cello. Both Haydn and Mozart wrote many string quartets, and Mozart also wrote for combinations of string quartet and a woodwind instrument. We speak, therefore, of "flute quintets," "clarinet quintets," and so forth. The basic unit for which most of the music is written, however, is the four string instruments.

We also mentioned that composers treated the string quartet as a miniature symphony. The form usually consists of four movements: the first, in sonata-allegro form; the second, a lyric song form; the third, a minuet; and the last movement, in sonata-allegro, rondo, or theme-and-variations form. The quartet, like the symphony, was a medium in which the Classical concern for structure and balance was foremost in the composer's mind and in which one can observe creative innovations in form.

Orchestration

One of the fascinating things about the string quartet literature is the composer's approach to orchestration. When a composer chooses a small group of instruments or otherwise limits his resources in the area of instrumental color, he poses for himself a special challenge in the disposition of the instrumental lines. All music must have variety to hold our interest. If the forces are limited to four instruments of like color, the composer must vary the ranges and texture, so that

Haydn leading a quartet in rehearsal.

we are not fatigued by the constant sameness of sound. The string instruments have the capacity for variety that the composer needs. All four, including the cello, are quite agile, capable of playing rapid melodies. They have a great dynamic capability, making it possible for any of the four players to play either the main melody or background accompaniment. They also have a very wide range, developed during the previous Baroque period, so that the ensemble can play high or low as a unit or can play very widely spaced lines. One effect possible on the string instruments that is often used is their capacity for playing **double-stops**, that is, simultaneous notes on two or more strings. When all four instruments play double- or triple-stops at once, the sound is that of a large string section, rather than of four instruments, and adds variety, as well as drama and intensity, for opening or closing chords.

A good quartet composer varies the texture and spacing of his writing constantly, an effect we can hear as well as see in a score. Typical spacings include the following: melody in the first violin, sustained bass line in the cello, and moving chordal parts in the two inner instruments; melody in the viola or cello, with light chords in the higher parts; polyphonic texture, with each instrument in turn having a prominent motive; and widely spaced writing alternating with sections in which all instruments play within the span of an octave. Listen for the variety of texture and spacing when you hear quartets. The medium works for the listener because of the varied capabilities of string instruments and players and the composer's creative solutions to the problem of variety and interest.

Performance

The challenges and pleasures of playing chamber music are different from those of playing orchestral music or solo concerto literature. In an orchestra, the player's basic responsibility is to be in control of his own part. It is the conductor's responsibility to decide details of dynamics, tempo, articulation, and so forth. Another player of roughly equal ability can substitute for almost any player in an orchestra on a moment's notice, provided there is sufficient rehearsal time for the conductor to make his particular demands clear. In a chamber music group, on the other hand, all are equal participants and must get along as a musical unit, if not as friends. Replacing one member is not always easy, any more than it would be in a jazz or rock group that has worked together for some time. The players must reach a consensus on the way the music should be played and cooperate in the production of a unified vision of it. All of the stylistic details of tempo, articulation, dynamics, and shading that produce that unified vision must be agreed upon by all four players. Rehearsals tend to include a lot of discussion of stylistic details, and agreement must be reached or imposed. Some players form groups that last for years. The pleasures of playing chamber music motivate musicians who play professionally as soloists or as orchestra members to meet in their spare time to play chamber music for their own enjoyment.

For the listener, chamber music provides a different sort of pleasure from orchestral music. The effects are smaller and more subtle. Some concertgoers and record collectors focus their attention on this specialized literature and are as knowledgeable about favorite performing groups and recordings as lovers of orchestral music or opera. When the famous quartets go on tour, enthusiastic audiences turn out in all of the cities they visit. Recordings provide a fine means of enjoying this smaller scale music in the home.

STRING QUARTET IN *E*-FLAT, OPUS 71, NO. 3

As we mentioned in the section on Haydn's life and music, he wrote about eighty string quartets. His early efforts in this medium tend to be more like sonatas for the first violin with accompaniment by the other instruments than like music for four equal instruments. As his style evolved, however, the instruments became more nearly equal, and the composer developed more ways of including variety of texture and sound in his quartets. The *E*-flat quartet is one of his later works and clearly illustrates his mature quartet style.

First Movement

Opus 71, No. 3, is in the expected four-movement form. The first movement is a sonata-allegro structure, of smaller dimensions than a symphonic first movement, but identical in structure. The listening guide (Figure 21-6) outlines the structure in more detail. After a single loud chord, which serves as introduction, the sprightly first theme (see Figure 21-1) is presented twice, the second time an octave higher.

Figure 21-1. First theme.

Transitional material modulates to the dominant key, *B*-flat major. In typical Haydn fashion, the first idea of the second group (see Figure 21-2) is a modified version of the first theme, in canonic treatment between viola and first violin. Most of the remaining material in the second group also consists of modifications of the first theme and transitional and cadential material.

Figure 21-2. Second group version of the first theme.

After the repeat of the exposition section, the brief development consists of reworking of fragments derived from the first theme and of moving through various related and remote keys, beginning in *E*-flat minor.

The recapitulation is quite regular and ends with a brief but busy coda section.

Second Movement

The second movement is in theme-and-variations form. The theme is first presented by the first violin, in the key of *B*-flat major (see Figure 21-3). Like the themes of most Classical theme-and-variations forms, it consists of two repeating halves, the first ending on the dominant (here, *F* major), the second, on the tonic.

The first variation has the melody in the viola, in *B*-flat minor. The first half ends on *F*; the second begins in *D*-flat major, the relative major of *B*-flat minor, and ends in *B*-flat minor. This section ends with a restatement of the theme as it

Figure 21-3.   Theme, second movement.

was first presented, in *B*-flat major. Another variation has the first violin playing running sixteenth-note triplets against staccato chords in the other parts. The next variation is in *B*-flat minor, and the texture is polyphonic, contrasting strongly with the preceding variations. The minor variation ends with a dominant pedal, after which another variation appears, in *B*-flat major, with the cello silent and the other three parts playing quiet high staccato chords. A final variation, or coda, begins like the first presentation of the theme and brings the movement to a close.

Third Movement

The third movement, as we would expect, is a minuet and trio, with some original surprises in its structure. The first repeating section of the minuet is twelve measures long; the second is thirty-five measures, lengthened by repeating sections and a short **codetta**. The trio is more symmetrical. The first section is sixteen measures long, and the second, twenty. The minuet is, of course, repeated after the trio. The minuet theme is given in Figure 21-4.

Figure 21-4.   Minuet, main theme.

Final Movement

The final movement, in a busy 6/8 meter, is an interesting version of rondo form. The returning A theme (see Figure 21-5) is easy to recognize because of its rhythmic swing and the oom-pah-pah accompaniment that goes with it.

   The A theme is presented in two repeating segments, the second much longer than the first. The first digression sounds like a variation of the theme rather

Figure 21-5.   The A theme, fourth movement.

Living room in the house of Haydn's birth in Rohrau, Austria.

than genuinely new material, because the main melody appears under running scale passages in the first violin. A brief return of four bars of the A section leads to another digression, which ends in the related but unusual key of C minor. A longer return of the A section ends inconclusively, trailing off into long pauses; and a busy coda, modeled again on the A theme, brings the movement to a headlong conclusion.

This lighthearted, pretty quartet tells us important things about Classical style and Classical forms. None of the themes we have listed are dramatic or heroic in feeling; nor do we find the soaring, lyric second themes beloved by Romantic composers like Brahms or Tchaikowsky. The music bubbles along delightfully, making no cosmic statements, but intriguing us with its inventiveness and variety. The forms employed are the same as for large symphonies but are used here in a different spirit, toward different ends. Listening to this work should make clear that standard forms are not molds or patterns that automatically produce similar works. Instead, they are ways of working with and organizing musical material that yield totally different works in the hands of different composers or in the different works of the same composer.

FIGURE 21-6. LISTENING GUIDE

FIRST MOVEMENT, STRING QUARTET IN E-FLAT, OPUS 71, NO. 3, BY HAYDN

INTRODUCTION
EXPOSITION

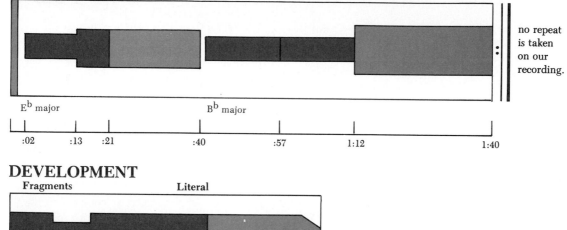

no repeat
is taken
on our
recording.

E^b major   B^b major

:02   :13   :21   :40   :57   1:12   1:40

DEVELOPMENT

Fragments   Literal

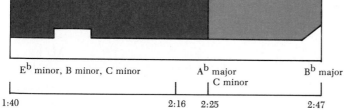

E^b minor, B minor, C minor   A^b major   B^b major
                     C minor

1:40   2:16   2:25   2:47

RECAPITULATION
                                         ## CODA

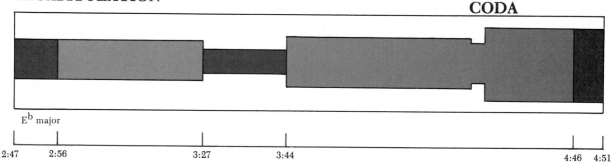

E^b major

2:47   2:56   3:27   3:44   4:46   4:51

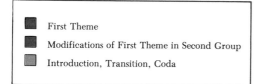

■ First Theme

■ Modifications of First Theme in Second Group

■ Introduction, Transition, Coda

Wolfgang Amadeus Mozart
Symphony No. 35 in D Major, K. 385

Wolfgang Amadeus Mozart (1756-1791) is one of the towering geniuses of Western music, a composer who ranks with Bach and Beethoven as an absolute master, and one of the greatest artists of Western culture. During his short life, he wrote more than six hundred compositions. Nineteenth-century writers romanticized his life and wrote glamorized accounts of it. This tendency is not surprising. He died young, neglected, and not quite sane, dividing his time between begging money from his friends and working on the *Requiem* planned for his own funeral. There is something deeply appealing about the genius who burns out early, and artists who die at the height of their powers are revered in a way different from those who live a full life. In the 1970s, figures like John F. Kennedy, Marilyn Monroe, James Dean, Elvis Presley, and Janis Joplin were all the objects of the sort of adulation they might never have received had they lived longer.

The unadorned historical facts of Mozart's life are astonishing enough without the romantic additions. His father, Leopold, was a respected violinist and composer at the court of the Archbishop of Salzburg, and he immediately recognized his small son's remarkable talent. The boy played the harpsichord by the age of three and composed short pieces when he was five. He studied keyboard instruments, the violin, and composition under the watchful eye of his father, who foresaw a great career for the prodigy. Like stage parents in any age, Leopold may have pushed the boy too hard, and Mozart's tragic later life may have been the result of these early pressures. But the talent was certainly there.

When Mozart was eight, and later when he was ten, the family toured the great courts of Paris, London, Italy, and Vienna. By the time he was a teenager, the young boy and his sister had performed for the nobility of Europe. He had a talent, not only for performing, but also for improvising and composing, and an astonishing memory for music. Stories are told of his hearing complex and lengthy compositions once and later writing them down note for note from memory. His musical mind was apparently unique. We know from his letters that his process of composing was certainly unusual. He regarded the actual writing down of a composition as a chore to be rushed through at the last possible minute. Apparently, he worked out entire symphonies in his head and then sat down and wrote out what already existed in detail in his mind. We know that on one occasion, he wrote down several symphonies in a few days.

After Mozart's early successes as a child prodigy, the remainder of his life was tragically unsuccessful. He was hired by a new Archbishop of Salzburg, but the arrangement was never satisfactory. The Archbishop was a man of little vision, who did not appreciate the genius in his employ, and Mozart resigned in anger in 1781. For the last ten years of his life, he lived in Vienna and supported himself as a freelance performer and composer. For part of that time, he was in the employ of Emperor Joseph II, who used him only to write dance music for court entertainments. Some of his operas were successes, but these last ten years, in general, were frustrating, impoverished, and unhappy. Mozart died in poverty and was not appreciated as a great genius until some time after his death.

Writers are fond of speculating about what Mozart might have accomplished had he had the advantage of a successful and satisfactory patronage arrangement like the one between Haydn and the Esterhazy court. That is, of course, idle speculation, because Mozart's personality was so much different from Haydn's and because the pressures created by Mozart's father in his early years and by his international celebrity as a child prodigy might have soured him for any opportunities that came along later. Except for his musical genius, Mozart seems to have been quite an ordinary person—jovial and fond of people, billiards, and good times. Perhaps he remained all his life the brilliant child, unprepared for the realities of business and professional life.

In any event, what Mozart accomplished in his short life is astonishing, both in quantity and quality. He left the world works that still remain the models of how to write symphonies, quartets, operas, wind music, and so forth. Many of his compositions are staples of the performing repertoire, as delightful now for us as they were two hundred years ago in an entirely different society. The enormous scope of his work is evident in our text which examines four different Mozart compositions: a symphony, a wind piece, a piano concerto and an opera, all excellent examples of the Classical style in music.

MOZART'S MUSIC

In his short lifetime, Mozart wrote more than six hundred works we now know of. Like many composers of the time, he was not very systematic or organized about collecting his own works. As we have mentioned, he worked most often under tremendous pressure, writing out works at the last possible moment, completing scores just in time for one run-through before the first performance. In 1862, a botanist and amateur musical scholar, Ludwig von Köchel, compiled a chronological list of Mozart's works. Several scholars have since worked at revising the Köchel catalog, as further information has come to light about the order in which works were actually written, or about works wrongly ascribed to Mozart. In its modern editions, the work is still known as *Köchel-Verzeichnis* ("Köchel-Catalog") and remains a basic source for Mozart scholarship. Programs and recordings generally list Mozart's works with their Köchel number. A typical listing is Symphony in *G* minor, K. 550.

Mozart's works include eighteen operas, several of which are frequently performed by opera companies. His operas are discussed in more detail in Chapter 25. He wrote extensively for solo keyboard instruments. Many of those works were written for his own performing tours in his youth. Also among his works are several dozen chamber works, mostly for string quartet, or string quartet plus a solo wind instrument. He composed forty-nine symphonies, one of which is discussed in detail later in this chapter, and many lighter works for instrumental ensembles, called divertimentos or serenades, one of which is discussed in Chapter 23. His works also include twenty-one piano concertos, five violin concertos, and several concertos for other solo instruments. Mozart performed the piano concertos himself, and they are still very popular works. One of his concertos for piano is discussed in Chapter 24. The bewildering variety and number of Mozart's musical works attest to his prodigious genius, and the fact that so many of his works are still frequently performed indicates that his music has an appeal far beyond the audiences and circumstances for which he composed it.

SYMPHONY NO. 35, IN *D* MAJOR, (*HAFFNER*), K. 385

The so-called *Haffner* Symphony is not the most famous or frequently played of Mozart's symphonies. The later works, especially the *G* minor, K. 550, and the *C* major (*Jupiter*), K. 551, are better known and more frequently discussed. But the *Haffner* is an interesting work because its history illustrates the way composers worked in those days and because of what it can teach us about approaches to form. The first and last movements are both sonata-allegro structures, but contrast greatly in the way the form is treated. We will look at both of those movements in detail.

History of the Work

This work did not first come into being as a symphony. It started as a serenade, commissioned by the Haffner family of Salzburg, for whom Mozart had written another serenade, which is also nicknamed the *Haffner*. The second piece was requested by Mozart's father shortly after Mozart had moved to Vienna. Although Mozart complained about being snowed under with work, he sent off a set of orchestral pieces, movement by movement, as he finished them. The original work consisted of the opening allegro movement, an andante, two minuets, a march, and the finale. Early in 1783, Mozart asked his father to send the music back to him, and he reworked it as the present symphony. The first and last movements remained intact, the march and one of the minuets were dropped, and Mozart reorchestrated the four remaining movements, adding pairs of flutes and clarinets to the original group. The revised symphony was performed in March 1783 and was very well received.

Forms

The first and last movements both consist of novel versions of sonata-allegro structure, combined with other structures. The first has elements of theme-and-variations form within its sonata structure, and the last can be considered either a sonata-allegro or a rondo. Innovation and wit were an important element in the way Classical composers dealt with structure.

Composers were fond of setting up harmonic or structural expectations, and then diverting them at the last moment. Because the Classical style is generally so symmetrical and balanced, these unexpected twists and turns are usually obvious and surprising. The typical audience reaction to them is an appreciative smile and a heightened awareness of the composer's wit and skill.

First Movement

Exposition

The first movement begins immediately with an aggressive theme consisting of octave leaps and a descending scale (see Figure 22-1). It resembles an introductory idea more than an actual theme, but its advantage is that it combines well with other material to form recognizable variations. The first variation (see Figure 22-2), still in the first group and key area, consists of a canon of the opening theme at an interval of two measures.

After a transitional section leads to the dominant key area, the first theme of the second group (see Figure 22-3) is another variation of the first theme, this time combined with running scale passages in the bassoon and cello. Another variation in this group sets the theme against yet another counter-melody in the violins (see Figure 22-4). The fourth variation, still in the second group, sets the main theme against a lyric counter-melody in the violins (see Figure 22-5). A

Figure 22-1.   First theme.

Figure 22-2.   First variation.

Figure 22-3.   Second Group, first theme (variation 2).

Figure 22-4.   Second group, variation 3.

Figure 22-5.   Variation 4.

number of closing ideas, including a dramatic series of ascending unison trills, bring the exposition to its conclusion.

Development

The development is relatively short, possibly because the opening idea has already been the subject of so much variation in the exposition section. As we would expect, the opening idea is presented again in various keys. Yet another variation appears in the second half of the development, when the opening theme is presented accompanied by a new counter-melody consisting of short phrases passed around the solo winds.

Recapitulation

The recapitulation brings back the exposition material and includes a descending section based on the second half of the development. All of the closing material is repeated in the tonic key of *D* major, and a short coda is added.

Although the variation principle is so important in this movement, it is clearly intended to be heard as a sonata-allegro structure. The most important thing in sonata-allegro form, as we have already seen, is not the identity of themes but the question of key areas. No matter how the materials relate to each other, or how many distinct themes there are, the succession of key areas—tonic for the first group, dominant for the second, remote keys for the development, and tonic for the recapitulation—is the real basis of sonata-allegro structure. That all of the melodic materials are variations of the main idea contributes to the coherence and unity of the movement.

A final question needs to be mentioned. The score I referred to for this discussion makes no reference to the repeat of the exposition section. Such repetition would, of course, blur the variation relationships, because one expects variations to appear in a series without repeats, but it is a standard part of sonata-allegro structure. The recording in our record set does repeat, therefore it is indicated in the listening guide. (Figure 22-6).

Final Movement

The final movement of the symphony is, as we mentioned, a combination of sonata-allegro and rondo forms. It is lighter in feeling, as is usual, than the first movement and bubbles along merrily. The question of its form is somewhat confusing and technical, but can be explained and diagrammed (see Figure 22-8) to make some sense. This recording is not in our record set, so the times on the recording you listen to may vary from those indicated.

Exposition

The exposition is quite regular. A first theme is presented in *D* major, a transitional section leads to the dominant, and a second theme appears in that key, followed by a brief closing section. The themes are shown in Figure 22-7.

FIGURE 22-6. LISTENING GUIDE

FIRST MOVEMENT, SYMPHONY NO. 35 IN D MAJOR, BY MOZART

EXPOSITION

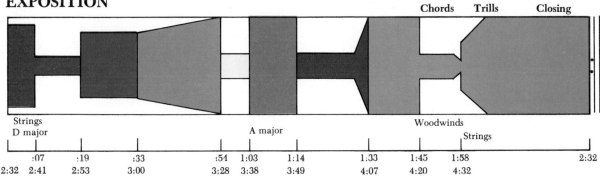

Chords   Trills   Closing

Strings
D major   A major   Woodwinds

Strings

| :07 | :19 | :33 | :54 | 1:03 | 1:14 | 1:33 | 1:45 | 1:58 | 2:32 |
| 2:32 2:41 | 2:53 | 3:00 | 3:28 | 3:38 | 3:49 | 4:07 | 4:20 | 4:32 | |

DEVELOPMENT

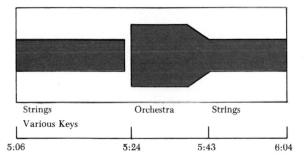

Strings   Orchestra   Strings

Various Keys

5:06   5:24   5:43   6:04

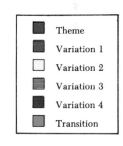

- ■ Theme
- ■ Variation 1
- □ Variation 2
- ■ Variation 3
- ■ Variation 4
- ■ Transition

RECAPITUALATION

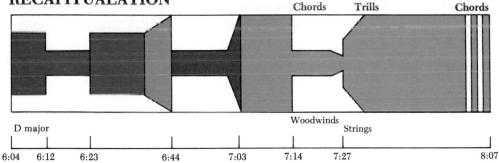

Chords   Trills   Chords

D major   Woodwinds

Strings

6:04   6:12   6:23   6:44   7:03   7:14   7:27   8:07

Figure 22-7. First and second themes, last movement.

Development

The development begins with some transitional material, and then the first theme appears, in the tonic key, which would be appropriate in a rondo form, as the return of the A section after a digression, but is *not* appropriate in the development section of a sonata-allegro form, which usually stays away from the tonic key to create suspense. This appearance is not really a recapitulation of the first theme, because the music then wanders off into other keys, presenting the second theme in *B* minor and gradually working back to the dominant to prepare for the recapitulation.

Recapitulation

After both themes are presented again in *D* major and the closing material has reappeared, the sonata-allegro form is complete. But the music continues, hinting again at rondo form by presenting the first theme once again in *D* major, followed by a headlong conclusion. We can best present the ambiguity of this final movement by outlining its progress in parallel interpretations, each section labeled the way it would be denoted in each of the two structural patterns. This short, bouncy, four-minute movement is filled with details and structural innovations which provide the delight and surprise that Classical period music alone can provide.

The *Haffner* Symphony is a far cry from the high drama of the *Jupiter* Symphony or the *G* minor, but it provides us an excellent example of Mozart's complete mastery of symphonic form, his ability with orchestral color, and his fertile creative imagination.

FIGURE 22-8.

DIAGRAM OF FINAL MOVEMENT, SYMPHONY NO. 35 IN D MAJOR, BY MOZART

Sonata Allegro

EXPOSITION

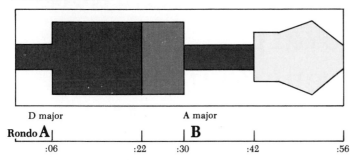

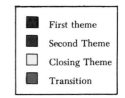

■	First theme
■	Second Theme
□	Closing Theme
■	Transition

D major   A major

Rondo **A**   **B**

:06   :22   :30   :42   :56

DEVELOPMENT

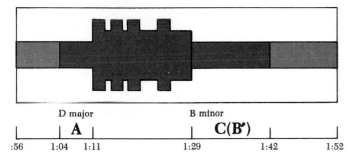

D major   B minor

A   **C(B')**

:56   1:04   1:11   1:29   1:42   1:52

RECAPITULATION

CODA   Chords

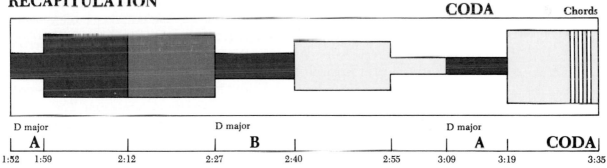

D major   D major   D major

A   **B**   **A**   **CODA**

1:52   1:59   2:12   2:27   2:40   2:55   3:09   3:19   3:35

CHAPTER 23

Wolfgang Amadeus Mozart
Serenade in B-Flat for Thirteen Wind Instruments, K. 361

DIVERTIMENTO, SERENADE, AND CASSATION

We have seen how the symphony evolved into a standard concert form, written with a sense of drama and seriousness and intended to be listened to with full attention. The string quartet, the most popular form of chamber music, evolved into a miniature symphony, with the same four movements as the symphony and the same sense of seriousness and drama. Midway between quartet and symphony, and distinct from both of them by function and purpose, is the general classification of lighter instrumental music for court occasions rather than for concert performance, works known by the generic titles of **divertimento** (music for entertainment), **serenade** (evening music), or **cassation** (outdoor music). These works were written for small ensembles of instruments and often opened with a march, instead of the more complex sonata-allegro form. They were played at court as light background music. We recall that Mozart was asked to write such music by Joseph II. That was the only assignment the Emperor could think of for the great composer of opera and symphony.

This type of music has its roots in the Baroque suite, written and performed for the same sorts of occasions, and divertimento and suite are similar in form. Although Baroque polyphonic texture is replaced by the pervasive melody-and-accompaniment texture of the Classic period, the overall design is much the same. A typical Classical divertimento consists of six or seven movements, the first and last being marches and the interior movements including minuets (the most popular stylized dance form at this period) and perhaps a lyric slow movement. We recall that the minuet movements in symphonies are places of relaxation. The repetitive, predictable forms serve as relief between the dramatic

In this painting by the Italian painter Francesco de Gardi we see a typically elegant Gala concert in Venice, 1782.

sonata-allegro structures and the intense slow movements. A work made up mostly of minuets and marches is obviously a lighter, less serious work than a symphony.

Many of these lighter instrumental works are seldom performed and are not of major interest to later listeners outside the situation for which they were written. Some of Mozart's works of this type have survived and are frequently performed because he often wrote better music than the situation demanded. His most famous serenade, *Eine Kleine Nachtmusik* ("A Little Night-Music") is frequently performed by small string orchestras. It survives because it is more symphonic than most works of this type. It consists of four movements: a sonata-allegro first movement, a lyric, slow movement, a minuet and trio, and a rondo finale. Like a string quartet, it is a mini-symphony in form and seriousness and, therefore, fits well in our concert setting. We will now look at another work called *Serenade,* which is more typical of this class of music.

SERENADE IN *B*-FLAT FOR THIRTEEN WIND INSTRUMENTS, K. 361

Scholars have discovered the circumstances surrounding the writing of most of Mozart's music. We assume this particular serenade was written for the wind ensemble at the Munich court because we know that there was no appropriate ensemble in Salzburg. It was probably another job application. Mozart sent it off to Munich to impress the court, hoping for future commissions or a permanent position. He over-writes for the occasion: the first movement is a full-fledged sonata-allegro structure instead of a simple march, and the slow movement is a remarkable triumph of writing over the natural limitations of such an ensemble.

Instrumentation

The instrumentation may strike us as strange. The work is scored for two oboes, two clarinets, two **basset horns** (a type of alto clarinet, a favorite instrument of Mozart's), four French horns, two bassoons, and a contrabassoon. The score states that a string double-bass may play the contrabassoon part, but it obviously makes more sense to use the bass wind instrument. Two things are striking about the ensemble: the absence of flutes, and the preponderance of low instruments (horns and bassoons). But the ensemble makes sense from two points of view. First, the group resembles the outdoor ensembles of the Renaissance and Baroque periods, which always consisted of the louder, double-reed family of winds, here represented by the oboes and bassoons. The clarinets and basset horns are new Classic additions, and the French horns are used in Classic fashion to fill in harmonies and sustain the sound. Flutes would not make sense because they are "indoor" instruments. Second, there was a Classical tradition of **Turkish** or **Janizary music** for winds, often with the addition of drums, and cymbals, a Classic version of the later Romantic fascination with the exotic. The music they played was not really Turkish at all, but the unusual colors were associated with that region and used in operas, such as *The Abduction from the Seraglio,* when that flavor was appropriate. In any event, Mozart wrote for a specific group of players which included all of those instruments. He treated them as solo instruments as well as an ensemble, and wind players today are still fond of the work because of its solo opportunities. The work exploits the sustaining lyric qualities of the oboe and clarinet, the dry, comic possibilities of the bassoon, and the agility of all the woodwinds.

A painting by Carmontelle, showing Mozart the child prodigy performing.

FIGURE 23-4. LISTENING GUIDE

RONDO MOVEMENT, SERENADE IN B-FLAT FOR THIRTEEN WIND INSTRUMENTS, BY MOZART

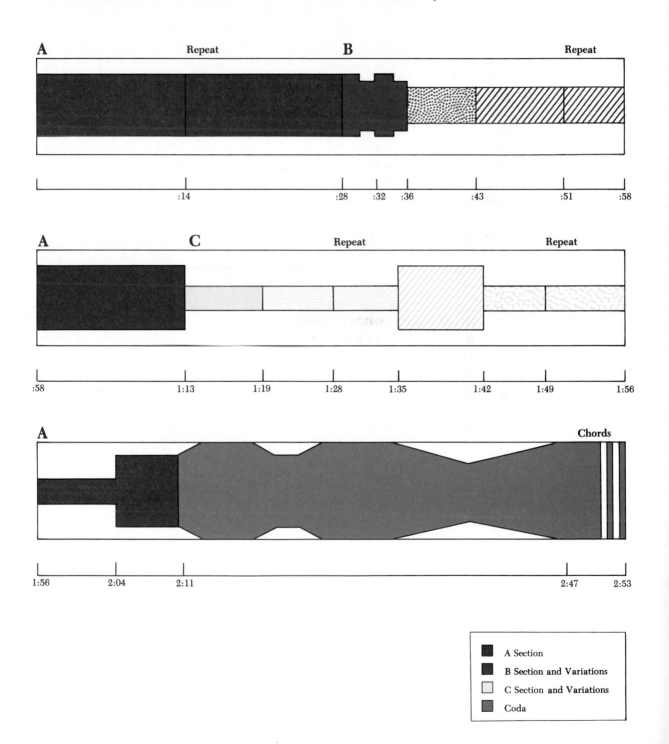

Form

The design of the overall work is fairly typical of divertimento-serenade form with some exceptions. The movements are as follows:

> I. Sonata-allegro, complete with a dramatic slow introduction. A march would be more typical of the form.
> II. Minuet, with two trios. A-B-A-C-A form, with many repeated sections within each large unit.
> III. Adagio, an unusual lyric slow movement.
> IV. Minuet, with two trios, another A-B-A-C-A form.
> V. Romanze, made up of a slow section, a faster allegretto, a repeat of the slow section, and a coda.
> VI. Theme and six variations.
> VII. Rondo, allegro molto.

Adagio

We will look at two contrasting movements of the work, the Adagio and the closing Rondo. The Adagio is an incredible triumph of mind over medium. Writing for a reedy, bottom-heavy band, Mozart manages to write a lyric slow movement of great intensity and beauty. He accomplishes this miracle by several means. First, he drops out two of the horns, keeping the other two for their sustaining ability to maintain the harmonies. That expedient reduces the loud and heavy sound only slightly; he could well have dropped out the contrabassoon and one of the bassoons as well. Then he arranges the pairs of higher instruments as two separate units; the first oboe, first clarinet, and first basset horn he uses as soloists, to sing the long, lyric, melodic lines. The first bassoon also plays the

Figure 23-1.   Arrangement of horns in Adagio.

melody occasionally; but generally, both bassoons, the contrabassoon, and the second oboe, second clarinet, and second basset horn are arranged in a tranquil but gently pulsing accompaniment, set up as shown in Figure 23-1. Over this accompaniment pattern, the first oboe, clarinet, and basset horn share a soaring, lyric melody (see Figure 23-2). The overall effect is astonishing. The sound is still heavy and thick, but Mozart manages to achieve an intense lyric feeling that by all rights should be impossible for the group at his disposal. One wonders why the Munich court did not hire him on the spot.

Figure 23-2. Adagio melody.

Rondo

The final Rondo is much more typical music for this sort of band. The oboes, clarinets, and basset horns clatter around in rapid sixteenth-note passages, over staccato chords from the thick accompaniment group. The A section of the Rondo melody is shown in Figure 23-3. The contrasting sections of the Rondo generally lighten the texture considerably and feature various solo instruments from the group. The contrasting sections are also generally made of simple eight-measure ideas which are repeated. The loud A section returns twice and is followed by a jolly coda, with the whole band clattering along to a bouncing conclusion, about as serious and intense as a Sousa march. Mozart could write whatever the occasion demanded, in the style typical for the group, but he proves in the wondrous Adagio that he could write far beyond the demands of typical styles and even beyond what most composers would consider possible, given the performing ensemble. One hopes that the work, if it did not get Mozart the commissions or position he wanted, at least livened up more than one court occasion. The form of the final Rondo movement is outlined in the listening guide (Figure 23-4).

Figure 23-3. Rondo, main melody.

CHAPTER 24

Wolfgang Amadeus Mozart Piano Concerto No. 23 in A Major, K. 488

MOZART'S PIANO CONCERTOS

The solo concerto with orchestra accompaniment became a popular concert form during the Classic period. Solo concertos had been written in the Baroque period, especially by Vivaldi, but the form settled into standard patterns and assumed new popularity during the Classic period. Like the symphony, the concerto was a concert piece, similar in intensity and seriousness to the symphony. As we might expect, Mozart, the child prodigy and virtuoso performer, wrote some fine concertos, especially for the piano, which he performed himself. Twenty-five piano concertos survive, and they constitute a varied and masterful body of work.

All of the concertos are still frequently performed. In recent years, we have witnessed a revival of interest in authentic Classic sounds, and therefore we have access to recordings of these concertos made on the softer, mellower pianos of the period, accompanied by small chamber orchestras. Even when performers play modern, brilliant pianos, they are sensitive to the fact that the Mozart sound is different from the nineteenth-century sound for which modern pianos are built. Mozart does not exploit the thick textures and dynamic extremes that nineteenth-century composers loved. More common in Mozart piano writing are legato runs, rapid passage-work, and lyric melodies. The piano parts for the concertos are not the virtuoso challenges that nineteenth-century concertos are, but they do require perfect control, a smooth legato touch, and a high degree of sensitivity. The two facets of Mozart's piano concertos that are the most interesting are orchestration and structure. We shall look at these two elements in some detail.

Another scene of the Mozart family performing; the portrait in the background depicts his late mother.

Orchestration

Consider the forces at Mozart's disposal in a piano concerto. The wind section of the orchestra had already become a separate unit, capable of functioning as an independent group to contrast with the strings in alternating phrases of distinct color. Mozart, as we have seen, was also a master of solo wind lines. To this rich orchestra he adds the piano, with all of its possibilities both as a solo and as an accompaniment instrument. As a performer, he knew its capabilities well and never wrote any passage that did not fit beautifully and idiomatically on the instrument. He now had at his disposal three sound sources of distinct color, each capable of playing as a fully independent unit and each capable of blending with the others in a wide variety of combinations. The piano can play melody to the accompaniment of either of the sections of the orchestra, or can play accompaniment to either of them. A solo wind counter-melody can be added to vary the return of familiar material in the piano, a favorite Mozart device to achieve variety. The winds can play as a homophonic group or weave a complex polyphonic texture; the strings can play as a small orchestra or provide delicate accompaniment figures. As you listen to works of this kind, listen for the endless variety and change in the dimension of orchestral color. The interplay of distinct colors almost becomes a foreground element, as it is in the Baroque concerto grosso.

Structure

The addition of the third independent force, the piano, to the orchestral texture also has a profound effect on form. Concerto form in this period, and into the Romantic period, is related to, but distinct from, symphonic form. First of all, the standard pattern becomes three movements, usually a sonata-allegro first movement, a lyric slow movement, and a finale in sonata-allegro, rondo, or theme-and-variations form. What is missing from symphonic structure is the minuet-and-trio third movement, the last remnant of the Baroque stylized dance forms and the least dramatic and intense of the symphonic movements. It is interesting to speculate about why the minuet was dropped from the concerto but retained in the symphony and string quartet. It seems reasonable to assume that the answer lies in the nature of the concerto, which is inherently more dramatic than the other structures, pitting soloist "against" orchestra, or that the minuet did not lend itself to the medium, although it seems that the numerous repetitions in minuet-and-trio structure would have provided opportunity for further exploitation of the varied color possibilities. Further, the addition of the solo instrument makes first movement sonata-allegro structure considerably longer and more complex. Last, the Baroque solo concerto and concerto grosso were generally three-movement forms, and this design may have simply been retained in the Classical concerto.

First Movement Form

For the first movement, a special concerto adaptation of sonata-allegro structure developed. The concerto version of the form is no more a rigid mold than the symphonic model, but certain standard tendencies did develop. The main changes were made to accommodate the concerto medium. First, there is a **double exposition**: the orchestra presents the main thematic materials, and then the soloist does, usually in varied form, more idiomatic for the instrument, or more ornamented. This double exposition should not be confused with the repetition of the exposition section in symphonic sonata-allegro form, because the crucial element of key area is different. In the orchestral exposition of a concerto first movement, the second group of thematic ideas is presented in the tonic, not the dominant or related key. The modulation to the second key area is delayed until the solo exposition. The recapitulation, as we would expect, is not a literal duplication of the double exposition, which would be too much of a good thing, but a compressed version of the exposition materials, involving both orchestra and soloist, often in alternating phrases.

Cadenza

Another concerto innovation is the **cadenza**, which has a double function. It extends and dramatizes a strong cadence near the end of the closing section of the movement, after the recapitulation, and it provides an opportunity for solo display. The orchestra stops on the second-to-last chord of a strong tonic cadence, and the soloist takes off in an improvised free section, using fragments of the thematic material in developmental fashion, with lots of passage-work, sequences, and modulations into remote keys, returning to complete the cadence, usually signaled by a trill. As the soloist arrives at the tonic chord, the orchestra joins in and usually plays a brisk coda, so that work ends shortly after the conclusion of the cadenza.

The cadenza presents an interesting stylistic challenge. Some sensitive performers improvise stylistically consistent cadenzas with great skill; others prefer to search out written cadenzas, especially the few Mozart himself wrote out. Many nineteenth-century cadenzas were published, and some of these do considerable stylistic violence to the concertos for which they were written. As you can imagine, the Romantic era, with its powerful pianos and its image of the demonic virtuoso hero, favored cadenzas somewhat different from the ones Mozart would have played or improvised. The extreme ones have the same jarring aesthetic effect that would be achieved by splicing a guitar chorus from an acid rock number into a gentle ballad. Fortunately, performers in our own day are more sensitive to the demands of Classical style and prepare or improvise stylistically sound cadenzas or find existing ones that are suitable for the work.

One last comment about Mozart's concertos—it is interesting to compare his concertos to the flamboyant nineteenth-century piano concertos that are such favorites of concert audiences. Mozart's are much more balanced and restrained; soloist and orchestra are much more equal partners, and display for its own sake does not exist. Textures are always clear and light, and the overall effect is one of balanced collaboration.

The young Beethoven playing for Mozart.

PIANO CONCERTO NO. 23 IN *A* MAJOR, K. 488

The *A* major concerto is a fine example of Mozart's concerto writing at its elegant best. He wrote it when he was working on *The Marriage of Figaro*, his most successful comic opera, and the concerto reflects the sunny Italian flavor of the opera.

First Movement

The first movement begins with the orchestral exposition of the first theme presented by the strings and then repeated by the wind ensemble (see Figure 24-1). A short transition leads to the second theme (see Figure 24-2), also in the tonic and also presented first by the strings and then by the winds. The orchestral exposition, slightly more than two minutes long, ends with a strong cadence in *A* major, the tonic key. The piano then enters for the first time, playing the first theme with some accompaniment from the strings. A transition section now modulates into the dominant, and the piano presents the second theme in that key area, first alone, and then with wind accompaniment. The second exposition ends without a strong cadence in the dominant key, and the development begins abruptly, with one of the preceding cadence ideas.

The development section is not so much thematic as it is modulatory, moving through a great number of related keys. It features scales and passage-work for the piano and contrapuntal writing for the winds. One last long run for the soloist, with sustained chords, first from the strings and then the winds, over a

Figure 24-1.   First movement, first theme.

Figure 24-2.   Second theme.

dominant pedal, leads to the recapitulation, begun by winds and strings together and continued by the piano in the second phrase. The piano reintroduces the second theme, now in the tonic again, and the orchestra repeats it. The closing ideas recur, followed by a piano cadenza of about a minute's duration, after which a brief and surprisingly quiet orchestral coda brings the movement to an end. A listening guide (Figure 24-5) outlines the main materials and design of this first movement.

Second Movement

The second movement is a lovely slow movement in *F*-sharp minor. It is in 6/8 meter, with dotted rhythm patterns. The meter indicates that it is a **siciliano**, a stylized Baroque dance pattern that appears frequently in the tragic arias of Baroque operas. The movement is filled with lovely chromatic harmonies, and features some lyric wind solos. The strings play mostly accompaniment. Figure 24-3 shows the theme of the second movement.

Figure 24-3.   Melody, slow movement.

Third Movement

The final movement is a bubbling rondo in five parts. The sections are not as clearly divided nor as symmetrical as in the rondo described in the previous chapter, and there are elements of sonata-allegro structure as well. But the movement still feels like a rondo. The contrasting sections are in various related keys, the transitions back to the A theme are extended and sometimes teasing with their delays, and the return of the A theme, always in the tonic key of *A* major, feels like a welcome return home. The A theme appears in Figure 24-4.

The *A* major concerto is a perfect example of Mozart at his best in this genre. It is satisfying to play, delightful to listen to, balanced, elegant, sophisticated, and endlessly fascinating in its wealth of beautiful detail.

Figure 24-4.   Rondo, A theme.

FIGURE 24-5. LISTENING GUIDE

MOZART, PIANO CONCERTO NO. 23   **220**

PIANO CONCERTO IN A MAJOR, K. 488,
BY MOZART

ORCHESTRA EXPOSITION   SOLO EXPOSITION

Trill

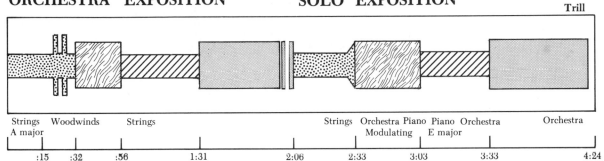

| Strings | Woodwinds | Strings | | Strings | Orchestra | Piano | Piano | Orchestra | Orchestra |
| A major | | | | | | Modulating | E major | | |

:15 :32 :56 1:31 2:06 2:33 3:03 3:33 4:24

DEVELOPMENT

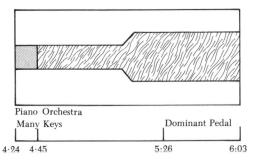

Piano Orchestra
Many Keys   Dominant Pedal

4·24 4·45   5:26   6:03

RECAPITUALATION

Trills Ritard

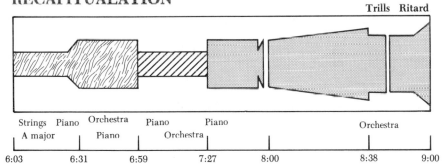

| Strings | Piano | Orchestra | Piano | Piano | | Orchestra |
| A major | | Piano | Orchestra | | | |

6:03 6:31 6:59 7:27 8:00 8:38 9:00

CADENZA   CLOSING

Trills

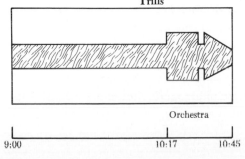

Orchestra

9:00   10:17   10:45

	First Theme
	Second Theme
	Closing Material
	Transition, Cadenza, Coda

CHAPTER 25

Mozart Opera
Don Giovanni

Besides the huge wealth of instrumental music Mozart composed in his short life, he also wrote eighteen operas of various sorts. Some of these stage works are among the great masterpieces of Western art; many remain timeless favorites of the opera repertory. Mozart's incredible achievements in the field of opera are the combined result of his superb talent for dramatic music and the fact that he came along at the right time. As is often true of great artistic achievements, the time was ripe for great Classic opera because of several circumstances.

OPERATIC REFORM

First, various reform movements had taken a critical look at the extravagances of Baroque opera and had established certain principles about musical drama. Christoph Gluck, a German composer, was one of the leaders of opera reform. Among his ideas was the principle of dramatic unity. He felt strongly that Baroque opera, with its emphasis on vocal pyrotechnics and display, had done disservice to drama. He supported the idea that all of the elements—plot, characterization, and music—should work together to produce believable drama about real people motivated by recognizable feelings and sentiments. Second, the sociological situation was right for certain types of opera, especially *opera buffa*. A new middle-class audience was emerging, ready to attend public performances of comic opera, with its emphasis on human foibles, stock characters, and the foolishness and pretense of arrogant characters from the upper classes. The popularity of such operas is a gentler form of the same impulse that eventually led to revolution and the overthrow of the aristocratic model of society. In Mozart operas, particularly in his comic operas, there is a fine sense of class distinction and a keen eye for pretense, particularly on the part of the aristocratic characters.

Another development that preceded Mozart's activity in the opera field was the development of German comic opera, called *Singspiel*, which featured spoken dialogue, believable characters, and nationalistic sentiments. It was the forerunner of German Romantic opera, as exemplified first by Carl Maria von Weber's *Der Frieschutz* and later by the works of Richard Wagner. An eager audience was ready for opera. Several types of opera existed with fairly standard outlines and expectations, and everything was ready for an operatic genius to come along and develop these possibilities.

This Metropolitan Opera performance of *The Magic Flute* with backdrops by twentieth-century artist Marc Chagall.

MOZART AS AN OPERA COMPOSER

But this historical moment, pregnant with possibilities for great opera, would not have produced great opera without the proper composer and his unique gifts. As we know from Mozart's orchestral music, he had a limitless gift for beautiful melody and complete control of orchestral writing. He also had an instinct for vocal writing, so that even those operas that do not seem exciting as staged drama are filled with gorgeous music.

Mozart's most telling gift was the ability to depict character and character development in music. In the comic operas, where class distinction is such an important element, he writes in distinct styles for the various social classes. Often the comic characters among the nobility sing in an exaggerated parody of highflown style, so that the comic element is in the *music*, not in the plot or stage business alone. The lower-class characters sing in a simpler, folk-like style, and comic servants sing in staccato patter style.

It was traditional in the comic opera of the time for each act to end with an ensemble. As you can imagine, it is extremely difficult to have five or six characters sing at the same time without imposing a homogeneous style on them. One of the marvels of Mozart's comic operas is that his characters always sing in character in the ensembles, so that their individual musical styles are maintained and somehow blended.

Mozart was also fortunate in his librettists. Although he worked with some rather silly stories and some troublesome librettists, he also worked with some fine ones, particularly Lorenzo da Ponte, the librettist of *The Marriage of Figaro*, *Don Giovanni*, and *Così Fan Tutte*. Incidentally, da Ponte is a fascinating man in himself. He later emigrated to the United States, where he surfaced at various times as a grocer, a bootlegger, and a professor of Italian at Columbia University. His memoirs are now available in English translation.

MOZART'S WORKS

Before looking at *Don Giovanni* in detail, we should mention a few of Mozart's works in each of the prevalent styles. At this time, *opera seria* continued to be more of a court entertainment than a public performance and maintained some of the earlier conventions, such as mythological plots and static action schemes more suited to pageant than to opera, *castrato* male roles, and a high moral tone designed to honor the aristrocratic patron. Examples of Mozart's *opera seria* are *Idomeneo* and *La Clemenza di Tito*, both commissioned for royal occasions. These works are occasionally revived by opera companies for their beautiful music. Much more popular are the examples of *opera buffa*, like *Figaro*, *Così Fan Tutte*, and *Don Giovanni*. Although the class distinctions on which the operas are based no longer apply, these works still delight opera audiences and work quite successfully as musical drama. They are favorites of all opera companies, enormously popular with both singers and musicians. In the *Singspiel* style, Mozart wrote *The Abduction from the Seraglio* and the complicated and endlessly fascinating *The Magic Flute*. Ingmar Bergman has made a film version of *The Magic Flute*, which depicts a small company's production of the work in Swedish. Despite the language (the film comes with subtitles) and some irrelevant film devices, like panning over the audience's faces during instrumental passages, the film works very well as one version of the opera and is well worth seeing.

This body of operatic work is astonishing, considering the short life of Mozart and his achievements in other areas. He has not only enriched the repertory of opera, but produced some of the finest masterpieces of all Western culture, especially in the work we now look at more closely.

DON GIOVANNI

Style

We saw in previous chapters that Mozart was quite capable of writing exactly what was required or desired for a particular occasion; he was also capable of over-writing, going so far beyond the demands of an established style that he created something entirely new, risking the loss of his audience or his patron in the process. So it was with *Don Giovanni*, regarded by most commentators as his supreme operatic masterpiece. It has elements of *opera buffa*—the comic servant Leporello, the charming seduction scenes, the cases of mistaken identity. But comic operas are not supposed to end with the hero's being snatched down to hell. Mozart invented a new term for this opera, calling it a **dramma giocosa**, which we might translate as "entertaining drama," halfway between *opera buffa* and the stylized solemnity of *opera seria*. There are elements of serious tragedy, in the tradition of Greek tragedy: the hero is inexorably pulled down by his tragic flaw and his defiance of the gods. From the moment early in the opera when the Don kills the Commendatore in the duel, his fate is sealed, and all of the subplots are mere filler between the tragic mistake and its inevitable punishment.

Characters

The characters of the opera, like the characters of Shakespeare's plays, are endlessly fascinating.

This scene from a New York Metropolitan Opera performance of Mozart's *Don Giovanni* features Elisabeth Schwarzkopf as Donna Elvira.

The Don

The Don is capable of many conflicting interpretations. In the various versions of the Don Juan story, he can be a destructive maniac, a sick compulsive, a comic figure always involved in the chase, or a jaded libertine, as he is portrayed in the Joseph Losey film version of the opera. Mozart presents him as simultaneously heroic, comic, and tragic. Leporello's famous "catalog aria," listing the thousands of conquests, presents the Don as a compulsive hunter, more interested in setting records than in love. Elsewhere in the opera, we feel some admiration for the Don. He seduces Zerlina, the peasant girl, with considerable skill and charm, and she is not exactly granite in her resistance. Their charming duet "La ci darem la mano," seems to represent genuine feeling. The Don is heroic in the final scene. Confronted with the statue of the Commendatore, he refuses to cower or repent, and takes his fate like a man. He has an ambiguity about him, like Hamlet or Macbeth, which is open to differing dramatic interpretations, and which has given the character its fascination for generations of audiences.

Leporello

The other characters are easier to understand. Leporello, the fat servant, is a stock character, in the tradition of Western comic servants going back to the Latin comedies of Plautus and Terence. The Zero Mostel character, Pseudolus, in the musical comedy *A Funny Thing Happened on the Way to the Forum*, is a perfect example of the original Roman version of this sort of character. Musically speaking, Leporello is a *basso buffo*, a fine role for a bass with comic acting ability and a voice that can sing staccato patter songs.

The Commendatore

The Commendatore is the next most important character, ordinary enough in the early scenes as the outraged father of Donna Anna, one of the Don's conquests. He comes into his own in the final scenes, when his statue miraculously comes to life to wreak vengeance on the Don. As the supernatural avenger, he sings ominous lines in octaves, accompanied by trombones that symbolize the terrifying netherworld (see Figure 25-1).

Figure 25-1. The Statue's opening phrases from the last act.

Other Roles

The other roles are more typical. Donna Anna, the outraged lover, is a soprano role. Her bethrothed, Don Ottavio, is a somewhat colorless character, sung by a tenor. Donna Elvira, another woman the Don has loved and left, is a strong soprano role and dramatically interesting. She seems to be the only woman who really loves the Don. She returns near the end of the opera to warn him about his fate, and vows in the Epilogue, after his death, to enter a convent. Donna Anna, on the other hand, is content to marry her patient Don Ottavio and live happily

This view of the San Benedetto theater in Venice illustrates how the horseshoe-shaped interior allowed opera goers to see and be seen.

ever after. There is also a peasant couple, Masetto and Zerlina. We have already mentioned the duet between the Don and Zerlina in which the Don sings in simple peasant style and rather easily wins Zerlina, while Leporello keeps Masetto out of the way. You can already sense the fundamental ambivalence of the opera. For a tragedy, there is much too much banter, too much mistaken identity, and too many hair's-breadth escapes—the typical business of *opera buffa*. But the basic plot—the murder and its revenge—is deadly serious.

Comic Sections

There are several clever musical moments in the opera that give it additional charm. At one point, the Don, idle between major seductions, sings a serenade to Donna Anna's maid, accompanying himself on the mandolin. This scene provides an interesting moment of comic relief. The Don seems to be mocking himself and his endless compulsive hunt. A female extra usually has some comic business as the maid, who does not take the wooing seriously but enjoys it anyway, and the Don mimes his mandolin playing, as the real mandolin player in the pit plays the charming solo. At the Don's fancy dinner in the last act, there is a wind ensemble on stage, which plays snatches of popular operas of the period, including some of Mozart's own. The Don's critical comments about the works set up complicated inside jokes for the audience, and there are interesting balance and synchronization problems between the stage band and the pit. Mozart obviously took great glee in composing these complicated lighter moments of the opera.

The Final Scene

The section we will listen to is far more serious. After the banquet scene with the on-stage band and the references to other works, and some comic business as Leporello sneaks bites of the food and then tries to sing with his mouth full, Donna Elvira enters to make one last plea to the Don to mend his ways. He laughs at her pleas and goes on in his swashbuckling way. But outside lurks menace, in the form of the Commendatore's statue. In an earlier graveyard scene, the statue spoke to the Don, who mockingly invited it to dinner. Now it has come; and as Elvira leaves, she screams, having encountered the statue outside. The rest of the scene has three characters on stage: the Don, continuing in his defiance; Leporello, scared out of his wits; and the statue of the Commendatore, singing in his threatening, otherworldly way. The Don refuses to repent and is snatched down to hell as an off-stage chorus of spirits sings of his doom.

The Epilogue

The Epilogue, added after the first performance, gives the other characters an opportunity to shine one last time, and wraps up all of the dramatic loose ends. Leporello repeats his comic account of the entrance of the statue, and then everyone makes his or her future plans. Leporello will find another master; Donna Elvira will enter a convent; Don Ottavio and Donna Anna will marry; and Masetto and Zerlina will live happily ever after. Then they sing a rousing, boisterous ensemble finale, on the moral of the tale, "Questo è il fin di chi fa mal" ("Anyone who does evil ends up this way").

The listening guide (Figure 25-2) gives the libretto of the final scene in Italian and English, with all the text repeats, so that you can follow the music. You should be aware of the musical characterization. All of the characters maintain their own styles, and we come to know the characters and how they feel and change through the way they sing, both in the dramatic final scene and the spirited Epilogue. With all of its seesawing between tragedy and comedy, with all of its conventional scenes and characters, *Don Giovanni* remains one of the great operatic masterpieces, not only for its beautiful music, but also because of its successful characterization and its timeless story.

FIGURE 25-2. LISTENING GUIDE

FINAL SCENE, DON GIOVANNI, BY MOZART

The stage orchestra finishes playing. The girls depart, and Donna Elvira rushes in.

DONNA ELVIRA
L'ultima prova dell'amor mio ancor vogl'io fare con te. Più non rammento gl'inganni tuoi, gl'inganni tuoi, pietade io sento!

DONNA ELVIRA
I want to prove my love for you one last time. I no longer remember your deceits, your deceits, I feel pity!

Don Giovanni waves away the musicans.

DON GIOVANNI AND LEPORELLO
Cos'è? Cos'è?

DON GIOVANNI AND LEPORELLO
What's the matter? What's the matter?

Donna Elvira kneels pleadingly

DONNA ELVIRA
Da te non chiede quest'alma oppressa della sua fede qualche mercè.

DONNA ELVIRA
This oppressed soul asks no thanks for its faithfulness to you.

DON GIOVANNI
Mi maraviglio! cosa volete? cosa volete? Se non sorgete, non resto in piè, non resto in piè.

DON GIOVANNI
How wonderful! what do you want? what do you want? If you don't get up, *I* won't stay on my feet, *I* won't stay on my feet.

He too kneels.

DONNA ELVIRA
Ah non deridere gli affanni miei!

DONNA ELVIRA
Ah, don't mock my sorrows!

LEPORELLO
Quasi di piangere mi fa costei, quasi di piangere mi fa costei!

LEPORELLO
She's almost making me cry, she's almost making me cry!

Don Giovanni gets to his feet and pulls Donna Elvira up too.

DON GIOVANNI
Io te deridere!

DON GIOVANNI
I, mock you!

DONNA ELVIRA
Ah, non deridere!

DONNA ELVIRA
Ah, don't mock!

DON GIOVANNI
Io te deridere?

DON GIOVANNI
I mock you?

DONNA ELVIRA
Ah, non deridere!

DONNA ELVIRA
Ah, don't mock.

DON GIOVANNI
Cielo! perchè? Che vuoi, mio bene?

DON GIOVANNI
Heavens! why? What do you want, my dear?

DONNA ELVIRA
Che vita cangi!

DONNA ELVIRA
That you change your life!

DON GIOVANNI
Brava!

DON GIOVANNI
Good girl!

DONNA ELVIRA
Cor perfido!

DONNA ELVIRA
Faithless scoundrel!

DON GIOVANNI (cont.)

DON GIOVANNI
Brava!

DON GIOVANNI
Good girl!

DONNA ELVIRA
Cor perfido!

DONNA ELVIRA
Faithless scoundrel!

DONNA ELVIRA AND LEPORELLO
Cor perfido!

DONNA ELVIRA AND LEPORELLO
Faithless scoundrel!

Don Giovanni laughs and sits down at the table again.

DON GIOVANNI
Lascia ch'io mangi, lascia ch'io mangi,
e se ti piace, mangia con me!

DON GIOVANNI
Let me eat, let me eat, and if you like, eat
with me!

DONNA ELVIRA
Restati, barbaro! nel lezzo immondo
esempio orribile d'iniquità!

DONNA ELVIRA
Remain, cruel man! a dreadful example
of evil in your filthy stench.

LEPORELLO
Se non si muove del suo dolore, di sasso
ha il core, o cor non ha!

LEPORELLO
If her sorrow doesn't move him, he has a
heart of stone, or he hasn't got a heart!

ACT TWO

Don Giovanni lifts his glass in a toast.

DON GIOVANNI
Vivan le femmine, viva il buon vino!
sostegno e gloria d'umanità, sostegno e
gloria d'umanità!

DON GIOVANNI
Long live women, long live good wine!
sustenance and glory of humankind, sustenance and glory of humankind!

DONNA ELVIRA
Restati, barbaro! nel lezzo immondo, restati barbaro! nel lezzo immondo! esempio
orribile d'iniquità! esempio orribile
d'iniquità, d'iniquità, d'inquità, esempio
orribile d'iniquità!

DONNA ELVIRA
Remain, cruel man! remain, cruel man,
in your filthy stench! in your filthy
stench! a dreadful example of evil!
a dreadful example of evil, of evil, of
evil, a dreadful example of evil!

LEPORELLO
Se non si muove del suo dolore, di sasso ha
il core, di sasso ha il core, o cor non ha.
Di sasso ha il core, o cor non ha! o cor non
ha, o cor non ha, di sasso ha il core, o cor
non ha!

LEPORELLO
If her sorrow doesn't move him, he has a
heart of stone, he has a heart of stone, or
he hasn't got a heart. He has a heart of
stone, or he hasn't got a heart! or he
hasn't got a heart, or he hasn't got a
heart, he has a heart of stone, or he hasn't
got a heart!

DON GIOVANNI
Vivan le femmine, viva il buon vino!
vivan le femmine, viva il buon vino!
sostegno e gloria d'umanità, sostegno e
gloria d'umanità, sostegno e gloria d'u-
manità, d'umanità, d'umanità, sostegno
e gloria d'umanità!

DON GIOVANNI
Long live women, long live good wine!
long live women, long live good wine!
sustenance and glory of humankind, sustenance and glory of humankind, sustenance and glory of humankind, of
humankind, of humankind, sustenance
and glory of humankind!

DON GIOVANNI (cont.)

*Donna Elvira rushes out one of the doors, starts back with a terrified scream,
turns, and rushes out the other door.*

DONNA ELVIRA
Ah!

DONNA ELVIRA
Screaming. Ah!

DON GIOVANNI
Che grido è questo mai? che grido, che
grido è questo mai?

DON GIOVANNI
Whatever is that scream? Whatever is
that scream, that scream?

LEPORELLO
Che grido è questo mai! che grido è
questo mai?

LEPORELLO
Whatever is that scream! whatever is that
scream?

DON GIOVANNI
Va a veder, va a veder che cosa è stato.

DON GIOVANNI
To Leporello. Go to see, go to see what's
happened.

Leporello goes to the first door, looks out, screams, and returns.

LEPORELLO
Ah!

LEPORELLO
Screaming. Ah!

DON GIOVANNI
Che grido indiavolato! che grido indiavolato! Leporello, che cos'è? che cos'è?
che cos'è?

DON GIOVANNI
What a devilish scream! what a devilish
scream! Leporello, what is it? what is it?
what is it?

LEPORELLO
Ah! Signor! per carità! non andate fuor di
quà! l'uom di sasso, l'uomo bianco, ah!
padrone! io gelo, io manco. Se vedeste che
figura, se sentiste come fa ta, ta, ta,ta!

LEPORELLO
Eyes bulging. Ah! Sir! for pity's sake!
don't go out of here! the man of stone,
the white man, ah! master! I'm freezing,
I'm faltering. If you had seen that form,
if you had heard how it goes, ta, ta, ta,
ta!

DON GIOVANNI
Non capisco niente affatto.

DON GIOVANNI
I don't understand anything at all.

LEPORELLO
Ta, ta, ta, ta!

LEPORELLO
Imitating the statue. Ta, ta, ta, ta!

DON GIOVANNI
Tu sei matto in verità, in verità, in verità!

DON GIOVANNI
In truth, in truth, in truth, you're crazy!

A hollow knock sounds on the door.

LEPORELLO
Ah! sentite!

LEPORELLO
Ah! do you hear!

DON GIOVANNI
Qualcun batte! Apri!

DON GIOVANNI
Impatiently. Someone is knocking! Open!

LEPORELLO
Io tremo!

LEPORELLO
I'm trembling!

DON GIOVANNI
Apri, dico!

DON GIOVANNI
Open, I say!

LEPORELLO
Ah!

LEPORELLO
Pleading, terrified. Ah!

DON GIOVANNI
Apri!

DON GIOVANNI
Open!

DON GIOVANNI (cont.)

LEPORELLO
Ah!

LEPORELLO
Ah!

DON GIOVANNI
Matto! Per togliermi d'intrico ad aprir io stesso andrò, io stesso andrò.

DON GIOVANNI
Madman! In order to clear up this mess, I'll go myself to open, I'll go myself.

Don Giovanni takes one of the candelabra from the table and goes to the door.
Leporello crawls underneath the table and cowers there.

LEPORELLO
Non vo' più veder l'amico, pian, pianin, m'asconderò, m'asconderò!

LEPORELLO
I don't want to see my friend again, quietly, very quietly I'll hide myself, I'll hide myself!

With a rumbling of tympani, the marble statue of the Commendatore
enters the room.

STATUE
Don Giovanni! a cenar teco m'invitasti! e son venuto!

STATUE
Don Giovanni! you invited me to dine with you! and I have arrived!

Don Giovanni is somewhat startled but conceals his surprise
under an air of bravado.

DON GIOVANNI
Non l'avrei giammai creduto; ma farò quel che potrò. Leporello! un'altra cena! fa che subito si porti!

DON GIOVANNI
I should never have believed it; but I'll do what I can. Leporello! another dinner! have it brought immediately!

Leporello peers dazedly out from under the table.

LEPORELLO
Ah, padron, ah, padron, ah, padron! siam tutti morti!

LEPORELLO
Ah, master, ah, master, ah, master! we're all dead!

DON GIOVANNI
Vanne, dico!

DON GIOVANNI
Go to it, I say!

Leporello begins to crawl out.

STATUE
Ferma un po'! non si pasce di cibo mortale, chi si pasce di cibo celeste! Altre cure più gravi di queste, altra brama quaggiù mi guidò.

STATUE
Wait a bit! one who partakes of celestial food does not partake of mortal food. Other matters more serious than these, another desire brought me down here.

Leporello crawls back under the table.

LEPORELLO
La terzana d'avere mi sembra, e le membra fermar più non sò, la terzana d'avere mi sembra, e le membra fermar più non sò.

LEPORELLO
I seem to have the ague, and I can't stop shaking, I seem to have the ague, and I can't stop shaking.

DON GIOVANNI
Parla dunque! che chiedi? che vuoi?

DON GIOVANNI
To Statue. Speak, then! what do you ask? what do you want?

STATUE
Parlo: ascolta! più tempo non ho.

STATUE
I speak: listen! I have not much time.

DON GIOVANNI
Parla, parla, ascoltando ti sto.

DON GIOVANNI
Speak, speak, I am listening to you.

DON GIOVANNI (cont.)

LEPORELLO
Ah le membra fermar più non sò; la terzana d'avere mi sembra, la terzana
d'avere mi sembra, e le membra fermar
più non sò!

STATUE
Parlo: ascolta! più tempo non ho!

Don Giovanni becomes more defiant.

DON GIOVANNI
Parla, parla, ascoltando ti sto.

STATUE
Tu m'invitasti a cena, il tuo dover or sai,
rispondimi, rispondimi, verrai tu a cenar
meco?

Leporello quavers from beneath the table.

LEPORELLO
Oibò, oibò; tempo non ha, scusate.

DON GIOVANNI
A torto di viltate tacciato mai saro.

STATUE
Verrai?

LEPORELLO
Dite di no, dite di no!

DON GIOVANNI
Ho fermo il core in petto, non ho timor,
verrò!

The Statue extends a hand toward Don Giovanni.

STATUE
Dammi la mano in pegno!

Still defiant, Don Giovanni gives the Statue his hand.

DON GIOVANNI
Eccola! Ohimè!

STATUE
Cos' hai?

DON GIOVANNI
Che gelo è questo mai?

STATUE
Pentiti, cangia vita, è l'ultimo momento!

Don Giovanni tries to withdraw his hand.

DON GIOVANNI
No, no, ch'io non mi pento, vanne lontan
da me!

LEPORELLO
Ah, I can't stop shaking; I seem to have
the ague, I seem to have the ague, and I
can't stop shaking!

STATUE
I speak: listen! I have not much time!

DON GIOVANNI
Speak, speak, I am listening to you.

STATUE
You invited me to dinner, you know your
obligation now, answer me, answer me,
will you come to dine with me?

LEPORELLO
Oh, oh; he hasn't got time, sorry.

DON GIOVANNI
Icily. I shall never be accused of coward-
ice.

STATUE
You will come?

LEPORELLO
Say no, say no!

DON GIOVANNI
My heart is steady in my breast, I am not
afraid, I shall come!

STATUE
Give me your hand as pledge!

DON GIOVANNI
Here it is! Ah!

STATUE
What is the matter?

DON GIOVANNI
How freezing cold it is!

STATUE
Repent, change your life, it is your last
moment!

DON GIOVANNI
No, no, I do not repent, get you far away
from me!

STATUE
Pentiti, scellerato!

DON GIOVANNI
No, vecchio infatuato!

STATUE
Pentiti!

DON GIOVANNI
No!

STATUE
Pentiti!

DON GIOVANNI
No!

STATUE
Sì!

DON GIOVANNI
No!

STATUE
Sì!

DON GIOVANNI
No!

With a desperate effort, he wrests his hand away from the Statue.

STATUE
Sì! Sì!

DON GIOVANNI
No! No!

STATUE
Repent, villain!

DON GIOVANNI
No, stupid old man!

STATUE
Repent!

DON GIOVANNI
No!

STATUE
Repent!

DON GIOVANNI
No!

STATUE
Yes!

DON GIOVANNI
No!

STATUE
Yes!

DON GIOVANNI
No!

STATUE
Yes! Yes!

DON GIOVANNI
No! No!

The Commendatore's Statue begins to move toward the door whence it entered.
Roaring flames begin to surround Don Giovanni.

STATUE
Ah! tempo più non v'e!

DON GIOVANNI
Da qual tremore insolito sento assalir gli
spiriti! dond'escono quei vortici di foco
pien d'orror?

STATUE
Ah! there is no more time!

DON GIOVANNI
I feel my strength gripped by such un-
wonted trembling! whence come those
horror-filled whirlpools of fire?

A chorus of ghostly demon voices sounds from below.

DEMON VOICES
Tutto a tue colpe è poco! vieni! c'è un mal
peggior!

DON GIOVANNI
Chi l'anima mi lacera? Chi m'agita
le viscere? Che strazio, ohimè, che
smania! Che inferno, che terror!

LEPORELLO
Che ceffo disperato! Che gesti da
dannato! che gridi! che lamenti! come mi
fa terror, mi fa terror!

DEMON VOICES
All is as nothing compared to your crimes!
come! worse is in store for you!

DON GIOVANNI
Who tears my spirit? who shakes my in-
nards? what twisting, alas, what frenzy!
what hell, what terror!

LEPORELLO
What a despairing grimace! What gestures of a damned soul! what shouts!
what wails! how terrified it makes me,
terrifed it makes me!

William Turner, *The Slave Ship*, a famous Romantic depiction of the demonic force of nature.

PART **V**

Music in the Romantic Era

CHAPTER 26

Social and Cultural Background

"ROMANTIC" AND "ROMANTICISM"

The term romantic or romanticism, like most of the terms for periods in the history of the arts, is a rather loose expression. Music historians usually use the term "the Romantic Era" to designate the period from about 1810 or 1820 until the turn of the twentieth century. The line between the Classic and Romantic eras, however, is not as clear a break as the line between the nineteenth and twentieth centuries or between the Renaissance and Baroque eras. Romantic music emphasizes different facets of style from Classic music; but in many ways the basic assumptions about music—harmonic language, texture, and structure—remain the same. Romantic tendencies appear in music slightly later than in literature and the other arts. For the purpose of understanding the course of Western music, it is useful to consider Beethoven as both the last great master of the Classic style and the first important Romantic composer. His lifetime (1770-1827) encompasses both the height of the Viennese Classical style and the early days of Romanticism; his musical style unites the Classical concern for form and structure with the power and individuality of Romanticism.

THE NINETEENTH CENTURY

The nineteenth century was a period of national and colonial expansion, a time of consolidating the ideas of freedom and equality that exploded in the American and French revolutions. The Industrial Revolution profoundly changed the ways society was ordered and gave rise not only to large cities and great industrial centers, but also to a new elite whose social position was based not on inherited wealth or noble birth but on commercial success. The backbone of the new society was the middle class, urban, somewhat sophisticated, educated, and hungry for a culture that embodied the values of the new society. Some of the concerns of nineteenth-century society are reflected in its innovations—labor unions, child labor laws, and educational opportunity for the children of all classes, not just the wealthy. The same egalitarian spirit is visible in the literature of the period, especially in the novels of Charles Dickens.

Nationalism

One of the important forces in nineteenth-century life was a new sense of nationalism. Germany became a unified country during this period, rather than a federation of independent territories; and German culture became a search for common roots in a shared literature, mythology, and art. Italy became a nation also and found expression for its patriotic feelings in the operas of Verdi (Chapter 36). The United States went through profound changes. The country began the nineteenth century as a small collection of federated states on the East Coast. After the continuous Westward expansion of the nineteenth century and the upheaval of the Civil War, the nation entered the twentieth century as a large country of what were thought to be unlimited resources and wealth, ready to take its place in history as a world power. In England, the long and prosperous reign of Queen Victoria and the immense resources of the Commonwealth promised endless prosperity. We now have appropriated Victoria's name as a label for the middle-class morality and sense of propriety established and guarded during the century. The nineteenth century was an exciting time in Europe and America, a time of discovery, change, and promise.

Naturally the arts of the nineteenth century reflected the ideas and events of the time. The aristocratic elegance and restraint that was so much a factor in the aesthetic ideas of the Classic period would no longer serve as the guiding idea for the arts of this new time. A new aesthetic was born that set the standards not only for the arts of the nineteenth century, but for many artistic creations of our own century as well.

THE ROMANTIC AESTHETIC

In some ways, Romanticism in the arts is visible in any age. One commentator has said that all art is Romantic in its early stages because it is in some way new and individual. Still, there are some common ideas that form the premises of nineteenth-century art. It is important that we understand these ideas because they are still the underlying assumptions in many areas of the arts today.

A sketch from Charles Dickens' *Barnaby Rudge,* a novel based on the Gordon riots in England.

Freedom

The most fundamental notion of Romanticism is the freedom of the artist to say what he wants to say, free from the strictures of previous styles and disciplines. This idea extended into the realm of the arts the fundamental social and political notion of the importance and freedom of the individual. The artist in previous ages had been in the service of the church or the nobility and had produced works of art on demand. The first well-known composer to work independently of church or aristocratic patronage, free to write whatever he wanted and sell his work to publishers, was Beethoven. The fact that we regard this freedom from patronage as a natural thing shows how much we have accepted the Romantic notion of the artist. We are amazed that great artists and composers worked under the patronage system without rebelling against the limitations it imposed upon them.

We regard the artist as an outsider, a rebel struggling to find expression for the tumultuous creative drive at work within him. This picture never existed before the nineteenth century, but it has lasted even into our own cynical day as the typical picture of the artist. We may reject the latest creation of the artist, we may laugh at his apparent madness or be shocked at his "different" behavior. Still, as a society, we assume that he has an inalienable right to struggle with his demons, and pursue his attempts at artistic creation—at least, for a while. We assume he should be financially independent, perhaps supported somehow by society, so that he can be free of mundane cares, able to dedicate himself totally to the work of artistic creation. We regard attempts by society to exclude some works from exhibition or performance as censorship, a crime in a free society.

Individualism

Allied to this notion of the artist's role in society is the Romantic notion of what art should be. As the artist is now presumed to be free from the laws that govern ordinary mortals, so the art he produces is assumed to be new, individual, even revolutionary, totally free from the restrictions imposed by earlier ages and traditions. More important than laws and accepted ways is the artist's freedom to say what he as an individual has to say, in new and startling ways if necessary. Romantic art is concerned with the expression of feeling, of sentiment, of man's deepest emotions, dreams, and fears. There is a fascination with the new in all the arts. It is startling for us to see a concert program from the nineteenth century. By our standards, audiences sat through incredibly long performances, and they listened mostly to new works. Because our own ideas about concert programming depend so heavily on music from the past and because, in our society, contemporary music is performed for a small, select audience, it is hard for us to visualize this mass fascination with new works.

Music as the Meeting Place of the Arts

Other fundamental ideas of Romantic culture had a profound effect on music. As all of the arts began to concern themselves with expression of deep feelings, music took on new importance because it was recognized as the art most suited for emotional expression. Music could portray Romantic ideas with warm sounds, great crescendos and exciting climaxes. It was regarded as the place where all of the arts met, where ideas from literature and the visual arts found their most effective expression. There was great interest in composing music based on literary themes or settings of poetry. Even orchestral forms like the symphony came to incorporate singers and choruses, particularly for their mighty, solemn finales, following the example of Beethoven, who used a chorus singing Schiller's "Ode to Joy" in the finale of his Ninth Symphony.

Program for a concert in April, 1800, featuring Beethoven in several roles—as composer, conductor, and pianist. The program includes a Mozart symphony, vocal excerpts from Haydn's *Creation*, a new piano concerto by Beethoven, played by the composer, more excerpts from the *Creation*, piano improvisations by Beethoven, and a new symphony, also by Beethoven.

Aesthetic Argument

Musicians were also more heavily involved in the aesthetic discussions and writings of the nineteenth century than were the composers of previous centuries, who seemed content to produce the music rather than to argue about its value and significance. Romantic musicians were passionately involved in heated and endless discussions about art. Hector Berlioz wrote extensively in French journals; Robert Schumann published a journal on music, in which he argued for one position concerning the proper course for German music to take; Richard Wagner wrote long tracts defending the opposite position. Many of these writings are now available to us in translation. The passionate seriousness with which composers defended positions on aesthetic questions is impressive. People cared deeply about the directions art should take and dedicated their lives to arguing aesthetic questions.

THEMES OF ROMANTIC LITERATURE AND ART

As you may already be aware from studies of nineteenth-century literature, there are some favorite subjects for all of the arts in the Romantic era. These themes are visible in the works of writers like Byron, Shelley, Keats, Wordsworth, and Poe, to name just a few, and are treated by painters, sculptors, and composers of the time.

The Struggling Hero

One of the favorite themes is that of the hero and his struggles against impossible odds to meet his particular challenge. Sometimes the hero is a contemporary figure, real or fictional, but often the artist reaches back into myth or legend to find a hero who will symbolize the continual human struggle for greatness.

Jacques-Louis David. *Oath of Horatio*, 1784 (The Louvre, Paris).

Faust

One of the favorite heroes of the Romantic arts was Faust. The story is very old and exists in several versions from various centuries. Romantic artists were familiar with the poetic version of the legend by Goethe, written in the late eighteenth century. According to the story, Faust is a medieval scientist who sells his soul to achieve superhuman illumination, but is saved by his love for Marguerite. The story had everything Romantic artists loved—a distant setting, cosmic questions about man's limits and his efforts to overcome them, a demonic character able to raise a shudder of horror in the reader, and the pure, redeeming love of an idealized woman. The *Faust* Symphony of Liszt, the *Damnation of Faust* by Berlioz, Gounod's opera *Faust*, and the Eighth Symphony of Mahler are examples of works based on the Faust story. The list of songs and other works based on the same story would be nearly endless.

Nature

Nature is another favorite Romantic theme. The Romantic idea of nature, however, was not the same as ours. The Romantics viewed nature not in the way a conservationist now views it, but rather as an idealized, magical, and even divine world, the source of either tranquility and peace or overwhelming demonic power. Romantic artists painted the sea—calm or stormy—or the woods or the glories of the Alps, and Romantic writers sang the praises of the endless, mysterious life and power of nature. Composers wrote works like the *Pastoral* Symphony of Beethoven, depicting several moods of nature, both stormy and peaceful, or endless songs and piano pieces depicting waterfalls, brooks, landscapes, and storms.

The Supernatural

The supernatural was another favorite theme, and one of the masters of Romantic horror is Edgar Allan Poe. Romantic artists of all media constantly strove for dramatic effect, and one of their favorite effects was a shiver of horror in the audience. Examples of musical works based on grotesque or supernatural stories include Carl Maria von Weber's opera *Der Freischütz*, whose midnight scene in the forest features tolling bells, demonic manifestations, and magic bullets. Other examples are *The Sorcerer's Apprentice* by Dukas, and Mussorgsky's *Night on Bald Mountain*.

The Exotic

Another favorite theme was the exotic—distant lands, glamorous and mysterious. Coleridge's "Kubla Khan" is a famous literary example. In the field of music, composers wrote music depicting faraway places and called for special

The Romantic interest in mythological themes provided dramatic subjects for paintings like *The Raft of Medusa* by Gericault.

instruments and other ways of depicting the Far East (gongs and Chinese scales), Spain (castanets and flamenco rhythms), and Eastern Europe (usually, gypsy melodies). These composers were not interested in serious study of the musics of other cultures, as some twentieth century composers are. All they wanted was a few standard effects to suggest faraway places, the way film and television composers now suggest particular countries or cities with a few brief musical ideas or by particular orchestral colors. Famous examples of Romantic music based on exoticism are Rimsky-Korsakov's *Scheherazade*, which depicts the magical world of the Arabian Nights, and Chabrier's *España*, which is filled with castanets and the fiery rhythms of Andalucia.

The Middle Ages

We mentioned already that, in their search for heroes, Romantic artists turned to earlier times and old legends. One theme that runs through the Romantic arts is the Middle Ages, glorified as an idealized age of beautiful damsels in distress, brave and selfless knights, wise kings, and demonic magicians. The legends of King Arthur and his knights of the Round Table, the quest for the Holy Grail, and other medieval tales were revived, modified to fit Romantic specifications, and used over and over as thematic material in the arts of the nineteenth century. Sir Walter Scott's *Ivanhoe* is a famous literary example; two of Richard Wagner's operas, *Tristan und Isolde* and *Der Meistersinger*, are based on medieval legends, and the four operas of the Ring cycle are based on old Norse mythology. This interest in the Middle Ages was not literally historical. Artists searched for stories and heroes that could be treated in Romantic fashion, and the Middle Ages they presented bore little resemblance to any real historical era. The quest was always for effect—for heroes larger than life, for a surge of exaltation, a shiver of fear, a wrenching tragedy, or a feeling of peace. At no time in the history of music has there been such a close connection between the ideals and themes of all the arts. Music gives the final and deepest expression to the ideas of the Romantic aesthetic.

Metropolitan Opera performance of Wagner's *Die Walküre*.

CHAPTER 27

New Musical Development

THE VIRTUOSO PERFORMER

The Romantic era saw the rise of a new type of performer: the traveling virtuoso. Previous ages, of course, had great performers whom they celebrated and honored. We have already discussed musicians like the *castrati* stars of Baroque Italian opera or Mozart the child prodigy, who performed for the courts of Europe. But this trend escalated in the Romantic era, with its love of dramatic effect and its search for new heroes of all sorts. A new type of virtuoso performer emerged, whose displays of unheard of technical ability appealed to worshiping audiences.

The pioneer star performer was Franz Liszt, the composer-pianist, who was the first performer to turn the piano sideways to the audience, so that at least some of its members could see his hands and all could appreciate his noble profile. Another star performer was Niccolo Paganini, a violinist who so astounded people with his technical agility that some suspected him of being in league with the devil and many wanted to examine his instrument to see if it was, indeed, a standard violin.

This new type of performer naturally needed a new type of music, designed to amaze and thrill the audience. Composers began to write music designed more for technical display than for musical value. When performers needed a new showpiece, they sometimes wrote their own. Virtuoso performers toured Europe all through the nineteenth century, and some even ventured to the New World. Both Ole Bull, a Scandinavian violinist, and Jenny Lind, a singer, had very successful tours of the United States during the nineteenth century. We still see evidence of the Romantic virtuoso idea in our present concert world. A few for-

Niccolo Paganini's technical agility on the violin astounded his audiences.

tunate and talented performers, like Van Cliburn and Jascha Heifitz, manage to become international celebrities. Star conductors share in this same sort of celebrity and fame. On another level, we have rock superstars, who can fill the largest stadiums in the country with adoring fans and who enjoy all of the advantages and problems associated with being famous.

NEW DEVELOPMENTS IN INSTRUMENTS

The Piano

The piano, as we have already seen, existed in the Classic period. Mozart wrote twenty-five concertos for piano and orchestra. But in the nineteenth century, the piano underwent some mechanical changes, so much so that we now realize it is not correct to use a modern piano to play the Mozart concertos or other literature

Artur Rubinstein, a virtuoso performer and a great interpreter of Romantic music, expertly handles the expressive possibilities of the piano.

from the Classic period. The changes had to do with making the instrument heavier and sturdier. This new kind of piano was much more capable of a sustained, singing tone, and a wide range of dynamics. The new expressive possibilities of the piano were immediately exploited by composers, and the piano became a favorite instrument in a variety of roles. It was the most common home instrument, and a large amount of music was written for solo piano with amateur performers in mind. It was also the standard accompaniment instrument for the many songs written in this period. Because of its new capacity for variety of color and dynamics, it was an ideal instrument for setting the mood and commenting musically on the ideas expressed in the song texts. It also continued to be a solo instrument with orchestra, and many showy Romantic piano concertos were composed, some of which are still played. The piano concertos by Tchaikovsky and Grieg are among the best-selling classical recordings. The piano also played a role in chamber music: a favorite Romantic chamber group was the piano trio, consisting of a piano, a violin, and a cello.

There was another kind of writing for piano that we have lost altogether in our age: piano transcriptions. In an age without recordings, television, or radio, the only ways to experience music were by attending the performance or by somehow recreating it at home. Symphonies, for example, were published both as orchestral scores and as transcriptions for piano, so that amateurs could make the music themselves. The transcriptions were usually for piano duet, called "piano four hands"—one piano with two players. The use of two players not only made the experience a shared one (and probably helped along many budding romances), but also made it easier for the arranger or composer to duplicate some of the richness and complexity of the orchestral version. Some of these transcriptions are still available, and pianists enjoy reading through these old versions.

The Orchestra

Expansion

The most obvious change in the orchestra from the Classic period to the Romantic era was its expansion. Some Romantic works added one or two brass bands and two or three choruses to the standard orchestra. The expanding forces called for by some composers were ridiculed as a trend that would lead (or had led) to situations in which the performers would outnumber the audience. The Eighth Symphony of Mahler was nicknamed "The Symphony of a Thousand," an exaggerated estimate of the number of musicians needed to perform it.

Brass Section

Aside from these extremes, however, the standard orchestra expanded in a number of ways. One was the development of the brass section as an independent group, on equal footing with the woodwinds and strings. The addition of valves to the brass instruments made them much more agile and freed them from the support role they often played in the Classic orchestra. In addition, the brass colors became very popular for other reasons. The French horn was a special favorite because of its heroic effect. The low brasses—trombone and tuba—were added to the standard orchestra, so that now the brass section—trumpets, French horns, trombones, and tubas—could function as a separate group. They could also add immensely to the richness and fullness of the ensemble sound and help to make climaxes loud and exciting.

Woodwind Section

In the woodwind section, new instruments, usually different sizes of the basic woodwind instruments, were added for their special possibilities as solo instruments. The English horn, the bass clarinet, and the piccolo all joined the standard orchestra during this period. Like the brasses, these new instruments added not only to the solo color possibilities, but also to the full orchestral sound. Occasionally more exotic instruments, some of which, like the **ophicleide**, do not even exist any more, were called for, and sometimes saxophones were added to the woodwind section.

String Section

The string section had to be greatly increased, of course, to keep up with the expanded brass and woodwind sections, and new techniques of string writing were used so that the strings would have something useful to do in the loud passages. Usually, composers wrote **tremolo** passages for strings (very rapid bowing, to strengthen the sound) or rapid scales and arpeggios which the strings played during loud wind passages.

Percussion Section

The percussion section was also greatly expanded from the two or three tympani which constituted a Classical percussion section. This expansion was partly to add to the increased sound of the larger orchestra, and partly to add the special effects needed in picturesque Romantic music. Besides the tympani, the Romantic orchestra included a bass drum, a snare drum, cymbals to add zing to the climaxes, and perhaps castanets, chimes, gongs, and other exotic instruments for special effects. Unusual percussion includes the cowbells called for in some of Mahler's symphonies and the artillery needed in some works on military themes, like the *1812* Overture by Tchaikovsky.

The orchestral demands of composers vary enormously, but it is safe to say that the average Romantic orchestra would contain seventy to eighty players, whereas the typical Classic orchestra would contain thirty to forty.

ROMANTIC FORMS

Symphonies

Like the orchestra, the forms inherited from the Classic period expand greatly in the Romantic period. Romantic symphonies and concertos are about twice as long as their Classic counterparts. Several factors work together to produce this change in mass. Romantic themes tend to be longer and more lyric than Classic ones, and Romantic composers are much more prone to vary and transform their themes as one of the basic means of musical development. Also, as one would expect, the more dramatic sections of the symphonic form are greatly expanded. Romantic symphonies tend to have moody or dramatic introductions, expanded

This contemporary caricature ridicules the colorful orchestration of Berlioz. Along with other Romantic composers, Berlioz extended the size and sound of the orchestra.

development sections, and long, ringing conclusions. Sometimes the forms are expanded almost beyond recognition, although detailed study reveals the Classical skeleton underneath all of the Romantic ornament. Following the example of Beethoven, composers often substituted another type of movement for the elegant Classical minuet and trio as the third movement of the symphony. It may be a scherzo, often with a demonic feel to it, or an additional slow movement. We have already mentioned the introduction of the chorus in the finale of Beethoven's Ninth Symphony. That work apparently posed a challenge to other Romantic symphonists; their final movements are frequently the longest part of the symphony and the favorite place for extremes of grandeur or cosmic philosophical statements, often with the aid of a chorus, or of a brass choir for solemn religious effects. Examples of symphonic movements by Beethoven and Brahms are discussed in Chapters 28 and 29.

Concertos

As we would imagine, Romantic concertos are longer than their Classic counterparts, partly because of the longer themes and looser structure they share with the Romantic symphony, and partly because of the desire to leave ample time for technical display on the part of the soloist.

New Forms

New forms for orchestra emerged in this period. Some composers wrote **program symphonies**, that is, symphonies in several movements, organized around a literary theme. Famous examples include the *Faust* Symphony of Liszt, in which each of the major characters of the story—Faust, Gretchen (the redeeming female figure), and Mephistopheles—are pictured in a separate movement, and the *Symphonie Fantastique* of Berlioz, discussed in Chapter 30. Another popular form is the **symphonic poem**, or tone poem, which is a single-movement work for orchestra on a literary or pictorial idea. Famous examples include *Les Préludes* by Liszt, discussed in Chapter 32, and *Till Eulenspiegel's Merry Pranks*, by Richard Strauss. Other composers wrote **overtures** and incidental music for dramatic presentations, such as the *Romeo and Juliet* Overture by Tchaikovsky (Chapter 31) and the music to *Midsummer Night's Dream* by Felix Mendelssohn.

Balancing the tendency toward larger and larger forms for orchestra, there is a corresponding tendency toward small forms, which we might call miniatures, for either piano or voice and piano. A very large number of pieces were written for solo piano, often for amateur performance, during this period, and most of them have picturesque titles. The aim of the composers was to paint a picture or to depict a single mood or feeling in a short work of a few minutes' duration. Generally there is little contrast in these works. Their purpose is to sketch a picture as economically as possible. A work for piano by Frédéric Chopin is discussed in Chapter 33.

Many of the songs in the large repertory written during this period work the same way: a single idea or mood is painted, simply and briefly, in a few pages of music. The songs are sometimes grouped in larger cycles, so that each song is one part of a unified larger work, but even more of them exist as isolated miniatures. Songs by Schubert and Schumann are discussed in Chapters 34 and 35.

Opera

Opera, as one might imagine, was a very popular form in the Romantic period. Because opera is a combination of music, drama, staging, and costumes, it truly represents the union of the arts so sought after in Romantic thought. The inherited, stylized forms of Classic opera would not do, however, for the Romantic sensibility, so new forms were developed. Characters became less mythical and

This New York Metropolitan Opera performance of Verdi's *Aida* shows the large dimensions which opera took in the Romantic era.

more representative of genuine human passion, although, of course, on a larger Romantic scale. The heroes were really heroic, and the villains were absolutely reprehensible. Romantic opera plots are filled with mad scenes, unrequited love, murder, infidelity, and tragic death. They are the staples of the opera repertory and can still move us to joy and tears, if we accept their conventions and their larger-than-life posture.

The two giants of Romantic opera are Giuseppe Verdi and Richard Wagner. Verdi developed a type of Italian opera that lets the singers star in their big numbers and surrounds them with effective stagecraft and drama (Chapter 36). Wagner invented a totally new type of work which he viewed as a perfectly unified fusion of the arts (Chapter 37).

Romantic composers, then, continued to write in standard Classical forms, but the forms were usually modified and stretched to contain the grandiose ideas and color effects of Romantic music. New forms were developed also, designed specifically to be adequate and attractive frameworks for Romantic musical ideas.

The following chapters in this part are organized not by chronology, although some attention is paid to the time dimension, but by medium of composition. Chapter 28 begins with Beethoven, the last Classicist and the first Romantic, and discusses a movement of one of his symphonies. Chapter 29 is about Brahms, who continued the symphonic tradition. The next three chapters deal with program music for orchestra, then three chapters look at music for solo piano and the *Lied*. The section closes with two chapters on the giants of Romantic opera, Verdi and Wagner.

CHAPTER **28**

Ludwig van Beethoven Symphony No. 3

Ludwig van Beethoven is probably the best-known composer in the history of Western music. Not only is the opening motive from his Fifth Symphony the best-known melody of all classical music but he has even broken into American pop culture. His unmistakable scowl glowers at us from T-shirts and sweatshirts; Schroeder, the pianist of the "Peanuts" comic strip, idolized Beethoven and plays his piano works for the unheeding ears of Lucy; and the Fifth Symphony has even appeared in a rock version, called "A Fifth of Beethoven."

Although Beethoven would be astounded at his position as a pop culture celebrity, there is good reason for his popularity and his position in people's minds as a "typical" figure in Western art music. There is something universally appealing about Beethoven as a man and about his music. He embodies the eternal struggle of the artist to "do his own thing." He was a commoner who insisted that an aristocratic world accept him not only as an equal but as a superior, because of his artistic gifts. He also struggled against impossible odds because of his deafness. He was the first well-known composer to survive as an independent businessman, negotiating directly with publishers and concert managers. He also clearly exemplifies the notion that the artist finds in the act of creating the satisfaction and sense of accomplishment

Figure 28-1. Opening motive from the first movement of Symphony No. 5, by Beethoven.

that eludes him in everyday life.

Beethoven's music has a universal appeal. There is no mistaking his style, with its power, its audible creative struggle, its mighty themes and dramatic climaxes. Although many historians classify him, with some justification, as a Classic composer in the tradition of Haydn and Mozart, his life and many of his best-known works are more Romantic than Classic. Acknowledging that some of his works, like the First, Second, and Eighth Symphonies and many of the quartets, are classical in outline and approach, we will consider him the first Romantic composer rather than the last Classic one. He exemplifies the fact that historical periods are helpful categories for students of an art but do not really reflect the complicated overlappings of artistic styles. He and many other great artists are impossible to categorize as representatives of one period or school.

BEETHOVEN'S LIFE

Beethoven was born in 1770. His father was an unsuccessful musician, who dreamed of his son having the musical career he never had. Ludwig, therefore, had considerable training as a performer. In his twenties, he was sent from Bonn, his birthplace, to Vienna to study with Haydn and Mozart. By the time he was thirty, he had made a reputation in Vienna as both a performer and a composer. At about that time, his hearing started to deteriorate, which did not seriously impede his composing but caused him enormous pain and embarrassment in dealings with others. He had always been a difficult person and a loner. Deafness drove him further into isolation and increased his suspicion and crankiness. Eventually, his hearing was completely gone, and he communicated only in writing. In fact, his conversation books have been preserved and are now being published. Late in his life, he adopted a nephew—he had never married or had children of his own—and his papers and conversation books reveal that he must have been a fearsome and frightening guardian. He was revered as a genius in his own lifetime, and thousands attended his funeral. In our own day, his fame was increased still more by the publication, in 1970, the bicentennial year of his birth, of a large number of new books about him and new recordings of his works. His place as one of the giants of Western music is secure, and no one, performer or scholar, can pretend to know music without having studied the works of Beethoven. If we had to select just a few recordings of Western music to

Portrait of Ludwig van Beethoven
by W. J. Mahler, (1804).

preserve in some science-fiction disaster scenario, the Beethoven symphonies
would probably be on everyone's basic list, along with selected works of Bach
and Mozart.

Beethoven's output as a composer is enormous, considering that his life was
relatively short: he died in 1827, at the age of 57. We also know from study of his
sketchbooks, which have survived, that he composed with great difficulty, constantly revising, crossing out passages, refining details. But remember that all he
did was perform and compose. He managed to support himself by securing aid
from his aristocratic admirers and negotiating shrewdly with his publishers. One
not very admirable custom of his was to sell exclusive publication rights for his
latest work to several publishers at once. His character and deafness kept him
from social life, family life, teaching, or any other distractions.

Historians love to divide events into threes. Beethoven's creative life is usually divided into three periods because the works of these periods are different in style and approach, although there is, of course, some overlapping of styles. The first period, until about 1802, comprises works in Classical style—the first ten piano sonatas, the first two symphonies, and the first six string quartets. The second period, 1802-1816, includes Beethoven's best-known works—Symphonies Three through Eight, the opera *Fidelio*, the bulk of the piano sonatas, concertos for piano and violin, and more quartets. During the final period, from 1816 until his death, Beethoven's style underwent considerable change, and his music became much more experimental as he groped for a new voice. The works of this period are fewer and are somewhat less well-known, but endlessly fascinating because of the composer's obvious struggle to make some sort of final artistic statement. The works of the third period include the last few piano sonatas and quartets, the *Diabelli* variations, the Ninth Symphony, and the *Missa Solemnis*.

Beethoven's works are still staples of the current concert repertoire. All serious students of the piano play his sonatas; the symphonies are constantly performed in concerts and recorded; the quartets are a basic part of the chamber music literature; and music students still analyze his works in minute detail to learn about musical structure, orchestration, and development of themes. As long as Western music is performed and studied, Beethoven will remain one of its best-known and most admired creative geniuses.

Johann Wolfgang von Goethe, a literary giant of the Romantic period.

SYMPHONY NO. 3, *EROICA*

Beethoven wrote his Third Symphony in 1803, and conducted the first public performance of it on April 7, 1805. There is a story, which seems to be true, that he dedicated this symphony to Napoleon and, in fact, first titled it the *Bonaparte* Symphony. When Napoleon had himself crowned Emperor, Beethoven was disgusted with his action, tore up the title page of the symphony, and retitled it, more generally, *Sinfonia Eroica*. This symphony is a perfect example of the Romantic fascination with the hero. It depicts, in a generalized way, the struggle and eventual triumph of any hero, perhaps of the composer himself.

The first performance puzzled many commentators, who viewed the new work as much too long and filled with bizarre and unrelated ideas. One critic wrote that connections between the various elements of the work were often disrupted entirely and that "the inordinate length of this longest and perhaps most difficult of all symphonies wearies even the cognoscenti, and is unendurable to the mere music-lover." Another wrote that, if Beethoven continued in this vein rather than returning to the more Classical style, "the public will leave the concert hall with an unpleasant feeling of fatigue from having been crushed by a mass of unconnected and overloaded ideas and a continuing tumult by all the instruments." It is interesting that critics, confronted by a novel work, always think it is too long, too loud, and too disorganized— criticisms leveled at many styles of music even today.

There are many novel elements in this symphony, at least for its time. It is exactly twice as long as either the First or Second Symphony, both of which were the length of a typical Classical symphony. The first movement, which we will look at in more detail, has many unorthodox things about it: the harmonies are often unusual; new material is introduced in the development; the coda is quite long; and the themes are not developed in standard ways. The second movement is a funeral march, rather than the expected lyric slow movement. The third movement is a boisterous scherzo, rather than a stylized minuet. The last movement is a set of variations with complicated fugal passages and abrupt shifts of tempo. Fifty years later, it would have been a fairly standard Romantic symphony; but, in the early years of the nineteenth century, it was revolutionary. Those who heard it either loved it or hated it—no one seems to have been neutral about it. All hearers felt its power: either they were frightened by it or it symbolized for them a new freedom in art, a freedom some welcomed as heralding the Romantic period.

First Movement

The first thing to notice about this first movement is that its proportions are skewed from the typical first-movement Classical form we discussed in the last section. In some performances, the exposition is not repeated, although the score clearly specifies that it should be. The exposition (not repeated) takes a little over three minutes. The development section takes over five minutes, or longer than the unrepeated exposition. The recapitulation, as we would expect, takes a little over three minutes, but the surprise is the coda, which takes two minutes and fifty seconds, almost as long as the recapitulation. The development, then, is expanded from Classic proportions, and the coda is greatly expanded into a second development section. This freedom to modify traditional forms was what upset the critics. Expecting a balanced Classical structure, they assumed that this new structure was a mistake or lapse on the part of the composer from whom they expected more skill and taste.

Exposition

The movement opens with two tonic chords and the main theme (see Figure 28-2), which consists mostly of an arpeggiated chord. It is the sort of theme that lends itself well to transformation and development because it is so undefined.

First Theme — Cellos

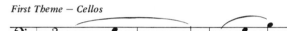

Figure 28-2. *Eroica,* first theme.

After modulating into the dominant key, Beethoven introduces the second theme (see Figure 28-3), a short idea that is passed around the woodwind section and first violins. Other ideas are stated along with these themes; the structural details of this movement can be argued endlessly. Some ideas are called major themes by some analysts and transitional material by others. For our purposes, it seems easier to concentrate on the major ideas which recur constantly in the work. A third important idea is the closing theme of the exposition (see Figure 28-4). Note that its rhythmic shape is the same as that of the second theme.

Figure 28-3. *Eroica,* second theme.

Figure 28-4. *Eroica,* closing theme.

Development

After the repeat of the exposition, the development begins with the second theme, then moves to a version of the first theme in various keys. A contrapuntal section, combining the second theme and a new counter-melody, comes next, followed by a long section based on syncopated transitional chords from the exposition. A new theme is introduced, in violation of Classical first-movement principles (see Figure 28-5). This new theme plays an important role in the long coda at the end of the movement.

Figure 28-5. *Eroica*, new idea in the development section.

Jean Gros. *Napolean Bonaparte*, 1790. (The Louvre, Paris)

FIGURE 28-6. LISTENING GUIDE

FIRST MOVEMENT, SYMPHONY NO. 3, *EROICA*, BY BEETHOVEN

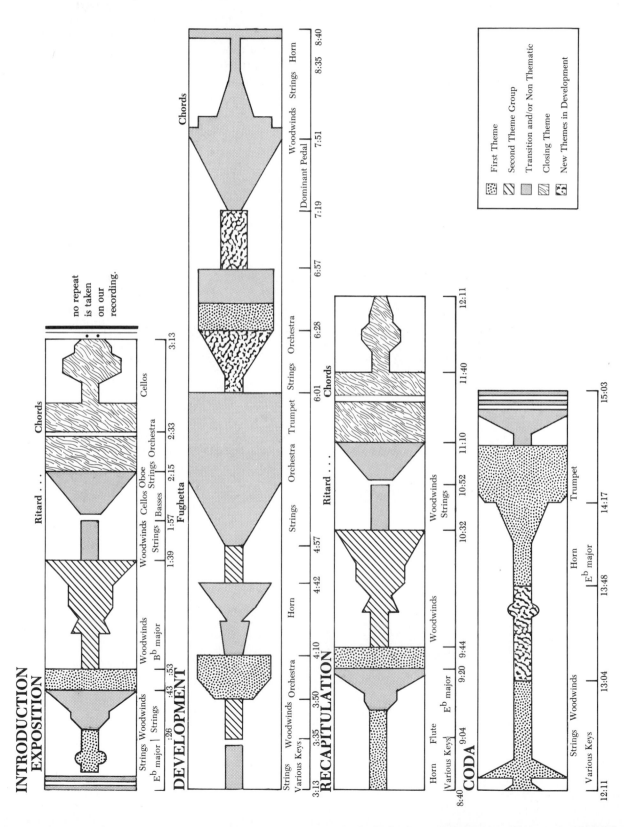

The end of the development is an interesting passage. While the strings are still winding down the tension of the development section and playing part of a dominant chord, one of the horns, as if by mistake, plays the beginning of the main theme, in the tonic key. The theme clashes harmonically, creating the impression that the horn player miscounted measures, and anticipates both the theme and key of the recapitulation. It is probably a rough joke, the Beethoven version of the tongue-in-cheek "wrong" turns and deceptive moves that were part of the Classic style.

Recapitulation

The recapitulation is quite regular. All of the main ideas return, now in the tonic key of *E*-flat. The beginning of the coda is another surprise. After the recapitulation of the closing material from the exposition, the coda begins by sliding down a minor third—*E*-flat, *D*-flat, *C*. This harmonic shift is the sort of move we expect at the beginning of a development section, and thus Beethoven signals his intention to write a modulatory second development instead of wrapping up the movement with a routine coda. During the coda, he uses the first theme, with counter-melodies we have not heard before, and the new idea introduced earlier in the development. Eventually, the coda winds down with a typical strong assertion and repetition of the tonic chord of *E*-flat. The movement, then, is clearly built on the Classical first-movement skeleton, but with a highly individual approach to structure and proportions and enough daring harmonies and bold strokes to make it a highly personal statement. Figure 28-6 is a listening guide to this first movement.

CHAPTER 29

Johannes Brahms
Symphony No. 3

Although Johannes Brahms was not born until six years after the death of Beethoven and died in 1897, on the threshold of the twentieth century, he is always linked with Beethoven. His best-known works are his four symphonies which are often considered a continuation of the symphonic approach of Beethoven. Romantic commentators were fond of calling Brahms's First Symphony "Beethoven's Tenth," and Brahms himself considered his symphonies to be a continuation of Beethoven's nonprogrammatic orchestral writing when other composers were turning to program music for orchestra.

BRAHMS'S LIFE

Brahms was born in 1833 in Hamburg, the son of a double bass player. As a youth, he received musical instruction and worked at various musical jobs, including playing the piano in dance halls. A tour as accompanist to a violinist,

This drawing by Wily von Beckerath shows Brahms at the piano.

Eduard Réményi, brought him to the attention of another violinist, Joseph Joachim, who introduced the young pianist and composer to Franz Liszt and Robert Schumann. This latter connection was extremely important in determining the course of Brahms's life. Schumann immediately announced to the world in an article in his journal that an exciting new composer had appeared on the scene. The article appointed Brahms the champion of the conservative school of German Romanticism, leading the struggle against Liszt and Wagner and their concept of the "New Music." One wonders what Brahms might have composed had his position in German culture not been decided for him by Schumann. Another lasting effect of this contact was the lifelong friendship between Brahms and Clara Schumann, Robert's wife, a performer and composer in her own right. While Schumann was still alive, Brahms was hopelessly in love with Clara. After Robert's death in 1856, when they could have married, they did not, but the friendship remained extremely important to Brahms.

View of Hamburg, Brahms's birthplace.

Brahms held several minor positions as a choral conductor. In fact, his reputation as a composer of choral and piano works was well established before his symphonic works were known. He was a diffident composer. He withheld his first symphony from publication or performance until 1876, long after it was completed. Nowadays he is best known for the four symphonies, which, although Romantic in breadth and color, are Classical in their lack of programmatic titles and effects and their concern for balanced structures. It is important to realize, however, that stylistically Brahms is not as far from Liszt or Wagner as one might assume from all the writings of the period. He is definitely a Romanticist, but by both his own inclination and appointment by the Schumann camp, he is on the Classical side of Romanticism. Liszt admired some of his works and vice versa, but their positions on opposite sides of the heated controversy about the future of German music kept them apart.

BRAHMS'S MUSIC

Besides his four symphonies, the works of Brahms include two concert overtures for orchestra and four concertos—two for piano, one for violin, and a double concerto for violin and cello. Among his compositions for smaller groups are a large number of piano works and works for various chamber groups. One of his better-known chamber works is a sonata for the unusual combination of French horn, violin, and piano. He also wrote about two hundred *Lieder* and songs for various combinations of solo voices. Famous among his choral works are the German Requiem and the *Schicksalslied* ("Song of Destiny").

SYMPHONY NO. 3, THIRD MOVEMENT

The orchestral style of Brahms is highly individual and immediately recognizable to a trained ear. His symphonies are marked by very broad themes, a fondness for rhythmic patterns that run counter to the established meter, and a particular style of orchestration. His orchestral sound is thick, particularly in the middle register: he consistently writes low parts for viola and the lower horns, giving his sound a dark quality.

The third movement of the Third Symphony is neither a Classical minuet and trio, nor a scherzo in Beethoven style, but a lyric slow movement. It features a broad, melancholy theme that is one of the most famous of Brahms's melodies (see Figure 29-1). The theme is played by the cellos in its first appearance, against gentle arpeggiated chords in the other strings, quiet wind chords, and pizzicato basses. When the theme is repeated, it appears in the first violins, against a new counter-melody in the cellos. After a transitional section, it appears again, this time in flute, oboe, and horn, with a descending counter-melody in the bassoons. A gentle contrasting section in A-flat major forms the B section, and then the A section returns. This time the theme is played first by a solo horn, then by the oboe; after the repeat of the transitional section, it returns once more, now in widely spaced octaves in first violins and cellos. A quiet coda concludes the movement. Like many Romantic slow movements, it consists basically of one melody, varied in orchestral color and given ample room to breathe and expand. Figure 29-2 outlines the structure and organization of this lovely movement.

Figure 29-1. Symphony No. 3, main theme, third movement.

FIGURE 29-2. LISTENING GUIDE

THIRD MOVEMENT, SYMPHONY NO. 3, BY BRAHMS

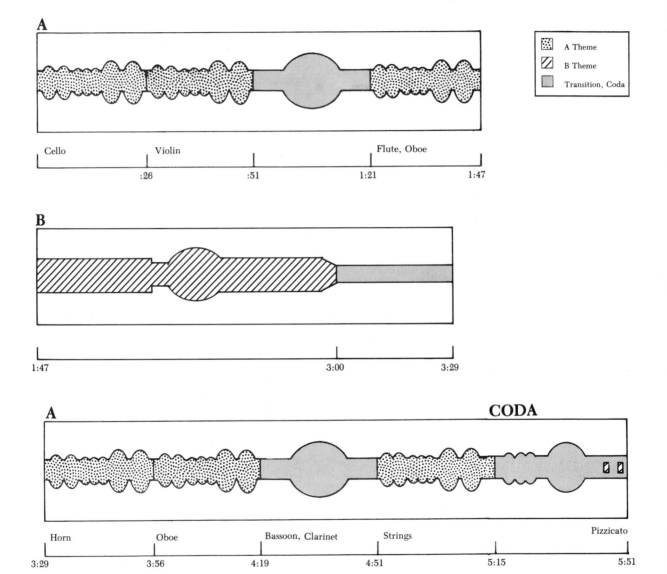

CHAPTER 30

Hector Berlioz
Symphonie
Fantastique

Chapter 27 discussed the Romantic tendency to deal with the orchestra not only as a vehicle for playing abstract symphonies, but also as a giant palette with which to portray literary stories, extremes of Romantic feelings, and colorful pictures. To this end, new symphonic forms were developed: the program symphony, the concert overture, and the symphonic poem. This chapter deals with a famous program symphony. Subsequent chapters will discuss the other new orchestral forms.

BERLIOZ'S LIFE

The life and career of Hector Berlioz illustrate the aims and intensity of artistic life in the Romantic era. Most of his musical works were written on literary themes, exemplifying perfectly the Romantic notion that music is the supreme art, the place where all of the other arts are joined and brought to their highest form. Berlioz was born in 1803 in a small town outside Grenoble. His father was a country doctor, who planned a medical career for his son. The boy had no musical instruction except a small amount of theory training and lessons on the flute and guitar. At eighteen he was sent to Paris to study medicine, but he dropped out of school to pursue his interest in music, eventually enrolling for study at the *Conservatoire* in Paris, where he concentrated on study of scores of great operas of the past.

He fell madly in love with Harriet Smithson, an Irish actress who starred in a touring Shakespeare troupe. When they married, his youthful ardor cooled somewhat, but the early years of their marriage were the most productive of his life. Besides working as a composer and conductor, he wrote musical criticism for Parisian journals and published an important treatise on orchestration and several other articles on various musical topics. His writings are now available in English translations. His *Memoires* make fascinating reading and give us great insight into the Romantic mind.

Berlioz never achieved in Paris the kind of recognition he thought he deserved, although French readers respected him as a literary figure. His music was better accepted in Germany and Russia, and his tours of those countries as a conductor were quite successful. His worst frustration was the long postponement of his opera *Les Troyens* ("The Trojans") which was never presented in its entirety in his lifetime. He died in 1869, a disappointed man.

BERLIOZ'S MUSIC

Berlioz is best known as a proponent of programmatic music, and most of his works have literary themes. *Les Troyens* is based on Vergil's *Aeneid*, the Latin epic about the fall of Troy and the founding of Rome. It is a huge work, which lasts more than six hours. One opera company devised the stratagem of presenting it in two parts, and the only section performed in Berlioz's lifetime was the first part, about the fall of Troy. The first full performance took place in 1969, to celebrate the centenary of Berlioz's death. Among his more frequently performed works are *Harold in Italy*, a program symphony with solo viola, based on Byron; *The Corsair*, an overture, also based on Byron; *The Damnation of Faust*, based on Goethe; and the dramatic symphony *Romeo and Juliet* and the *King Lear* Overture, based on Shakespeare. Besides *Les Troyens*, Berlioz wrote two other operas, *Béatrice et Bénedict* and *Benvenuto Cellini*. The introduction to the second act of the latter work is often performed as a separate orchestral piece, under the title *Roman Carnival* Overture. Berlioz also composed two massive works for chorus and orchestra, the *Te Deum* and the *Requiem*; one of the great moments in Romantic music is the brass entrance in the "Tuba mirum" of the *Dies Irae* section of the *Requiem*.

Metropolitan Opera production of *Les Troyens* by Berlioz.

Berlioz had great influence on late Romantic composers; his brilliant orchestral effects, his genius for transforming a theme to represent different moods, and his fondness for literary themes were characteristic of music of the second half of the nineteenth century.

SYMPHONIE FANTASTIQUE

Berlioz composed the *Symphonie Fantastique* in the early stages of his consuming love for Harriet Smithson. It was completed in 1830, three years before their marriage. He describes the story of the work in these words:

J. H. Fuseli, *The Nightmare*, 1781.

> A young musician of morbid sensibility and ardent imagina-
> tion in a paroxysm of lovesick despair has poisoned himself
> with opium. The drug, too weak to kill, plunges him into a
> heavy sleep accompanied by strange visions. His sensations,
> feelings, and memories are translated in his sick brain into
> musical images and ideas. The beloved one herself becomes for
> him a melody, a recurrent theme that haunts him everywhere.

The five movements of the work are depictions of the various images that flood
the musician's fevered brain. The first depicts his unhappiness and melancholy
before meeting his beloved and the volcanic love she inspires in him. The second
is a ball, during which he meets her again. The third is a pastoral scene of great
tranquility, but he becomes agitated as he worries about losing her. The fourth
movement is a march to the scaffold; he dreams he has killed his beloved and is
being marched to the guillotine. The final movement, called the "Dream of a
Witches' Sabbath," is his vision of hellish punishment after his death: the beloved and a troop of grotesque spirits torture and mock him. This program is so
typically Romantic as to be almost a parody of Romantic sentiments. It provides
opportunity for all of the great Romantic themes—love, melancholy, horror.

Two characteristics of the symphony are especially notable. First, the melody
representing the beloved appears in all five movements, but changed radically in
each appearance to represent different feelings. Figure 30-1 shows the melody in

its original form. Figure 30-2 shows the same melody as it appears in the final movement. It is recognizable as the same tune, but its meaning is entirely different. Instead of a broad, lyric theme, it is now a trivial dance tune in 6/8 meter. The grace notes and trills impart a mocking quality to the melody.

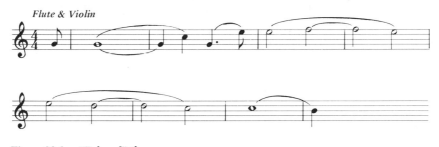

Flute & Violin

Figure 30-1. "Beloved" theme.

Figure 30-2. "Beloved" theme, fifth movement.

The second important characteristic of this symphony is its brilliant orchestration. Every page of the score has unusual effects that tellingly convey the extremes of feeling with which the work is concerned. The orchestra Berlioz writes for is huge. The woodwinds include two flutes and piccolo, two oboes and English horn, clarinets in various keys, and bassoons. The brass section includes four French horns, two cornets, two trumpets, three trombones, and two tubas, and often functions as an independent brass band. The percussion section includes two sets of tympani, bass drum, snare drum, cymbals, and bells. The large string section is used in a variety of imaginative special effects, and two harps are added for particular passages. The score is a compendium of Romantic orchestral effects, and the work can be enjoyed as a study in orchestral sound.

"DREAM OF A WITCHES' SABBATH"

The final movement of the symphony is a classic example of the Romantic fondness for the grotesque. It opens with an eerie introduction: divided and muted strings play high tremolo sounds, and woodwinds and a muted horn play fanfares. The first main section is the parody of the beloved's theme, already discussed. It is scored for E-flat clarinet, an unusual instrument with a piercing, sassy sound. A transitional section winds down to ominous low string unisons, and we hear the bells tolling, which introduce a section based on the *Dies Irae* chant from the Requiem Mass. Figure 30-3 is the opening of the original chant. The theme appears first in long notes, for two tubas and bassoons (Figure 30-4). Then it appears in notes of half that length, for horns and trombones (Figure 30-5). Finally, it appears in woodwinds and strings, in still shorter notes, in the meter of a jig (Figure 30-6). This process of **diminution**, making the note values shorter and shorter, here serves the function of turning a somber, ominous idea into a grotesque mockery.

Di - es i - rae, di - es il - la

Figure 30-3.   Original *Dies Irae* chant.

Figure 30-4.   Introduction of theme, tubas and bassoon.

Figure 30-5.   For horns and trombones.

Figure 30-6.   For woodwinds and strings in jig meter.

Cello

Figure 30-7.   Subject of fugato section, Witches' Round Dance.

The next section of the movement is the Witches' Round Dance, **a fugato** section based on the subject shown in Figure 30-7. This section illustrates well the special uses to which polyphonic writing was put in the Classic and Romantic periods. It generally serves to heighten tension in a developmental section. Here, the thick polyphonic texture and the fast meter combine to create a feeling of gathering tension and inevitability. Later in the movement, the *Dies Irae* and Witches' Dance themes are combined, after which a loud and brilliant coda brings the work to a dramatic conclusion.

FIGURE 30-8. LISTENING GUIDE

BERLIOZ 285

FIFTH MOVEMENT, *SYMPHONIE FANTASTIQUE*, BY BERLIOZ

■	"Beloved" Theme
■	Dies Irae Theme
□	Witches' Sabbath Fugato
■	Introduction, Coda, Transition

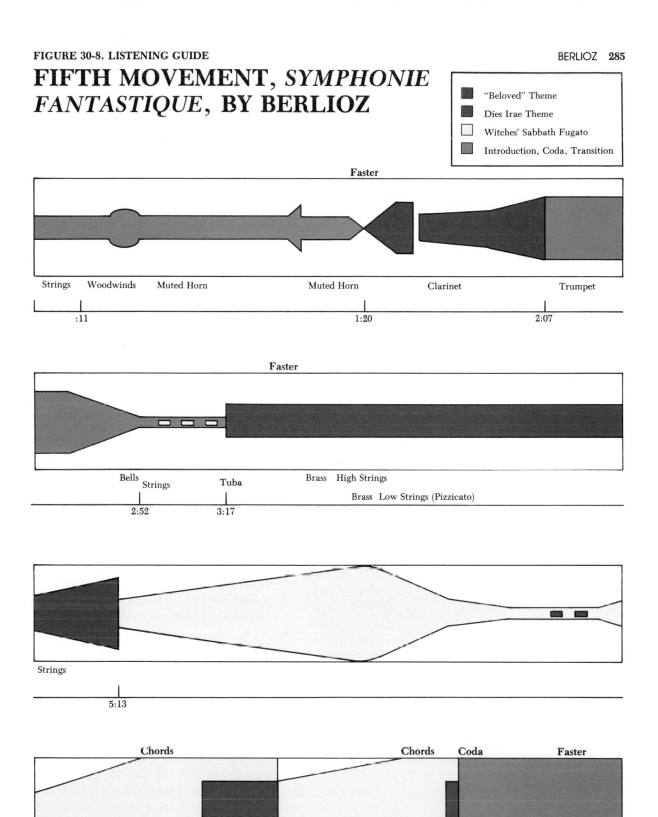

Faster

Strings Woodwinds Muted Horn Muted Horn Clarinet Trumpet

:11 1:20 2:07

Faster

Bells Strings Tuba Brass High Strings Brass Low Strings (Pizzicato)

2:52 3:17

Strings

5:13

Chords Chords Coda **Faster**

Brass

7:53 8:13 8:52 8:59 9:34

CHAPTER **31**

Peter Ilyich Tchaikovsky Romeo and Juliet

TCHAIKOVSKY'S LIFE

Peter Ilyich Tchaikovsky lived from 1840 until 1893. He was born in a remote province of Russia, the son of a government official. He was trained for a career in civil service and did not begin formal music study until he was twenty-three, when he commenced composition studies with Anton Rubinstein at the Conservatory of St. Petersburg. After graduation, he taught harmony for twelve years at the Moscow Conservatory. At that point began an important relationship for him. Matilda von Meck, a wealthy woman, decided to support him so he would be free to compose. The relationship lasted for thirteen years, although, in Victorian fashion, both parties agreed that they should not meet. They left a lengthy correspondence, which provides another glimpse into the fascinating relationships in the lives of Romantic composers. Tchaikovsky was also married briefly to a former student; the marriage ended in a legal separation, which caused him great depression.

Tchaikovsky achieved considerable fame. His music appealed both to the rising tide of nationalism in Russia and also to Western tastes. He was invited to America in 1891 to take part in the ceremonies to open Carnegie Hall and was

Edouard Manet. *Luncheon on the Grass*, 1863 (The Louvre, Paris).

impressed by the cordiality and generosity of the Americans. At the age of fifty-three, he traveled to St. Petersburg to conduct his Sixth Symphony and, while there, contracted cholera and died.

Tchaikovsky is a fine example of the tension in the nineteenth century between nationalism and the standard European musical language. Although composers like Chopin, Liszt, and Tchaikovsky made much of their "foreign" backgrounds—foreign to Central Europe, at least—they were all composers in the European tradition. Occasionally, they used folk themes or rhythms in their works, but their training was in the standard European tradition, and their fame was international. The conservatories that sprang up outside Central Europe, in places like Budapest, Warsaw, and Moscow, were carefully designed to be copies of the older conservatories in places like Paris and Vienna, and Central Europeans were imported to head these institutions. It is clear that the countries surrounding Central Europe had a cultural inferiority complex, as did the United States in the nineteenth century. The hallmark of cultural maturity was always the presence of artists and composers who had already been recognized in the major cultural capitals. Later in the century, composers began to turn their backs on the European tradition and to study their own cultures for musical ideas. Tchaikovsky is not a "Russian" composer in the sense that Mussorgsky and other later Russian composers are; Liszt is not a Hungarian composer in the same way that Bartók is in the twentieth century.

TCHAIKOVSKY'S WORKS

Tchaikovsky wrote music in many genres. Among his best-known works are the symphonies. The most famous is the Sixth, the *Pathetique*, which is filled with the melancholy for which he is famous. He also wrote ten symphonic poems, of which the best-known are *Romeo and Juliet* and the *1812* Overture. Of his eight operas, only *Eugene Onegin* is performed regularly. His ballet music is immensely popular. The best-known ballet scores in the entire repertoire—*Swan Lake*, *Sleeping Beauty*, and *The Nutcracker*—were composed by Tchaikovsky. His Piano Concerto in *B*-flat Minor and the Violin Concerto in *D* Major are still performed frequently; the Piano Concerto is one of the most frequently recorded works in the entire classical repertoire. Tchaikovsky also wrote more than one hundred songs, and numerous works for piano solo and chamber groups.

There is good reason for the popularity of Tchaikovsky's music for orchestra. First of all, it is accessible and gloriously Romantic. It is filled with bittersweet melancholy, themes of great lyricism or grandeur, thunderous climaxes, and passages of great drama. He is also a master of orchestration. The beautiful and novel effects in the suite from the *Nutcracker* ballet are a well-known example of his skill with orchestral colors. Another facet of his compositional style is his fine instinct for structure. His works are generally balanced, coherent, and tightly knit—qualities that are not always present in late Romantic music of similar expressive power. He generally knows when to stop, although he has an annoying tendency to resort to long passages of his trademark violin scales to stretch transitional sections. The scales in the *1812* Overture are a famous example.

ROMEO AND JULIET

Romeo and Juliet is not only one of Tchaikovsky's best-known works, it is also a fine example of Romantic program music, based on Shakespeare's story of the star-crossed lovers. While Tchaikovsky called the work an "overture-fantasy," classifying it exactly is not an important question. It could have been entitled a symphonic poem, because it is a one-movement orchestral work based on a literary theme. Because the story is so timeless and familiar—as you know, the story has been the basis of several films and of a musical, Leonard Bernstein's *West Side Story*—it provides a perfect example for us of how Romantic composers used literary materials as the basis for their compositions. The music is not a literal depiction of the story, because music is not the best medium for narrative details. What music does depict effectively are the feelings behind a story, and *Romeo and Juliet* is very successful at that level. If the work were not presented with a specific literary title, however, it could refer just as well to any

Performance of Tchaikovsky's ballet *The Sleeping Beauty*.

Romantic story, provided it contained the elements of conflict, love, and tragedy that are so strong in the music.

Themes

Tchaikovsky depicts only the main feelings of the story: the doomed love, the conflict between the families, and a generally religious or tragic feeling we can identify with Friar Laurence. Each of these feelings is portrayed by a definite theme. What strikes us strongly in the work is the breadth and spaciousness of the main themes, the way Tchaikovsky transforms and develops those themes, and the eloquent way they convey our feelings about the tragic story.

Edgar Degas, well-known for his impressionistic interpretations of theater life, creates in *The Musicians of the Theater* an interesting relationship between dancers and the orchestra.

Orchestration

The other foreground element that strikes us immediately is his effective use of orchestral colors. Among the striking effects are the organ-like woodwind writing in the Friar Laurence music; the use of harp for soft, lyric effects; the solo English horn passages; the biting attacks in the strings to depict conflict; the use of muted strings in the introduction to the love theme; the addition of piccolo, bass drum, and cymbals to the climactic sections; the soaring strings in the love theme; the opposition of wind and string choirs for color contrasts; and the use of trumpets and horns throughout the work. As you listen to the work, you may notice other striking effects. The entire piece is filled with skillful orchestral writing.

Structure

The structure of the work is clear and easy to follow, once we realize that the dimensions of the main sections are very large. Listening to Romantic music demands that we grant the composer sufficient time to paint in the broad and sweeping strokes that are characteristic of the Romantic style. This one-movement work is about twenty minutes long, as long as an entire Classical symphony. In many ways, it resembles a Classical sonata-allegro form, with an exposition, development, and recapitulation; but each section is quite long. What we interpret as an introduction, for example, is about five minutes long, as long as most movements of Classical symphonies. Granting the composer the time to repeat and transform his materials, however, we can hear a very clear structure, which utilizes a few main musical ideas that are easy to recognize. This work illustrates that the focus of the Romantic style is not on tight motivic structure and development, but on color, lyricism, and feeling.

Introduction

The work begins with a somber religious idea, stated by two clarinets in the low range and two bassoons. That ideas builds gradually, interspersed with different ideas, to form a very long introduction (see Figure 31-1).

Figure 31-1. Friar Laurence theme, introduction.

Exposition

What feels like the exposition section begins with a new theme, brusque and aggressive, which represents the conflict between the two families (see Figure 31-2). After a mini-development section, which presents the conflict theme in canonic form, string scales (the Tchaikovsky trademark) and syncopated chords build to a large climax, and the conflict theme is repeated by the full orchestra.

Figure 31-2.   *Romeo and Juliet* conflict theme.

Having wound the tension tight, Tchaikovsky must then release it slowly, by gradually diminishing the number of instruments, the dynamic level, and the rhythmic activity. When things are wound down almost to nothing, he introduces a lyric love theme, presenting it first in the English horn, doubled by muted violas (see Figure 31-3). Muted strings play a crescendo passage, which leads to a repeat of the love music, this time for full orchestra. We could predict that any Romantic composer would not simply state a sighing, aching theme like this one; naturally he would repeat it several times in varied orchestral colors.

Figure 31-3.   *Romeo and Juliet* love theme.

Development

The rest of the piece works out the possibilities of these three themes. The development section combines the theme from the introduction with fragments of the conflict theme; we feel the tension increasing. Note that the love theme does not appear in the development: it would not work well in this fragmentary, combinatorial technique. Besides, the function of the development is to increase the tension, preparing for the return of the tonic key at the beginning of the recapitulation; lyric themes dissipate tension rather than tightening it. The development reaches a climax in a series of syncopated full orchestra chords, after which another section of Tchaikovsky's string scales leads to the recapitulation.

Recapitulation

The recapitulation begins with the conflict theme in full orchestra. The love theme returns, in a somewhat different orchestration, and itself builds to a secondary climax. It gradually dissolves into the conflict theme, which again builds to a climax of great power. That tension is again wound down and reduced to a drum roll, which introduces the coda, based on fragments of previous material—the love theme, now in a tragic version, against muffled drums, the Friar Laurence music, and then the love theme again. After a peaceful ending, Tchaikovsky tacks on a few loud chords, in a rhythm reminiscent of the conflict theme.

This work is a perfect example of the Romantic approach to structure. In one sense, the work is self-indulgent; the structure is expanded to make space for the long crescendos and diminuendos, and to build toward the crashing climaxes. Themes are presented and repeated with the details of the orchestration changed. But the structural underpinning is still there, to keep the music coherent and to keep us involved in its progress. If there are dead spots where the music seems not to be going anywhere, we are beguiled by the skillful surface details. The more we understand this work, the better we can appreciate the fine balance Tchaikovsky achieves between coherent structure and Romantic expression. We can also understand how the Romantic ideal of expression, in the hands of less skillful composers, could produce works of endless repetition and tiresome striving for effect. For all its length and power, *Romeo and Juliet* seems shorter than it really is and perfectly logical and coherent.

The listening guide (Figure 31-4) outlines the structure, so that the coherence of the work will be clear as you listen to it.

FIGURE 31-4. LISTENING GUIDE

ROMEO AND JULIET, BY TCHAIKOVSKY

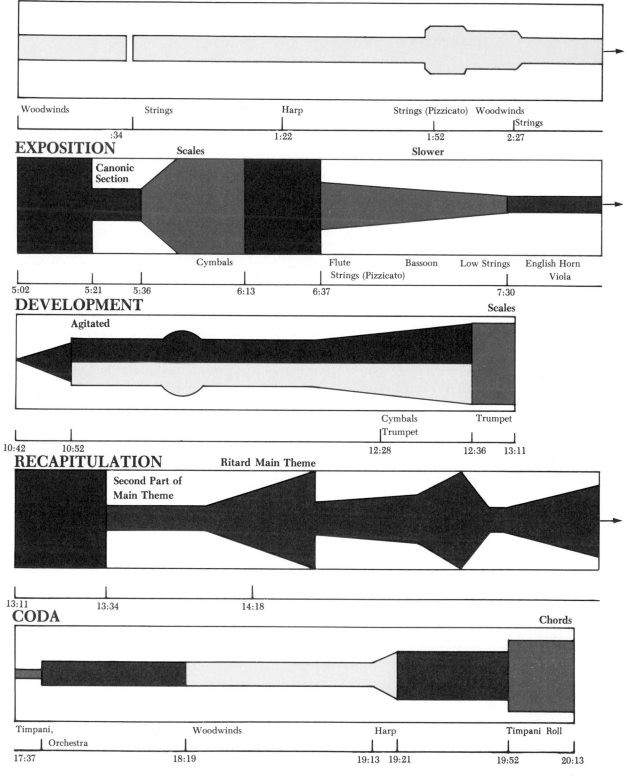

INTRODUCTION

Woodwinds   Strings   Harp   Strings (Pizzicato)   Woodwinds

Strings

:34   1:22   1:52   2:27

EXPOSITION

Scales   Slower

Canonic Section

Cymbals   Flute   Bassoon   Low Strings   English Horn

Strings (Pizzicato)   Viola

5:02   5:21   5:36   6:13   6:37   7:30

DEVELOPMENT

Scales

Agitated

Cymbals   Trumpet

Trumpet

10:42   10:52   12:28   12:36   13:11

RECAPITULATION

Ritard Main Theme

Second Part of Main Theme

13:11   13:34   14:18

CODA

Chords

Timpani,   Woodwinds   Harp   Timpani Roll

Orchestra

17:37   18:19   19:13   19:21   19:52   20:13

Friar Lawrence Theme
Conflict Theme
Love Theme
Transitional Material

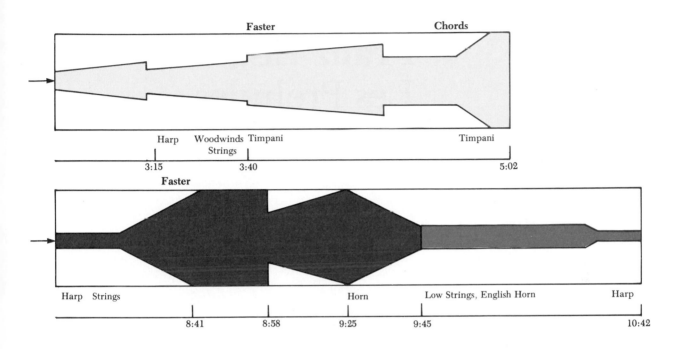

Faster   Chords

Harp   Woodwinds Timpani   Timpani
        Strings
       3:15   3:40   5:02

Faster

Harp   Strings   Horn   Low Strings, English Horn   Harp
            8:41   8:58   9:25   9:45   10:42

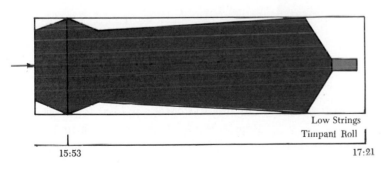

Low Strings
Timpani Roll
15:53   17:21

CHAPTER 32

Franz Liszt
Les Préludes

Besides the program symphony and concert overture, Romantic composers developed another genre of orchestral composition—the symphonic poem or "tone poem," a way of utilizing the orchestra to portray literary or pictorial themes without the limitations of traditional structures. The composer most closely associated with the symphonic poem is Franz Liszt.

LISZT'S LIFE

The life and career of Liszt read like a Romantic novel. He was born in 1811 at Raiding, a town in what was then Hungary. His father was a cellist who had played in Haydn's orchestra at the Esterhazy court. At the age of ten Liszt studied the piano for one year with Carl Czerny in Vienna. Czerny had been a pupil of Beethoven's and was the author of important technical studies for the piano. Liszt then began a career as a virtuoso pianist. He lived for eleven years in Paris, where he was welcome in the salons and rubbed shoulders with all of the great artists, writers, and musicians of that period, including Berlioz and Chopin. His fame as a virtuoso spread rapidly. He also met the Countess Marie d'Agoult, who wrote novels under the pen name of Daniel Stern. He and the

Countess lived together for five years in Switzerland and had three children. The second was Cosima, who later became the wife of Richard Wagner. After separating from the Countess, Liszt continued his triumphant concert tours. He met another noblewoman, Princess Carolyne Sayne-Wittgenstein, and lived with her for thirteen years at Weimar, where he accepted a post as music director for the Grand Duke. During the Weimar years, he worked tirelessly to see that the works of composers he admired, notably Berlioz and Wagner, were performed.

Upon leaving Weimar, Liszt traveled to Rome, studied theology, and was received into a monastic order. He continued to compose and perform. With his dramatic mane of grey hair and the black robes of a priest, his appearance became even more theatrical, and his fame continued to spread. He also held piano classes for unusually talented young people. Some of his students have left accounts of his teaching, testifying to his unfailing patience and helpfulness. He lived long enough to see the eventual triumph of his son-in-law, Wagner, and attended the opening of the opera house at Bayreuth built specifically for performances of Wagner's operas. Liszt died in Bayreuth in 1886, at the age of seventy-five.

It is hard for modern people to appreciate the life and importance of Liszt. Few performers have had as successful a virtuoso career as he did. Adoring women swooned at his appearance and fought for souvenirs. His love affairs seem like incidents from a Romantic novel. But he was also an influential teacher, a performer who changed the world's notions of piano performance, a great composer, and a selfless supporter of generations of younger composers. As one of the first "nationalists," proud of his Hungarian birth, he helped to set in motion that important trend in Romantic music.

LISZT'S MUSIC

For Piano

As we would expect, Liszt wrote many important works for the piano, most of them combining Romantic lyricism and expressiveness with difficult technical demands. Among his best-known works for solo piano are the *Transcendental Etudes*, several sonatas, and nineteen *Hungarian Rhapsodies*. He also wrote for piano and orchestra. The most frequently heard of these works are the Concerto in *E*-flat major, and the *Totentanz* ("Dance of Death"), consisting of variations on the *Dies Irae* theme.

For Orchestra

His compositions for orchestra consist entirely of program music. He wrote two program symphonies, the *Faust* and *Dante* symphonies. His best-known works for orchestra are his twelve symphonic poems; he invented both the term and the

This painting by J. Danhauser depicts Franz Liszt and his friends Musset, Victor Hugo, George Sand, Berlioz, Rossini and Countess D'Agoult.

genre. As mentioned earlier, a symphonic poem is a one-movement orchestral work on a literary or pictorial theme, which derives its structure not from any traditional musical structure, but from the story with which it is associated.

Liszt also composed a number of songs and large choral works, including several Masses and three oratorios on religious themes. His most famous works, however, remain the compositions for piano and for orchestra. His chief compositional technique is **thematic transformation**, a way of varying a musical idea of neutral meaning, by changing harmonies, rhythmic shape, orchestral color, and other musical details, so that the same theme has totally different meanings in different contexts. Later in the chapter, we will see how Liszt uses this technique in one of his symphonic poems. One striking example of thematic transformation is the *Faust* Symphony. In that work, there are three movements, each representing one of the major characters of the legend: Faust, Gretchen, and Mephistopheles. In the third movement, no new themes appear; all of the Mephistopheles music consists of parodies of the earlier Faust themes. This technique makes the philosophical point that man's destruction comes not from an external supernatural power, but from the dark side of his own humanity.

The same point needs to be made here that was made earlier in our discussion of Tchaikovsky's *Romeo and Juliet*. The music of these and similar composers moves at a very leisurely pace by our standards. Themes are repeated and varied, using all of the resources of the large Romantic orchestra, and at times the musical rhetoric seems padded. Liszt has a tendency to stretch the loud climaxes, causing an overly grand, bombastic feeling. Still, we can permit his self-indulgent moments; his genius for thematic transformation and his skill at orchestration keep us interested at all times.

LES PRÉLUDES

Les Préludes, the best known of the Liszt symphonic poems, was orginally written as the overture to a larger work for male chorus. In 1856, Liszt published the present independent version, revised and enlarged from the earlier overture. The program comes from a poem by Alphonse de Lamartine, which deals in a general way with heroism and the Romantic notion of the meaning of life. The work is long and dramatic. It consists entirely of a few musical ideas, transformed and varied, and transitional material to connect the large sections.

Themes

The germ motive (Figure 32-1) of the entire work is three notes, a descending half step and a rising fourth. In the introduction, the motive appears as the beginning of a string passage (see Figure 32-2). Later in the first section, the motive appears in two thematic guises, the first, majestic (see Figure 32-3), and the second, lyric (see Figure 32-4). In the second theme, the motive's opening half step has become a whole step, but the motive's identity is still clear.

Figure 32-1.   The germ motive.

Figure 32-2.   Introduction.

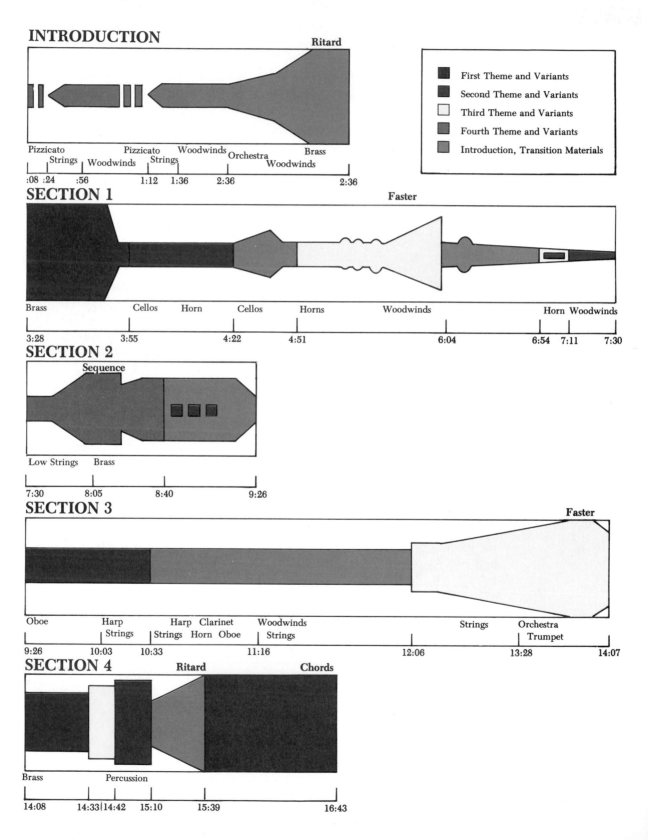

FIGURE 32-6. LISTENING GUIDE
LES PRÉLUDES, BY LISZT

Figure 32-3. Theme A, first section.

Figure 32-4. Theme B, first section.

A contrasting lyric theme (see Figure 32-5) is important throughout the entire work. Although we hear this melody as a new idea, it may also be viewed as an expanded version of the germ idea, with a descending whole step instead of the original half step and intervening neighboring notes.

Figure 32-5. Theme C.

Structure

The work falls into clearly divided large sections, which are not organized into any of the Classic forms, although we can hear a definite logic and coherence to the work. After the introduction, a long first section presents all three themes, at great leisure and with repetitions in varied orchestral colors. A second section feels like a sort of development; it is agitated and utilizes fragments of previous materials, although the major material is a fourth version of the germ motive. A third section is peaceful and brings back the B and C themes from the first section, thus functioning as a sort of recapitulation. The final section brings back material from the B and C themes, now in a martial guise. The work ends with one last loud presentation of the majestic A theme, back in the home key of C major.

Keys do not define structure in this work. Like most late Romantic composers, Liszt is fond of sudden shifts into other keys, often a third away from the original key. Modulating by a third, instead of by a fourth or fifth, as was common in Classic compositions, gives the music a feeling of surging forward that was dear to late Romantic composers. The overall key of this piece is C major. Other important keys are E major, a major third up from C; A-flat major, a major third downwards; and A minor, a minor third down from C. But keys are not used

This caricature of Franz Liszt shows him performing one of his flamboyant compositions.

structurally; Liszt is as likely to change keys in the first or last sections as he is in the developmental one.

Despite all of the repetitions in all of the sections and the overuse of the sequence technique in the second section, this work is coherent and satisfying, marked by strong, recognizable themes and colorful orchestration. The listening guide (Figure 32-6) outlines the major structural events in the work. Remember that each of the themes is derived from the three-note germ motive.

CHAPTER **33**
Frédéric Chopin
Polonaise in A-Flat

So far in this section, we have dealt with Romantic music for orchestra. Other media of performance were also extremely important during this era. We turn in this chapter and the next two to small forms, music for piano and for solo singer. The first composer to consider is Frédéric Chopin, one of the most important composers of Romantic piano music.

CHOPIN'S LIFE

Frédéric Chopin was born near Warsaw, Poland, in 1810, the son of a French father and a Polish mother. His father taught French to the children of Polish aristocrats, and young Frédéric had a fine education and early musical training. He performed on the piano as a child prodigy, and by the age of twenty had achieved fame as both a performer and composer. In 1831, he settled in Paris, where he lived until the end of his life.

In some ways, Chopin's life does not fit the standard tragic Romantic pattern; in other ways, it does. He was never troubled by poverty and enjoyed considerable fame and adulation throughout his life. In Paris he became the darling

A fan caricature of famous Paris personalities shows Chopin and George Sand in the center.

of several salons, where people like Victor Hugo, Dumas, Balzac, Liszt, and Berlioz met to discuss Romantic art. One of these salons was presided over by a woman novelist, Aurore Dudevant, who was a shockingly liberated woman for her time. She wrote under the pen name of George Sand and is famous for dressing in men's clothes and smoking cigars. Chopin's relationship with George Sand was complex and stormy. Apparently, she was a combination mother, lover, nagging manager, and nemesis. It was one of those Romantic relationships that invites speculation and Freudian analysis, and Chopin has been the subject of at least one sentimental film, *A Song to Remember*, an opus of the 1940s starring Cornel Wilde as Chopin and Merle Oberon as a somewhat idealized George Sand. Late in his short life, Chopin contracted tuberculosis and died at thirty-nine, at the height of his fame. In grisly Romantic fashion, he left instructions that his body should be buried in Paris, but that his heart should be removed and sent home to Poland for burial.

CHOPIN'S MUSIC

Although Chopin tried his hand at composing songs and some works for piano with other instruments, his fame rests on his works for solo piano. Two concertos for piano and orchestra are sometimes performed, but are not regarded as his greatest works: he was no master of writing for the orchestra. But he was a master of the piano, both as performer and composer. His works have a personal style that is immediately recognizable, a combination of beautiful melodies and a highly individual approach to harmony. He frequently writes chromatic passing harmonies within a clear harmonic progression, so that momentary strokes of harmonic color delight the ear without interrupting the broader flow of harmonic logic. His writing is always what musicians call "pianistic," that is, he knows exactly what will work on the piano. His passing harmonies, for example, seem to result from the natural movement of the fingers along the keyboard.

There are two other facets of Chopin's style that we must understand to appreciate his music. His structures are fairly simple. He does not develop themes motivically, as Beethoven does, but usually presents one idea, then a constrasting idea, then the first again. The foreground elements are the important ones—the melodies, the harmonic touches, the varied use of the instrument—and the structure is usually a very clear A-B-A. Second, his approach to rhythm is very individual. His waltzes are not dance music, and his music loses all meaning and expressive power if it is played in strict time. He requires that the performer use **rubato**, a subtle approach to time in which the rhythm shifts sensitively. Like many Romantic techniques, rubato playing is hard to master and easy to overdo, but necessary to make the music make any sense. Overdone, it deprives the music of any rhythmic drive or forward propulsion; without it, the music is lifeless. Performances of Chopin's music vary considerably from performer to performer; it would be interesting to compare the subtle differences between two performances of the same piece.

Chopin's music for solo piano exhibits great variety. He composed lyric miniatures with long, singing melodic lines, études which stretch the limits of both instrument and performer, waltzes of bittersweet charm, nocturnes of almost impressionistic gentleness, and dramatic, show-stopping recital pieces. His works are still studied and performed by pianists. They require mature sensitivity, variety of touch and expression, and perfect technical control at all speeds and dynamic levels. He developed the possibilities of the new piano more than any other single composer, and many other Romantic composers for the piano learned from his approach to composing for this instrument.

In the last few years, there has been a renewal of interest among music historians in Romantic music in general and in the ways Romantic composers worked in particular. Studies are being made of composers' sketchbooks and working papers to see how they actually conceived and developed their works. To their surprise, historians have discovered that Chopin worked with extreme care and precision, revising and rewriting as much as Beethoven did. His works often create the impression of spontaneity, as if they came to him in a reverie on some gloomy afternoon as he mused at the piano. Like the works of skillful song composers, Chopin's piano pieces often have an artless simplicity that results from his complete mastery and careful working out of musical ideas and structures.

POLONAISE IN A-FLAT

The Polonaise in *A*-flat is one of Chopin's best-known works, satisfying both to play and to hear. The title means "Polish," which actually applies only to the rhythmic pattern of the main theme. There is no attempt to quote native Polish melodies, harmonies, or dance forms. The piece shows off all of the piano's possibilities for big sounds: there are lots of two-fisted chords, rapid octaves, runs, and rolled chords. Although there are contrasting sections in more lyric style, the overall effect is assertive and majestic (the piece is marked *Maestoso*, "majestic"), and provides the challenge of technical difficulty without ever resorting to effects for their own sake.

Structure

A Section

Structurally, the piece falls into three large sections of uneven proportions. A dramatic introduction with drum-roll effects leads to the main theme (see Figure 33-1). The first theme is then repeated in a louder version, written in widely spaced octaves. A transitional section leads to a quieter theme in *F* minor (see Figure 33-2). The second idea is followed by a repeat of the main theme, in its louder, widely spaced setting.

Main Theme

Figure 33-1.   Polonaise, first theme.

Figure 33-2.   Polonaise, second theme.

B Section

The middle section begins with an abrupt shift into *E* major, a harmonic shift of a major third, a favorite Romantic move. The two keys are related more than one might think. *A*-flat, the tonic of the A section, is the same note as *G* sharp, which is the third of a chord in *E* major, the tonic of the B section. The first section of this middle part consists of a quiet but strong melody (see Figure 33-3), played against a background of rapid left-hand octaves which continue for a long time. This theme, after being presented and repeated, ends in *D*-sharp major, and another abrupt harmonic shift leads us back into *E* major for another repeat of the first theme of the B section.

Figure 33-3. Polonaise, *B* section, first theme.

Two subsidiary melodies are briefly presented. The second one is the more important, because it is a typical lyric Chopin theme, filled with ornamental dissonant notes and interesting turns (see Figure 33-4). It is also important because it leads back into the return of the A section.

Figure 33-4. Polonaise, transitional theme of B section.

A Section

The A section is greatly curtailed when it returns. We hear one statement of the main theme; as we would expect, it appears in its louder, more dramatic form. Next comes a coda built out of fragments of the A theme. The lack of symmetry in the form is not at all disturbing as one listens to the piece. The long opening A section (which itself is a kind of A-B-A form with contrasting material in the middle) and the long B section seem to require no more of a return of A than Chopin provides. The piece works very well, provided it is played by someone who can handle the technical demands comfortably and who is aware enough of the style to play the piece as freely as it should be played.

Daytime social activity, in the Paris of Chopin's time centered around fashionable cafés such as this.

FIGURE 33-5. LISTENING GUIDE

POLONAISE IN A-FLAT, BY CHOPIN

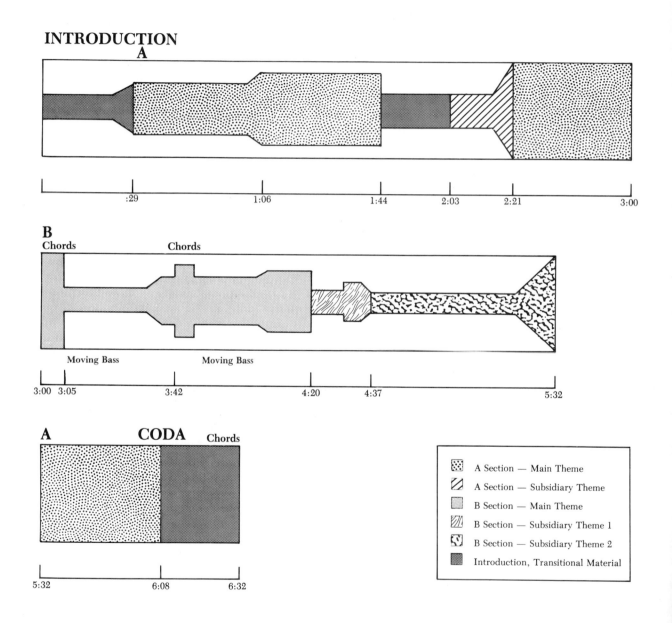

CHAPTER 34

The Romantic Lied
Franz Schubert,
Erlkönig

SCHUBERT'S LIFE

In many ways, the life of Franz Schubert is an embodiment of the Romantic notion of the artist as a lonely, tragic figure, outside the main currents of society. Schubert was born in 1797 to a humble family who lived near Vienna. His father was a schoolmaster, and Franz was trained for the same profession, which he pursued for three years. He was also trained in music. When he abandoned school teaching, he turned to music full-time, composing, performing, and giving private lessons. He lived continually on the edge of poverty and was helped and appreciated only by a small circle of friends. He battled illness constantly and died in 1828 at the age of thirty-one.

SCHUBERT'S MUSIC

During his short life, Franz Schubert managed to work with great discipline, composing an astounding number of works. He wrote nine symphonies; the early ones are Classical in spirit, but with some surprising harmonic turns. The best known are the Eighth, the *Unfinished*, and the Ninth, in *C* major. The *Unfinished* Symphony has been the subject of many legends and some crude jokes about what might have distracted Schubert from finishing it. Actually, he composed only two movements, never writing the usual third and fourth movements. Because he continued to compose after the Eighth Symphony, we know that the Eighth was not left unfinished because of his death or lack of creative spark. In any event, both the Eighth and Ninth symphonies are frequently performed, and some of the themes of the Eighth are among the best-known melodies of Western art music. Schubert also composed twenty-two piano sonatas, many short pieces for piano, about thirty-five chamber works, six Masses, and seventeen operatic works. He is known chiefly for his beautiful songs (called *Lieder*), of which he wrote more than six hundred, sometimes working, we are told, at the rate of several songs a day.

LIEDER

Schubert did not invent the *Lied*; as happens so often in the history of music, the genre had been around for years, in Germany, but the right combination of atmosphere and creative genius had never been present to raise the art song to a major genre. Poetic works in other languages also were set as songs; there is a considerable repertory of songs in French, English, and even Polish. The strongest impulse to Romantic song, however, was in Germany, and the first prominent song composer was Schubert. He was the composer whose personal creative gifts were perfectly designed for bringing this type of composition to a higher level of creativity and success. The specific things Schubert does so well in his songs are two: first, he had a gift for simple, expressive melody, natural to sing and perfectly suited to the ideas of the texts; second, he does wonderful things with the piano accompaniments. He composed at a time when the piano was coming into its Romantic prominence as an instrument of great expressive power, and he gives it a role equal in importance to the singer and the text. Often a short piano introduction establishes the mood skillfully, before the singer even begins, so that the feeling he wants to communicate is evident even to listeners who miss some of the text.

Schubert writes his songs in several different forms. Some are strophic, that is, they have the same melody for each verse of text, perhaps varied somewhat in both the singer's line and the accompaniment. Strophic form is familiar to us because it is the usual structure of modern folk and popular songs. Some of Schubert's songs are through-composed, that is, the melodies do not repeat, but are constructed as a developing unit from beginning to end. Some of his songs exist as **cycles**, that is, he has selected several individual poems from a collection and has written the songs in a group with each group or cycle constituting a larger unit. All of Schubert's songs remain staples of the vocal literature; all singers learn them, just as all pianists learn the Beethoven sonatas.

Schubert plays for a private audience in this sketch by Moritz von Schwind.

We should comment here on the place of the *Lied* in our present musical life. The *Lied* is a genre of subtle nuance. To appreciate a performance of *Lieder*, the listener must know German and must be sitting close enough to the singer to see facial expressions clearly and to appreciate small gestures. Because words and music are carefully matched, it is impossible to translate the poetry and then sing the translation to the same melody. In other words, the *Lied* is an intimate genre for small and sophisticated audiences. *Lieder* recitals bear the same relationship to opera that chamber music or solo recitals bear to orchestral concerts. Singers who specialize in *Lieder* seldom achieve the same international fame as opera stars: they perform for smaller audiences who can appreciate subtle nuances, both textual and musical. Listening to recordings of *Lieder* has advantages and disadvantages. Recordings provide a wonderful opportunity to hear the great singers of the past and present interpret these works and allow us to compare performances. We do lose something in recording, however, because a *Lieder* performance is, in part, a visual, dramatic experience.

ERLKÖNIG (''THE ELF-KING'')

The poem Schubert set to music is by Goethe. Goethe and Heinrich Heine were the favorite poets of Schubert and other Romantic song composers. This poem is a perfect example of the Romantic fascination with grotesque and supernatural themes. It is a fireside ghost story, filled with shivers of horror, and, to our twentieth-century minds, interesting Freudian implications.

Story

The story is quite simple: a father and his son are riding through the night, and the son is terrified by the King of the Elves, whom he sees and hears, but who is invisible to the father. The Elf-King sings his siren song, inviting the child to unimaginable delights and threatening force if he does not come along willingly. When the father reaches home, the boy in his arms is dead.

Musical Problems

Mood

The text poses interesting problems for composer and singer. The shifting moods of the poem present some interesting choices. Should the composer write slow ghostly music, fast riding music, a tragic lament, or a series of contrasting sections? Schubert chooses to have the music of the whole song rush along like the ride. The piano starts, with pounding triplets and a sinister melody in the bass; before the singer begins, the mood of agitation and terror is established.

Characters

There are four distinct characters to be depicted: the narrator in the first and last verses, the father, the boy, and the wicked king of the Elves. The composer depicts the four different characters in several ways. First of all, the breaks between the words of the three main characters and the narrator often come between verses, so the composer chooses to utilize this natural pause to signal changes of speaker. This gives the song a somewhat strophic feeling, although it is technically a through-composed form. In addition, the different characters are assigned musical lines of distinct style. In the second verse, for example, which consists of dialogue betweeen father and son, the composer uses the obvious device of range to differentiate the two: the father sings in the low range; the son, in the higher range. The Elf-King sings in a wheedling way, pleading, then threatening. The son's increasing fear is depicted musically by setting each repetition of "Mein Vater, Mein Vater" ("my father, my father") higher, so that the musical climax of the song is the third "Mein Vater" at the end of verse seven (see Figure 34-1). Long after we have heard the song, this dissonant plea is what sticks in our mind. The last verse releases the tension as it completes the story. The narrator's conclusion is placed lower in the singer's range and sung more quietly. The galloping triplet rhythm in the piano finally stops before the last line. Because it has been maintained without interruption since the opening of

Figure 34-1. Musical climax of *Erlkönig*.

the song, the brief moment of silence is deafening and dramatic. The last line is interrupted by a pause of indefinite length, as if the narrator can barely bring himself to pronounce the last two words, "was dead." *Erlkönig* is a fine example of the art of the Romantic song. We should remember, however, that not all *lieder* are this dramatic or frightening. Many are soft and lyric, concerned with beauty, nature, or tranquility.

Both the German text of Goethe's poem and an English translation appear below. Figure 34-2 is a listening guide.

Wer reitet so spät durch nacht und Wind?
Es ist der Vater mit seinem Kind;
er hat den Knaben wohl in dem Arm,
er fasst ihn sicher, er hält ihn warm.

"Mein Sohn, was birgst du so bang dein Gesicht?
"Siehst, Vater, du den Erlkönig nicht?
den Erlenkönig mit Kron' und Schweif?"
"Mein Sohn, es ist ein Nebelstreif."

"Du liebes Kind, komm, geh' mit mir!
gar schöne Spiele spiel' ich mit dir;
manch' bunte Blumen sind an dem Strand;
meine Mutter hat manch' gülden Gewand."

"Mein Vater, mein Vater, und hörest du nicht,
was Erlenkönig mir leise verspricht?"
"Sei ruhig, bleibe ruhig, mein Kind;
in dürren Blättern säuselt der Wind."

"Willst, feiner Knage, du mit mir geh'n?
meine Töchter sollen dich warten schön;
mein Töchter führen den nächtlichen Reih'n
und wiegen und tanzen und singen dich ein."

"Mein Vater, mein Vater, und siehst du nicht dort
Erlkönigs Töchter am düstern Ort?"
"Mein Sohn, mein Sohn, ich seh' es genau,

es scheinen die alten Weiden so grau."

"Ich liebe dich, mich reizt deine schöne Gestalt,
und bist du nicht willig, so brauch' ich Gewalt."
"Mein Vater, mein Vater, jetzt fasst er mich an!
Erlkönig hat mir ein Leid's gethan!"

Dem Vater grauset's, er reitet geschwind,

er hält in Armen das ächzende Kind,
erreicht den Hof mit Müh' und Noth:
in seinem Armen das Kind war tödt!

Who rides so late through the night and the wind?
It is the father with his child;
he folds the boy close in his arms,
he clasps him securely, he holds him warmly.

"My son, why do you hide your face so anxiously?"
"Father, don't you see the Elf-king?
The Elf-king with his crown and his train.?"
"My son, it is a streak of mist."

"Dear child, come, go with me!
I'll play the prettiest games with you.
Many colored flowers grow along the shore;
my mother has many golden garments."

"My father, my father, and don't you hear
the Elf-king whispering promises to me?"
"Be quiet, stay quiet, my child;
the wind is rustling in the dead leaves."

"My handsome boy, will you come with me?
My daughters shall wait upon you;
my daughters lead off in the dance night,
and cradle and dance and sing you to sleep."

"My father, my father, and don't you see there
the Elf-king's daughters in the shadows?"
"My son, my son, I see it clearly;

the old willows look so gray."

"I love you, your beautiful figure delights me!
And if you are not willing, then I shall use force!"
"My father, my father, now he is taking hold of me!
The Elf-king has hurt me!"

The father shudders, he rides swiftly on;

he holds in his arms the groaning child,
he reaches the courtyard weary and anxious:
in his arms the child was dead.

FIGURE 34-2. LISTENING GUIDE
ERLKÖNIG, BY SCHUBERT

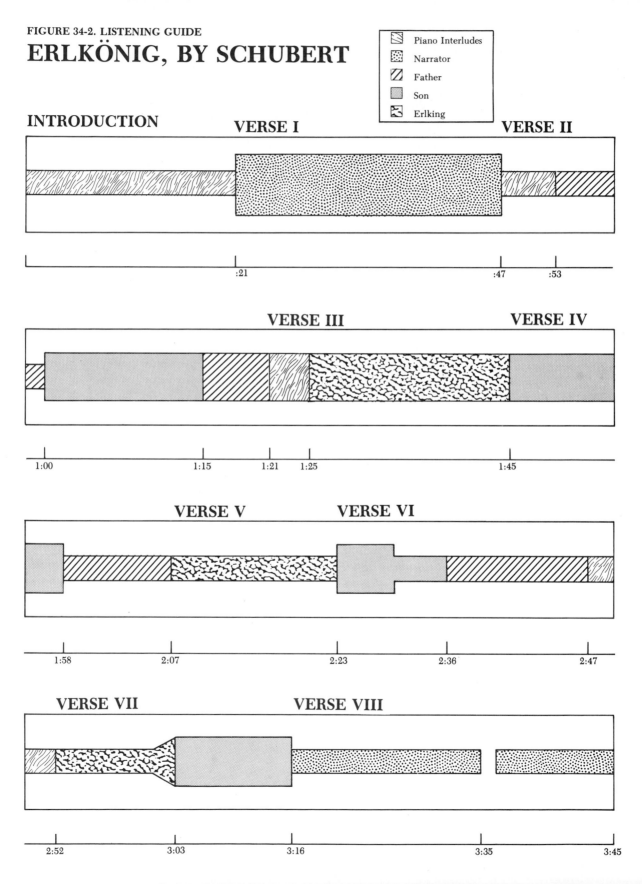

CHAPTER 35

Robert Schumann
Widmung from
Myrtles, Opus 25

SCHUMANN'S LIFE

The life of Robert Schumann was filled with tragedy and madness, broken by periods of feverish musical activity, during which he composed a large body of music for piano solo and many songs, as well as works of other types. Schumann was born in 1810 in Zwickau, a small town in Germany. His father was a publisher and bookseller. Robert grew up in an atmosphere of learning and developed a lifelong love of literature. He was sent to Leipzig, then Heidelberg, to study law, but showed more interest in literature and music. He returned to Leipzig to study the piano with Friedrich Wieck. Eager to make up for lost time, he devised a contraption to immobilize the fourth finger of his right hand, hoping to promote independence of finger movement. The device permanently injured that finger, and he had to abandon any thought of a career as a pianist. He turned, instead, to composing and wrote most of his works for the piano while in his twenties.

During the same period, he helped to found a musical periodical, the *Neue Zeitschrift fur Musik* ("New Journal on Music"), which became an important standards. He often used pen names, which appear in his music also, representing different sides of his character: Florestan, the impetuous romantic; Eusebius, a poetic, gentle person; and Raro, a logical intellectual.

Schumann fell in love with Clara, the young daughter of his teacher, Wieck. Clara was a fine pianist herself and the apple of her father's eye. He violently opposed any thought of marriage to the young composer and even took Robert and Clara to court to prevent the union. Finally, they were married; and in the first year of their marriage, he composed more than a hundred *Lieder*. For a while, things went well. The couple had several children, and Clara performed Robert's piano works, helping to spread his fame. But four years after their marriage, in 1844, Robert had a nervous breakdown, and they moved to Dresden to start their life anew. In 1850, he accepted a position as music director at Dusseldorf, but he was not suited for such a post. In 1854, he attempted suicide by throwing himself into the Rhine. He was rescued and put in an asylum, where he died two years later without recovering his sanity. Clara survived him by forty years and remained a staunch champion of his music and his ideas.

SCHUMANN'S MUSIC

Like many other Romantic composers, Schumann seems to have been more skillful at writing miniatures than at organizing larger works. His piano works are still frequently played. They include many character pieces—short works depicting one picture or mood—with fanciful titles such as "Papillons" ("Butterflies") or "Romances." Larger piano works include several sonatas, the Fantasy in *C*, the *Symphonic Etudes*, and a concerto. The best known of his piano works is *Carnaval*, a set of pieces intended to represent various characters and events at a masked ball.

Songs

Schumann's songs, as was mentioned earlier, were written largely in the early years of his marriage, and he seems to have written *Lieder* as fluently and effortlessly as Schubert. Among his well-known song cycles are *Frauen-liebe und Leben* ("Woman's Life and Love") and *Dichterliebe* ("A Poet's Love"). His favorite poetic theme was love; his favorite poet was Heine. The songs are generally lyric rather than dramatic, and often feature important postludes for the piano, in which the feelings of the song or cycle are summarized musically.

Symphonies

Schumann also wrote some chamber works and four symphonies. The first symphony, called *Spring*, is the most frequently performed. Schumann is usually regarded as not a very strong symphonic composer. Melodies came easily to him,

Clara Schumann, famed pianist, and interpreter of her husband Robert's work.

but large structures were not his natural medium. He is also regarded as weak in orchestration because of a fondness for unrelieved thick textures and multiple doublings of all the lines. These flaws also mar his dramatic music, which includes scenes from *Faust* and Byron's *Manfred*, and *Genoveva*, an unsuccessful opera.

In the smaller forms—solo piano music and songs—Schumann was a very skillful composer, and many of those works are greatly admired and frequently performed.

WIDMUNG ("DEDICATION") FROM *MYRTLES,* OPUS 25

Widmung, one of the many Schumann songs from 1840, his "song year," is a setting of a lovely Romantic poem by Frédrich Ruckert. It is in A-B-A form; the B section is quieter, calmer, and in a lower register than the A section, which is more ardent and ecstatic. Note that the second A section consists of a repeat of the poem's first four lines, plus the final line from the B section. The piano plays a short postlude, which provides a musical summary of the feelings of tender love set forth in the work.

This beautiful song contrasts strongly with Schubert's *Erlkönig* and demonstrates that the *Lied* is an effective medium for conveying tenderness and ardor, as well as more dramatic feelings and stories.

FIGURE 35-1. LISTENING GUIDE

"WIDMUNG" FROM "MYRTLES," OPUS 25, BY SCHUMANN

Musical Sections	German Text	English Translation
A	Du meine Seele, du mein Herz,	You my soul, you my heart,
	Du meine Wonn', o du	You my joy, you my grief;
	mein Schmerz,	
	Du meine Welt, in der ich lebe,	You my world, in which I live,
	Mein Himmel du, darein	You my heaven, into which
	ich schwebe,	I soar;
	O du mein Grab, in das hinab	You my grave, in which I bury
	Ich ewig meinen Kummer gab!	forever my sorrows.
B	Du bist die Ruh, du bist der	You are peace, you are
	Frieden,	consolation;
	Du bist vom Himmel mir	You are given me by heaven;
	beschieden,	
	Dass du mich liebst, macht	That you love me, makes me
	mich mir wert,	worth something in my own
		eyes;
	Dein Blick hat mich vor mir	Your glance transfigures me in
	verklärt,	my own sight;
	Du hebst mich liebend über	You raise me lovingly above
	mich,	myself;
	Mein guter Geist, mein	My guardian spirit, my
	bessres Ich!	better self.
A	Du meine Seele, du mein Herz,	You my soul, you my heart,
	Du meine Wonn! o du	You my joy, you my grief;
	mein Schmerz,	
	Du meine Welt, in der ich lebe,	You my world, in which I live,
	Mein Himmel du, darein	You my heaven, into which
	ich schwebe,	I soar;
	Mein guter Geist, mein	My guardian spirit, my
	bessres Ich!	better self.

CHAPTER 36

Giuseppe Verdi
La Traviata

The last two chapters of this part deal with Romantic opera and with the two great masters of the late Romantic period, Giuseppe Verdi and Richard Wagner. The works of both men are frequently performed and are regarded as masterpieces of the complicated medium of opera. Their aims and approaches to operatic style are entirely different, but each left works in his own personal style that have enriched our Western musical culture.

VERDI'S LIFE

Giuseppe Verdi, unlike many of the Romantic composers discussed so far, had a long and successful creative life. His operas were immensely popular, and he was regarded as a national hero. Not only are his operas perfectly designed musical works, they are also successful theater; and they gave voice to the patriotic feelings of Italians. During the nineteenth century, Italy worked itself loose from Austrian domination and became a unified country under King Victor Emmanuel, the first of the Savoy kings of the new country. Whatever historical period Verdi chose as the background for his operas, and however remote the Austrian censors insisted he make them from the current political situation, his audience understood that his tyrants represented the Austrians and his heroes stood for Garibaldi and other Italian nationalists.

Nabucco, Verdi's first successful opera, is based on a biblical story about the Jewish people in exile in Babylon, but the Italian audience naturally interpreted the choruses about longing for their own country as patriotic Italian anthems. Late in his life, after the unification of the country, Verdi was elected to the chamber of deputies in the new parliament. He is one of the few musicians in history to occupy a political position of any importance.

Verdi was born in 1813 in the village of Le Roncole, near Parma. In his youth, a benefactor supported his musical studies. He later married his benefactor's daughter and had two children. His wife and both children died before 1839, causing a severe crisis for the composer. The commission to write *Nabucco* came after he had vowed in despair never to write music again. The success of *Nabucco* launched one of the most successful careers in the history of Western music. After his successes with *Rigoletto* (1851), *Il Trovatore* (1853), and *La Traviata* (1853), Verdi married Giuseppina Strepponi, a soprano who had starred in several of his operas, and settled on a country estate near his birthplace.

Some of Verdi's greatest works were written late in his life. He wrote *Aida* on a commission from the Egyptian authorities to celebrate the opening of the Suez Canal in 1870. It was first performed in Cairo in 1871, when the composer was fifty-eight years old. Three years later came the *Requiem*, more of an opera than a liturgical service, written in memory of Alessandro Manzoni, a patriotic writer. *Otello*, a magnificent work based on Shakespeare's play, was first performed in 1887, when the composer was in his seventies. After again vowing to retire from writing opera in his eighties, he composed *Falstaff*, another Shakespearean opera, this one a rollicking comedy. We are told Verdi was contemplating a setting of *King Lear* late in his life; it is too bad he did not complete it. He died in 1901, at the age of eighty-eight.

Verdi's operas have remained as popular and successful in our own century as they were in his own country during his lifetime. It is interesting that several of his works have been performed recently in televised versions, and they hold up well even in this medium for which they were not designed. The televised performance of *Otello* reached a very large audience, at least for a cultural program, and the drama worked as well on the small screen as it does in a large opera house. In fact, some scenes play better in a closeup than they do from the balcony.

VERDI'S APPROACH TO OPERA

Human Drama

Verdi's operas are successful for several reasons. First and foremost, they are profoundly human dramas. They deal with strong human feelings and plots that involve the audience in the drama. Heroism, unrequited love, murder, conspiracy, selfless sacrifice, ardent yearning, and cruel fate are still appealing dramatic themes. Despite the fact that operatic characters tend to be larger than life and that the plots are sometimes overly melodramatic, audiences are still moved by the drama, as well as the music, of Verdi operas. Even the faintly comical conventions of opera—people sing for ten minutes after being fatally stabbed, and the action is constantly interrupted for big arias—somehow do not vitiate the force of Verdi's drama.

Like Shakespeare, whom he greatly admired, Verdi understood the necessity to please a variety of tastes. His operas always have variety: bustling crowd scenes alternate with intense confrontations or love scenes between the main characters. There are always pleasant choruses, often drinking songs with a robust peasant feeling. Everything is carefully spaced and planned so that people of different levels of taste can all enjoy the experience. Verdi's operas work, even for listeners who are not opera fans.

Singer's Opera

The second basic characteristic of Verdi opera is that it is singer's opera. The Italian tradition of opera has always nurtured and admired the great solo voice. Verdi knew how to write great choruses, and he was a master orchestrator; but the big moments in his operas are for the solo voices. The chorus moves offstage on some pretext, the orchestra is reduced to a background accompaniment role, and one or two singers have the stage to themselves for their big numbers. These arias are written so that the singer has a great deal of freedom to hold the dramatic high notes and opportunity to put his or her personal touches on the florid cadenzas. If they are well performed, the big arias bring members of the adoring audience to their feet at the end of the number. In his later operas, Verdi adopted a more continuous style of writing, without clearly separated arias; but the star singer is still the main ingredient, and the performance succeeds or fails on how well the stars sing on a particular night.

VIOLETTA'S SCENE, *LA TRAVIATA*, ACT I

The plot of *La Traviata*, based on a story by Alexandre Dumas, may sound melodramatic in a brief summary. Violetta, the heroine, is a Parisian beauty who, dying of consumption, has decided to live her last months in the pursuit of pleasure. Much to her surprise, she suddenly falls in love with Alfredo, a young man of good family, whose father naturally opposes this liaison with a woman of questionable virtue. By the time the father's opposition to their love eventually dissolves and he comes to respect Violetta, it is too late. At the end of the opera, she dies in Alfredo's arms.

The opera opens with a party, at which Violetta meets Alfredo and during which one of Verdi's famous drinking songs is sung. Near the end of the first act, everyone conveniently goes offstage, leaving Violetta onstage alone to muse about this sudden passion she feels, so contrary to her cynical pursuit of pleasure. The rest of the act is her soliloquy about her feelings and her big number in the opera. She occupies the stage for about nine minutes, in one of the great scenes in all opera.

She begins quietly, in recitative, singing of her surprise at the strength of this sudden love. The first aria section, in *F* minor, is gentle and hesitant—"perhaps he is the one." A crescendo on the last note of that section leads to a new section, in *F* major, in which she repeats the love music she and Alfredo sang earlier. So far she seems to be accepting this new love; note the lyric emphasis on the line which describes love as *"croce e delizia,"* "torture and delight." In a sudden shift of mood, she dismisses the whole thing as madness—*"follie"*—in an angry and dramatic section in recitative. The final aria section, *"Sempre libera,"* is in A-flat, and reasserts her vow to pursue pleasure at all cost, avoiding anything, including love, that might interfere with her freedom. This section is completely different from the earlier sections. It is fast and assertive, rather than slow and melting. In a nice dramatic touch, we then hear Alfredo, singing the love theme offstage. For a moment, Violetta hesitates, moved; then, in a shorter version of the *"follie"* recitative section, she reasserts her devil-may-care attitude and repeats the *"Sempre libera"* section. After that, Alfredo sings a few phrases of the love theme again, but this time it does not stop Violetta: she goes right on with her very florid singing. The section ends with a ringing climax and several opportunities for stellar high notes. Then the orchestra has several concluding loud chords, and down comes the curtain to thunderous applause. The scene has everything a big number should have—dramatic changes of mood, ravishing love music, challenging high notes and florid passages, the offstage love music by Alfredo, several dramatic climaxes, and the emphatic closing position in the act, providing everything necessary for a triumphant ovation. Finally, because it closes the act, the singer has the chance to rest during the following intermission, after nearly ten minutes of demanding solo singing.

On the following pages is an outline of the scene, with the Italian text, an English translation, and comments about the music. The florid cadenzas are marked also. Note as you listen to the recording that Verdi has carefully written pauses for the orchestra in those places and, in general, allows the singer considerable latitude and freedom. The singer is given the spotlight, both dramatically and musically; the success of the scene depends entirely on the soprano.

FIGURE 36-1. LISTENING GUIDE

VIOLETTA'S SCENE, ACT I, *LA TRAVIATA*

Music	Italian Text	English Translation

Recitative	VIOLETTA
	È strano! È strano! in core
	scolpiti ho quegli accenti!
	Saria per me sventura un
	    serio amore?
	Che risolvi, o turbata
	    anima mia?
	Null'uomo ancora t'accendeva . . .
	
	O gioia ch'io non connobbi,
	essere amata amando!
	E sdegnarlo poss'io
	per l'aride follie del
	    viver mio?
		VIOLETTA
		How strange! How strange! Those
		words are engraved upon my heart!
		Would serious love be a misfortune
		    for me?
		What do you say, my troubled
		    spirit?
		Until now no man has ever set
		    you on fire . . .
		Oh joy that I never knew,
		    to love and be loved!
		And can I spurn it
		    for my life of sterile pleasure?

A. F Minor (Soft)	Ah, fors'è lui che l'anima
	solinga ne' tumulti
	solinga ne'tumulti
	godea sovente pingere
	de' suoi colori occulti!
	
	Lui che modesto e vigile
	all'egre soglie ascese
	
	e nuova febbre accese,
	destandomi all'amor—
		Ah, perhaps he is the one my
		    heart, solitary among the crowd,
		    . . .
		often delighted to depict
		in dim uncertain colors!
		
		He who, modest and watchful,
		haunted the threshold of sickness
		
		and kindled a new fever,
		awakening me to love—

B. F Major (Love Music From Earlier Duet) (Soft)	A quell' amor, quell' amor
	    che palpito
	dell' universo, dell'
	    universo intero,
	misterioso, misterioso
	    altero,
	croce, croce e delizia,
	croce e delizia,
	delizia al cor!
	croce e delizia,
	delizia al cor!
	Ah!
	delizia al cor!
		To that love, that love
		which is the pulse
		of the whole world,
		    . . .
		mysterious, mysterious and
		    lofty,
		torment, torment and delight,
		torment and delight . . .

Music	Italian Text	English Translation
Recitative (Loud)	Follie! Follie! delirio vano e questo! Povera donna, sola, abbandonata in questo popoloso deserto che appellano Parigi . . . Che spero or più? Che far deggio? gioire! di volluttà ne vortici, di volutta perir! Gioir! Gioir!	Madness! Madness! This is vain delirium! A poor woman, alone, abandoned in this teeming desert they call Paris . . . What more do I hope for now? What must I do? Plunge into the vortex of pleasure, engulfed in pleasure to die! Revel! . . .
C. A Flat Major (Loud)	Sempre libera deggio folleggiare di gioia in gioia vo' che scorra il viver mio pei sentieri del piacer. Nasca il giorno o il giorno muoia, sempre lieta ne' ritrovi, ah! a diletti sempre nuovi dee volare il mio pensier. dee volar, dee volar, dee volare il mio pensier, dee volar, dee volar, il mio pensier!	Forever free, I must flit dizzily from pleasure to pleasure I want my life to skim along the purple path of pleasure. Whether the day is dawning or dying, always merry in company to pleasures ever new my thoughts must fly. . . .
B. A Flat-Love Music Repeated **(Soft)**	ALFREDO Amor, amor è palpito . . . VIOLETTA Oh! ALFREDO A. . . . dell' universo intero . . . VIOLETTA Oh amore! ALFREDO misterioso, altero, croce e delizia al cor!	ALFREDO Love, love is the pulse . . . VIOLETTA Oh! ALFREDO Of the whole world . . . VIOLETTA Oh love! ALFREDO mysterious, strange, torment and delight my heart!

Music	Italian Text	English Translation
Recitative	VIOLETTA Follie!, Follie! Gioir! gioir! Ah! si!	VIOLETTA Madness! Madness! Revel! Revel! Ah! Yes!
C. Repeated (Loud)	Sempre libera deggio folleggiare di gioia in gioia, vo'che scorra il viver mio pei sentieri del piacer. Nasca il giorno o il giorno muoia, sempre lieta ne'ritrovi, Ah! a diletti sempre nuovi dee volare il mio pensier. Dee volar, dee volar, dee volare il mio pensier, dee volar, dee volar il mio pensier.	Forever free, I must flit dizzily from pleasure to pleasure I want my life to skim along the purple path of pleasure. Whether the day is dawning or dying, always merry in company to pleasures ever new my thoughts must fly. . . .
B. Repeated	ALFREDO Amor è palpito VIOLETTA dee volar, ALFREDO dell' universo. VIOLETTA dee volar. ah! ah! dee volar il pensier.	ALFREDO Love is the pulse VIOLETTA They must fly, ALFREDO Of the whole world. VIOLETTA They must fly. Ah! Ah! my thoughts must fly.
B. Repeated	ALFREDO Amor è palpito. VIOLETTA dee volar, ALFREDO dell'universo. VIOLETTA dee volar, dee volar il mio pensier, il mio pensier . . . il mio pensier.	ALFREDO Love is the pulse. VIOLETTA They must fly, ALFREDO Of the whole world. VIOLETTA They must fly, they must fly, My thoughts . . .
Loud Orchestral Chords		

CHAPTER 37

Richard Wagner
Die Walküre

Richard Wagner's life was a long, unswerving struggle to bring into reality his vision of a new kind of opera, which he called "music drama." The chromatic style of his later works so stretched the tonal system on which Classic and Romantic music is based that composers after him had to face the question of whether the system had any further usefulness. The man and his music caused a tremendous stir in the late Romantic artistic world; all of Europe divided into pro-Wagner and anti-Wagner camps.

WAGNER'S LIFE

Wagner was born in Leipzig in 1813. His father, a police clerk, died shortly after Richard's birth. Not long thereafter, his mother married Ludwig Geyer, an actor, painter, and dramatist. The boy was raised in Dresden and showed no particular interest in music as a youth except for a great admiration for the works of Carl Maria van Weber, an earlier German Romantic composer. In 1827, Geyer died, and the family returned to Leipzig. There, Wagner became fascinated with the symphonies of Beethoven, began to teach himself harmony, and enrolled for six months of formal study in music theory. Immediately thereafter, he worked in a series of positions in provincial opera companies. He was forced to leave the last of these after accumulating huge debts which he could not pay, a lifelong habit of his. Next followed one of the low points of his life. He found no positions and supported himself and his wife by hack work in journalism and music arranging. Things changed in 1841. His opera *Rienzi* was performed at Dresden and was a great success. He was appointed music director at Dresden, were he revived works by Gluck, Mozart, and Beethoven. There he composed two more operas, *Tannhauser* and *Lohengrin*.

Wagner became involved in revolutionary political activity; and when the insurrection was suppressed in 1849, he was forced to flee Germany. For the next eleven years, he lived in Switzerland. Those were very productive years for him, although they also began his estrangement from his wife, who did not understand his visions. He wrote *Opera and Drama*, his two-volume work on his notions of opera, and began work on the libretto for his masterwork, the four-opera cycle *Der Ring des Nibelungen* ("The Ring of the Nibelung"). These years of exile were the most important of Wagner's creative life. He pursued and refined his vision, working in total seclusion for the entire time, and emerged with his giant masterpiece clearly worked out in his mind.

In 1857 he interrupted his work on the Ring operas to compose another opera. Inspired by an affair with a married woman, Mathilde Wesendonk, he composed *Tristan und Isolde*, which was completed in 1859 and first performed in 1865. During this period, he and his wife separated and he also composed *Die Meistersinger von Nurnberg*. These last two operas are the most frequently performed of his works. *Tristan* is written in his new chromatic and continuous style; *Die Meistersinger* is a traditional comic opera.

In 1864 two important people entered Wagner's life. The first was Ludwig, the young king of Bavaria, who was so taken with Wagner and his ideas that he was ready to bankrupt the Bavarian treasury to support him. The other was Cosima von Bülow, daughter of Liszt and wife of Hans von Bülow, a conductor who was an ardent supporter of Wagner's. Cosima was a strong, independent woman. She went to live with Wagner in 1866, causing a great scandal and turning King Ludwig against Wagner. They were finally married in 1870. With the support of Cosima and the help of Wagner Societies all over Germany, the composer finally was able to bring his vision to completion. He finished the composition of the Ring operas and designed and built his special opera house at Bayreuth in Bavaria, where the four great operas were performed in 1876. After the composition and performance of one more opera, *Parsifal*, Wagner died in 1883 in Venice and was buried in Bayreuth.

Wagner is a difficult man for us to understand. There are certainly some very unattractive facets to his character. In his conviction that he was destined to be

The *Festspielhaus* was Wagner's dream; it was opened in 1876 in Bayreuth, West Germany.

the savior of German culture, he was incredibly arrogant and ruthless in his exploitation of friends, their money, and their wives. He considered himself an expert not only on music and culture, but on a number of other subjects. Among his extensive writings are some anti-Semitic tracts which reflect the German thinking of the time. Still, there is no denying that he was a musical genius and that his impact on the history of music was tremendous. Despite the way he used people to pursue his goals, we must admire his lifelong dedication to his artistic vision. In the view of some historians, it was Wagner's music that brought Romanticism to its final state, and the twentieth century and its musical experiments can be viewed as a massive reaction against Wagner. After him, composers had to develop entirely new ways of conceiving and organizing music.

MUSIC DRAMA

Wagner's view of opera is entirely different from Verdi's. Wagner viewed opera as *Gesamtkunstwerk*, "total art work." He sought control of every element: plot, drama, libretto, singing, staging, orchestra. No one element is spotlighted at the expense of the others; all are to work together to further the unified vision.

Librettos

Wagner wrote his own librettos, creating a new German mythology that he assumed would be the basis of the culture of the new unified Germany. In doing so, he reached back into medieval legend and Norse sagas, but freely rewrote these tales to serve his cultural vision.

Singers

Wagner conceived a new role for the singer. His music dramas are not broken up into separate numbers, but are continuous: there are no arias that can be performed separately at a concert. The singer usually has a line that is a combination of speech and song, and rarely soars into prominent, memorable melody. Wagner makes extraordinary demands on singers; some scenes are very long and require unusual stamina. The singer is not performing against accompaniment patterns in the orchestra, either; his is just another line in a rich, complex orchestral texture. Particular types of voices are called for, and singers usually specialize in either Wagnerian roles or traditional opera. There are even special terms to classify Wagnerian voices, such as *Heldentenor* ("heroic tenor"), a kind of bright, strong tenor voice, required for Wagnerian roles.

Orchestra

The main character in Wagnerian opera is the orchestra. Wagner wrote for a huge orchestra with a very large brass section. One of his reasons for designing his own opera house was the question of balance between singers and orchestra. He wanted the orchestra out of sight beneath the stage, where their sound would be somewhat muffled. In a standard opera house, where the orchestra is in front of the stage, the acoustics work out differently, necessitating adjustments for balance. In Wagnerian opera, the orchestra usually plays the main melodies and produces the surging, chromatic musical texture into which the singers must fit. Often, it is the orchestra that communicates the emotional meaning of a scene. The characters may be singing about inconsequential matters, while the orchestra is communicating the underlying dread, love, or tragedy toward which events are heading.

Leitmotifs

One of Wagner's chief compositional techniques is the use of recurring melodies which represent persons, ideas, or events—the *Leitmotifs*. Wagner did not invent this technique; many Romantic composers had made effective use of reminiscence themes, especially in program music, to communicate the stories behind the music. But Wagner used the technique more extensively than any other composer, and this device became one of the main ways in which his music was organized and held together. Wagner was greatly influenced by Liszt and his technique of thematic transformation. When the *leitmotif* reappears, it is likely to be changed to reflect the mood of the moment, although it is still recognizable as a specific melody representing a specific idea or person. Liner notes for recordings and program notes for live performances generally identify the main *leitmotifs* for us; they have been identified and given their standard names not by Wagner, but by later commentators.

Massive Scale

One last important facet of Wagner's style is the massive scale on which he works. With other composers, it is possible to single out one aria from their operas and to use it to form a fairly accurate notion of the way they work. With Wagner, it is much harder to do so. The four Ring operas, according to some commentators, are organized as a coherent unit, with a logical overall musical plan. But each of the four lasts for five or six hours, and it is not likely that anyone will sit down to listen to the entire cycle at once. When we listen to excerpts, we must bear in mind that fifteen minutes of Wagner is a brief moment extracted from a unified larger work. At any given moment, we hear his chromatic style, shifting and surging, evading cadences, approaching climaxes and then receding, never reaching a conclusion with any finality. To sense the overall logic, we must listen to entire works.

EXCERPT FROM *DIE WALKÜRE*

The excerpt we will focus on is taken from the end of the first act of *Die Walküre* ("The Valkyries"), the second of the four Ring operas. All of the elements of Wagner's style are present here: rich orchestration, fluid rhythm, chromatic harmony, the feeling of seamless flow. The plot at this point concerns the accidental meeting of Siegfried and Sieglinde, who are beginning to discover that there is some bond between them. The orchestra tells us that they are falling in love. From the rest of the cycle, we are aware, although they are not, that they are actually brother and sister.

The excerpt begins with Siegfried singing a lyric song against subdued accompaniment. This section sounds like a traditional aria. But then the orchestra moves into the yearning love music, and the rest of the excerpt is in more typical Wagnerian style as the voices compete with a rich orchestral texture. The love music is built around the melodic idea shown in Figure 37-1. Figure 37-2, the listening guide, consists of the German text, a translation, and some comments on the ongoing musical style.

Figure 37-1. Love motive.

FIGURE 37-2. LISTENING GUIDE

DIE WALKÜRE, BY WAGNER

—Orchestra
—Voices

Introduction—	German Text	English Translation
Harp, Muted Strings	(drawing Sieglinde down beside him)	
Song Style	Winterstürme wichen	The storms of winter have yielded
Subdued	dem Wonnemond,	to the month of May,
Orchestra	in mildem Lichte	the gentle light
	leuchtet der Lenz;	of Spring shines forth;
	auf linden Lüften	on the soft breeze
	leicht und lieblich,	light and lovely,
	Wunder webend	Spring is wafted,
Clarinet Melody	er sich wiegt;	working marvels;
	durch Wald und Auen	through wood and meadow
Crescendo	weht sein Atem,	blows his breath,
	weit geöffnet	his eyes are bright
	lacht sein Aug'.	with laughter.
	Aus sel'ger Vöglein Sange	In the merry song of birds
	süss er tönt,	his voice resounds,
	holde Düfte	he exhales
	haucht er aus;	sweet fragrance;
	seinem warmen Blut entblühen	from his warm blood
	wonnige Blumen.	burst forth flowers;
	Keim und Spross	buds and shoots
	entspringt seiner Kraft.	spring up from his strength,
Faster	Mit zarter Waffen Zier	Arrayed with fragile weapons
	bezwingt er die Welt.	he conquers the world.
	Winter und Sturm wichen	Winter and storm give way
	der starken Wehr;	to his attack:
	wohl musste den tapfem Streichen	his bold blows
	die strenge Türe auch weichen,	break down the rough doors even
Love Music-Strings	die trotzig und starr	that, rigid and defiant,
	uns trennte von ihm.	parted us from him.
	Zu seiner Schwester	To his sister
	schwang er sich her;	hither he has flown;
Crescendo	die Liebe lockte den Lenz;	Spring was drawn to Love;
	in unsrem Busen	deep in our breasts
	barg sie sich tief:	Love lay hidden—
	nun lacht sie selig dem Licht.	now she smiles at the light.
	Die bräutliche Schwester	The sister-bride
	befreite der Bruder;	is freed by the brother;
	zertrümmert liegt,	what kept them apart
	was je sie getrennt;	now lies in ruins;
	jauchzend grüsst sich	the young couple
Climax—	das junge Paar:	greet one another joyfully:
Cadence	vereint sind Liebe und Lenz!	united are Love and Spring!

Voice as Part of Orchestra (Until End)

Quiet—Orch. Subdued

Crescendo

Cadence (Climax)

SIEGLINDE

Du bist der Lenz,
nach dem ich verlangte
in frostigen Winters Frist;
dich grüsste mein Herz
mit heiligem Grau'n,
als dein Blick zuerst mir erblühte.
Fremdes nur sah ich von je,
freundlos war mir das Nahe;
als hätt' ich nie es gekannt
war, was immer mir kam.
Doch dich kannt' ich
deutlich und klar:
als mein Auge dich sah,
warst du mein Eigen:
was im Busen ich barg,
was ich bin,
hell wie der Tag
tauch' es mir auf,
wie tönender Schall
schlug's an mein Ohr,
als in frostig öder Fremde

zuerst ich den Freund ersah.

SIEGLINDE

You are the spring
for which I yearned
in the days of frosty winter;
my heart greeted you
with holy dread
when your look first lighted on me.
All I had ever seen was strange,
I never found a friend near me;
All that happened
seemed as if I had never known it.
Yet I knew you
clearly and plainly:
as soon as my eyes beheld you,
you were mine.
What I hid in my heart,
what I am,
came to light
as clear as day,
it struck my ears
like the peal of a bell,
when in this cold, strange, desert place
I first beheld my friend.

(She clings rapturously to Siegmund.)

SIEGMUND

(carried away)

O süsseste Wonne!
Seligstes Weib!

SIEGMUND

Oh sweetest bliss!
Most blessed of women!

SIEGLINDE

O lass in Nähe
zu dir mich neigen,
dass hell ich schaue
den hehren Schein,
der dir aus Aug'
und Antlitz bricht,
und so süss die Sinne mir zwingt!

SIEGLINDE

O let me press
closer to you,
that I may see clearly
the glorious light
that shines from your eyes
and your face,
and so sweetly rules my senses!

Crescendo

Climax — Evaded Cadence

SIEGMUND

Im Lenzesmond
leuchtest du hell;
hehr umwebt dich
das Wellenhaar;
was mich berückt
errat' ich nun leicht —
denn wonnig weidet mein Blick.

SIEGMUND

In the spring moonlight
your face shines brightly;
framed by your lovely
waving hair;
what bewitched me
now I see clearly —
for I feast my eyes in rapture.

Soft

Crescendo

Soft

SIEGLINDE

(pushing back the hair from his brow)

Wie dir die Stim
so offen steht,
der Adern Geäst
in den Schläfen sich schlingt!
Mir zagt es vor der Wonne,
die mich entzückt!
Ein Wunder will mich gemahnen:
den heut' zuerst ich erschaut,
mein Auge sah dich schon!

SIEGMUND

Ein Minnetraum
gemahnt auch mich:
in heissem Sehnen
sah ich dich schon!

SIEGLINDE

Im Bach erblickt' ich
mein eigen Bild —
und jetzt gewahr' ich es wieder:
wie einst dem Teich es enttaucht,
bietest mein Bild mir nun du!

SIEGMUND

Du bist das Bild —
das ich in mir barg.

SIEGLINDE

O still! lass mich
der Stimme lauschen;
mich dünkt, ihren Klang
hört' ich als Kind—
doch nein! ich hörte sie neulich,
als meiner Stimme Schall
mir widerhallte der Wald.

SIEGMUND

O lieblichste Laute,
denen ich lausche!

SIEGLINDE

(gazing rapturously into his eyes)

Deines Auges Glut
erglänzte mir schon:
so blickte der Greis
grüssend auf mich,
als der Traurigen Trost er gab.
An dem Blick
erkannt' ihn sein Kind —
schon wollt' ich beim Namen ihn
    nennen . . .

SIEGLINDE

How broad and open
is your brow,
how the veins twist
in your temples!
I shiver with the ecstasy
that fills me with rapture!
My memory is strangely stirred:
you, whom I first saw today—
my eyes have beheld you before!

SIEGMUND

A dream of love
reminds me, too:
in fervent longing
I have seen you before!

SIEGLINDE

In the stream I perceived
my own image —
and now I perceive it again:
as once it rose from the pool,
you present my image now to me!

SIEGMUND

You are the image
that I preserved within me.

SIEGLINDE

Oh let me
listen to your voice.
methinks I heard its sound
as a child—
but no! I heard it of late
when my own voice
echoed in the wood.

SIEGMUND

Oh how sweet are the sounds
to which I listen!

SIEGLINDE

The glow of your eyes
has shone on me before:
thus did the old man
look kindly at me
when he consoled me in my grief.
By that glance
his child did recognize him —
I almost spoke his name . . .

Pablo Picasso. *Nature morte á la guitare*, 1921. (Galleria d'Arte Moderna, Parigi)

PART VI

Music in the Twentieth Century

CHAPTER **38**

Social and Cultural Background

The twentieth century is totally different from the Romantic age that preceded it, and this difference is visible in the contrast between the cultures of the nineteenth and twentieth centuries. Our century is a period of sweeping change. Revolutions in the fields of transportation and communication have accelerated the pace of change. The globe has shrunk, so that developments in one country immediately affect life in another, and it has become increasingly hard to maintain one's views of the world and society in a rapidly changing world. Psychologists have observed that many people suffer from "future shock," a generalized feeling that society is changing too rapidly for them and that they cannot adjust to what they regard as the constant assaults on their beliefs. Change takes place so rapidly in the culture of this century that we find it easier to characterize separate decades, like the twenties or the sixties, than we do to generalize about the whole century.

TECHNOLOGICAL DEVELOPMENTS

The most obvious and sweeping change that has determined the course of history in this century is the rapid advance of technology. Our lives are filled with gadgets that did not even exist in 1900. The automobile, the airplane, and the computer have changed society forever, and new generations of technological advances appear with astonishing rapidity. It is fascinating to note how many seeds of sweeping change appear early in this century. Queen Victoria, the symbol of the nineteenth century, died in 1901. Two years later, the Wright Brothers flew their spindly prototype plane a few yards, beginning the revolution that was to lead to jet travel, a shrinking globe, new kinds of warfare, and even to man's walking on the moon in 1969. In 1903, Henry Ford established his automobile company; General Motors was formed in 1908. The automobile determined the shape of society in ways we did not fully understand until oil began to grow scarce in the seventies. In 1905, Einstein published his special theory of relativity, the first step in post-Newtonian physics, and a milestone in twentieth-century science.

THE NATURE OF MAN

Another important development early in the century was a new understanding of the nature of man. In 1900, Sigmund Freud published his *Interpretation of Dreams*; in 1909, he visited the United States on a lecture tour. Psychology and psychiatry changed forever our visions of the nature of man. We learned that man was a struggling product of heredity and environment, pulled by unconscious urges and fears, and probably needing counseling at some point in his life. The world of dreams and nightmares became an important subject for the arts. Entire professions and new industries were created, as messiahs and gurus sprang up at an astonishing rate in the sixties and seventies, each promising new heights of development, happiness, and fulfillment.

WAR AND VIOLENCE

This is also a century of war and violence. Technology revolutionized the way man wages war. Total war, saturation bombing, and nuclear war are all inventions of this century. America began World War II with an air corps consisting of a few old biplanes and a cavalry corps that still used horses. Ten years later, jet fighters and bombers had increased the capacity for efficient destruction immeasurably. Earlier, World War I was a profound shock to the societies of Europe and America. It proved that war was not glamorous and heroic, but absurd and insane. Unfortunately, the lesson was lost on the world, and we went on to even greater horrors. We have witnessed atrocities that previous generations thought man was incapable of. We have seen attempted genocide. Since 1945, we have lived under the constant shadow of the possibility of nuclear holocaust. It follows that the literature and art of this century are concerned with themes that are different from those that inspired the arts of the Romantic era.

INDIVIDUAL FULFILLMENT

One more general trend deserves mention. In the last quarter of the century, people have been very concerned with individual fulfillment and lifestyle. We have a huge range of choices about how to spend our leisure time; and services such as self-help programs, fitness centers, and groups of people pursuing similar interests abound. The new individualism also raises interesting questions about the makeup of our society. We seem to be splintering into an assortment of special interest groups. This fragmentation makes some observers worry about the future of the larger groups that once provided cohesion, such as traditional political parties, organized churches, and nuclear families. Leisure time commitments and activities have become increasingly important issues to all of us.

THE ARTS IN THE TWENTIETH CENTURY

It follows from our brief discussion of the twentieth century that the arts and the artists of this century would have to be defined differently from the way they were defined in the nineteenth century. The arts always mirror the age in which they exist; the anger, confusion, technology, and violence of the twentieth century are mirrored in the arts of this period.

Themes

The Romantic artist pursued beauty as his goal, and dealt with themes like the hero, nature, exotic adventure, and the wonders of romantic love. None of these themes would be adequate for the self-conscious twentieth-century artist. He is more likely to deal with the victim or the anti-hero than with the hero.

Characters

The main character of a modern novel or film is more likely to be neurotic than heroic, and the demons he struggles with are more likely to be his own fears or the impersonal society around him than the dragons or evil wizards of the Romantic tale. The setting is more likely to be a decaying city than an imaginary forest or exotic wonderland. The women in the story (or in the art) are probably not the idealized madonnas of Romantic stories; the feminine component in modern literature is much more likely to be the crippling mother, the angry crusader, or a complex person struggling to find and express her individuality.

Vestiges of Romanticism

Twentieth-century readers smile at the too-perfect heroes and heroines of Romantic literature, although such larger-than-life heroes persist in some form, as we can see from the success of films like *Superman* and *Star Wars.* These films illustrate an important fact. When we generalize about the differences between the Romantic arts and those of our own century, it is easy to form the impression that Romanticism died, once and for all, at the turn of the century. But it did not. We can find typical Romantic impulses at work in much of the music, art, and literature of our own century. Although there are still some romantic heroes in our culture, much more typical is the anti-hero, the product and victim of his age, caught in his lonely struggle to hold on to and live by his principles.

The City Versus Nature

Nature, at least in the Romantic sense, is no longer a popular theme, although there is a growing appreciation of the importance of our remaining wilderness areas. The background in a modern story, or in modern art, is more likely to be the city or the factory than an idealized glen or forest. The city appears constantly as a theme in the visual arts, and its nervous rhythms, if not its mechanical sounds, appear in most modern music. Some of the other popular Romantic themes—the idealized Middle Ages, adventure in exotic lands—seem dated, and are not likely to reappear as artistic themes. Instead, the arts in this century mirror the ideas of this age—technology, psychology, and violence.

Technology and the Arts

Twentieth-century technology has changed the arts forever in a number of ways. It has created new art media, such as film—*the* twentieth-century art—still photography, and television. It has created new industries involved in the arts: the movie business, the recording industry, the television industry. Technology has created a mass market of a size unimaginable in the nineteenth century; film, radio, and television penetrate every remote corner of the globe. Technology has given us access to the arts of the past, through full-color reproductions and recordings. New technologies are just over the horizon—videodiscs, digital recording—which will provide even greater access to drama, music, and performances of all kinds. Technology always outstrips its intelligent application, and inventions like recording and television can deaden our lives with mindless mass culture of no lasting value. But the possibilities are limitless and become more exciting with each new development. Even educational television, reaching audiences that are quite small in comparison with the millions who watch network shows, can bring performances of drama or opera to large numbers of people, more than could possibly attend live performances.

Fragmentation of the Audience

The other side of this rapidly expanding access to a wide variety of cultural experiences is the fragmentation of the audience for culture. In one sense, the arts will never again unify society the way they did in other cultures. To cite one example, three films of the late seventies tried to give Americans some vision and understanding of an experience they all shared, the Vietnam conflict. The films—*The Deer Hunter, Coming Home,* and *Apocalypse Now*—can be viewed as a trilogy, recreating the war for the American people and allowing them to grow through an artistic, cathartic experience of it. These three films, however, will reach only a relatively small segment of the population. Some people apparently no longer go to the movies; of the group that does attend films, many avoid serious films, preferring to use the medium for escapist fare. Variety provides access but also splinters the audience into a bewildering array of special interest groups.

Elitism

Another effect of wider access to culture and fragmentation of the audience is that the artist or composer no longer feels any need to appeal to a wide segment of the population. There is an elitist tendency in the arts of this century, an attitude that to produce a work of art that has a large appeal is to fail one's responsibility to art. It is now possible for writers, artists, and composers to work only for each other and a small group of students and initiates. The fact that artists of all sorts are often associated with universities encourages this tendency, at least in the opinion of some commentators. A position on a university faculty may be viewed as a modern form of the patronage system, which encourages artists to work in some areas and discourages them from pursuing others. It is now possible to work in a very rarified atmosphere, removed from the demands of the popular market, and to produce works of intellectual interest, leaving the masses to their popular culture. If this view is true, then artists are not having the challenging effect on the society in general that artists should have.

Anti-Romanticism

One characteristic common to all of the arts in the twentieth century is an attempt to move away from the premises and assumptions of Romanticism and to discover new ways of organizing, structuring, and judging artistic works. The history of the arts in the twentieth century is a jumble of schools and theories, revolutionary ways of organizing one's work, and questioning of the whole function and purpose of art. Constant change and discovery are the rule. Much of the art of this century is concerned with redefining art rather than with communicating some message or idea from artist to audience. Twentieth-century art is liable to have art itself as its theme.

Connections Among the Arts

The connections among the arts established in the nineteenth century continue in the twentieth, so that some schools and "isms" first pop up in one form of art and then spread to others. This tendency toward unity of the arts is balanced by the struggle within each art for new techniques and organizing principles. Many works in all of the arts are, therefore, experimental, concerned with trying a new technique in that particular art, rather than with pursuing some thematic idea borrowed from another art. Within twentieth-century music, for example, we have some works that use literature, visual arts, and drama in their organization. In fact, mixing of media is an important trend in twentieth-century art. But there are also a number of works that are interesting solely for musical reasons, because of their experimentation with new techniques, new instruments, and new organizational principles.

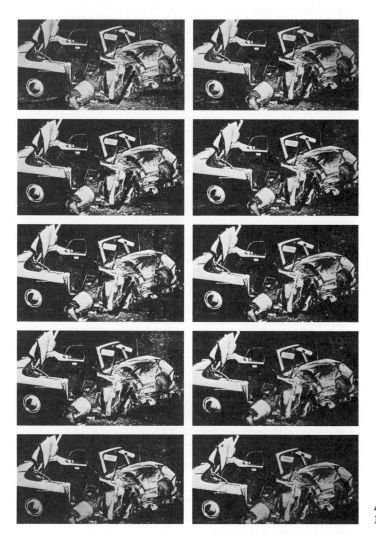

Andy Warhol. *Green Disaster #2,* 1963. (Collection of Karl Stroher)

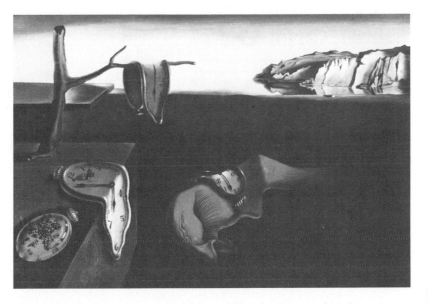

Salvador Dali. *The Persistence of Memory*, 1931. (The Museum of Modern Art, New York)

Twentieth-Century Painting

The tendency to question the whole function of art is very easy to observe in twentieth-century painting. The discovery of photography created a new art which depicted reality more faithfully than painting could; therefore, painters pursued goals other than merely creating realistic images. The Impressionists experimented with the phenomenon of light and tried to paint what the eye actually sees, rather than the object as object. Consequently, they developed the technique of breaking up colored areas into pinpoints of bright color, leaving the mind to organize these points of color into objects. Surrealists sought to depict, not the real world around us, but the world of dreams and the unconscious. Expressionism sought first to depict feelings, things as we *feel* them rather than as we *see* them; later, abstract expressionism sought to eliminate the object altogether and to play with line, color, and space. Cubism focused on the mass of the object and, therefore, simultaneously depicted several planes, or the same object or sight from several viewpoints. Op art took optical illusions and other phenomena of vision as its subject matter. Pop art started with the dross of popular culture and made larger or endlessly duplicated versions of those artifacts. The list could go on, but it is easy to see, just from these few examples, that all of the artists involved are trying to redefine the nature and function of art. It is also clear that there is no basis for comparing the works of these different schools. They must be accepted on their own grounds, and the only fair critical question is how well they succeed on their own terms.

The arts in the twentieth century are a faithful reflection of the concerns, fears, and endless change of this century. All premises are open to question; and the arts, if not always beautiful in the Romantic sense, are endlessly fascinating.

CHAPTER **39**

Major Musical
Developments

Just as practitioners of the visual arts sought new ways of depicting reality and argued whether or not depicting reality was even the purpose of the visual arts, so music has gone through enormous changes in the twentieth century. Although some composers, as we have already noted, continue to compose in something similar to Romantic style, most have accepted the idea that Romanticism is over and have searched for new ways of organizing and structuring music. As we might imagine, the hallmarks of Romanticism were the first stylistic traits to disappear.

In place of the huge Romantic orchestra, twentieth-century compositions are more typically for smaller groups, chamber groups of various types or a small orchestra. The instrumental family that comes into prominence is the percussion family. Sometimes works are written entirely for percussion instruments; the percussion section has a more important role in ensembles of all types. Another hallmark of twentieth-century music is jagged rhythm. Even instruments like the piano and violin are played more percussively and less lyrically.

NEW TECHNIQUES

All sorts of new effects and new playing techniques are asked of instrumentalists and vocalists. The piano, used by Romantic composers as a miniature orchestra, is viewed as the potential source for all sorts of new and strange sounds by the twentieth-century composer. He may ask the player to reach inside the instrument and pluck the strings, use his fists and elbows to create "clusters" of notes, or play an instrument that has been "prepared" by the addition of various materials to the strings, so that the instrument sounds like a percussion section, or at least not like a traditional piano. Violinists are instructed to bow in unusual places to create new sounds—on the bridge, below the bridge, and elsewhere. They are also asked to use the body of the instrument as a percussion instrument, playing it with their hands or bows. Wind players are asked to produce "multiphonics," two sounds at once, or percussive key clicks. Brass players are sometimes asked to speak through their instruments, and singers, to sing into instruments. They are asked to sing some very unvocal melodies and to produce other special effects as well.

ELECTRIC AND ELECTRONIC INSTRUMENTS

One new technological possibility is the electrifying of instruments, just as the guitar has been electrified. Works have been written for electric piano, electric violin, and electric versions of most other instruments. Short of the electric instruments, amplification of various sorts is a resource used by composers to produce new sounds. The last class of new instruments, of course, is the electronic instruments, instruments that produce the original sound electronically, as

Milton Babbitt developing an electronic composition.

distinguished from the electric instruments, which produce the sound in one of the usual ways and then amplify it electronically. In the pioneer days of electronic instruments, they were cumbersome. It took a room full of equipment and huge amounts of time to put together a short electronic composition. Now, however, the synthesizer has been hooked up to a keyboard and the circuitry has been miniaturized, so that today's electronic instruments are portable, and can do much more, more quickly, than the early versions. Some electronic instruments have been designed to duplicate the sounds of acoustic instruments or voices. Much more fascinating are the ones designed to produce entirely new types of sound, the only limits being the imagination of the composer.

MUSICAL STYLE

Melody

Some of the other hallmarks of Romantic style are abandoned in twentieth-century music. The long, arching melodies of a Brahms or Tchaikovsky are not much in evidence in this century's music. Melodies now are more marked by wide leaps, irregular phrasing, and a conscious effort *not* to be stepwise and lyrical.

Rhythm

Rhythm, as we have already indicated, is much more in the foreground as a crucial element of musical style. The rhythmic patterns of this century are more likely to remind one of the city or the factory than of the Romantic babbling brook. Rhythm was not a foreground element in late Romantic style, which explains why so much music in that style is soothing and peaceful. Twentieth-century music is more likely to have the jagged, staccato rhythm patterns we are used to in our big cities, or from our physiological responses to the stresses in modern life.

Harmony

As we have seen, one of the strongest elements in late Romantic style is a creative approach to standard harmony. In the works of Liszt and Wagner especially, the constant modulations, evaded cadences, and generally rich chromatic harmony extended the standard harmonic system to its limits. As we would expect, twentieth-century composers abandoned that chromatic style and created new harmonic underpinnings for their music.

Impressionism

One new approach seems like an extension of late Romantic harmony, but is actually a large step away from traditional functional harmony. In this style, called **Impressionism**, seen most clearly in the works of Claude Debussy (Chapter 40), dissonant chords do not lead to resolution, but are used in series or "streams," weakening any sense of harmonic gravity and function. Some Impressionistic composers also use scales other than the standard Western scales to escape from their implied harmonic direction.

Polytonality

Another approach, called **polytonality**, sounds two or more tonalities at once, defying the listener's ear to keep its sense of harmonic bearings in the traditional sense. Famous examples of polytonality appear in the early works of Igor Stravinsky, such as *Petrushka*.

Pan-diatonic System

Still another approach, called **pan-diatonic**, makes no distinction between what would formerly have been regarded as "consonant" and "dissonant" notes. All notes are equally valid, and a sense of musical logic and shape is created by other than harmonic means. In this system, for example, a cadence would be signaled through means other than harmony, such as articulation, rhythm, or movement from thick, complex chords to more simple ones. Paul Hindemith, a German-born composer who taught at Yale for years and influenced several generations of American composers, developed a new theory of harmony based on this concept. He tried to create a theory of musical logic that would work for all music, including the music composed before the development of standard-practice tonality and the new twentieth-century music. Whether his theories actually work for all music is doubtful, but the pan-diatonic system has been used by a large number of twentieth-century composers.

Atonality

Obviously, the next logical step from polytonality is atonality, the total absence of a tonal center. Atonal music is liberated from any sense of harmony; all notes are equally important, and there are no consonant or dissonant chords.

Twelve–Tone or Serial Composition

Since atonality removed the basic principle of musical organization in use since 1700, new ways of organizing music had to be created. One of the most important is twelve-tone or serial composition, developed by Arnold Schoenberg, who had composed earlier in a nontonal, post-Romantic style. The twelve-tone, or serial, method is one of the crucial innovations of this century and is a system of organizing music that is beautiful in its simplicity and logic. The fundamental principle is that all twelve notes of the chromatic scale are equal in importance; none takes the position of tonic or dominant. For that reason, the twelve notes are arranged in a series or row selected by the composer and then appear always in that order with no note repeated, so that none takes precedence as a tonal center. Every aspect of the composition is then to be derived from the row—chords, melodic ideas, accompaniment patterns, and so forth.

Besides its original form, the row exists in three other possible versions: the **inversion**, which keeps the intervals of the original row but reverses their direction, so that it is the original row upside down; the **retrograde**, which reverses the order of the twelve notes, so that it is the original row backwards; and the **retrograde inversion**, which combines the two previous versions, producing an upside-down and backwards version of the original row. All four versions can be transposed to any other pitch level. Thus there are forty-eight different series available: each of the four versions can begin on any of the twelve chromatic pitches. Figure 39-1 is the row from Schoenberg's Suite for Piano, Opus 25, in its original, inversion, retrograde, and retrograde inversion forms.

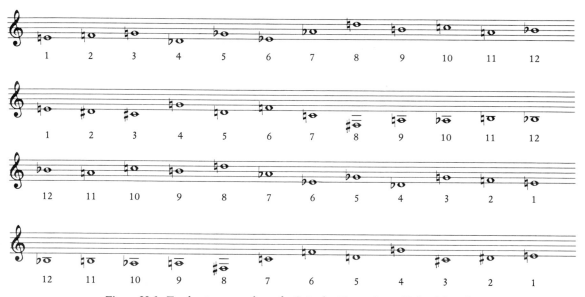

Figure 39-1. Twelve-tone row from the Suite for Piano, Opus 25, by Schoenberg.

Students sometimes get the impression that the twelve-tone method is some sort of music-making machine: pick a row, turn the crank, and out comes a prefabricated work. It is important to realize that the twelve-tone method does not determine the style of a piece or eliminate compositional choices. The twelve-tone works of Schoenberg do not sound like the twelve-tone works of others. One of his disciples, Alban Berg (Chapter 44) tended to select rows that facilitated traditional-sounding harmony and wrote in a very lyric, accessible style. Anton Webern, another Schoenberg disciple, chose nontonal rows and wrote in a sparse, concentrated style that isolates each note within an envelope of surrounding silence. It is questionable whether Schoenberg himself wrote completely atonally, because he composed phrases that ended on a particular note, thus turning that note into a temporary tonal center. He also shaped his compositions in traditional ways, so that one can hear structural events—sections, cadences, phrases—whether or not one can pick out the permutations of the row by ear. Other composers have experimented with extending the serial principle to dimensions other than pitch: rhythm, articulation, instrumental color. However it has been used, the serial principle is one of the important original contributions to music in this century and a highly significant answer to the problem of tonality in post-Romantic music.

Structure

Neoclassicism

The element of structure has been the subject of considerable discussion and innovation in the twentieth century. One approach, popular in the thirties and forties and audible in the works of Hindemith and middle-period Stravinsky, was called Neoclassicism. This style revived the tight, logical structures of the Baroque and Classic periods, but in a twentieth-century, usually pan-diatonic harmonic idiom. Forms like fugue, rondo, sonata-allegro, and theme and variations were popular. What these forms provided for composers was an intellectually satisfying, abstract framework for their musical ideas, usually stated in a rhythmically complex, busy texture for a chamber group of some sort. Neoclassicism provided the necessary relief from the heroic themes, overblown orchestras, and loose structures of late Romanticism. Works in this style often convey a spirit of sardonic wit which was the perfect response to the cosmic seriousness of Romanticism. Like the Baroque and Classic works whose forms they imitate, Neoclassic compositions are generally fun to play, and exploit the delightful possibilities of unusual combinations of instruments.

Aleatoric or Chance Music

Another revolutionary approach to structure is called **aleatoric** or **chance music**. Some composers, reacting against the minutely controlled structures of others, create "happenings" in which some elements of the musical structure are left to the performers, usually with some guidance provided by either composer or conductor. Like the splattered paintings of Jackson Pollack and others, aleatoric music upsets some observers, who view the abandonment of control over every detail as a capitulation to random chance, or a put-on of the audience. But to restore some element of improvisation and choice to the performer is not to abandon the great Western rational tradition or to contribute to the downfall of Western civilization. It simply restores to the performer a role in the creative process that he has always had in popular music and in the folk traditions of every culture, as well as in the art musics of some cultures.

New Principles

The most common approach to structure in twentieth century music is to create new structural principles and organization with each new composition. Composers now speak of "events" in their music, a neutral term that allows them to escape from the assumptions of traditional forms. Sometimes they provide explanations of how the piece is structured; sometimes the explanations are longer and more puzzling than the music itself. Sometimes no clues are given, and the listener organizes the events himself as they reach his ear. Often it takes repeated listening to sense the underlying logic behind the work.

Older Forms

Symphony and Concerto

Some forms from the past have persisted in the twentieth century, besides the ones adopted by Neoclassic composers. The symphony is a pliant enough form to have lasted from its inception in the Classic era until the present day. As we saw, it remained a viable form in the Romantic era, although modified by the Romantic spirit, and it has persisted in twentieth-century music also. Like Romantic symphonies, twentieth-century symphonies tend to be highly individual in organization and spirit. Among composers who have devoted a major part of their attention to the symphony are Dmitri Shostakovich, Roy Harris, and Charles Ives. The concerto has survived also, but not as a showy Romantic display piece. A twentieth-century concerto is generally an exploration of the new possibilities of an instrument or of unusual instruments or combinations of instruments.

Opera

Opera in the twentieth century is a fascinating subject, worthy of another book in itself. Although few twentieth-century operas have found their way into the standard repertoire of the major opera houses, some, like Berg's *Wozzeck* and several of Benjamin Britten's operas—*Peter Grimes, Death in Venice, Turn of the Screw*—are performed with some regularity. The usual fare of opera houses is still the eighteenth and nineteenth-century repertory, just as the concerts of major orchestras consist almost entirely of masterworks from those same periods. As we would expect, opera in the twentieth century is not about great heroic deeds and unrequited love. It tends to focus, instead, on anti-heroes,

Metropolitan Opera performance of Stauss's *Salome*.

psychological drama, violence, and Katkaesque plots. *Salome* by Richard Strauss, which shocked the world in 1905, is still shockingly violent and Freudian, at least if it is performed well. Berg's *Wozzeck* (Chapter 41) is concerned with man's inhumanity to man, madness, and violence.

Most opera lovers want star singers and familiar tunes; twentieth-century opera is much more likely to be performed in a university or workshop setting than in the major houses. It is a genre worth studying; some of the works are masterful dramatic statements of the ideas and fears of our age.

Musical Theater

One important new form in this century is musical theater, sometimes called, not very accurately, "musical comedy." There had always been lighter musical stage presentations alongside opera; but in this century these lighter works took on new dramatic validity, new seriousness, and better plots and music. In one sense, musicals moved into the gap left by twentieth-century opera, which became more esoteric, and provided musical theater for a broader audience. Works like *South Pacific*, *The Sound of Music*, *Oklahoma!*, *Brigadoon*, *Chorus Line*, *Annie*, and the hundreds of other musicals have had enormously long runs

The University of Kansas Contemporary Percussion Ensemble.

and successful revivals. Film versions reached a huge audience and made some of the songs quite popular. Chapter 48 surveys the history of American musical theater in this century.

Popular Music

Straying further from the art music field, this century also saw the rise of popular music as a separate genre and a separate industry. Not only have jazz, pop, and rock been important facets of our own popular culture, but they constitute our best-known and most successful exports as well. Chapter 49 deals briefly with this important realm of music.

Generalizing about this century is extremely difficult. Not only is it a jumble, filled with rapid change and endless innovation; it also is too recent for any reliable historical perspective. Performers and composers do not necessarily agree with the historian's attempt to assess what has been significant in the music of this century. Composers are still creating the century's style and have understandably strong feelings about the relative importance of what has happened so far. It is more useful to look in detail at some of the milestone works of the century (not everyone would agree, of course, on the selection) and see how composers have worked in this fascinating and tangled period.

CHAPTER 40

Impressionism Claude Debussy, Prélude à l'après-midi d'un faune

DEBUSSY'S LIFE

Claude Debussy was born near Paris in 1862. As a boy he studied piano with a woman who had been a pupil of Chopin's, at the age of ten he enrolled as a piano student at the Paris Conservatoire. He graduated in 1880, having distinguished himself as a pianist but not as a composition student, because he insisted on his own personal style, rather than following the traditional rules of harmony and counterpoint. Upon graduation, he was hired as household pianist and tutor for her children by the same woman who had been Tchaikovsky's patroness. In her employ he traveled to Switzerland, Italy, and Russia; and the new music of the Russian composers Mussorgsky and Borodin influenced the development of his own style. In 1884 he won the Prix de Rome for a cantata, *L'Enfant prodigue*. The prize granted him several years in Italy, so that he could devote himself to composing. Not much came of those years, and he returned to Paris before the subsidy ended. He became fascinated with Wagner's works and was also greatly influenced by the Oriental music he heard at the Paris Exposition of 1889. He later turned away from Wagner's ideas and became involved with the symbolist poets. Association with their ideas further refined his unique musical style. In 1902, his opera *Pelléas et Mélisande*, based on a symbolist drama by Maurice Maeterlinck, caused a great sensation but was gradually accepted into the opera repertoire. He continued composing and performing as a pianist and conductor of his orchestral works. Illness forced him to abandon musical activity around 1914. He died of cancer in 1918, just before the liberation of Paris and the end of World War I.

WRITINGS ABOUT MUSIC

Like Berlioz, Debussy wrote extensively on musical aesthetics and the current musical scene. He is especially interesting in his criticism of Wagner. Although he realized the genius and importance of Wagner and had been fascinated as a youth with his music, he later rejected what he regarded as the ponderous Teutonic seriousness of Wagner's operas. Of the four Ring operas he wrote, "My God! How unbearable these people in skins and helmets become by the fourth night!"

IMPRESSIONISM

The musical style called Impressionism, associated with Debussy, is a musical analog to Impressionist painting and the works of the symbolist poets. Impressionist painters were interested in depicting the effect of light on the eye rather than in painting realistic pictures of objects. The Symbolist poets had a similar aim: to evoke an object or feeling by means of allusive words in a deliberate atmosphere of shadow and ambiguity. Impressionist music moves in the same veiled, pastel world: hard edges of rhythm and structure are removed or blurred, and the resulting music is vague, dreamy, and shimmering.

In one sense, it is hard to separate Impressionism from late Romanticism: both are concerned with expressing feelings, and both use orchestral color as an important means to that end. But the style of Debussy and the other Impressionists goes so far beyond Romantic style that many historians view this school as the first stage of twentieth-century style, rather than as the last gasp of Romanticism.

IMPRESSIONIST MUSICAL STYLE

The special style of Impressionism is the result of a unique approach to each of the elements that make up musical style.

Orchestral Color

Orchestral color is crucial to the overall effect intended by Impressionist composers. The colors are delicate and shimmering, rather than bold and assertive. In place of the dramatic color shifts of late Romanticism, we now hear carefully shaded and blended changes from one color to another. Favorite Impressionist instruments include the solo woodwinds, the combination of flute and harp, muted French horns, and muted strings divided into eight or ten separate parts.

Rhythm

Rhythm is dealt with very freely. In most of Debussy's music, the rhythmic movement is kept fluid by shifting meters, deliberately blurring rhythmic and metrical patterns, and constructing asymmetrical melodic phrases.

Harmony

Most important of all, the harmonic patterns of the nineteenth century are extended or abandoned altogether. As was mentioned earlier, Debussy attended an International Exposition in Paris in 1889, at which he was greatly impressed by performances of Asian music by native performers. Apparently what he heard was Javanese gamelan music, a type of Asian court music characterized by static harmonies, large groups of gongs of various sizes, and an approach to structure much less directional and less organized than Western musical structures. Debussy used some scales foreign to Western music. Their effect is to eliminate the sense of harmonic directionality inherent in Western scales. Two of his favorite "exotic" scales are given in Figure 40-1. Note that both lack the half-steps that give our Western scales their harmonic flavor.

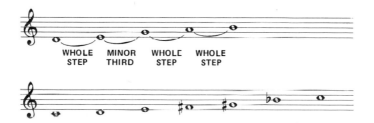

Figure 40-1.   Two of Claude Debussy's favorite "exotic" scales.

Another harmonic device that defeats any sense of harmonic direction is the use of streams of dissonant chords. Each dissonant chord, instead of resolving to a consonant chord, becomes one member of a series of parallel dissonant chords, thus eliminating its harmonic function. The resulting effect is pleasant, dreamlike, and tranquil.

DEBUSSY'S MUSIC

Debussy is important in several areas of composition. He wrote numerous works for the piano, generally with picturesque titles, often referring to scenes of water or moonlight, like the titles of Impressionist paintings. His most famous piano piece is *"Claire de Lune"* ("Moonlight"), from the *Suite Bergamesque*. To play his piano pieces requires a sensitivity to subtle dynamics, fluid rhythm, and skillful pedaling. He is one of the composers who has extended the expressive capacities of the piano and added immensely to its literature.

Debussy is also important for his songs, which are settings of the poems of writers like Baudelaire, Paul Verlaine, and Stéphane Mallarmé. He also wrote the opera we have already mentioned, *Pelléas et Mélisande*, based on a play by the symbolist poet Maurice Maeterlinck. Although the plot revolves around the doomed love of the title characters and superficially resembles the story of Tristan and Isolde, the story, the music, and the staging are completely faithful to the Impressionist aesthetic. Debussy is also well known for his orchestral music; the best-known works are the *Prélude à l'après-midi d'un faune*, ("Prelude to The Afternoon of a Faun"), and three nocturnes, *La Mer*, ("The Sea"). and *Iberia*.

PRÉLUDE À L'APRÈS-MIDI D'UN FAUNE, 1894

The *Prelude to the Afternoon of a Faun* is a perfect example of Impressionist orchestral music. It is based on a poem of Mallarmé, which depicts a moment in the life of a faun, the mythical half-man, half-goat. It is not so much a story that the poet and composer depict as it is a mood. Dulled by wine, the faun lies dreaming by a stream on a hot summer afternoon. Wavering between sleep and wakefulness, he is not sure whether the erotic visions he sees are real or imagined.

Orchestration

The music matches the picture perfectly. It is all silken shimmer, sliding harmonies, and fluid rhythm. All of the sharp edges of meter, structure, and harmony are blurred and veiled. In the foreground is color—the solo flute, solo oboe, English horn, muted strings, solo French horn, harps. Gone is the Romantic brass section; the only brasses here are three French horns. The only percussion instruments called for are two antique cymbals, percussion instruments of definite pitch and exotic effect. The dynamic range is subtle, moving from almost inaudible to medium soft; there are a few crescendos, all carefully controlled. The harmony is full of vague chords, whose function in the harmonic

Leon Bakst's famous poster of *Prelude to the Afternoon of a Faun* captures the Impressionistic spirit of Debussy's composition.

scheme is elusive, and surprising movements in and out of tenuously related keys. The melodies are vague and asymmetrical, and keep recurring in what seems to be random order. Cadences are carefully avoided; in the nearly nine minutes of music, there are only three cadences we hear with any sense of finality, and they occur at odd intervals. In between, our impression is of a continuous, organic flow, like water or sunlight.

Opening Melody

The piece begins with one of the most famous openings in all music: a vague melody for solo flute in the breathy lower octave (see Figure 40-2). The melody is vague in several ways: in its first two measures, it outlines an augmented fourth, an interval devoid of harmonic identity. It also has a very free rhythmic shape, as if the player were improvising. That opening melody keeps recurring throughout the piece, usually with details freely changed—played by different instruments, against a different harmonic background, or with some notes changed. Another melody appears in what we hear as the A section; this one is more animated (see Figure 40-3). A third melody in *D*-flat forms the B section of the overall form (see Figure 40-4). Note the way the meter shifts, dividing the six half-beats of the measure first as three sets of two, then two threes. The return of the A section is marked by a return of the flute melody in several modified versions that sound more harmonically stable than the original one, then in a duplication of the original version. After a cadence on *E* major, there are a few measures of coda, bringing the piece to a very quiet close. The work is subtle, refined, perfumed, almost decadent in its controlled, delicate effects.

Figure 40-2. A section, first theme.

Figure 40-3. A section, subsidiary theme.

Figure 40-4. B section, theme.

The listening guide (Figure 40-5) outlines the main events in the work, identifying the major themes.

FIGURE 40-5. LISTENING GUIDE

PRÉLUDE À L'APRÈS-MIDI D'UN FAUNE,
BY DEBUSSY

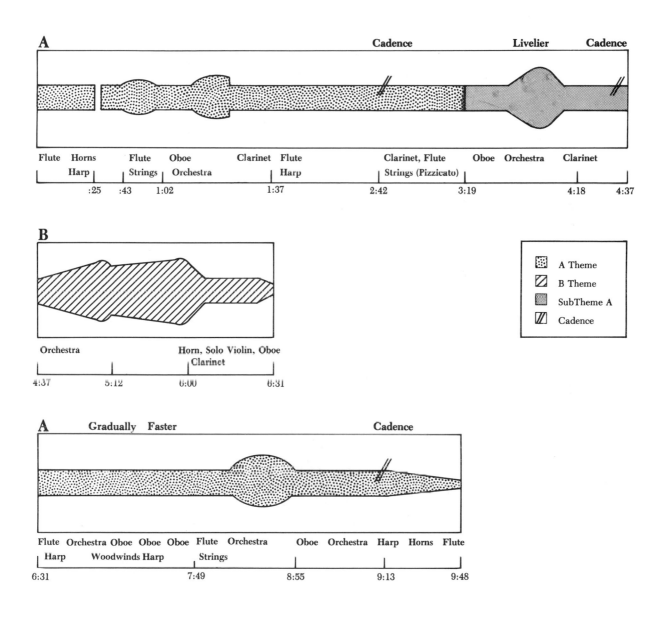

CHAPTER **41**

Igor Stravinsky Le Sacre du Printemps

STRAVINSKY'S LIFE

Igor Stravinsky is probably the best-known composer of art music in the twentieth century. He is often compared to the artist Pablo Picasso, both because the two men are the best-known artists of this period in their respective fields and because Stravinsky, like Picasso, moved through several phases in his creative life and worked in several different styles.

Stravinsky was born in 1881 near St. Petersburg (now Leningrad) in Russia. His father was a bass in the Imperial Opera. Like so many composers before him, his education was in the field of law rather than music, although he was a musical amateur in his youth. At twenty, he abandoned law for the formal study of music. He became a pupil of Nicolai Rimsky-Korsakov, one of the nationalist Russian composers.

Success came early to the young composer. Serge Diaghilev, the impresario of the Ballet Russe in Paris, commissioned a work from Stravinsky. The association with Diaghilev brought Stravinsky immediate fame. Diaghilev had gathered at the Ballet Russe an incredible assembly of creative geniuses: Nijinsky was the leading male dancer and one of the choreographers; Piccaso and Jean Cocteau worked on stage design and scenery. Among the famous ballets for which Stravinsky wrote the music were *The Firebird* (1910), *Petrushka* (1911), and the scandalous *Rite of Spring* (1913), which we will discuss in more detail later in this chapter. Many of Stravinsky's early works have a Russian nationalist flavor. They are also written for large, colorful orchestras, reflecting the composer's training with Rimsky-Korsakov, who was a master orchestrator.

STRAVINSKY'S MUSIC

Smaller Works

After the early ballets, Stravinsky wrote for much smaller ensembles, partly as a result of the limitations imposed by World War I and the impossibility of ballets on the grand Diaghilev scale, and partly because of a change in his approach to creating music. A cantata, *Les Noces* ("The Wedding"), based on Russian peasant marriage customs, was scored for four pianos and percussion. A more famous small-scale work is *L'Histoire Du Soldat* ("A Soldier's Tale"), scored for speaker and seven instruments.

Neoclassic Period

The next phase of Stravinsky's creative life was the Neoclassic period, which lasted from about 1920 until 1951. As was explained in Chapter 30, Neoclassicism sought to escape from Romantic excess by returning to abstract Baroque and Classic forms and reestablishing a spirit of pungent wit, clear textures, and a pan-diatonic harmonic vocabulary. Among Stravinsky's better-known Neoclassic works are the ballet *Pulcinella*, based on music by Pergolesi, an eighteenth-century Italian composer; the Octet for Winds; *Oedipus Rex*, an opera-oratorio; the ballet *Apollon Musagetes*; the Symphony in *C*; the Symphony in Three Movements; the Dumbarton Oaks Concerto for chamber orchestra; the *Symphony of Psalms*; and *The Rake's Progress*. The last work is an opera based on Hogarth's famous drawings and utilizes many of the conventions of eighteenth-century comic opera—recitative and aria, ensemble numbers, harpsichord accompaniment, and a typical finale, in which the main characters sing in front of the curtain, discussing the moral of the story.

The Serial Period

From 1952 on, Stravinsky moved from the Neoclassic style into a type of serial writing, a shift that some of his admirers regarded as selling out to the Schoenberg forces. The people around these two composers regarded them as antagonists and kept them apart, despite the fact that they both lived in Los Angeles for some time. Stravinsky's version of serial technique was different from Schoenberg's, and he worked in that style for his last twenty years. Among his serial works are the *Canticum Sacrum*, the ballet *Agon*, and the *Requiem Canticles*. Stravinsky died in New York in 1971 and was buried in Venice.

STRAVINSKY'S WRITINGS

Stravinsky left several accessible accounts of his ideas. He wrote an autobiography, a work entitled *Poetics of Music*, and several books of *Conversations*, written with Robert Craft, a composer and conductor who worked as his assistant during the later years of his life. Like Schoenberg, Stravinsky had a strong sense of his mission as a twentieth-century composer, an uncompromising critical view of the artistic life of his time, and the biting wit to express his ideas in memorable phrases.

STRAVINSKY'S APPROACH TO COMPOSITION

Stravinsky was a dedicated composer. On his frequent concert tours as a conductor he always made time to work on his compositions. Bedridden in his final days, he insisted on composing every day, if only for a few minutes. He worked with immense care, and his creative mind was always searching out new topics for inspiration, new texts to set, and new languages to work with. He set some texts in Latin and Hebrew because the sounds of the languages, as well as their antiquity and sacredness, fascinated him.

A story is told of a brush with the film industry, which is typical of the wealth of Stravinsky stories that musicians love to tell. It seems that the head of one of the studios thought it would be a feather in his cap to hire a composer of Stravinsky's stature to write the music for one of the studio's films. A meeting was arranged, during which the magnate asked the composer how long he thought he would need to score an important film that had just been completed. The composer's answer, "Two years," brought the potential association to an abrupt halt.

Stravinsky is one of the giants of twentieth-century music; every younger composer and student of contemporary music must understand his work. Stravinsky contributed major works in most important contemporary styles, with the exception of electronic music and avant-garde experimental style. His consummate craftsmanship set high standards for all other composers.

STRAVINSKY'S STYLE

It is impossible to generalize about Stravinsky's style because his output is so varied. The early ballets do not sound like the late works, and he got very tired of being introduced or thought of as the "the *Firebird* man." But some aspects of his style remain constant throughout his creative life. Chief among them is rhythmic drive. His approach to rhythm is always strong and creative, marked by shifting meters, ostinato patterns, and constant freshness and surprise. He also was a master of orchestration, whether he chose to write for a swollen late Romantic orchestra or a small group. And his works in any style always have a freshness and vitality about them that testify to his genius and care.

LE SACRE DU PRINTEMPS ("THE RITE OF SPRING")

The audience that attended the first performance of *The Rite of Spring* at the Ballet Russe in Paris in 1913 was not prepared for the revolutionary aspects of the work. It caused a great scandal. The audience created such an uproar that Nijinsky and the other dancers could not hear the music from the pit, and the critics had a fine time inventing new levels of disdain for the shocking work. The scandal may have been caused more by the costumes and the dancing than by the music, because a performance the following year of the music without the dancing was a great success.

There was reason to regard the music as revolutionary, particularly in comparison with the nationalistic works that preceded it. Stravinsky invented a totally new style for *The Rite of Spring*, a style often described as primitivism. Although a few subsequent works were written in this style, the idea of the composer's freedom to create a totally new style for each new work was revolutionary and changed the course of Western music forever. The first performance also established the idea that the composer could not or, perhaps, should not expect his ideas to mean anything to the general audience, at least at first. Thus was established the composer's obligation to himself and to his experiments with new styles, rather than his obligation to the audience to provide what they wanted to hear—a fundamental notion in Stravinsky's writings, and in the ideas of nearly all twentieth-century composers. Stravinsky regarded the standard Romantic repertoire as nice sounds in which members of the audience could wallow. What he wanted to provide was a more challenging experience, forcing them to think and listen carefully. Charles Ives, an American experimental composer, spoke of writing "muscular" music, which would force audiences to work; he regarded Romantic music as "sissy" music, and once exhorted a complaining man next to him at a concert to "use his ears like a man."

Style

Stravinsky certainly created a new style in this work, one that carefully avoids anything that would smack of Romanticism or the familiar. While he continues in the *Rite* to use the large Romantic orchestra, with its array of special woodwind sounds and its percussion equipment, he uses instruments in new ways, asking the violins to use the wood of their bows in places, grouping and doubling the instruments in new ways and creating grating, percussive effects rather than the lyric sounds and lush colors of late Romanticism. Most original is his approach to harmony and rhythm. We already noted that vital rhythm is a Stravinsky trademark in any of his styles. In this work, rhythm is crucial. All of the sections abound with pounding ostinato patterns; syncopated, nervous rhythms, and shifting meters. At times, all we hear is rhythm, to the exclusion of harmony and melody in the standard sense of those terms. In the harmonic sphere, traditional harmony is avoided altogether for long stretches in favor of melodic ideas that are restricted to a few notes, hypnotically repeated. In one famous passage, the string section plays staccato groups of notes that together form a simultaneous combination of an *E*-flat chord and an *E* chord. The effect is a far cry from the typical lush, lyric writing for the string section in the Romantic era. Sections of the *Rite* are in recognizable keys, but other long stretches juxtapose or superimpose notes or groups of notes that are "dissonant" in traditional harmonic terms. The critics who found the work barbarous and savage were simply pointing out the obvious. Stravinsky asked the listener to forget all previous music and to listen with ears free of traditional expectations. Accepted on its own terms, the *Rite* is a work of enormous power. Although it no longer sounds revolutionary to us, it was a seminal work in the ongoing revolution that is the history of Western music in this century.

Structure

Introduction

The work opens with a famous solo for bassoon, at the upper limits of its range (see Figure 41-1). The sound is tight and pinched, and the notes played are few and repetitive. The effect is one of dawn or the beginning of time.

The introductory section features mostly woodwinds, playing what sound like random bits of melody, like birds waking up in the jungle and beginning to sing.

Figure 41-1. Opening bassoon melody.

Every note is actually carefully written out in complex rhythmic patterns, but the effect is random, as more and more instruments are added. Near the end of the introduction, a four-note idea first appears (see Figure 41-2). It later becomes an important ostinato pattern.

Figure 41-2.   Ostinato idea, end of introduction.

First Ballet Section

The first ballet section, "Dance of the Adolescents," begins with the polytonal string chords already mentioned, with the syncopated accents reinforced by eight horns (see Figure 41-3). Later in the section, a prominent melody appears, first in the horn (see Figure 41-4). Note that it moves within a narrow range of five notes.

Figure 41-3.   Rhythmic pattern.

Figure 41-4.   Horn Melody.

The listening guide (Figure 41-5) outlines the main events of the introduction and first section. To get a sense of the dramatic contrasts in the work, one should listen to the next two sections, the "Dance of Abduction" and "Spring Dance." The "Dance of Abduction" consists of nervous patterns in winds and strings, punctuated by hunting calls in the brass. The "Dance of Spring" has a heavy, solemn feeling, depicting ancient religious rites. Unfamiliar harmonies and strange instrumental colors create the impression of antiquity. The entire work merits several listenings. It is powerful, colorful, and completely original for its time.

FIGURE 41-5. LISTENING GUIDE

INTRODUCTION AND THE "DANCE OF THE ADOLESCENTS" FROM *RITE OF SPRING*, BY STRAVINSKY

■	Ostinato
■	Horn Melody
■	Other

A INTRODUCTION

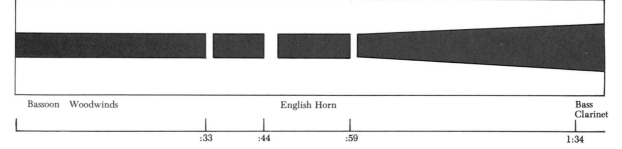

Faster   Thicker

Bassoon   Woodwinds   English Horn   Bass Clarinet

:33   :44   :59   1:34

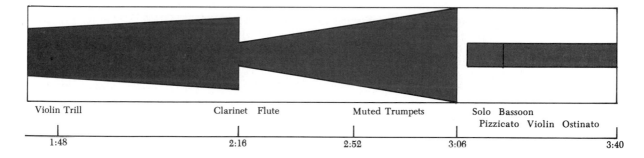

Violin Trill   Clarinet   Flute   Muted Trumpets   Solo   Bassoon
                                                                            Pizzicato   Violin   Ostinato

1:48   2:16   2:52   3:06   3:40

B DANCE OF THE ADOLESCENTS

Chords   Chords

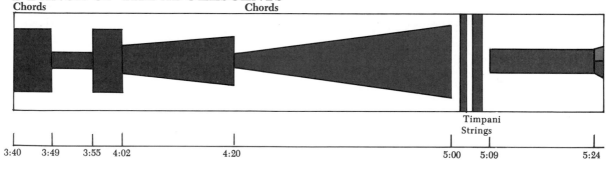

Timpani
Strings

3:40   3:49   3:55   4:02   4:20   5:00   5:09   5:24

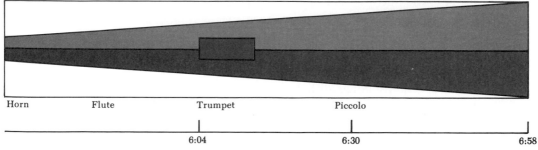

Horn   Flute   Trumpet   Piccolo

6:04   6:30   6:58

CHAPTER 42

Béla Bartók
Concerto for
Orchestra

In many ways, the life and career of Bartók parallel those of Stravinsky, but Bartók never achieved during his lifetime the fame he deserved. Since his death, he has come to occupy a position similar to Stravinsky's in the estimation of musicians. He too was a consummate craftsman, a person of uncompromising commitment to his art and his personal style, and a pioneer who has had a great influence on many later composers.

BARTÓK'S LIFE

Bartók was born in 1881 in a small town in Hungary and studied piano and composition at the Royal Academy in Budapest. Liszt was the national hero of the time, and Bartók's first compositions owe a great deal to the earlier Hungarian master. In 1906, Bartók turned to studies that completely changed his approach to composing. Along with Zoltán Kodály, another composer, he began to study folk musics of the various ethnic groups inhabiting Hungary. He soon discovered that what pass for "Hungarian" touches in nineteenth-century music were really a few simple ideas borrowed from café Gypsy music.

The real music of the region was actually quite different, based on different scales and structural patterns, which he and Kodály studied and cataloged. They were pioneers in serious field studies of folk music. Out of efforts like theirs has developed a new branch of the study of music, **ethnomusicology**, which combines the methods of anthropology and sociology with musical scholarship to study folk musics and musics of other cultures with accuracy and discipline, and without the Western bias that prevented serious study in the past.

Besides uncovering information about the folk musics of his country, Bartók's studies provided him with new ways of thinking about his own musical style. Without quoting literally from folk music, he began to incorporate some of the folk scales and patterns into his own compositions. They provided fresh ways to organize music and escape from the clichés of late Romanticism. He combined those fresh ideas with a knack for strong rhythms and free counterpoint and with a Neoclassical interest in tightly organized structures. All of these elements, plus a talent for driving rhythms and great skill at orchestral color, combine to make Bartók's music fascinating to listener and scholar alike. Like Stravinsky's music, Bartók's always has drive and power; unlike Stravinsky, however, Bartók never went through clear stylistic metamorphoses and never became an international celebrity.

The end of Bartók's life was tragic. Depressed by the devastation he saw coming in World War II, and unwilling to compromise with the limitations imposed on artists by the spreading fascism of the Third Reich, Bartók left Hungary in 1940 and moved to the United States. Almost unknown in his new country, and suffering from leukemia, he died in 1945.

BARTÓK'S MUSIC

Among Bartók's important contributions to the music of this century are several works for the piano. He remained active until late in his life as a performer on this instrument. Included in his piano works are three concertos and several collections of shorter pieces for piano solo, the most important being the six books called *Mikrokosmos*, studies ranging in difficulty from pieces for beginners to technically demanding virtuoso pieces. He also composed six string quartets, which are regarded as the most significant addition to quartet literature since Beethoven. The quartets are significant both for their use of new string techniques and their creative structures, and are frequently performed. Among Bartók's orchestral works are the Music for Strings, Percussion, and Celesta, and the Concerto for Orchestra. He also wrote a primitivist ballet score, *The Miraculous Mandarin*, and an opera, *Bluebeard's Castle*. All of his works show the various traits—folk ideas, virgorous rhythms, **ostinato** patterns, clear structures, a talent for dissonant counterpoint—that he welded into a strong personal style.

CONCERTO FOR ORCHESTRA

The Concerto for Orchestra was written in 1943, on a commission from Serge Koussevitsky, the conductor of the Boston Symphony. Bartók was hospitalized when the commission was arranged, and the eventual performance of the work afforded him one of the few successes of his years in New York. The title is interesting. "Concerto" generally indicates a soloist with orchestral accompaniment; here it refers to a symphonic design that treats all of the members of the orchestra as virtuoso soloists. This intent is clearest in the second movement—*Giuocco delle Coppie* ("Game of Pairs")—which features the various wind instruments in pairs. There are five movements altogether, the third, "Elegy," being an example of the tragic and desolate mood Bartók's music sometimes evokes. The entire work is a fine example of the variety of expression within his style and has become a favorite twentieth-century work for orchestral concerts.

First Movement

One of the hallmarks of Bartók's style is tight construction. His ideas relate to one another in several ways, and the same idea or motive may appear in several guises in the same work. Students of musical structure analyze his works closely. Like Beethoven, he merits close study for his motivic unity and the way he relates and expands ideas. The first movement of the Concerto for Orchestra makes extensive use of the melodic interval of the fourth, an interval used more in Eastern European folk musics than in Western art music. The form of the movement is similar to a Classical sonata-allegro structure.

Introduction and Exposition

The movement begins with a long introduction, which serves as an introduction not only to the first movement, but to the entire work. It opens with a melody constructed mostly of fourths in the cellos and basses (see Figure 42-1), answered by tremolo string sounds and twitters from the flute. After several alternations of cellos and higher strings and flute, the fourths continue, now interspersed with smaller intervals and becoming faster and more insistent. Another idea appears, first in the trumpets, then in the whole orchestra. It sounds, at first, like the first

Cellos and Basses

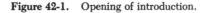

Figure 42-1. Opening of introduction.

main theme, but turns out to be more introductory material. The cello fourths now have become an **ostinato** (an insistent repeating rhythmic idea) in major and minor seconds. The ostinato gets faster and faster, and leads into the first theme (see Figure 42-2), a vigorous idea made up of the materials set forth in the introduction: fourths and scale patterns. Note that the second half of the theme feels like the inversion of the first half, although the parallels are not exact. Note, too, that it is made up entirely of seconds and fourths; the third, with its strong feeling of traditional harmony, is avoided.

Figure 42-2. Main theme.

The trombone introduces another idea, also constructed of fourths and seconds (see Figure 42-3). This subsidiary idea will become important in the development section. There is a contrasting second theme, static and pastoral in feeling, played by the oboe (see Figure 42-4). Note that this theme consists entirely of two notes, a major second apart.

Figure 42-3. Trombone idea.

Figure 42-4. Contrasting theme.

Development

Although there is no traditional harmonic cadence, the contrasting section winds down to a peaceful conclusion. The beginning of the development section introduces the aggressive first theme, or the rising scale section of it, after which the strings have a fugato section on still another idea made up of seconds and fourths. The subsidiary trombone idea appears again and becomes the subject for two fugato sections in the brass, the second constructed on the inversion of the trombone idea.

Recapitulation

After a deceptive reference to the main theme, which trails off in a sustained unison high note, the real recapitulation begins with the pastoral second theme. Following a tense transition that features the opening scales from the main theme, the theme itself returns, in a short version. One last reference to the trombone idea and a quick descending scale bring the movement to a brilliant conclusion.

It is significant that we can hear this movement as a sonata-allegro form, the traditional form for the first movement of a symphony, despite the absence of harmonic cadences and traditional key areas to define the sections. Bartók organizes the music in his own version of this structure. The logic and coherence of the movement and its amazing unity come from his strong, memorable themes and from the clear relationships among them. From two intervals— seconds and fourths—he has crafted several themes of contrasting character and developed them in a clear, Classical structure. Although the Concerto for Orchestra is written in a calmer, less primitivist style than some of Bartók's earlier works, it is a fine example of his craft and genius, and is one of the masterpieces of twentieth-century orchestral literature.

Fernand Léger. Adieu New York. (National Museum of Modern Art, Paris)

FIGURE 42-5. LISTENING GUIDE

FIRST MOVEMENT, CONCERTO FOR ORCHESTRA, BY BARTÓK

INTRODUCTION

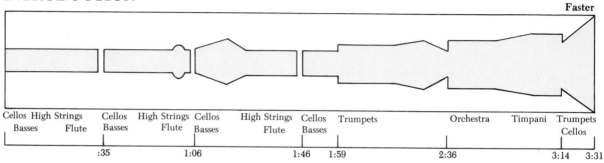

Faster

| Cellos | High Strings | | Cellos | High Strings | Cellos | | High Strings | Cellos | Trumpets | | Orchestra | Timpani | Trumpets |
| Basses | | Flute | Basses | Flute | Basses | | Flute | Basses | | | | | Cellos |

:35   1:06   1:46   1:59   2:36   3:14   3:31

EXPOSITION

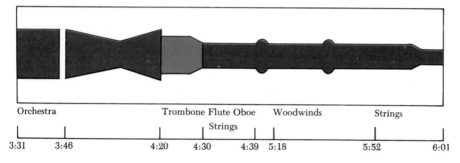

| Orchestra | | | Trombone | Flute | Oboe | Woodwinds | | Strings | |
| | | | | Strings | | | | | |

3:31   3:46   4:20   4:30   4:39   5:18   5:52   6:01

DEVELOPMENT

Fugato Inversion

| Timpani | Strings | Clarinet | Woodwinds | Brass | High |
| Trumpet | | | | | Unison |

6:01   6:13   6:31   7:13   7:31   8:05

RECAPITULATION

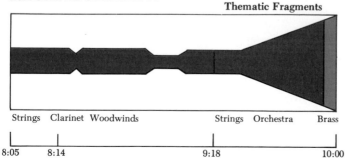

Thematic Fragments

| Strings | Clarinet | Woodwinds | Strings | Orchestra | Brass |

8:05   8:14   9:18   10:00

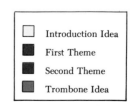

	Introduction Idea
	First Theme
	Second Theme
	Trombone Idea

CHAPTER 43

Arnold Schoenberg
Quintet for Winds, Opus 26

Arnold Schoenberg, along with Stravinsky, stands as one of the most influential composers of this century, a man rooted in the long European musical tradition, but seeking all his life for new ways of organizing music. We have already spoken of his twelve-tone method (Chapter 39), a way of composing that finally promised a new type of organization to replace the worn-out chromaticism of the late nineteenth century while avoiding what Schoenberg saw as the threatening danger of chaos and anarchy in the art.

SCHOENBERG'S LIFE

Schoenberg was born in Vienna in 1874. As a musician, he was largely self-taught, except for a few months of lessons in counterpoint. The compositions of his twenties reveal the influence of turn-of-the-century Vienna, with its fondness for Wagnerian chromaticism; the string sextet *Verklarte Nacht* ("Transfigured Night"), usually heard in a transcription for string orchestra, and his first songs are Wagnerian in style. Another early work, a huge composition for voices and orchestra called *Gurrelieder*, stretches the harmonic system still further, while exploiting the grand effects of the late Romantic orchestra. Schoenberg was a friend of expressionistic painters such as Oscar Kokoshka and Wassily Kandinsky, and painted as an avocation throughout his life.

In his forties, Schoenberg was drafted for military service in World War I and ceased to compose for a time. He worked out his new twelve-tone system for the "emancipation of dissonance" and began a teaching career in Berlin. He also joined with other musicians anxious to get new music performed, and performed correctly, to found the Society for Private Musical Performance, which ran its own series of concerts for members interested in the new music. This society was the first of many such groups dedicated to new music, evidence of the gulf between the composers and performers of new music and the larger concert world.

In 1933, Schoenberg came to the United States. He eventually settled in Los Angeles, where he taught composition and music theory at the University of California, Los Angeles. After his retirement from this post at the age of seventy, he continued to compose until his death in 1951. The centenary of his birth in 1974 led to renewed interest in studying his writings and his music and to the establishment of the Arnold Schoenberg Institute on the campus of the University of Southern California. The Institute is a center for the study and performance not only of Schoenberg's works, but also of the works influenced by his revolutionary ideas.

SCHOENBERG'S MUSIC

Following the early works in post-Romantic style, there is an intermediate group of works that abandon tonality in the traditional sense but do not replace this fundamental premise with another system. Among those post-tonal works, sometimes called atonal or expressionistic, are the *Five Pieces for Orchestra* (1909), and *Pierrot Lunaire* (1912). This latter work, settings of poems by a symbolist poet, Albert Giraud, caused a minor scandal. The poetry is in a strange, haunted style, for which Schoenberg invented a new musical style or expression. The singer half-speaks, half-sings, in a technique called **Sprechstimme** ("speech-song"). Rhythms are written out exactly, but pitch is not fixed. The singer is to aim generally at certain pitches in the line, but not to sustain them. The effect is like stylized recitation. Against the singer, a small chamber group plays nontonal polyphony in fragmented style. The work is an important twentieth-century milestone and is often performed, frequently with the aid of some staging, scenery, or projections. It is interesting that the performance of this work coincided rather closely with the much larger scandal caused by Stravinsky's *Rite* *of Spring.* Although both composers went on to write in much different styles, both works signaled that the nineteenth-century style was over and new things were in the air.

In the mid-twenties, the first of the compositions in the new twelve-tone style began to appear, among them the Suite for Piano, opus 25; the Wind Quintet, which will be discussed in more detail; and several string quartets. Later twelve-tone works include the Variations for Orchestra (1928), concertos for piano and violin, the Fantasy for Violin and Piano (1949), and the severe unfinished opera, *Moses und Aron.* Late in his life, Schoenberg also composed several works that are more tonal in organization, including the *Ode to Napoleon*, the Second Chamber Symphony, and a setting of *Kol Nidre.*

SCHOENBERG'S INFLUENCE

Two important comments must be made about Schoenberg and his effect on the course of Western music. First, he may be more important as a thinker and theorist than as a composer. The twelve-tone system was one of the pivotal discoveries in twentieth-century music, and the serial principles it embodies may be extended much further than Schoenberg himself extended them. He was by nature a traditionalist: generations of his students report his insistence on rigorous analysis of works by Bach and Brahms. Composition students who expected to write in atonal or experimental styles were surprised by his unbending traditional rigor. Although he organized pitch selection by the twelve-tone method, he structured his compositions along Classical lines and wrote abstract Classical music for traditional instruments, played in traditional ways. His leading students, Alban Berg and Anton Webern, soon showed that the system could be used to create widely divergent styles. Although Webern's twelve-tone style, succinct and pointilistic, has had more influence on composition in the sixties and seventies than Schoenberg's, the fundamental insight was Schoenberg's. It remained for Schoenberg's disciples and a later school of mathematically oriented composers—Milton Babbitt and Yannis Xenakis among them—to explore the possibilities and ramifications unleashed by his prophetic discovery.

A second comment, and interesting field for speculation, concerns comparisons between Schoenberg and Stravinsky. Their disciples emphasize the contrasts between them—Schoenberg, the rigorous teacher and thinker, versus Stravinsky, the ballet composer and celebrity, living in fame's spotlight. As is so often true, the generalizations are not entirely fair. Both men were rooted in the nineteenth-century European tradition; both chose divergent new paths that opened up new modes of musical thought; and both were dedicated seekers and creators who pursued their creative destinies throughout their lives. From the vantage point of the late seventies, it seems tragic that zealous disciples and opposing schools of thought kept them apart. In different ways, each is a towering genius; together, they changed the course of Western art music.

QUINTET FOR WINDS, OPUS 26

Schoenberg's Wind Quintet, opus 26, is one of the first works to utilize the twelve-tone system. It was completed in August 1924 and first performed the following month. The Quintet is a fine illustration of the way the system works as a compositional method and also illustrates the fact that Schoenberg's style is not so much a result of the twelve-tone method as it is a result of his Classical approach to the organization of musical structures.

The wind quintet—a flute, oboe, clarinet, French horn, and bassoon—has been a standard chamber group since the Classic period. Although the literature for wind quintet is not as extensive as the string quartet repertory, it remains the standard wind chamber group, an ensemble of unique appeal for composer and listener alike. The five instruments are of completely distinct color, but blend very well. The four woodwinds are among the most agile instruments of the modern orchestra, capable of long lyric melodies, rapid virtuoso flights, and dry and sardonic passages. The French horn has the widest range and dynamic variety of all the brasses, and its mellow tone blends with other instruments better than do the tones of any of the other brasses.

Small wind groups have a special attraction for twentieth-century composers. One of the fundamental thrusts of twentieth-century music is a reaction against the overblown lyricism of the late nineteenth century. Composers wanted to escape from the lush string sections and huge brass choirs of Wagner and Liszt. The woodwinds are favorite instruments for the atmosphere desired by contemporary composers, whether it is the abstraction of twelve-tone styles, the wit and clarity of neoclassicism, or the jazz-tinged flavor of some other styles. In this particular work, the wind quintet is perfect for the abstraction, variety, and dense polyphonic texture that Schoenberg wanted.

The Row

The first step in the composition of a twelve-tone piece is the selection of **a row**, a unique arrangement of all twelve notes of the chromatic scale. The row of the wind quintet is shown in Figure 43-1. There are some surprising things about this particular row. Note that the first and last intervals are thirds, an interval usually avoided by Schoenberg in his rows because of its tonal and harmonic implications. The interval between notes 7 and 8 is another third. The rest of the intervals are the more common seconds and sevenths.

Selecting the row is not writing the music. Although the row becomes the basic source material of all of the musical lines within the piece, the same row could be used to produce entirely different compositions. Some composers use segments of the row, units of four or six notes. Others select rows that are mirror images of themselves in the second half, or have other internal relationships that are exploited as the basis of the composition. Schoenberg, especially at this period of his life, generally used his rows in literal form to create melodic ideas heard as

Figure 43-1. The row.

themes. Figure 43-2 shows the first appearance of the row in a melody for the flute, which opens the work. Note how Schoenberg has disposed the notes of the row in this melody. He has chosen a relatively calm and orderly rhythmic shape, but the very wide spacing of the notes makes the melody angular and unusual. One of the basic rules about serial composition is that **octave displacement**—that is, placing a *C*-sharp, for example, in any range possible on the instrument—does not affect the basic series.

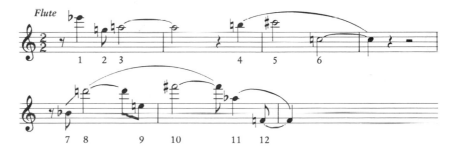

Figure 43-2. Opening flute melody.

The same row can produce melodies of totally different contour and effect. In what we hear as the second section of a modified sonata-allegro form, the oboe has a different theme, another version of the row (see Figure 43-3). Note how this melody differs from the opening flute melody. First, it is an inversion of the flute melody. That is, all of the same intervals appear, but upside down. The interval between notes 2 and 3, for example, is a major second in both versions, but in the flute version it is a descending second, and in the oboe version, an ascending second. The intervals are the same, discounting octave positions, but upwards instead of downwards, and vice versa. It also covers a narrower range and is more lyric in its rhythmic design.

Figure 43-3. Oboe melody, measure 42.

FIGURE 43-4. LISTENING GUIDE

FIRST MOVEMENT, QUINTET FOR WINDS, OPUS 26, BY SCHOENBERG

EXPOSITION

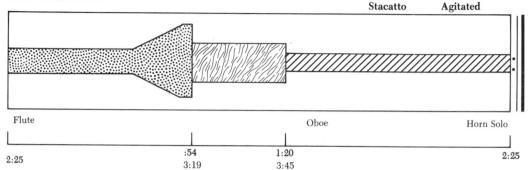

Stacatto Agitated

Flute   Oboe   Horn Solo

2:25   :54   1:20   2:25
           3:19 3:45

DEVELOPMENT

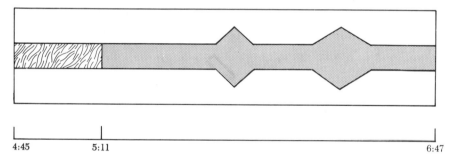

4:45   5:11   6:47

RECAPITULATION

Stacatto Agitated

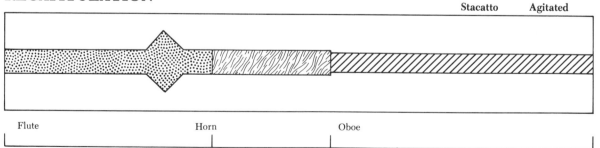

Flute   Horn   Oboe

6:47   7:47   8:22   9:36

CODA
Slower

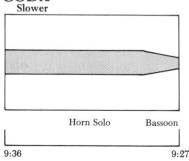

Horn Solo Bassoon

9:36   9:27

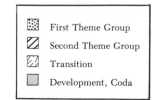

  First Theme Group

  Second Theme Group

  Transition

  Development, Coda

Structure

The structure of the first movement results from compositional choices entirely separate from the twelve-tone process. The twelve-tone system regulates only the matter of pitch choices; and, as we have said, a different composer would have produced an entirely different piece from this row. Schoenberg chooses to use standard Classical structures, confining his "revolutionary" ideas to the matter of pitch. He forms his row into recognizable themes that appear in related groups and lets us know when he is moving from one section to another by means of standard signals—changes of texture and dynamics, shifts in meter and rhythm, and melodic cadences. It is intriguing that he can construct a recognizable sonata-allegro form without the most basic means used by Classic and Romantic composers to do so, the tonal areas that define the various sections. He has even denied himself the possibility of a harmonic cadence, but he still creates cadences that make sense to us, so that his works seem to end satisfactorily, rather than just stop. Later composers have used the serial idea to create entirely new approaches to form and structure, as well as to pitch organization.

It may not be easy at first to hear the sonata-allegro structure of this movement because of the absence of harmonic cadences or key areas to define the sections. The texture makes it difficult, also, because Schoenberg generally writes polyphonic, relatively busy textures that tire our ears after a while. Texture is actually the key to the structure of this piece, because climaxes of large sections and the increased tension of the development section result from marked increases in the denseness of the texture. With the aid of the listening guide (Figure 43-4), you should be able to hear an exposition section, made up of several varied presentations of material, then a more fragmentary, dense development section, and finally a return to the clearer texture of the beginning, and a release of the tension in a sort of coda.

At first listening, people sometimes find Schoenberg's music opaque and confusing. He was actually a Classicist, seeking a new approach to musical organization, free from the domination of tonal harmony and free from the anarchy that had resulted from the extreme chromaticism of late Romantic music.

CHAPTER 44

Alban Berg
Wozzeck

Schoenberg's two most important students, Alban Berg and Anton Webern, developed highly personal styles of twelve-tone music, different not only from Schoenberg's but from each other's as well. Webern developed a terse style, abstract and fragmentary, that had a great influence on postwar avant-garde music. Berg, on the other hand, combined the twelve-tone system with a Classical instinct for structure and an intense Romanticism to produce an accessible, emotionally expressive version of twelve-tone style.

BERG'S LIFE

Alban Berg was born in Vienna in 1885. He studied with Schoenberg from 1904 until 1910, and remained a lifelong friend and correspondent of the older composer's. Like Schoenberg, Berg was drafted into military service. Because of ill

Metropolitan Opera performance of Berg's opera *Wozzeck.*

health, he served at a desk in the War Ministry. The first performance of his opera *Wozzeck* in 1925 caused a great sensation. He spent the rest of his life composing, teaching, and defending the new twelve-tone school and its ideas. He died in 1935 of blood poisoning brought on by an insect bite.

BERG'S MUSIC

Berg's works are few but important. Besides *Wozzeck,* he composed another opera, *Lulu,* which was left unfinished at his death. It was completed from the sketches he left and has recently been performed. Among his other well-known works are the *Lyric Suite* (1926), originally written for string quartet, but now performed more often in a version Berg adapted for string orchestra.

One of Berg's best-known works is the Violin Concerto (1935), a fine example of his eclectic style. In it he combines elements of twelve-tone thinking, Classical structures, and even quotations of Bach to produce a work of lyric expression and great emotional intensity. It was written to mourn the death of Manon Gropius, the daughter of Walter Gropius, the famous architect, and Alma Mahler, the composer's widow. Berg interrupted his work on *Lulu* to write the concerto. It was the last work he completed before his death.

Figure 44-2 shows the twelve-tone row Berg chose for the concerto. Note that the row is not at all like those of Schoenberg or Webern. It consists almost entirely of thirds and triads. The tonal interval of the third, studiously avoided in Schoenberg's rows because of its harmonic implications, is everywhere in this row. The last three intervals are major seconds; the last four notes of the row are the first four notes of a Lutheran chorale, "Es ist genug," which is quoted in the last part of the concerto. The work utilizes the twelve-tone system freely and uses folk tunes Lutheran chorales, parodies of Viennese café music, and difficult solo writing to produce a work of intense Romanticism and programmatic content. There is no mistaking Berg's mourning for the dead girl or the passionate intensity of his style.

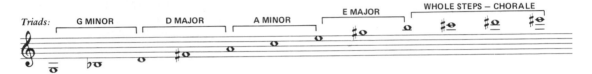

Figure 44-1. Row of the Violin Concerto.

WOZZECK

Story

Wozzeck, Berg's best-known work and one of the few twentieth-century operas to find its way into the standard repertory, is based on fragmentary writings by Georg Büchner. It is a work of protest, as far from the heroics of nineteenth-century drama and opera as possible. The main character is not a hero at all, but an inarticulate soldier, bullied and used as a guinea pig in medical experiments by his superiors, who represent all of the authorities and bureaucrats of the modern world. Wozzeck represents all of the poor and downtrodden of this world, the victims the twentieth century has produced in such great numbers. Wozzeck loves Marie, a woman of the street, with whom he has fathered a son. Marie, although a tender mother, cannot resist swaggering men in uniform and falls in love with the arrogant Sergeant Major. Wozzeck, in a jealous rage, kills Marie, goes mad, and drowns himself.

Out of this brutal story, Berg has fashioned an opera of enormous power. We feel the inarticulate rage of Wozzeck, a twentieth-century Everyman, at the mercy of an anonymous, unfeeling societal structure. The murder and suicide have the universal force of Greek tragedy.

Musical Style

Berg makes his powerful statement through remarkably eclectic means. He uses not only angular twelve-tone writing, but also Viennese café music and children's songs and lullabies. Complex Baroque and Classical structures organize the music without being obtrusive or distracting from the dramatic unity and power of the opera. Figure 44-2 is a standard analysis of the musical form of the opera in relation to the dramatic events. From the outline, one would think the com-

Dramatic	**Musical**

Act I

EXPOSITION

Wozzeck and his relation to his environment.	Five Character Sketches.
Scene	*Scene*
1. The Captain	1. Suite
2. Andres	2. Rhapsody
3. Marie	3. Military March and Cradle Song
4. The Physician	4. Passacaglia
5. The Drum Major	5. Andante affetuoso (quasi Rondo)

Act II

DENOUEMENT

Scene	*Scene*
Wozzeck is gradually convinced of Marie's infidelity.	Symphony in five movements.
Scene	*Scene*
1. Wozzeck's first suspicion	1. Sonata form
2. Wozzeck is mocked	2. Fantasie and Fugue
3. Wozzeck accuses Marie	3. Largo
4. Marie and Drum Major dance	4. Scherzo
5. The Drum Major trounces Wozzeck	5. Rondo Marziale

Act III

CATASTROPHE

Wozzeck murders Marie and atones suicide.	Six Inventions
Scene	*Scene*
1. Marie's remorse	1. Invention on a Theme
2. Death of Marie	2. Invention of a Tone
3. Wozzeck tries to forget	3. Invention of a Rhythm
4. Wozzeck drowns in the pond	4. Invention of a Key (D minor)

(Instrumental interlude with closed curtain)

5. Marie's son plays unconcerned	5. Invention on a President Rhythm (Perpetuum Mobile)

Figure 44-2.   Diagram of the opera's structure.

plex musical structures would detract from the unity of the drama, but Berg proudly observed that what people remembered from the work was not the structures but the drama and its universal implications. Note that the borrowed older structures serve dramatic purposes as well. The Doctor, for example, obsessed with his experiments on humans, including Wozzeck, is represented by the **passacaglia**, a repetitive Baroque form based on an insistent repeating bass.

Two striking musical devices that add to the drama deserve mention. First, at the climactic moment of Marie's murder by Wozzeck, the orchestral comment, instead of being a tangle of twelve-tone polyphony, is a unison *B*-natural. Somehow, in the context, that simple sustained *B* is more horrible than anything else Berg might have devised. Second, he breaks the action several times with orchestral interludes, the longest of which follows Wozzeck's suicide by drowning. These interludes are not breaks in the dramatic tension, although they take place while the curtain is closed between scenes. Rather, they resemble the orchestral writing in Wagner's operas, because they comment on the action and its significance. The real meaning is in the orchestral passages.

Act III, Scenes 4 and 5

The recorded excerpt includes scenes 4 and 5 of Act III. After stabbing Marie, Wozzeck goes to a tavern, where he dances with Margaret, Marie's friend, to an out-of-tune café band. She notices blood on his hands and uniform. He lurches out, half-mad, to return to the pond where the murder took place. In *Sprechstimme*, Wozzeck's guilt-crazed mind rambles: he cannot wash off the blood, even the moon is bloody. He walks into the pond. The Doctor and Captain enter and discover the body of Marie, and the scene ends with the final orchestral interlude. In the fifth scene, Wozzeck's son is playing with other children when news reaches them of his mother's death. They run off, as the son, uncomprehending, continues his little game. The childish music at the final curtain makes a wrenching conclusion to one of the masterpieces of expressionist musical drama.

The listening guide (Figure 44-3) includes the German and English text for the fourth and fifth scenes of the third act, with comments about the musical style.

FIGURE 44-3. LISTENING GUIDE

WOZZECK, ACT III, SCENES 4 AND 5, BY BERG

Music	German Text	English Translation
Sprechstimme Fragmentary Dissonant, Sinister	**VIERTE SZENE** *(Waldweg am Teich. Mondnacht wie vorher. Wozzeck kommt schnell herangewankt. Bleibt suchend stehen.)* WOZZECK Das Messer? Wo ist das Messer? Ich hab's dagelassen . . . Näher, noch näher. Mir graut's! Da regt sich was. Still! Alles still und tot . . . Mörder! Mörder! Ha! Da ruft's. Nein, ich selbst. *(wankt suchend ein paar Schritte weiter und stösst auf die Leiche)* Marie! Marie! Was hast Du für eine rote Schnur um den Hals? Hast Dir das rote Halsband verdient, wie die Ohrringlein, mit Deiner Sünde! Was hängen Dir die schwarzen Haare so wild? Mörder! Mörder! Sie werden nach mir suchen . . . Das Messer verrät mich! *(sucht fieberhaft)* Da, da ist's *(am Teich)* So! Da hinunter *(wirft das Messer hinein)* Es taucht ins dunkle Wasser wie ein Stein. *(Der Mond bricht blutrot hinter den Wolken hervor. Wozzeck blickt auf)* Aber der Mond verrät mich . . . der Mond ist blutig. Will denn die ganze Welt es ausplaudern?!—Das Messer, es liegt zu weit vorn, sie finden's beim Baden oder wenn sie nach Muscheln tauchen. *(geht in den Teich hinein)* Ich find's nicht . . . Aber ich muss mich waschen. Ich bin blutig. Da ein Fleck . . . und noch einer. Weh! Weh! Ich wasche mich mit Blut! Das Wasser ist Blut . . . Blut . . . *(Er ertrinkt.)* *(Der Doktor tritt auf, der Hauptmann folgt ihm.)*	**SCENE FOUR** *(Forest path by the pool. Moonlit night as before. Wozzeck staggers on hastily, and then stops as he searches for something.)* WOZZECK Where is it? Where has the knife gone? Somewhere here I left it . . . Somewhere here, somewhere. Oh! Horror! There something moved! Still! All is still and dead! . . . Murder! Murder! Ah, who cried? No, 'twas me. *(Still searching, he staggers forward a few more steps, and comes on the corpse)* Marie! Marie! What is that so like a crimson cord round your neck? And was that crimson necklace well earned, like the gold earrings: the price of sinning? Why hangs your fine black hair so wild on your head? Murder! Murder! For me they'll soon be searching . . . That knife will betray me! *(seeks it feverishly)* Ah! It's here! *(at the pool)* Down to the bottom! *(throws the knife in)* It sinks through deep dark water like a stone. *(The moon comes up blood-red through the clouds)* See how the moon betrays me . . . the moon is bloody! Must then the whole wide world be blabbing it?—The knife there, too near the shore! They'll find it when bathing, maybe when they are mussel gathering. *(He wades into the pool)* It's gone now. I ought to wash my body. I am bloody. Here's a spot . . . and here . . . something. Woe! Woe! I wash myself with blood! The water is blood . . . blood . . . *(He drowns)* *(After a short time the Doctor enters, followed by the Captain.)*
Recitation Ascending Scales in Various Groups of Instruments	HAUPTMANN Halt! DOKTOR *(bleibt stehen)* Hören Sie? Dort! HAUPTMANN Jesus! Das war ein Ton. *(bleibt ebenfalls stehen)* DOKTOR *(auf den Teich zeigend)* Ja, dort!	CAPTAIN Stop! DOCTOR *(stands still)* Do you hear? There! CAPTAIN Heavens! There was a sound. *(stands still)* DOCTOR *(pointing to the pool)* Yes, there!

Scales in Contrary Motion	**HAUPTMANN** Es ist das Wasser im Teich. Das Wasser ruft. Es ist schon lange Niemand ertrunken. Kommen Sie, Doktor! Es ist nicht gut zu hören. *(will den Doktor mit sich ziehen)*	**CAPTAIN** It is the water in the pool. The water calls. It is a long time since anyone was drowned. Come, Doctor, this is not good to hear. *(He tries to drag off the Doctor.)*
	DOKTOR *(bleibt aber stehen und lauscht)* Das stöhnt . . . als stürbe ein Mensch. Da ertrinkt Jemand!	**DOCTOR** *(stands still and listens)* It groans . . . like a dying man. There's someone drowning!
	HAUPTMANN Unheimlich! Der Mond rot und die Nebel grau. Hören Sie? . . . Jetzt wieder das Achzen.	**CAPTAIN** It's uncanny! The moon is red, and the mist is grey. Do you hear? . . . That groaning again.
	DOKTOR Stiller, . . . jetzt ganz still.	**DOCTOR** It's getting softer . . . and now quite gone.
	HAUPTMANN Kommen Sie! Kommen Sie schnell. *(zieht den Doktor mit sich)*	**CAPTAIN** Come away! Quick! *(drags the Doctor off with him)*
Interlude		
Light Sounds—High Strings, Celesta	**FUNFTE SZENE** *(Strasse vor Mariens Tür. Heller Morgen. Sonnenschein. Kinder spielen und lärmen. Mariens Knabe auf einem Steckenpferd reitend.)*	**SCENE FIVE** *(Street before Marie's door. Bright morning. Sunshine. Children are playing and shouting. Marie's child is riding a hobby-horse.)*
Children's Song	**DIE SPIELENDEN KINDER** Ringel, Ringel, Rosenkranz, Ringelreih'n! Ringel, Ringel, Rosenkranz, Rin . . .	**CHILDREN** Ring-a-ring-a-roses, all fall down! Ring-a-ring-a-roses, all . . .
Recitation	*(unterbrechen Gesang und Spiel, andere Kinder Stürmen herein)* **EINS VON IHNEN** Du Käthe! . . . Die Marie . . .	*(They stop, and other children come rushing on.)* **ONE OF THESE** Katie! . . . Marie . . .
Fragmentary Lower Dissonant Ideas	**ZWEITES KIND** Was is?	**SECOND CHILD** What is it?
	ERSTES KIND Weisst' es nit? Sie sind schon Alle 'naus.	**FIRST CHILD** Don't you know? They've all gone out there.
	DRITTES KIND *(zu Mariens Knaben)* Du! Dein Mutter ist tot!	**THIRD CHILD** *(to Marie's child)* Hey! Your mother is dead.
Singing; Recitation	**MARIENS KNABE** *(immer reitend)* Hopp, hopp! Hopp, hopp! Hopp, hopp!	**MARIE'S CHILD** *(still riding his horse)* Hop, hop! Hop, hop! Hop, hop!
	ZWEITES KIND Wo is sie denn?	**SECOND CHILD** Where is she now?
	ERSTES KIND Draus' liegt sie, am Weg, neben dem Teich.	**FIRST CHILD** Out there, on the path by the pool.
	DRITTES KIND Kommt, anschaun! *(Alle Kinder laufen davon.)*	**THIRD CHILD** Let's go and look! *(All the children run off.)*
Singing **Quiet Ending-Strings and Celesta**	**MARIENS KNABE** *(reitet)* Hopp, hopp! Hopp, hopp! Hopp, hopp! *(zögert einen Augenblick und reitet dann den anderen Kindern nach.)*	**MARIE'S CHILD** *(continues to ride)* Hop, hop! Hop, hop! Hop, hop! *(He hesitates a moment, and then rides off after the other children.)*

CHAPTER **45**

American Music
Aaron Copland,
Appalachian Spring

NORTH AMERICAN MUSIC

The history of music in the United States in the twentieth century is a complex and fascinating subject. Serious music in America in the nineteenth century was largely imported from Europe, although there were a few American composers who made use of American musical traditions in their music. The first American composer to achieve fame in Europe was Louis Moreau Gottschalk (1829-1869), a piano virtuoso and composer, who used the rhythms of Creole music to create a successful American version of nineteenth-century exoticism. Stephen Foster (1826-1864) composed over two hundred American songs. Some of them have become American classics, like "My Old Kentucky Home." Edward MacDowell (1860-1908) was an important composer, whose best-known works are character pieces for piano. MacDowell was admired as a serious composer in Europe and taught composition both in Germany and in this country.

The first important American composer of the twentieth century was Charles Ives (1874-1954), an independent Yankee composer whose music found little acceptance among members of the musical establishment during his lifetime. His father had been a Civil War bandmaster, interested in acoustic experiments. Charles maintained a lifelong love for patriotic band music, experiments with acoustical phenomena like the simultaneous sound of two different bands in a parade, and music that evoked the American experience. He wrote often in collage fashion, superimposing different tunes and rhythms, creating a dense texture that many professional musicians considered impossible to play accurately.

Ives supported himself all of his life as an insurance executive. By the time his music was first performed in public, he had ceased composing. Among his important works are four symphonies, many songs, and his two best-known compositions: the *Concord* Sonata for piano and *Three Places in New England* for orchestra. His works embody the American spirit perfectly. He was outside the

European tradition altogether, fiercely independent, and completely rooted in New England's history and thought. He was by personal philosophy a transcendentalist in the tradition of Ralph Waldo Emerson and Henry David Thoreau. Ives envisioned music as the uniting force of a great people, rather than as the entertainment of the rich. We now recognize his importance as a great American composer and a thoroughly original musical thinker.

Composers working in a specifically American style later in the century are a diverse and interesting group. Besides Aaron Copland, a number of others deserve mention. Roger Sessions (b. 1896) is known for his eight symphonies and *Montezuma*, an opera about the conquest of the Aztecs by Cortez. Virgil Thomson (b.1896) is known for an opera on a Gertrude Stein story, *Four Saints in Three Acts*, symphonic music with an American tinge, and several film scores. Roy Harris (1898–1979) is known for his twelve symphonies; the Third is especially popular. George Gershwin (1898–1937) was a versatile American composer who worked successfully in several areas, including Tin Pan Alley popular songs, musical comedy, film music, and "serious" composition. His most enduringly popular works are the *Rhapsody in Blue*, combining jazz and symphonic styles, and the opera *Porgy and Bess*. Samuel Barber (b.1910) is an American Neoromantic known especially for his *Adagio for Strings*, which appears often on symphony programs. Gian Carlo Menotti (b.1911), who was born in Italy but has lived in America during his creative life, is a well-known composer of popular operas, many of them chamber operas suitable for workshop and university groups. His best-known work, now an annual fixture of the Christmas season, is *Amahl and the Night Visitors*. Other works often performed include *The Medium* and *The Consul*. Although some critics dismiss him as a composer "who writes contemporary music for people who don't like contemporary music," it has always been characteristic of "American" style to appeal to the common man and avoid excessive intellectualizing.

A list of American composers would be incomplete without the name of Leonard Bernstein (b.1918), famous as a conductor, composer, lecturer, television celebrity, and spokesman for the arts in America. He has written works as diverse as the musical *West Side Story* and the *Mass*, which combines elements of several major religions and several popular and symphonic styles to make a powerful statement about man in the late twentieth century. Like Copland, Bernstein has used his fame and celebrity to encourage performance of contemporary works and to explain music to a wider audience.

LATIN-AMERICAN MUSIC

The other Americas were also represented in the nationalistic movement of the thirties and forties. Mexico was represented by Carlos Chávez (1899–1978), who used Indian rhythms and ideas in his operas and symphonic works. The best known of these is the *Sinfonia India*. Brazil had its nationalistic composer, Heitor Villa-Lobos (1887–1959), who wrote an enormous amount of music incorporating Brazilian rhythms and themes, and who worked tirelessly to create a Brazilian musical culture and a music program in the Brazilian schools. His best-known piece, often performed, is the *Bachianas Brasilieras*. He also wrote a huge amount of colorful piano music. Like most of their North American counterparts, Latin-American composers, after the nationalistic surge of the thirties and forties, turned to a more abstract international style following World War II.

AARON COPLAND

Copland's Life

The best-known American composer of this century is Aaron Copland (b. 1900). Trained in the European tradition, Copland wrote in several twentieth-century styles, and he has done more than anyone else to establish an "American" style of music and make that music accessible to a wider audience. He represents the search for an authentic, independent American voice and style. He studied composition in Paris with Nadia Boulanger, a famous teacher who trained several generations of American composers. Copland studied in Paris in the twenties, the Paris of Ernest Hemingway and Igor Stravinsky. His early works combine the jazz idiom with an abstract Neoclassic style. In the thirties and forties, he turned to his more popular "American" style in the works which are his best-known— *Appalachian Spring, Rodeo, Billy the Kid*, and *A Lincoln Portrait*. He also wrote scores for several films in this period, most of them based on American literary classics—*Of Mice and Men, Our Town*, and *The Red Pony*.

After World War II, Copland turned to a more universal style of twelve-tone writing, as seen in such works as the *Piano Fantasy* and *Inscape*. Although he has utilized the innovations of Stravinsky and Schoenberg, his fame rests on the appealing "American" works of the middle period. He is also to be admired for his tireless, lifelong efforts to explain twentieth-century music to the general public and to see that twentieth-century American composers got their works performed. He became the unofficial spokesman of American composers, and used his fame and widespread acceptance to educate American audiences.

Copland's Musical Style

Copland's style is an amalgam of several elements of twentieth-century style that we have seen already, particularly in the works of Stravinsky, plus some unique elements. The familiar elements include a muscular approach to rhythm, marked by complex meters, syncopation, and ostinato patterns. Harmonically, Copland is fond of bitonality, the simultaneous sounding of two different triads. Missing from his music are the complex modulations and the lush chromaticism of late Romanticism. Generally, his music is diatonic. His melodies are filled with wide intervals and large leaps. In other words, his style, while not forbidding or overly complex, avoids anything that would detract from its strength and directness. Sometimes he quotes American hymn tunes, frontier songs, and patriotic melodies; sometimes he uses jazz or ragtime rhythms and melodic ideas as well. He also writes often in a solemn, declamatory style. When his music is not dancing along in his rhythmically complex style, it often has a solemnity and prophetic strength that is appealing and somehow quite American.

The famous American conductor/composer Leonard Bernstein conducts a piece by Strauss.

APPALACHIAN SPRING

Appalachian Spring, one of Copland's best-known works, was written as music for a ballet by Martha Graham, first performed in 1944. Graham is a pioneer of American ballet who departed from the European ballet tradition to incorporate naturalistic movements and American stories into modern dance.

The Story

The story of the ballet concerns the celebration of a young couple's wedding and their moving into their new home in Western Pennsylvania in the nineteenth century. It is a nostalgic look backwards at an idealized time when pioneer virtues and strengths were the guiding principles of people's lives. Like many ballet

The Martha Graham Dance Company performs *Appalachian Spring*.

scores, the music was later adapted as a concert suite by the composer, and it is perhaps his most widely performed orchestral composition.

The Structure

Introduction

The work begins with a peaceful introduction, made up largely of arpeggiated chords over a sustained unison *A* in the bass. The chords are laid out in such a way that superimposed *A* and *E* triads sound together. The polytonality keeps the introduction from being Romantically sweet. The feeling it creates is one of space and newness.

Second Section

The second section, a fast dance movement, begins with startling suddenness and is built on a wide-spaced, energetic melody that has a "hoedown" feeling (see Figure 45-1). That melody is developed in various ways and in various keys. Copland breaks it into distinct motivic sections and presents it in varied rhythmic shapes. He also combines it with a more solemn, hymn-like tune (see Figure 45-2). The latter appears first in the winds, as the strings play the main dance tune. Later the groups reverse, the winds playing the dance tune and the strings, the hymn.

Figure 45-1. Main melody, dance section.

Figure 45-2. Counter-melody, hymn-like tune.

The various sections of the work continue without a break. The whole work deserves to be heard. The final section quotes a Shaker hymn, "Tis the Gift to be Simple." *Appalachian Spring* is a masterpiece of Copland's American style, original yet accessible and appealing.

FIGURE 45-3. LISTENING GUIDE

OPENING, *APPALACHIAN SPRING,* BY COPLAND

▦	Introduction
Dance:	
▦	Main Theme
▨	Hymn Like Theme

INTRODUCTION

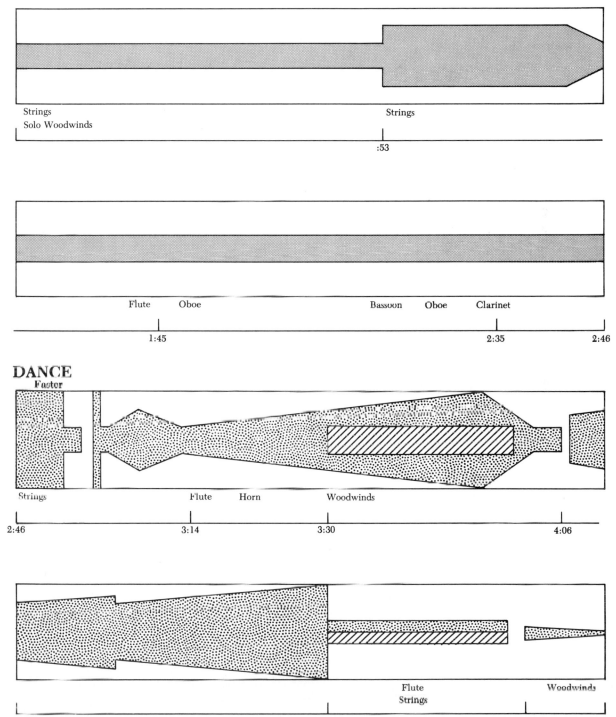

CHAPTER 46

Electronic Music Milton Babbitt, Composition for Synthesizer

ELECTRONIC MUSIC

The production of sounds by electronic means and the organization of those sounds into musical structures were logical extensions of several ideas that were in the air during the mid-twentieth century. Composers had already used instruments and voices in new ways, extending the range of tonal colors. Many of them had juxtaposed otherwise unrelated sound masses or musical ideas in a collage effect. Schoenberg's idea of serialization and Webern's extension of his ideas into miniature, tightly organized structures led naturally to the possibilities of electronic sound sources and sound modifiers.

The use of electronic sound generators increases color possibilities enormously. Electronic equipment can produce a theoretically infinite variety of sounds, pitches beyond the range of natural instruments or voices, a theoretically infinite range of dynamics, and complex and rapid rhythmic patterns that are impossible for human players to play or singers to sing.

Another facet of electronic music that was exciting to the pioneers was the possibility of total composer control. Once the composer has organized the sounds on tape, they are frozen forever, without any worry about available performers and their limitations.

Electronic instruments can be used to generate new sounds or to modify existing ones. Electronic sound generators produce sounds of a particular pitch, duration, intensity, and articulation, as the composer orders. They can be used to duplicate the sounds of traditional acoustic instruments or to produce a whole new range of sound possibilities. Electronic equipment can also be used to modify existing sounds. Any sound—a musical note, a noise from nature, sounds of a city or a factory—can be taped and then modified electronically. One school of electronic composition, called **Musique Concrète**, worked with modified natural sounds, and others modified singing or speaking voices.

Electronic modification of voices is an intriguing process, since it tampers with basic notions of meaning and communication. Words can be broken down to their individual elements or phonemes, changes in tape speed can transform the voices into entirely different sounds, or words can be treated, as some writers treat them, as sounds rather than as symbols of ideas. An example of a work based entirely on modification of word sounds is Luciano Berio's *Tema: Omaggio a Joyce*, which consists of electronic modification of a reading of a single paragraph from James Joyce's *Ulysses*.

Notation

One of the interesting sides of electronic music is composers' solutions to the problem of notation. Conventional notation, of course, will not work, because it indicates pitch, rhythm, phrasing, and articulation for conventional instruments. The whole purpose of an electronic "score" is different from that of a conventional score, because it is intended to tell a musician in an electronic studio how to duplicate the effects and structure the composer had in mind. Electronic scores usually look more like the graphic listening guides in this book than like standard musical scores: they often use time lines and graphic or schematic symbols to indicate the type and duration of the various events. They also incorporate, either in preliminary notes or in the course of the score, verbal explanations of the various effects. Compare the electronic score excerpt in Figure 46-1 with the standard music notation you have seen.

History

Since its inception in the late forties, electronic music has moved through several phases. The early, pioneering works tended to be abstract, extremely complex, and blindingly rapid; composers were excited about the possibilities of total control and speed beyond the capacity of the live musician. Recent works have utilized electronic means in different ways: in combination with live performers; in lyric, relaxed compositions; and even in a style that is almost Romantic or Impressionistic, such as the *Butterfly* series by Morton Subotnick.

The development of the portable keyboard electronic instrument, the familiar Moog or Arp synthesizer, has made electronic composition much less cumbersome and made possible live electronic performances. Composers of the seventies and eighties regard electronic composition not as a radical experiment, but as one more creative possibility.

MILTON BABBITT

One of the leading pioneers of electronic music in the U.S. is Milton Babbitt (b.1916). Born in Philadelphia, Babbit pursued his musical studies at New York University and Princeton, where he studied composition with Roger Sessions. At Princeton, he studied and taught mathematics as well as music. Babbitt's influence on young Amerian composers rests not only on his music, but on his work in applying modern mathematical theory to the process of composition. He has received several honors, including a Guggenheim grant and membership to the National Institute of Arts and Letters. He was one of the organizers of the Columbia-Princeton Electronic Music Center, the first major center for electronic music in this country.

Babbitt's compositions are not exclusively electronic—in fact, the majority of his compositions use standard instruments and voices, either in conjunction with taped electronic sounds or by themselves. Whatever the medium, however, he consistently composes in a tightly organized style that is the antithesis of the aleatoric style of a composer like John Cage. Babbitt extended the principle of serialism to elements other than pitch, such as rhythm, dynamics, and instrumental color.

Babbitt's interest in mathematics has led not only to compositional experiments, but also to a body of important theoretical writings in which mathematical ideas like set theory and variability are applied to the field of music.

With the help of Iannis Xenakis, another mathematically oriented composer, Babbitt moved away from chance music and deliberately loose structures into the direction of minutely structured and controlled musical events. His writings are dense and scientific, and may seem remote from the way most listeners approach music, but they represent an important trend in twentieth–century music.

COMPOSITION FOR SYNTHESIZER (1961)

Our listening example of electronic music is not typical of the way most composers now utilize electronic sounds; it is not even typical of Babbitt's writings, which are more likely to use electronically generated sounds in conjunction with

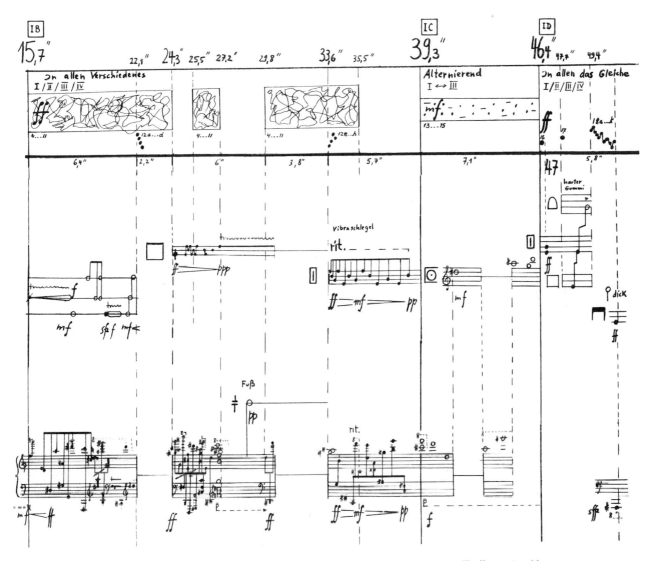

Figure 46-1. Part of an electronic score, Nr. 12 Kontakte, by Karlheinz Stockhausen.

live performance on traditional instruments. The work, however, in its abstract title and its handling of electronic sound resources, illustrates both the possibilities of electronic sound and Babbitt's abstract approach to musical organization.

This work, like many contemporary compositions, may need to be heard more than once for it to make sense to us. Probably the most striking element of the musical experience is color. The synthesizer is capable of an enormous range of timbre. We hear percussive sounds, which seem to be without definite pitch. Some sounds remind us of traditional instruments; still others use the extreme high and low ranges. The tone quality ranges from delicate to snarling.

Structure

The element of structure is the most intriguing element in this music. We know that Babbitt is interested in complex, minute structures; it is clear that his intent in this work was to experiment with serialized rhythmic units and tone colors. Even if we cannot follow all the precise details of Babbitt's design, it is quite clear that there are strong design elements in the piece.

The distinct colors already mentioned are a strong element of design. Color changes identify sections and announce new ideas that are developed and modified until the color changes again. The percussion effects and trills, punctuate sections and take on structural meaning in our minds. Melodic ideas form structures also. Several pitch patterns take on the force of motives, and form the unifying material for sections. Rhythm is a strong structural element. There are pauses and rhythmic cadences, or cessation of rapid motion, between sections. We can even hear harmony of a sort; combinations of tones are heard as chords, distinct from the prevailing linear, polyphonic texture of the work. Thus, those moments take on structural significance as well.

In other words, we actually process electronic music in the same ways we process other musical experiences. Although events sometimes move past our ears with blinding speed, and although we may not comprehend all the details of the composer's design, we hear motives, similar colors, sections, cadences, and development of related musical ideas.

This experience should point out the exciting new possibilities available to the modern composer. Used as an independent resource, or in conjunction with live performers, electronic technology has expanded the world of sound and the composer's range of choice.

CHAPTER 47

George Crumb
Ancient Voices of Children

It is impossible to generalize about art music in the sixties and seventies, not only because this period is too recent to allow much historical perspective, but also because these decades are so eclectic and diverse. Some composers continue to write in the major styles of the earlier part of the century, the styles we have already described, and some struggle to break new ground. At a concert of new music, listeners may hear works in "Classical" Schoenbergian twelve-tone style; works of Neoclassic wit and structural tightness; works that are mixed-media "happenings" and incorporate poetry readings, staging, and slide or film projections; experimental works using instruments in new or unusual ways; or works that mix taped and live performances. Perhaps the most significant trend is a tendency to incorporate diverse elements—musics of other cultures, popular or rock music combined with "serious" music, music combined with other media. Because communication is so rapid in this age and because the musical scene, having abandoned the nationalism of the thirties and forties, is again an international forum, styles and innovations are immediately known around the world. Some seem to come and go in a matter of months; others become part of the composer's range of choice, available for incorporation into his personal style. In summary, the composer is faced with incredible diversity and freedom, and can develop a new style with each work if he chooses or continue to explore one concept or mode of organization.

GEORGE CRUMB

George Crumb (b.1929) is a current American composer who works in a free, eclectic style. He is typical of the current composition scene in other ways also: he studied in this country with Ross Lee Finney at the University of Michigan, and he is currently Professor of composition at the University of Pennsylvania. He has earned numerous awards, including a UNESCO prize for his work *Ancient Voices of Children*.

ANCIENT VOICES OF CHILDREN

Crumb's best-known work is *Ancient Voices of Children*, a cycle of songs for mezzo-soprano, boy soprano, and a small group of instruments. It is based, as are several of Crumb's works, on the poetry of Federico García Lorca, a Spanish poet who was killed by the Fascists during the Spanish Civil War. Lorca's poetry, spare and powerfully evocative, has been set to music by many recent composers. Crumb is not interested in setting the Lorca texts literally or declaiming them so that we can easily follow the words. His goals are different than those of Romantic composers who tried to paint musical pictures of texts. Like most modern composers who use texts, Crumb is more interested in the feeling and essence of the text than in its literal declamation. Lorca poetry is already quite compressed and deals with elemental realities like (in Crumb's words) "life, death, love, the smell of the earth, the sounds of the wind and sea." Crumb's work is a meditation on the meaning behind the texts, rather than a straightforward presentation of the words in musical form.

Instrumentation

Crumb calls for a number of unusual instruments and effects in *Ancient Voices*. The voice is used not only for standard singing, but also as a purely "instrumental" sound. The singer is asked to sing wordless passages into an open amplified piano, which produces a vague shimmer of sympathetic vibrations. The soprano must also produce a wide range of sounds, such as whispers, sneezes, coughs, and percussive sounds. The boy soprano sings offstage, through a cardboard speaking tube, to give his part an ethereal remoteness. The accompanying instruments include a wide array of unusual percussion instruments; a mandolin, sometimes mistuned, and sometimes asked to produce bent pitches; an oboe, asked to sound like a Middle Eastern shawm; a harp, sometimes played with paper threaded in its strings; and a piano, sometimes with the strings muted inside by means of the player's hand or a chisel. The mandolin player doubles on musical saw, the pianist on toy piano.

Structure

The work includes five songs and two interludes in dance rhythms; the composer asks that a dancer be included in the performance. The work thus becomes an example of several twentieth-century trends: mixed media; new sounds, including electronic amplification (but not electronically produced sounds); new ways of using voice and instruments; and free creation of new modes of musical organization.

The entire work deserves attention, but we will focus on the first three parts: the first song, the first interlude, and the second song. Crumb's structures are clear and easily audible, based on an alternation of vocal and instrumental sounds.

First Song

El niño busca su voz.	The little boy was looking for his voice.
(La tenía el rey de los grillos.)	(The king of the crickets had it.)
En una gota de aqua	In a drop of water
Buscaba su voz el niño.	the boy was looking for his voice.
No la quiero para hablar;	I do not want it for speaking;
me haré con ella un anillo	I will make a ring of it
que llevará me silencio	so that he may wear my silence
en su dedo pequeñito. . . .	on his little finger . . . .

The first song begins, not with the soprano singing the words of the text, but with wordless, free singing from the soprano, in a style that calls to mind the improvisatory, intense sound of flamenco singing. Three vocal phrases are each punctuated with drumming sounds from piano and harp; the fourth vocal entrance begins the text. The boy soprano sings the second stanza offstage, through a speaking tube, in a simple, folk-like style.

First Interlude: "Dances of the Ancient Earth"

The first interlude features the solo oboe and creates a primitive feeling that combines elements of flamenco improvisation and Oriental scales and effects. The oboe alternates with the mistuned mandolin, stones, and other instruments.

Second Song

Me he perdido muchas veces por el mar
con el oido lleno de floras recién cortadas,
con la lengua lleno de amor y de agonia, . . .
Como me pierdo en el corazón de algunos niños . . .
Muchas veces me he perdido por el mar.

I have lost myself in the sea many times
with my ear full of freshly cut flowers,
with my tongue full of love and agony, . . .
As I lose myself in the hearts of certain children . . .
I have lost myself in the sea many times.

In the second song, the alternation scheme remains the principle of the structure; but here it is the instruments that have the main line, and the soprano whispers bits of the text as the punctuation. Only the last line is sung in normal style and volume. The instruments in this section include the piano, vibraphone, musical saw, electric piano, and harp.

Figure 47-1 is a listening guide that diagrams the structure of the first song. The alternation schemes of the first interlude and second song are quite clear and easy to follow by ear.

FIGURE 47-1. LISTENING GUIDE

ANCIENT VOICES OF CHILDREN, BY CRUMB

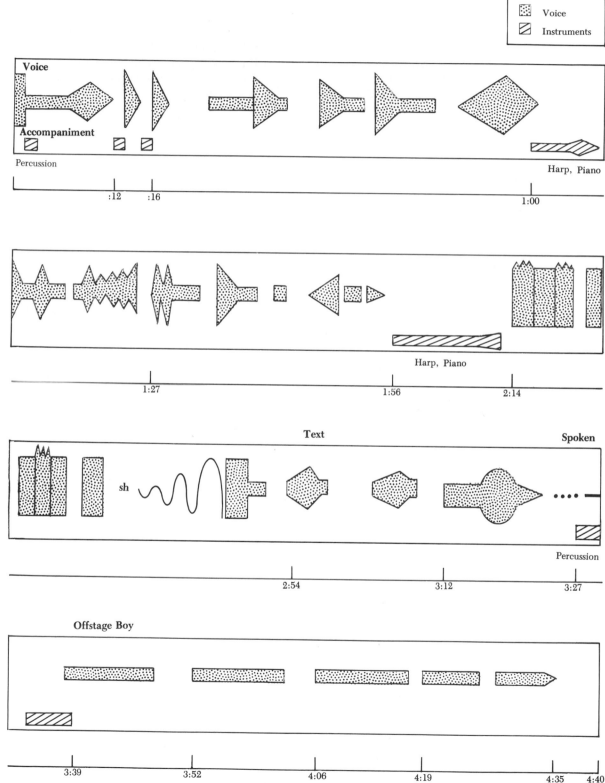

CHAPTER 48

Musical Theater in America

So far, the discussion of music in the twentieth century has concentrated on the world of serious art music and on the new styles of music in this century. In all periods of culture, parallel types of music—folk and popular music—have flourished alongside art music. In the twentieth century, two kinds of music distinct from "serious" or "art" music have become extremely important. This chapter and the next survey these musical worlds. This chapter discusses musical theater, sometimes called "musical comedy"; the following chapter considers the world of popular music and jazz.

The term "musical theater" includes a wide variety of shows—works as diverse as *Showboat*, *Oklahoma!*, *Cabaret*, and *Hair*. It distinguishes these shows as a class from other types of theater that include musical numbers, such as vaudeville, burlesque, and revue. These types of shows were enormously popular and important in our country's cultural history, but they are fundamentally different from musical theater. In a vaudeville show or revue, a succession of acts is presented, often including such elements as a featured star singer, dance numbers, animal acts, and perhaps a magician or acrobat. Chorus lines of scantily clad girls are important also and sometimes are the main element of the show's appeal. What distinguishes these types of entertainment from musical theater is that there is no attempt to connect the various numbers in any logical plot. The acts simply appear, one after another, and musical numbers are changed when one artist leaves the company and another joins. In musical theater, however, there is a definite plot, however flimsy it might be, dialogue that stays the same in all productions of the show, and a definite order of specified musical numbers that remains the same even when the cast changes. Plots get more interesting and lifelike as the century progresses, but all examples of musical comedy are similar in so far as they have a plot at all.

Musical theater, then, means "book shows"—stage presentations with a plot, dialogue, specially written new music, and special choreography for the dance numbers. Musical theater productions go through long rehearsals, perhaps out-of-town tryouts, and maybe extensive modifications. Once they open, however, they remain the same no matter how long the run or how many road companies present the show with different casts in several cities. The shows must remain the same, from the very nature of the medium, because they are designed with commercial success in mind. People who pay to see the show throughout its run expect to see the same show they have read about and heard about.

CHARACTERISTICS OF AMERICAN MUSICAL THEATER

Shows that come under the general heading of "musical comedy" or "musical theater" are an incredibly diverse group, including works as different in intent and tone as the lighthearted shows of the twenties and thirties and the more sophisticated presentations of later years. The genre is general enough to include shows like *Hair* and rock operas like *Tommy* and *Jesus Christ Superstar*, as well as the Rodgers and Hammerstein classics more typical of the genre. Certain characteristics, however, are common to all of the shows in this tradition.

Collaborative Effort

First, musical theater productions are *collaborative* efforts. When people discuss musical theater, they always speak of the great teams that created the important shows: George and Ira Gershwin, Rodgers and Hammerstein, Lerner and Loewe. It is, perhaps, significant that the major art form of this century —film—is also collaborative, requiring the services of a number of artists and craftsmen to bring the creator's vision to the screen. It is true that earlier forms of musical theater, like opera, were also group efforts and that great composers sometimes had the aid of fine librettists and had to rely on singers, musicians, staging and lighting directors, and a host of others. But in opera, the major appeal is the music. We speak of the operas of Verdi, Wagner, and Puccini and sometimes forget these composers' less famous collaborators. The balance of the elements in musical comedy is more even. Because the songs are intended to be "hits," the lyrics are more important than they are in opera, and lyricist and composer work on a much more equal footing. Dance is another element more important in musical comedy than in opera. People from the world of dance— Jerome Robbins, Agnes de Mille, Bob Fosse, Gower Champion—have played an important and widely recognized role in the success of many shows. Musical comedy has also relied on the services of another type of specialist who does not even exist in the world of opera—the "show doctor." Occasionally, a show does not jell by opening night, and specialists are called in to make changes, so that

Here, the successful team of George and Ira Gershwin work with Fred Astaire for the 1937 film *Shall We Dance*.

the revised effort has some chance at success. These specialists are given total power, and they are paid well for their efforts. A famous example of the work of a show doctor is *Camelot*, which opened to very mixed reviews. Moss Hart, the best-known of these specialists, was called in to make changes, and the show went on to become a success.

Stars

Musical theater has also created a special kind of star. A musical comedy star needs a trained voice, capable of projecting successfully in a large theater, but does not need the kind of vocal training demanded by operatic roles. Conversely, musical comedy stars must act more convincingly than opera stars, because

The successful team of Oscar Hammerstein II and Richard Rodgers collaborated on many popular shows.

musical comedy audiences expect more than gorgeous voices. They also have to look the part. A middle-aged, overweight heroine may be acceptable within the conventions of opera if her voice is right, but the more naturalistic conventions of musical comedy would not permit such casting. Interestingly, the best-known stars of musical comedy have been women—Ethel Merman, Carol Channing, Florence Henderson, Gwen Verdon, Julie Andrews. Some male stars have specialized in this medium—Robert Goulet, Alfred Drake—but the focus is more often on the female star. While many musical comedy stars have gone on to success in other media—film, television, nightclub singing, or dramatic acting, an astonishing number of familiar stars got their start as singer-dancer-actors in the world of musical comedy.

Mass Appeal

Another general characteristic of musical theater is that it is consciously designed to appeal to a mass audience. While the opera world caters to the educated tastes of its special audience and the world of "serious" twentieth-century music explores exciting new directions, musical theater continues its quest for a show of universal appeal that will run forever. Shows with any sparkle and creativity involve tremendous investments of time and money before a single ticket is sold; shows that close rapidly lose large sums of their backers' money. The striving for mass appeal has both good and bad effects. On the good side, great inventiveness and a tremendous amount of talent are invested in the struggle to create a hit show. On the bad side, there is the temptation to put together a formula show, a routine combination of appealing elements, or to revive a surefire hit from a previous era, rather than risk something really new. The 1980 Broadway season included one successful show regarded by some as a formula piece—*Annie*, with its cute orphans, the dog, and a relentlessly upbeat feeling—and two revivals, *Peter Pan* and *Oklahoma!* It also included *Evita*, a totally new and risky kind of show, which was a great success. On the good side, the search for mass appeal has inspired lyricists and composers to produce hundreds of wonderful songs that have become part of our mass culture and have enriched our musical life. Many songs that we regard as masterpieces of popular music, songs as diverse as "My Funny Valentine," "You'll Never Walk Alone," "The Impossible Dream," "Embraceable You," "Getting to Know You," and "The Age of Aquarius," were all composed for musicals. Composers of musicals try to come up with at least three hit songs: a love song; a catchy, upbeat, rhythmic number; and, perhaps, an inspiring dramatic song. The search for mass appeal also determines the style of the music. Musical theater works within the standard harmonic system and, at its best, produces songs you and I can remember and sing ourselves. Innovation is welcome and freshness is necessary, but always within the limits of audience appeal.

Themes

Nostalgia

The search for audience appeal and a long run determines everything about musical theater, including the popular themes and plotlines. Nostalgia is a surefire theme, at least with those people who have the interest and income to spend an evening in the theater. Many of the best known and most successful musical comedies look back to an idealized, earlier time, when things were simpler and principles mattered. *Show Boat* was set in an idealized South of riverboats and weeping willows, although it did deal with such issues as interracial marriage and slavery—revolutionary ideas for a 1927 musical. *Oklahoma!* dealt with the days when that region was still a territory, on the brink of becoming a state. *Music Man*, a show of great originality, was set in an idealized small town of nineteenth-century America. The numerous flag-waving patriotic shows can also be considered as a type of nostalgia, exalting the simple virtues of an earlier day. Revivals and new versions of the shows of the twenties, like *No, No, Nanette*, are further signs of nostalgia as a pervasive theme.

Cinderella Stories

Another popular theme is a kind of fairy tale, usually centered on a girl who overcomes impossible odds to win the man of her dreams. One commentator says that most successful musicals are versions of the Cinderella story. Anna in *The*

Showboat, Jerome Kern.

King and I, Maria in *The Sound of Music*, and Eliza Doolittle in *My Fair Lady* are all examples of this kind of heroine: they all win over male leads who are stern father figures, and then live happily ever after.

Realistic Plots

Not all musical theater is based on Cinderella stories or fond looks backward at the "good old days." One of the most interesting developments in musical theater is the gradual rise of shows with realistic or pessimistic stories. The genre can survive without happy endings, as evidenced by shows like *Pal Joey*, whose hero is a small-time hoodlum. *Cabaret* deals with a decadent world and uses the sleazy night club as a metaphor of decaying prewar Germany. Bernstein's *West Side Story* is a modern version of the tragic Romeo and Juliet story and concerns street gangs and racial strife. Stephen Sondheim, the leading lyricist-composer of the seventies, has created shows like *Company*, *Follies*, and *A Little Night Music* that deal with a weary cynicism and the ambiguities and poses of modern society. Musical theater is a very flexible genre, capable of dealing with a wide variety of themes.

Film Adaptations

One last general characteristic of music comedy deserves discussion. These shows are written for the stage, and their success depends on the excitement generated between performers and audience. Successful musicals are often adapted for film. This transfer from one medium to another deserves some discussion because most people's experience of musical theater is restricted to the film versions. As is usually true when a work moves from one medium to another, there are gains and losses in the transfer of musical theater from stage to film. Sometimes the planners of the film version hedge their bets by hiring famous film stars, whether or not they have experience in musical comedy or can even sing. Even in those instances when good singers are hired for the film, the film version reaches so many people that the star of the film version is forever identified with the role in the popular mind. In the film version of *Hello, Dolly*, Barbra Streisand, for example, created a Dolly quite different from the original Carol Channing version. Julie Andrews is forever identified with the role of Maria in *The Sound of Music* from the film version, although Mary Martin created the role on stage. Examples of nonsinging stars are Deborah Kerr in the film version of *The King and I* and Audrey Hepburn in *My Fair Lady*. A soprano named Marni Nixon did the singing for both of them.

The chief advantage of the film versions is, of course, their ability to escape the limitations of the stage. The film version of *Oklahoma!* could show real wide open spaces; *The Sound of Music* made a beautiful film, set amid gorgeous Alpine scenery and Baroque castles; the parades in the film versions of *Music Man* and *Hello Dolly* surpassed anything possible on a stage. The most important advantage of the film versions is that they reach a tremendous audience, far more numerous than the group that sees the shows live.

Television

In a final irony of transfer from one medium to another, even more people have seen the film versions that were shown on television. *The Sound of Music* has reached huge television audiences several times, and thus more people have seen the televised film than saw the film in a theater. Rodgers and Hammerstein wrote the show first for the stage; they did not have film in mind. The producers of the film did not have television in mind when they made the beautiful film version. The show eventually reached people in a medium even more cramped for space than a stage. One wonders whether a tape of a stage performance might not work better on television than the film version.

Stage Adaptations of Films

Now the medium transfer is reversing on occasion. *A Little Night Music* is a musical version for the stage of a film by Ingmar Bergman; and *Forty-Second*

A Little Night Music, voted best Broadway musical in 1973.

Street, a Busby Berkeley film musical of the 1930s, has been transformed into a stage show. Certainly the film versions of musical theater are important, not only for making the shows known to many more people, but also as a sign of the vitality and adaptability of musical theater.

HISTORY

The history of American musical theater in this century divides neatly into four major periods, each including a number of works that are similar in basic ways. As is always true with these subdivisions dear to historians, there is considerable overlap between periods, and there are individual composers and shows that stubbornly refuse to be neatly categorized. Still, these four periods are a helpful way to understand the long and involved history of the genre.

First Period

The first period consists of musicals that are American versions of the European operetta, a type of light opera popular in Europe in the late nineteenth century. Plots were generally simple and unrealistic, with a great emphasis on romanticized, exotic locations. Composers of this period included Victor Herbert (1859–1924), Rudolf Friml (1879–1972), and Sigmund Romberg (1887–1951). The best-known Herbert operettas are *The Red Mill* (1906), *Naughty Marietta* (1910), and *Sweethearts* (1913). Well-known works by Friml include *Rose-Marie* (1924) and *The Vagabond King* (1925). Romberg's contributions include *Maytime* (1917), *The Student Prince* (1924), and *The Desert Song* (1926). All of these composers also wrote for revues and other types of shows, but their famous works are these operettas in European style.

The Student Prince is set in romantic Heidelberg and features dashing students with dueling scars and lovely coffeehouse waitresses. *The Desert Song* is concerned with glamorized Bedouins of the Rudolph Valentino type, who rob from the rich and give to the poor. These two shows are typical of the operetta genre.

Second Period

The second period consists of specifically American versions of musical theater. The composers who created this new American type of musical theater include George M. Cohan (1878–1942), Jerome Kern (1885–1945), Irving Berlin (b. 1888), and George Gershwin (1898–1937). These composers were somewhat

George M. Cohan (left) and Irving Berlin (above), great composers in the second period of American musical theater.

Written by George Gershwin, *Porgy and Bess* was originally considered a serious musical comedy, but is now considered opera.

different from those of the first period; all wrote popular songs as well as musical comedies, and their musical comedies were truly American shows. Cohan is famous for his World War I songs like "Over There" and "You're a Grand Old Flag." His other famous tunes include "Give My Regards to Broadway," "Mary," and "Yankee Doodle Dandy." *George M!*, a musical of 1968, put together all of Cohan's hits, which originally appeared in several different shows, and revived the Cohan mystique once again. Kern is best known for *Show Boat* (1927), which really belongs in the next category because its plot is considerably more realistic than most stories of this period. Another of Kern's famous shows is *Roberta* (1933), which includes the classic song, "Smoke Gets in Your Eyes." Irving Berlin wrote a number of revues, many classic hit tunes, a patriotic World War II show—*This Is the Army* (1942)—and two timeless hit shows designed for Ethel Merman: *Annie Get Your Gun* (1946) and *Call Me Madam* (1950). Gershwin, like Berlin, wrote scores of hit tunes, many revues, and several famous musical comedies, including *Funny Face* (1927), *Strike Up the Band* (1930), and *Of Thee I Sing* (1931). He also wrote a genuine American opera, *Porgy and Bess* (1935), regarded for some time as an unusually serious musical comedy, but now thought of as an opera and performed by opera companies.

Third Period

The third period of the history of musical theater in America is the best-known. Works of this period were enormously popular. Many had very long runs on stage and were made into successful motion pictures as well. The shows of this third period are based on better, more realistic plots, including great works of literature, and the elements are in better balance. Most commentators agree that the songs and dances from shows of this period are much better integrated into the drama than before; they help to establish character, advance the plot, and involve the audience in the drama. Songs and dance numbers in the previous types were sometimes dragged into the story without much dramatic justification. Even when they were fitted into the action smoothly, they rarely advanced the progress of the story. They tended, instead, to interrupt its flow. They could be omitted or changed without materially affecting the story; whereas, in the third period, the musical numbers are an integral part of the show, which would not make sense without them.

The composers of this period are such great teams as Rodgers and Hammerstein, Lerner and Loewe, and Styne, Comden, and Green. Rodgers and Hammerstein were incredibly successful and changed the genre forever. After the phenomenal success of *Oklahoma!* (1943), discussed in more detail later, they went on to write a string of hits, including *Carousel* (1945), *South Pacific* (1949), *The King and I* (1951), *Flower Drum Song* (1958), and *The Sound of Music* (1959). Nothing either member wrote with other lyricists or composers approached the success of the hits they wrote together, although Rodgers and Lorenz Hart wrote some great songs and fine shows like *Pal Joey* (1940) and *A Connecticut Yankee* (1943). The team of Alan Jay Lerner and Frederick Loewe produced *Brigadoon* (1947), *My Fair Lady* (1956), and *Camelot* (1960). Jule Styne, Betty Comden, and Adolph Green produced such shows as *Gentlemen Prefer Blondes* (1949), *Peter Pan* (1954), *Gypsy* (1959), and *Funny Girl* (1964). Meredith Wilson (1902-1980) wrote *The Music Man* (1957) and *The Unsinkable Molly Brown* (1960).

Fourth Period

The fourth period in this history includes totally new approaches to musical theater.

New Characters and Stories

Sociological change and the emergence of new attitudes and ideas were reflected in new kinds of musical theater, often opposed to the romance, glamor, and happy endings of the hit shows of the forties and fifties. *Pal Joey* (Rodgers and Hart, 1940) is often viewed as an early forerunner of this fourth type of musical

One of the longest running musicals ever, *Fiddler on the Roof*, dealt with the life of a Russian peasant and his family.

theater because it dealt with unheroic characters from the nightclub world. *Guys and Dolls* (Frank Loesser, 1950) also dealt with the Damon Runyon world of low-life gamblers and molls. Loesser's *How to Succeed in Business Without Really Trying* (1961) and *The Pajama Game* (Adler and Ross, 1954) dealt in comic ways with the unlikely world of business.

Rock Musicals

In the late 1950s, rock burst upon the popular music world, and this new style of music proved suitable for musical theater also. *Bye, Bye, Birdie* (Adams and Strouse, 1960) celebrated the rock craze, and *Hair* (Ragni, Rado, and MacDermot, 1968) celebrated the revolution of the sixties. Two rock musicals appeared in 1971 that told the story of the life of Christ in rock music: *Godspell* (Tebelak and Schwartz) and *Jesus Christ Superstar* (O'Horgan, Rice, and Webber). There was even a rock musical based on nostalgia for the "good old days" of the fifties—*Grease* (Jacobs and Casey, 1972).

Other New Approaches

Man of La Mancha (Leigh and Darion, 1965) is one of the most interesting of the new types of musical. It is more a theatrical than a musical experience. The staging is brilliant, and the show combines the squalid world of Don Quixote's prison with his dream world of heroic knights and innocent damsels. *Fiddler on the Roof* (Bock and Harnick, 1964) also dealt with unlikely material for a musical. Based on stories written by Sholom Aleichem about the Jewish inhabitants of an impoverished peasant town in czarist Russia, *Fiddler* ran longer than any other musical. We have already mentioned *Cabaret* (Kander and Ebb, 1966), which uses the atmosphere of the cabaret as a metaphor for the decadence and menace of prewar Berlin. The most successful show of the late seventies was another unlikely story for musical comedy. *Evita*, the story of the rise to power of Eva Peron, the wife of the Argentinian dictator, won several awards and had a very long run.

The composer who most typifies the new musical is Stephen Sondheim, who wrote such shows as *A Funny Thing Happened on the Way to the Forum* (1962), *Company* (1970), *Follies* (1971), and *A Little Night Music* (1973). Sondheim's lyrics are filled with a wry spirit reminiscent of Cole Porter songs, and the stories of his shows often focus on middle-aged characters looking backward at the folly of their youth. He catches perfectly the foibles of modern society, with its pretenses and games, and has created still another type of musical theater, quite distinct from the classics of musical comedy and from the other types of new musical theater.

The wide variety of hit shows in this last period testifies to the flexibility and durability of musical theater as a genre. It can delight us with magic and fairy tales; it can transport us back to idealized, better times; and it can also deal with biography, great literature, and serious thinking about contemporary society. Musical theater continues to be a viable and successful art form and to attract inventive minds and superb lyricists, composers, and choreographers.

The remainder of this chapter looks in detail at two shows, *Okalahoma!* and *A Little Night Music*, and attempts to analyze one important song from each.

OKLAHOMA!

Oklahoma!, the first collaboration of Rodgers and Hammerstein, was a phenomenal success. It opened in 1943, when the country was at war, and it celebrated a nostalgic vision of pioneer virtue and nineteenth-century American life. Contemporary accounts of the New York run speak of the servicemen in uniform crowded into the standing room at the rear of the theater, seeing the show before shipping out for the war. The national road company tour ran for ten years; the Chicago run alone lasted for more than a year.

Besides its timely theme, the show had a number of other factors in its favor. The collaboration of Richard Rodgers and Oscar Hammerstein II was a magic one, as their string of hits was to testify. The show, although it may seem dated by modern standards, departed courageously from many of the previous musical theater stereotypes. The choreography by Agnes de Mille integrated the dancing into the story, rather than merely providing decoration or big production numbers. The plot hinges on the heroine's difficult choice between two men: Curley, a typical hero, and Jud, a villain who somehow fascinates the innocent girl. She ends up with Curley, of course, but the dream ballet makes clear that

Oklahoma! featured the choreography of Agnes de Mille.

there is a struggle going on within her. Instead of providing lighthearted diversion, the dance tells us more than the dialogue and reveals her subconscious fears and drives.

The songs of the show have a natural charm about them and great variety. "People Will Say We're in Love" is a fresh twist on the obligatory love duet; the couple agree on what they will not do, so that their friends will not suspect their growing love. The title song is a rousing big number. "I'm Just a Girl Who Can't Say No" is a comically bawdy number, slightly wicked but still well within the bounds of the show's general tone of small-town morality. "Kansas City" is a wide-eyed account of the wonders and dangers of the big city, seen through the eyes of a small-town citizen. "Surrey with the Fringe on Top" is a charming song in Western rhythm. All of the songs are catchy and hummable; several have become standards of the popular repertoire.

"Oh, What a Beautiful Mornin' "

The song that sets the mood for the whole show is "Oh, What a Beautiful Mornin', " sung by Curley, the hero, as the curtain opens on the first act. This beginning was a departure; the standard opening was a big dance number. Instead, the curtain opens to reveal a stage that is nearly empty. Aunt Eller, an older woman, is doing her chores. Offstage, Curley begins singing the song and enters in the course of it. The song tells us something about Curley's character and sets the tone for the show by extolling the wide open country in folksy description. This song was the first one Rodgers and Hammerstein wrote for the show. Legend has it that, when Rodgers first received the lyrics, he recognized that the show, and the team, would work well.

In this scene from *Oklahoma!* Curley sings "Oh, What a Beautiful Mornin'."

There are two musical sections in the song. The chorus melody moves mostly by thirds (see Figure 48-1). The chorus is sixteen measures long and divides symmetrically into two eight-measure halves, divided further into four-measure segments. The verse consists of a contrasting idea, whose last four measures lead into the repeat of the chorus (see Figure 48-2). The verse is a stepwise melody, sixteen measures long and subdivided into four segments of four measures each. Both sections are in a lilting waltz tempo. The combination of the lyric melody, familiar harmony, and homespun text successfully creates the country mood that sets the tone for the whole show.

Oh, what a beau-ti-ful morn-in',

Oh, what a beau-ti-ful day.___

Figure 48-1.   Chorus melody.

There's a bright gold-en haze on the mead-ow,___ there's a

bright gold-en haze on the mead-ow.___

Figure 48-2.   Verse melody.

FIGURE 48-3. LISTENING GUIDE

"OH, WHAT A BEAUTIFUL MORNIN'," *OKLAHOMA*, BY RODGERS AND HAMMERSTEIN

Introduction:
Sustained Chords
Solo Woodwind
Bird Calls

Verse I Voice Alone	There's a bright, golden haze on the meadow,
	There's a bright, golden haze on the meadow,
	The Corn is as high as an elephant's eye.
Orchestra Enters	And it looks like it's climbin' clear up to the sky.
Chorus	Oh, what a beautiful mornin',
	Oh, what a beautiful day,
	I got a beautiful feelin',
	Everythin's goin' my way.
Four—Bar Interlude	
Verse II	All the cattle are standin' like statues,
	All the cattle are standin' like statues,
	They don't turn their heads as they see me ride by,
	But a little brown maverick is winkin' her eye.
Chorus	Oh, what a beautiful mornin',
	Oh, what a beautiful day,
	I got a beautiful feelin',
	Everythin's goin' my way.
Verse III	All the sounds of the earth are like music,
	All the sounds of the earth are like music,
	The breeze is so busy, it don't miss a tree,
	And an ol' weepin' willer is laughin' at me.
Chorus	Oh, what a beautiful mornin',
	Oh, what a beautiful day,
	I got a beautiful feeling',
	Everythin's goin' my way.
	Oh, what a beautiful day.
Slowing—	
Last Line Repeated	

A LITTLE NIGHT MUSIC

As we mentioned earlier, Stephen Sondheim (b. 1930) is one of the leading composer-lyricists of the last, or experimental phase of the genre. He is a well-trained composer who commands a wide variety of musical styles, and is a lyricist of trenchant wit who captures the cynicism and pretense of modern speech perfectly in his songs. He broke into musical theater as the lyricist for *West Side Story (1957)* and *Gypsy* (1959) and wrote both lyrics and music for *A Funny Thing Happened on the Way to the Forum* (1962). *Company* (1970) and *Follies* (1971) further enhanced his reputation.

A Little Night Music (1973) is as far as possible from the spirit of *Oklahoma!* It is a reworking of *Smiles of a Summer Night*, a 1957 film by Ingmar Bergman. The plot centers on upper-class, sophisticated characters and their search for love. The main characters include Fredrik Egerman, a lawyer who has recently remarried; his eighteen-year-old wife, still a virgin after eleven months of marriage; his son Henrik, a divinity student bothered by his helplessness with women; Desiree Armfeldt, an attractive actress who has been Fredrik's mistress; and Madame Armfeldt, a wonderful old bawd, Desiree's mother, who at one point laments that liaisons aren't what they used to be in the good old days. Obviously, we are in a world far different from the usual musical comedy world. There is comedy, but it is the rueful sort, as the various characters reflect on life, love, and their entanglements. One of the first songs is Fredrik's "Now," in which he muses on possible strategies to consummate his marriage. One short section of lyrics illustrates both the tone of the work and Sondheim's skill with sophisticated lyrics and original rhymes. Fredrik is considering the possible effectiveness of reading Romantic literature to his modest bride.

> In view of her penchant
> For something romantic,
> De Sade is too trenchant
> And Dickens too frantic,
> And Stendhal would ruin
> The plan of attack,
> As there isn't much blue in
> *The Red and the Black*
> De Maupassant's candor
>
> Would cause her dismay.
> The Brontës are grander
> But not very gay.
> Her taste is much blander,
> I'm sorry to say,
> But is Hans Christian Ander-
> sen ever risqué?
> Which eliminates A . . .

The music is as original as the lyrics. Sondheim created a unique style for this show. All of the music is in triple meter: 3/4, 6/8, or 9/8. Some of his unusual metrical tricks are possible only because both lyrics and music were composed by the same person. The harmonies are unusual, more impressionistic than standard, and so are the muted, delicate orchestral colors. Every element of the show contributes to the air of upper-class decadence.

The best-known song from the show is "Send in the Clowns," a haunting ballad that achieved some success as a hit song apart from the show. It appears twice in the show. The first time, it is sung by Desiree after she and Fredrik have met at Madame Armfeldt's estate in the country. The meeting did not go well. He chattered about his lovely wife, and they parted without reestablishing their old love affair. The song is Desiree's reaction to the meeting, weary musings about the foolishness of love. The song appears again at the end, after Fredrik's wife has decided to run off with her stepson. In the second context, when Fredrik and Desiree are free to love one another again, the tone of the lyrics is not so weary, but there still is a wry sense of the comedy and foolishness of love.

Musically, the song has a haunting quality (see Figure 48-4). The harmonies are unusual, particularly in the middle section. The melody moves in a relatively narrow compass and never reaches the sort of climax we associate with the "big" love song of a show, but stays tentative and floating in its feeling. The restrained orchestral accompaniment, filled with sustained chords, harp arpeggios, and solo passages in the low range of the clarinet, reinforces the gentle, musing quality of the song.

Figure 48-4. Opening of "Send in the Clowns."

CONCLUSION

The creativity and talent that has fueled a century of musical theater in America shows no signs of flagging. It seems safe to predict that the world of musical theater will continue as long as this country has any musical life. Somehow, we need the magic of musical theater. We hunger to be whisked away from our routine lives. We are revitalized and delighted by the exuberance and vitality of a good show. The astounding success of revivals of older shows like *Oklahoma!* indicates that there will always be a market for traditional musical comedies, both old ones and new shows designed on the traditional patterns. The success of more experimental shows, like *Fiddler on the Roof, Man of La Mancha*, and *Evita* opens the way for other nontraditional, experimental musicals. Producers and composers will strive to supply the shows audiences want, and the theater and music produced will be deserving of serious and intelligent listening.

FIGURE 48-5. LISTENING GUIDE

"SEND IN THE CLOWNS,"
A LITTLE NIGHT MUSIC,
BY SONDHEIM

A Section

Isn't it rich?
Are we a pair?
Me here at last on the ground,
You in midair.
Send in the clowns.

A Repeated

Isn't it bliss?
Don't you approve?
One who keeps tearing around,
One who can't move.
Where are the clowns?
Send in the clowns.

B Contrasting Material

Just when I'd stopped opening doors,
Finally knowing the one that I wanted was yours,
Making my entrance again with my usual flair,
Sure of my lines
No one is there.

A

Don't you love farce?
My fault, I fear.
I thought that you'd want what I want.
Sorry, my dear.
But where are the clowns?
Quick, send in the clowns.
Don't bother, they're here.

A Repeated

Isn't it rich?
Isn't it queer?
Losing my timing
This late in my career?
And where are the clowns?
There ought to be clowns.
Well, maybe next year.

CHAPTER 49

Popular Music and Jazz

Writing a brief history of popular music in twentieth-century America is a formidable task. The history of popular culture of any kind—music, movies, television—involves sociological considerations at least as much as aesthetic ones. Pop culture responds instantly to sociological change and social pressures of all kinds. Some angry commentators blame popular culture for what they view as the decline of moral values; others associate rock music in particular with the atmosphere of drugs and promiscuity that they imagine always accompanies it. But rock does not cause moral decay any more than the permissiveness of theme and language in movies of the past ten years has caused a breakdown in moral standards. The popular arts respond to whatever is going on in the culture and reflect changes of mood or standards already present in society. The history of American jazz, for example, is largely a history of blacks in America. The stages of black history, from slavery through urban assimilation to consciousness of African roots and pride in a unique cultural heritage, are all represented in major style changes in jazz. Anxiety during wartime, patriotism in times of crisis, and prevalent moods of sentimentality and anger can all be traced in our popular music. Music cannot become popular unless it speaks to a large audience and gives expression to a mood or feeling shared by a fairly large segment of the population.

CHARACTERISTICS OF POPULAR MUSIC

Rapid Change

Pop music changes with extreme rapidity, responding to the rapid changes in twentieth-century society. As we already mentioned, modern technology and mass communication media have greatly increased the pace of change. Television and the numerous magazines devoted to mass culture can create a new celebrity overnight. Saturation advertising campaigns can bring a new face or voice to everyone in America. Unless the manufactured celebrities develop a loyal following, however, they disappear as quickly as they appeared, and newly created celebrities take their place. It is astonishing to see the dizzying speed with which some stars rise and burn out in popular culture.

Some individual stars and groups achieve unusual longevity, proving that the appeal of real talent does last, even in our fickle age. Frank Sinatra has managed to maintain his position as a star singer for nearly forty years by doing what he does extremely well. Although he has ignored several major style changes in pop music, his fans are still loyal. The Rolling Stones first appeared on the pop scene about the same time as the Beatles, in the sixties, and are still going strong, selling records and filling stadiums for their live concerts. But singers and groups who can stay on top for years are merely the exceptions that prove the rule of rapid change.

Multiplicity of Styles

Another unique characterisitc of popular music, as opposed to classical music, is that there is no one style common to all performers. The world of pop music is a world of bewildering diversity. The audience for pop music is huge. Billions of records are sold each year, and billions of dollars are spent to attend live performances. A singer or group needs to capture only a small segment of the market to make large amounts of money, and there is always room in the market for another singer or group. As we begin the eighties, for example, the popular recording artists of the moment include disco groups like the Village People; country and western favorites like Willie Nelson, Dolly Parton, and Loretta Lynn; middle-of-the-road singers like Barry Manilow and Olivia Newton-John; and rock groups of all sorts, including heavy metal groups, New Wave groups, and mainstream groups like the Stones. It is difficult to generalize about any moment in the history of popular music; it is impossible to predict what might happen in the next five years.

Performer's Music

One generalization made in the first pages of this book bears repeating here. Popular music is performer's music: it depends for its success on the energy flowing between performer and audience. The composer of the material is not nearly as important as the way the performer projects that material. The forties crooner gently shaping a ballad, the following of the sixties intoning his poetic or angry text, the rock guitarist stalking the stage of an arena, and the soul group prancing in its complicated movement patterns are all quite similar, despite the divergencies of their musical styles. Like jazz musicians, they impose their own shape and style on their material, and they project a message and an energy to their audience.

This final chapter will not attempt a detailed history of American popular music in this century, and will certainly not try to evaluate all of the various styles in that history. Instead, it will outline some of the major styles and artists in twentieth-century American jazz and popular music and present a few examples of jazz and popular tunes in detail.

JAZZ: POPULAR MUSIC OR NOT?

Jazz, a unique and important native American art form, has always had an ambiguous relationship with popular music. Jazz began as one style of popular music, but it is now generally regarded as sophisticated art music, rather than as a class of pop music. Jazz is improvised music, involving more risk and creativity than most pop music. Since about 1940, it has become a highly individual art form, forsaking mass appeal for personal expression and authenticity. Jazz still has devoted fans, but they are a specialized, knowledgeable, and somewhat elite group. There are jazz FM stations in most large cities, but the audience for jazz is quite small in comparison with the larger pop audience.

It is difficult to separate jazz entirely from the popular music world. Occasionally, a jazz artist breaks into the pop world. Such artists, however, run the risk of being written off as sellouts by devoted jazz fans. Other groups exist somewhere in between the "pure" jazz and pop worlds. In this chapter, we will treat jazz and pop as related parallel developments. The more sophisticated styles of jazz which emerged after its separation from pop music are musically fascinating and deserving of serious study. In this chapter, however, we are more interested in the major developments in both worlds.

BEFORE 1900

Jazz and popular music did not spring up in a vacuum around 1900; both were built on developments that had taken place earlier. Since the days of the American Revolution, there had been popular patriotic songs, hymns, and work songs. In the latter half of the nineteenth century, several developments took place that had a great influence on the later history of jazz and popular music.

Vaudeville and Minstrel Shows

The first important development of the period between the Civil War and 1900 was the rise of vaudeville and other forms of popular musical entertainment. Minstrel shows were very popular. Although we now regard their blackface humor as hopelessly racist, this form of entertainment was extremely important in the evolution of our popular culture. Revues were popular also. In 1866 a show called *The Black Crook* opened in New York. It combined a melodramatic plot, some French dancers stranded in America, and elaborate stage sets to produce the first musical extravaganza. It had a very long run—474 performances. It developed a reputation as a wicked show, featuring the French dancers in costumes that were shocking, and its scandalous reputation naturally helped to ensure the show's success. It was followed by other types of popular musical entertainments, burlesque and vaudeville. Burlesque was originally a type of musical entertainment featuring parody and caricature, and only later came to denote entertainment consisting mostly of strippers and comics.

Sheet Music

These types of musical entertainment had a powerful effect on the business of popular music. The great number of vaudeville troupes needed large amounts of musical material, providing an opportunity for songwriters to have their material performed. When one of the vaudeville stars introduced a new song, it stood a very good chance of becoming popular. The performance created a demand for the sheet music so the audience could sing the song at home. Then, as now, it became important to sell your song to the most popular performers, and early sheet music always features a picture of the performer on the cover. "As sung by" and the performer's name and picture are much more prominently displayed than the composer's name.

The same practice continues throughout the history of popular songs. Even today, the covers of sheet music and collections emphasize the association with particular performers, and the implied promise, seldom really true, is that the sheet music accurately represents the way the famous performers sing it.

To fill this demand for sheet music, publishers began to specialize in popular music and sentimental ballads, rather than merely printing them as a sideline. Among the songs published in the late decades of the nineteenth century are a large number of sentimental ballads, filled with sad tales of drunken fathers, sudden death, and tragic slides into lives of sin and shame. Other types of songs that appeared were Irish songs, songs introducing new dances such as the cakewalk, and "Negro" songs glamorizing the racial stereotype of the happy "darky."

Jazz

The third important development prior to 1900 was the birth of jazz in New Orleans. The origins of jazz are not entirely clear. Scholars argue about its sources and their relative importance. Work songs of black slaves, simple rural blues, and the music of the minstrel shows all seem to be involved in the origin of jazz. The important fact is that a new style arose in Storyville, the red-light

Early sheet music cover. Performers became an important factor in the sucess of popular music.

quarter of New Orleans. Pianists like "Jelly Roll" Morton and bands like "King" Oliver's played a new type of music, featuring strong rhythm, improvisation on the melody line, and "blue" notes outside the standard scale, such as the flatted third and sixth. Thus began the long and complex history of this important art form. New Orleans jazz is well preserved in recordings, as well as in live performances by groups, such as the Preservation Hall Jazz Band, who keep the early tradition alive.

The Preservation Hall Jazz Band continues to keep the early jazz tradition alive.

1900–1920

The years between 1900 and 1920 saw a continuation of the three important trends of the late 1800s.

Sheet Music

The sheet music publishing business expanded greatly. One area of New York, where the publishers were concentrated, became known as Tin Pan Alley, after a chance remark by a newspaper writer comparing the sound of their tinny pianos to that of tin pans being banged together. Among the big publishers of popular music were Witmark and Sons, Joseph Stern, Jerome Remick, and Shapiro and Bernstein. The publishers employed numerous musicians as pianists to demonstrate songs for performers seeking new material. They also hired arrangers to help composers get their ideas down on paper, and orchestrators who arranged new songs for performance by instrumental ensembles. As late as the 1940s, the last remnant of the trade of "song plugger" could be seen and heard in the music sections of large department stores, where a pianist was employed to demonstrate sheet music for customers. Among the hit songs that sold a million copies in that period were such perennial favorites as "A Bird in a Gilded Cage," "Let Me Call You Sweetheart," "Down By the Old Mill Stream," and "Put on Your Old Gray Bonnet." Many of these songs are still known and sung, at least by people over forty.

Jazz

Among the material published in this thriving music business were songs and piano pieces from the world of jazz. Scott Joplin's piano rags, like "Maple Leaf Rag" and "The Entertainer," were published in that period. Joplin's music enjoyed a revival after it was used as background music in *The Sting*, a popular film of the seventies. Among the other materials published were the first commercial versions of the blues. W. C. Handy, a black composer who had performed in minstrel shows, published "The Memphis Blues" and "The St. Louis Blues," the most famous blues song ever written. Jazz was breaking into the commercial, popular world, perhaps in watered-down versions, lacking the honesty and strength it had in its original setting, but still reaching thousands of people through the music publishing business.

Opposition to jazz arose in proportion to its popularity outside the black quarters of southern cities. It was denounced as wicked, demoralizing to the young, and generally not respectable. This outraged reaction is an early example of another trend in the history of popular music in America; each new style is denounced at its first appearance as a corrupting, uncivilized influence on the young. Such protests, however, never deter the course of popular taste; rather, the outrage of parents and the establishment seems to help new styles catch on among the rebellious youth of the moment.

Vaudeville

Vaudeville enjoyed its greatest heyday in the early decades of this century. Stars like Bert Williams, Jimmy Durante, Sophie Tucker, Fred Astaire, Eddie Cantor, and Al Jolson reached the height of their popularity during this period. Many vaudeville stars had long subsequent careers in nightclubs and films. Sophie Tucker, billed as "the Last of the Red-Hot Mamas," appeared in Las Vegas, where the crowds tend to be somewhat older than the record-buying public, as late as the fifties.

World War I

World War I produced a crop of patriotic songs and brought to prominence George M. Cohan, mentioned in Chapter 48 as a musical comedy composer. Before America's entry into the war, some English songs associated with the war, such as "Keep the Home Fires Burning," "It's a Long Way to Tipperary," and "Pack Up Your Troubles in Your Old Kit Bag," became popular here. When America joined the fight in 1917, Tin Pan Alley immediately cranked out the songs required for bond rallies, including defiant, patriotic tunes like "We're Going to Whip the Kaiser" and sentimental ballads of separation and farewell, such as "Till We Meet Again" and "There's a Long, Long Trail a-Winding." The most successful World War I song was Cohan's "Over There," which sold two million copies of sheet music and one million records, and won for Cohan the Congressional Medal of Honor. The war even produced humorous songs about our boys' adventures in France, such as "How Ya Gonna Keep 'Em Down on the Farm, After They've Seen Paree?" The war songs were featured in musicals, revues and vaudeville. They also appeared in the war films that the new movie industry cranked out with energy equal to that shown by Tin Pan Alley.

1920–1940

The twenties and thirties were a time of great changes in American society. The Roaring Twenties, a time of flappers, bootleg gin, and a pervasive cynicism as portrayed in the literary works of F. Scott Fitzgerald, created a different type of society with tastes quite different from those of more innocent earlier decades. The Great Depression of the thirties ended the party atmosphere of the twenties and changed national tastes once again.

Technological Changes

Technological changes revolutionized the popular music business also. American homes suddenly contained radios and phonographs, both of which created a demand for new popular singers and groups. Movies added sound tracks, eliminating the theater orchestras but creating new work for musicians in Hollywood.

Jazz

Around 1920, jazz migrated from New Orleans to Chicago and New York, finding a new audience and branching off into several distinct styles, each still based on improvisation and strong rhythm. **Boogie-Woogie**, a style of piano playing combining repetitive bass patterns in the left hand with blues melodies in the right, arose in this period, as did **scat singing**, a style of jazz singing that uses nonsense syllables instead of lyrics and imitates the virtuoso flights of instrumental soloists. Among the well-known proponents of these new styles are the pianist Earl "Fatha" Hines, trumpeter Bix Beiderbecke, and the best-known jazz soloist of them all, Louis Armstrong. This was also the era of the great female blues singers, such as Ma Rainey and Bessie Smith. Because all of these artists flourished when the recording industry had already begun, many of their classic performances are still available on records.

The Big Bands

An extremely important development in both jazz and popular music was the rise of the big bands. Instead of the five or six instrumentalists in the standard jazz ensemble, the big bands had sixteen or twenty players, consisting of a reed section—four saxophones, usually doubling on clarinet—a brass section consisting of six or eight trumpets and trombones, and a rhythm section consisting of piano, guitar, bass, and drums. The best bands achieved a precision that made them as flexible as a smaller ensemble, but also had a much greater variety of color and a much wider dynamic range.

It is interesting to argue whether "jazz" is an appropriate term for many of these bands. Because mass improvisation with sixteen or twenty players is obviously impossible, some bands used "charts," arrangements that were worked out in detail but left some room for improvisation by a featured soloist. Other dance bands left nothing to chance and wrote out every note, thus eliminating all improvisation, which is the essence of jazz. Everyone agrees that the Count Basie bands played jazz, and so did the groups led by Benny Goodman, Woody

Caricature of band leader and clarinetist Benny Goodman.

Glenn Miller and his Orchestra.

Herman, and the Dorsey brothers. At the other extreme, Glen Gray, Guy Lombardo, and Glenn Miller played a kind of "sweet" popular music that no one would label jazz. In between these extremes, many bands are not as easy to classify, although some commentators would put most of them in the pop music, rather than the jazz, classification.

The big bands were very important in popular culture. They toured constantly, played for dances, appeared in musical movies, and sold great numbers of recordings. They provided steady employment for large numbers of instrumentalists and a start for most popular singers. Artists as diverse as Doris Day, Frank Sinatra, Billie Holliday, and Ella Fitzgerald began their careers as band singers, and many musicians ascribe their later success to the training and discipline of their years working with bands.

Popular Music

The period between 1920 and 1940 was a heyday for popular music. Great composers like George Gershwin, Cole Porter, Jerome Kern, Vincent Youmans, and Vernon Duke wrote popular songs, musical comedies, and material for the new movie musicals. On Tin Pan Alley, composers like Hoagy Carmichael and Sammy Fain added to the stream of great tunes. The phonograph, radio, and juke box brought the songs and singers to everyone in the country. Singers like Bing Crosby, Rudy Vallee, and Kate Smith began their careers as radio singers. Groups like the Mills Brothers and the Andrews Sisters were heard in millions of homes. Some radio shows were constructed entirely around hit tunes. *Your Hit Parade* was the first in a long line of radio and television shows that presented nothing but the "top ten" songs of the moment.

Hillbilly, or Country, Music

Two other developments in this period were important. "Hillbilly," or country, music reached a much larger audience also, thanks to radio and recordings. Artists like the Carter Family and Jimmie Rodgers, "the Father of Country Music," were broadcast all over the country. Their songs sound more like folk music than like the country music we are familiar with, because early groups played only acoustic instruments, but they began the country trend that exploded in later decades. *Grand Ole Opry*, a radio show featuring country music, was a big hit, and the first of numerous radio and television shows built around country artists.

Folk Music

During the thirties, folk music, featuring songs of protest, songs of the new union movement, and blues and protest songs of earlier days, first gained popular notice. Singers like Josh White, Woody Guthrie, and Burl Ives were the first wave of the folk movement that became much more important in popular music in later decades.

1940–1950

World War II

The most important event in America's social history during the forties was, of course, World War II. Just as popular culture celebrated World War I, World War II became the subject of numerous films, stage musicals, and popular songs. The films included heroic tales of action, with the inevitable volunteer patrols consisting of representatives of several ethnic groups, films about the USO and its efforts to entertain the troops, and films filled with sentimental scenes of parting, the tragic arrival of news of the hero's death in action, or tearful returns home. Among the songs popular during World War II were fighting songs like "We Did It Before" and "Praise the Lord and Pass the Ammunition," and sentimental ballads like "White Christmas," "You'll Never Know," "Sentimental Journey," and "I'll Never Walk Alone." Nonsense songs, for some reason, enjoyed great popularity during both wars. The nonsense hits of the forties included "Flat Foot Floogie," "Three Little Fishies," and "Mairzy Doats."

Jazz

In the forties, jazz took some interesting turns and started on its journey away from being mass appeal music to becoming an art music for an elite audience. A new type of small ensemble jazz emerged, called "bebop" or "bop," which was

Two leading proponents of bebop were saxophonist Charlie "Byrd" Parker and trumpeter Dizzy Gillespie.

characterized by a much lighter beat, faster tempos, complex chord patterns, and a rapid, swirling kind of melody line. Leading proponents of the new style included Dizzy Gillespie, Charlie "Bird" Parker, and Thelonius Monk. While dance bands became more popular, some bands, like Woody Herman's succession of "herds" and Stan Kenton's organization, played a more adventurous kind of big band jazz, featuring complex chord progressions, unusual instrumental colors, and creative melodic ideas. Both bop and the new big bands were moving in intellectually exciting directions, leaving simplicity and mass appeal behind.

Pop Artists

The forties featured solo singers, who became important stars in the growing recording industry. Their records sold in great numbers and were constantly heard on radio and jukeboxes. Bing Crosby became increasingly popular; "Accentuate the Positive" and "Swinging on a Star" were among the decade's greatest hits. His chief rival was a skinny young man named Frank Sinatra. He crooned ballads to crowds of bobbysoxers, who rivaled today's rock audiences in numbers and enthusiasm. Other male singers of the decade included Frankie

Laine, Perry Como, Billy Eckstine, and Nat "King" Cole. Cole was a fine jazz pianist but is better known as a crooner of ballads like "Mona Lisa." The female singers of the forties included Doris Day, Dinah Shore, Peggy Lee, and Sarah Vaughan.

Folk singers continued to carve out a portion of the popular audience. During the forties some clubs began to feature live folk music as the entertainment, and folk music could be heard more on the radio. Among the popular artists in this style were the Weavers and Oscar Brand. The most important folk singer of this time was Pete Seeger, the composer of two songs that became big folk hits in the sixties, "Where Have All the Flowers Gone" and "If I Had a Hammer."

Other important influences on the popular music scene at this time were musical comedy and the movies. Remember that the forties were the heyday of Rodgers and Hammerstein, whose hit songs moved from their stage contexts into the pop realm. Movies served to introduce both artists and songs.

1950–1960

The fifties were wonderful times for popular music. Postwar prosperity and the exodus to the suburbs created a great demand for leisure activities. The development of the long-playing record made record collecting much more convenient, and suddenly album sales soared toward the astronomical figures already reached by singles sales. Television provided another outlet for popular songs and artists, and created singing stars just as radio had. *Your Hit Parade* moved from radio to television; *American Bandstand* began its incredibly long run, emceed by the ageless Dick Clark; and television variety shows, like Ed Sullivan's and Arthur Godfrey's, featured popular singers and songs.

When the function of radio drama was taken over by television, radio stations turned to their present formats, playing a steady diet of hit records and news programs, and the disc jockey became an important force in the creation and dissemination of popular hits. So crucial was his position in making or breaking a new record that record companies began rewarding DJs under the table for pushing their products. The "payola" scandals of 1959 revealed the creative and costly methods used by promoters to persuade disc jockeys to play certain tunes on the air.

Singers

Among the pop singers who owe their initial fame to television are Dean Martin, Rosemary Clooney, Tony Bennett, Steve Lawrence and Eydie Gorme, Pat Boone, Andy Williams, and Wayne Newton. The new recording artists of the first half of the decade continued in earlier traditions. Johnny Mathis and Eddie Fisher were crooners in the Bing Crosby-Nat Cole mold. Teresa Brewer and Connie Francis were not much different from the girl singers of the forties. Some new recording artists were unusual, however. Les Paul and Mary Ford recorded complex guitar instrumentals through creative use of overdubbing and pioneered the use of a studio sound that could not be re-created in live performance. Johnnie Ray, who agonized through his recording, "Cry," was a good example of an overnight hit. Unfortunately for him, he disappeared after one or two recordings, as quickly as he had appeared.

Rock and Roll

The big news of the fifties was, of course, rock and roll. This important new style, eagerly absorbed by teenagers, and violently opposed by parents, was an outgrowth of rhythm and blues, which had been an exclusively black style of music until that time. Rhythm and blues songs were generally in the twelve-bar blues pattern, with simple harmonies and strong rhythmic underpinnings. The lyrics often consisted of not very subtle double entendres about sexual matters. The songs were recorded by specialized companies for the urban black market and were played on equally specialized small radio stations. Rock and roll was a slightly cleaned up white version of rhythm and blues, made commercial for the mass white audience. Crucial to its appeal was the energy and strong rhythm borrowed from the black style. The establishment opposition to this new wicked music, designed to undermine morality and Western civilization, also helped to make it popular. Bill Haley and the Comets, Fats Domino, Buddy Holly, and Jerry Lee Lewis were pioneers in this style.

The undisputed king of rock and roll was, of course, Elvis Presley, whose slicked-back hair, pouting expression, and stage acrobatics became the focus for both the adoration of his young fans and the opposition of parents, schools, and churches. Presley came to rock and roll through country music, and his performances illustrated clearly the influence of country music on rock and roll style. Presley sold millions and millions of records and became enormously wealthy. He went on to star in several films, in which he usually played more or less himself and always got the girl at the end. When Presley appeared on Ed Sullivan's television show, Sullivan insisted that Presley be shown only from the waist up, so that his pelvic gyrations would not upset the censors or outrage adult viewers.

Popular culture knows a bandwagon when it sees one. Scores of rock and roll movies were cranked out to capitalize on the new fad. In the seventies, nostalgia for the fifties produced television shows, like *Happy Days*, purporting to portray life in the fifties. The sound track and musical numbers faithfully recapture the sounds of early rock and roll.

Country and Western

Another strain of popular music changed greatly in the fifties. Hillbilly music became known as "country and western" and developed a more commercial sound, with amplified instruments and more sophisticated arrangements.

(Clockwise) Elvis Presley, king of rock and roll, Dave Brubeck, a leading jazz musician, and Johnny Cash, a popular country star.

Nashville became the capital of country recording and gathered a large group of talented studio musicians. The country stars of the fifties included Hank Snow, Eddie Arnold, and Johnny Cash. Throughout the era of rock and roll, and the rock of the sixties and seventies, country music went its own way, continuing to be enormously popular with a large segment of the country's population.

Jazz

Although jazz enjoyed some revival in the fifties with the Newport Jazz Festival and other such gatherings, it stayed pretty much out of the popular realm, which was taken over by rock. Jazz continued to move in specialized directions. Bop developed into "cool" jazz, created by superb musicians interested in creative expression rather than in mass appeal. The leading jazz musicians of the decade included Dave Brubeck, Gerry Mulligan, Miles Davis, and the Modern Jazz Quartet. The jazz of this period is fascinating to musicians. Sociologically, it was related to the intellectualism of the Beatnik movement. Performances combining cool jazz and poetry readings were popular in Beatnik coffeehouses of the day.

1960–1970

The sixties were a time of social revolution. The assasinations of John F. Kennedy, his brother Robert, and Martin Luther King, Jr., and the war in Viet Nam produced bewilderment, anger, and protests among the young and the black. The civil rights movement made hard-won advances in southern cities, fueled by voter registration drives, marches, and civil disobedience. Segments of the establishment condemned all militants and war protesters as drug-crazed hippies; but eventually, enough of the country turned against the war in Viet Nam to unseat Lyndon Johnson from the presidency and force the country out of the conflict. These social revolutions were naturally reflected in popular culture. Rock and folk music became the anthems of the young protesters, and a new awareness of black pride and black power led to a revival of rhythm and blues, "soul," and sweeping changes in the field of jazz.

Rock

An invasion of English groups started the American rock revolution. One of the most influential groups was, of course, the Beatles, who toured the United States in 1964, causing the same adulation among the young and disapproval among the establishment that Presley had caused earlier. Early Beatles tunes were not much different from rock and roll, but their lyrics were much more interesting than the mindless "Rock Around the Clock" type of the fifties. Genuine poetry and a new social consciousness emerged in their lyrics. Rock was the symbol of the disillusioned young in England much earlier than in the United States. Eventually, the Beatles experimented with unusual styles and innovations, like George Harrison's use of the Indian sitar. Finally they experimented with creative studio techniques, turning in their *Sergeant Pepper* album to a complex experimental style fascinating to musicians, but somewhat removed from the pop mainstream.

In 1964 The Beatles toured America and began the American rock revolution.

Perhaps more influential were the Rolling Stones, whose energy and anger were much more obvious and more upsetting to the establishment. The Stones are, of course, still performing, and their angry, nihilist stance makes the Beatles look quite tame in retrospect.

American rock bands began to proliferate in bewildering numbers, and several styles of rock branched out from the basic style. The Fillmore West in San Francisco featured bands like the Grateful Dead who played "acid rock" or "heavy metal," with the accent on "fuzzed" guitar sounds and incredible volume levels. Sixties rock was an uncompromising style, with very long numbers, intensely performed. It changed the music business. The emphasis in record sales shifted to albums rather than singles, and AM radio stations played little rock, because the tunes were too long. Rock groups produced albums in long studio sessions and then toured the country to promote the new product. Radio stations concentrated on more commercial "top forty" tunes in other styles. Rock festivals drew huge crowds and featured large numbers of groups. Of these, Woodstock was the most successful. Young rock fans idolized the stars, especially the few who burned out early and died young, like Janis Joplin and Jimi Hendrix.

Folk music became popular in the 1960's through artists like Joan Baez.

Folk Music

Folk music was also very much a part of the revolution of the sixties. Composed folk songs like Dylan's "The Times They Are A-Changin' " and true folk songs like "We Shall Overcome" were anthems of both the civil rights movement and the anti-war protests. Bob Dylan, Joan Baez, Joni Mitchell, Judy Collins, and Buffy Sainte-Marie performed to huge audiences and sold millions of albums to fans who viewed their songs as the expression of their own feelings.

Musically speaking, folk is totally different from rock. The emphasis is on the words, and the songs are generally rather simple, playable by amateurs at home, and usually accompanied by a single acoustic guitar. Although most of the folk stars were soloists, Peter, Paul, and Mary were a successful folk group. Simon and Garfunkel developed a successfully commercialized version of the folk style and broke into the top forty, AM radio, and film background music, with hits like "Scarborough Fair" and "Sounds of Silence."

Country Music

Things changed in other pop areas as well. Most pop artists moved into a rock-tinged style of some sort. Country music moved into the "Nashville sound," with electrified instruments and more involved arrangements, and reached a wider audience. Several country performers, like Roger Miller, Glen Campbell, and Kris Kristofferson, became pop stars. Country music invaded the top forty charts, and some AM radio stations began to play nothing but country hits.

Soul and Motown

The new black consciousness led to changes in black pop music. Old-fashioned rhythm and blues, from which rock and roll had sprung, was revived, and a new black style called "soul" emerged, as seen in the work of artists like Ray Charles, James Brown, Sam Cooke, and Aretha Franklin. A new style of commercial pop emerged around Detroit, called the "Motown Sound," exemplified by Diana Ross and the Supremes.

Jazz

Jazz moved in new directions also, and left the mass audience even farther behind. Artists like John Coltrane tried more complex and experimental styles. One school, searching for the African and Afro-Cuban roots of jazz, took on an angry, nationalist tinge, utilizing rhythms and sounds from the musics of Africa. The school called "free jazz" abandoned the tyranny of 4/4 rhythm and pre-arranged chord patterns, and relied on totally free group improvisation.

When soul music emerged in the 1960s stars like Aretha Franklin became popular.

1970–1980

The seventies were calmer and more individualistic than the sixties. The pop music scene was a jumble of continuing styles from earlier days plus new styles and artists.

Rock

Rock continued to move in several different directions at once. High-energy groups like the Rolling Stones continued to perform in much the same way they did in the sixties. Groups like Alice Cooper and Kiss moved into a bizarre, macabre style that was more theater than music. One hesitates even to try to classify someone like David Bowie. One widespread style is "soft rock," also called "middle-of-the-road" or "adult contemporary" music—rock without the noise, energy, or threat of some of the other styles. The Carpenters and the Captain and Tenille upset no one, nor do they seem to have the loyal followings of the more energetic rock styles. Late in the decade, punk rock and New Wave became the music of a new generation of young rebels. The style is deliberately crude musically, featuring simple chord patterns, narrow-range melodies sung in dull, flat voices, and robot-like movements. The instrumental backing usually consists of staccato chords and science-fiction sounds from a synthesizer.

The bizzare theatrics of groups like Kiss added a new dimension to rock music in the 1970s.

Disco

Disco became a very popular style. Its demise has often been proclaimed by derisive rock fans, but it continues to be successful. The disco sound is an interesting one, possible only in a studio. The main elements are a heavy beat in a fast 4/4 tempo, endless repetition of two or three musical ideas, and a heavy overlay of elaborate brass and string parts, accomplished through the recording studio technique of overdubbing. It is single-purpose music, of course, designed to accompany dancing, and is a good example of a style that has hardened into a successful formula with which no one wants to tamper.

Country Music

Country music continued to be a more and more important part of the pop market. Pop culture in the seventies adopted truckers as folk heroes, the apparent successors of the cowboy. Overnight, CB jargon and the world of the long-distance trucker became the subject of popular television shows. Country music is the popular music of this world, and country tunes about trucking began to appear on the charts. There is no end in sight for the new popularity of country music. Films, television shows, and popular music have adopted the trucker and the urban cowboy as major themes.

Fusion Styles

One interesting trend of the last decade is the fusion of different styles. One can hear jazz-rock, country rock, Latin rock, country pop, folk-rock, and various other combinations. The only prediction that seems safe, based on the recent history of popular music, is that all past trends will continue, and new trends and styles will spring up overnight, fueled by the media's fascination with the world of pop music. The new styles, if they are of any musical or sociological value, will carve their own place in the endlessly varied world of pop music.

This survey has been sketchy, mentioning only some major trends within the very complicated world of popular music and jazz. It remains now to look at a few examples from the worlds of jazz and pop to see how the music is created.

CLASSIC ENSEMBLE JAZZ: LOUIS ARMSTRONG AND HIS ALL-STARS, "BASIN STREET BLUES"

The first jazz recording to study in detail is a live recording of a 1956 concert by Louis Armstrong and his All-Stars. The rest of the personnel include Ed Hall on clarinet, Trummy Young on trombone, Billy Kyle on piano, Dale Jones on bass, and Barrett Deems on drums. Although the recording was made in the fifties, it is a typical example of small group jazz from the twenties or thirties. Armstrong was criticized by musicians (and loved by audiences) for not changing his style of playing as time went on. He continued to do what he did well and took seriously his role as a showman and entertainer. By the time of this recording, jazz had moved through bop into the cool and progressive styles, and jazz performers no longer considered themselves entertainers. One of the characteristics of pop music, however, has always been the simultaneous existence of different styles, the old ones persisting while new ones evolve. "Satchmo" Armstrong is revered as the best-known and best-loved proponent of classic jazz styles.

Louis Armstrong.

"Basin Street Blues"

Structures

"Basin Street Blues" is an old tune. Spencer Williams wrote it in the twenties, and it has been a jazz standard since. It is not in the traditional twelve-bar blues form. Rather, it consists of two parts, a verse made up of two similar eight-bar phrases and a chorus constructed the same way. The basic material, then, is simple and regular, with very traditional chord patterns. The point of classic jazz is to start with materials like this and improvise something unique and individual.

Organization

The general division of responsibility is as follows. The piano, bass, and drums are the **rhythm section**, providing a steady rhythmic and harmonic foundation over which the trumpet, clarinet, and trombone can weave their melodic patterns. Sometimes the rhythm section men become soloists—in this particular number, everyone gets his chance—in which case the horns play accompaniment to keep the rhythm and chord changes going.

This number is structured in typical jazz fashion. The entire ensemble plays at the beginning and end, and the middle choruses are a series of improvised solos by the various instruments. This number is more complex because of a tempo shift in the middle, but it still follows the basic outlines of standard jazz structure.

After Armstrong announces the number to the crowd in his inimitable fashion, the rhythm section plays a four-measure introduction of no particular distinction, setting the key and tempo. The ensemble plays the two phrases of the verse, with Armstrong's trumpet as the prominent instrument; everyone else is silent for the last two measures of each phrase. Then the group moves to the chorus, still playing as an ensemble with the trumpet leading; the trombone and clarinet play counter-melodies around and between the segments of the main trumpet melody. Next Armstrong sings a chorus in his gravelly voice; in the middle he abandons the lyrics and sings in scat style, using his voice like an instrument. The next chorus is given to Kyle's piano. Then a drum solo establishes a faster tempo. The ensemble plays a chorus in the new tempo. Note the quotation of "Jingle Bells" near the end of the ensemble chorus, bringing a laugh from the crowd. Then the clarinet has a chorus, followed by a chorus for bass, during which the trumpet and trombone play quiet chords, becoming the rhythm section for the moment. Then the trombone has a solo chorus; Young is a master of old-style, assertive trombone playing. Next, there are two ensemble choruses, wrapping everything up. The group moves into the second one as if one chorus were not enough to balance the long series of solo choruses. The drums have another eight-measure solo, and then the ensemble plays a short, busy closing. That sort of ending, with a short drum solo and the reentry of the ensemble, was traditional in early jazz styles. The music is fun, and the cumulative effect of the series of solos, followed by the whole group, is exciting. The listening guide (Figure 49-1) outlines the structure of the number.

FIGURE 49-1. LISTENING GUIDE

LISTENING GUIDE, "BASIN STREET BLUES," PLAYED BY LOUIS ARMSTRONG AND HIS ALL-STARS

Intro: Rhythm Section

Verse: Ensemble, Trumpet Lead _____

Chorus: Ensemble, Trumpet Lead _____

Chorus: Vocal _____

Chorus: Piano _____

Drum Solo

New Faster Tempo _____

Chorus: Ensemble, Trumpet Lead _____

Chorus: Clarinet _____

Chorus: Bass _____

Chorus: Trombone _____

Chorus: Ensemble _____

Chorus: Ensemble _____

Drum Solo _____ Ensemble Ending

BIG BAND JAZZ: DUKE ELLINGTON, "WILD MAN"

Duke Ellington

The example of big band jazz was recorded in 1962, at a studio date that combined the bands of Duke Ellington and Count Basie, two of the best of the big bands. This particular number, from Ellington's repertoire, features mostly Ellington's men, but some of Basie's soloists appear also and play along in the ensemble parts. The big bands added several new elements to small ensemble jazz: the arranger who wrote the ensemble sections, a larger number of virtuoso soloists, and the excitement that large reed and brass sections can generate. Ellington was a man of great creativity himself, and he gathered fine composer-arrangers like Billy Strayhorn, the composer of "Take the A Train." Because Ellington was successful for so long, he kept his personnel for unusually long periods and built an ensemble that played like one person. He provided ample room for good soloists, building in the improvisation that is the basis of jazz. He also wrote some numbers that have no improvisation, or very little, and some music that is symphonic in conception and scope. This particular tune is very much on the jazz side, with many improvised choruses, but also illustrates the unique ensemble sound of big bands and the unusual touches that marked Ellington's music.

"Wild Man"

"Wild Man" begins in an unusual way. The first thing we hear is a complex Latin or Afro-Cuban beat on drums played by hand and a tambourine. After the rhythm is established, a flute and clarinet play a simple, repetitive melody, with no accompaniment other than the percussion. Then there is a radical shift of rhythm. Within the same basic pulse, the complex Latin rhythm dissolves into a swinging jazz 4/4 tempo, and we are in the familiar territory of the twelve-bar blues. There are twelve choruses of this pattern, some of them played by ensemble and soloist in alternating phrases and some of them given entirely to soloists, accompanied only by the rhythm section. The first chorus is for muted trombone alone; the second, for saxophone and ensemble. Then there are sets of choruses in threes. Thad Jones plays a trumpet chorus, followed by a chorus by Cat Anderson on trumpet, and then a chorus for both, alternating. Anderson, in the joint chorus, throws in a quote from Chopin's "Minute Waltz." Then there are three saxophone choruses, the first by George Foster, the second by Paul Gonsalves, and the third shared by both. Next, there are two choruses for ensemble and soloists, in the relative minor of the main key. The first features Lawrence Brown on trombone, and the second features Cat Anderson again. After a return to the main key, there are two more choruses for Johnny Hodges's saxophone with the ensemble. Then the Latin beat returns, with the flute and clarinet. After a couple of those choruses, the beat continues for a while, then dissolves to a quiet ending, punctuated by a strange low note from Ellington at the piano. The listening guide (Figure 49-2) outlines the structure of "Wild Man."

FIGURE 49-2. LISTENING GUIDE

LISTENING GUIDE, "WILD MAN," PLAYED BY THE COMBINED BANDS OF DUKE ELLINGTON AND COUNT BASIE

Latin Section

Rhythm Intro

Chorus 1: Flute

Chorus 2: Clarinet and Flute

Medium Jazz Tempo, 12–Bar Blues

Chorus 1: Muted Trombone (Brown)

Chorus 2: Sax (Hodges) and Ensemble

Chorus 3: Trumpet (Jones)

Chorus 4: Trumpet (Anderson)

Chorus 5: Trumpets (Jones, Anderson)

Chorus 6: Sax (Foster)

Chorus 7: Sax (Gonsalves)

Chorus 8: Saxes (Foster, Gonsalves)

Chorus 9: Trombone (Brown) and Ensemble (Relative Minor)

Chorus 10: Trumpet (Anderson) and Ensemble Minor (Back to Main Key)

Chorus 11: Sax (Hodges) and Ensemble

Chorus 12: Sax (Hodges) and Ensemble

Return to Latin Section

Chorus 13: Flute and Clarinet

Chorus 14: Rhythm Continues, Dissolves

Tony Bennett.

THE POP SINGER: TONY BENNETT, "THE BEST IS YET TO COME"

Our example of the polished work of a good pop singer is a tune recorded by Tony Bennett in 1962, although the song, written by Carolyn Leigh and Cy Coleman, a musical comedy writing team, is older than that. The style is older also, and represents the style of the pop songs of the forties and fifties. Bennett is known mostly as a modern crooner. His best-known hit is "I Left My Heart in San Francisco." Bennett is a singer in the Sinatra mold. He has the band singer's sense of rhythm and respect for the lyrics.

"The Best Is Yet To Come"

The song is an interesting one. It moves in a comfortable, insinuating medium tempo, and the main melody has an interesting rhythmic structure that moves counter to the main beat. Figure 49-3 shows the rhythm of the first phrase of the

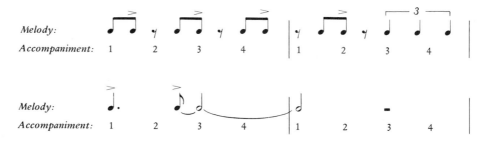

Figure 49-3. Rhythm of the first phrase of the main melody in "The Best Is Yet to Come."

main melody and the way it works against the basic pulse of the rhythm section. It avoids the usual A-A-B-A or A-B-A-C structure of most pop tunes and is pleasantly assymetrical.

Style

This performance is a fine example of a polished studio recording. Bennett does nothing fancy or personal to the song. The pop singer is different from the jazz soloist; the latter improvises something new, whereas the former presents the song literally, respecting the lyrics and melody as the composer wrote them.

The accompaniment is interesting also. The orchestra behind Bennett is an unidentified large studio group. Besides the rhythm section, brass, and reeds of a big jazz band, there is also a large string section. The accompaniment is arranged to create a long crescendo. The opening section is accompanied only by the bass and drums, and the other instruments come in gradually. The high sounds of the trumpet section are saved for the climactic part near the end of the piece. The band creates a pulsing, driving background, carefully arranged and controlled, over which the singer's voice can float. Some techniques of big band jazz are employed, but always in the service of the song, never for their own sake.

Structure

The song starts quietly, with a two-measure introduction by bass and drums. The first section is twelve measures long, consisting of three four-measure phrases, still backed by just bass and drums. The next section modulates up a major third and is sixteen measures (four phrases) long. The accompaniment becomes more complex: a guitar is added to the rhythm section; muted trombones play chords and answers to the vocal phrases; a string section plays sustained chords. The next section sounds like a varied version of the opening section, in the original key, but this time it consists of two phrases (eight measures) and brings the song to an apparent conclusion. A contrasting section with new melodic material then continues the ongoing crescendo, and the whole ensemble plays at full volume, including staccato chords of punctuation. The climactic sixteen-measure section follows, beginning with a version of the opening main melody, but this time in the relative minor. For the first time, we hear loud chords from the trumpet section, high in their range. The closing section returns to the opening phrases, with the rhythm section playing but with a muted trumpet embellishing the vocal phrases. The song could definitely end at that point, but Bennett and the muted trumpet begin the opening again and soon fade into silence. The fade ending is quite common in pop music. One assumes that this kind of ending is intended to make the listener continue the song in his head after the record fades. Figure 49-4 outlines the events in this fine pop performance.

Figure 49-4. LISTENING GUIDE

LISTENING GUIDE, "THE BEST IS YET TO COME," SUNG BY TONY BENNETT

Intro 2 bars

Bass, Drums

A: D^b major 12 bars

Voice, muted trumpet

Bass, Drums

B: F major 16 bars

add: Guitar, Strings, Trombones

A: D^b 8 bars

C: B^b 8 bars

Crescendo

A′: Main melody, B^b minor-G^b major-16 bars

Loud chords

A: D^b major 8 bars

Voice, Muted trumpet

Fade Ending

Chicago.

SIXTIES ROCK: CHICAGO

Just as it is impossible to convey a sense of the nearly infinite variety of styles within the world of pop music in one example, it is hardly fair to the complex world of rock styles to analyze only one example. This single example, however, illustrates several important facets of sixties rock: its base in social revolution, its seriousness of intent, and several prominent characteristics of the musical style of the time.

The group, first known as the Chicago Transit Authority, and later simply as Chicago, is one of the rock groups that expanded the guitar-dominated instrumental color to include horns. Another such group is Blood, Sweat, and Tears.

"Prologue" and "Someday"

Style

The rhythm of this number is a tight 4/4 with a strong, driving pulse maintained by the drums and electric bass. The phrases are all four measures long, creating familiar symmetry. The harmonic progressions, however, are unusual, and avoid the repetitive I-IV-V harmonies of rock and roll. Many rock groups utilize unusual chord progressions in this fashion. The singer is typical also. He sings high in his range, creating an urgent effect that matches the tone of the lyrics. Note, also, that he sings frequently just before the main beats played by the instruments. The lyrics are typical of sixties rock. They view the world as dissolving and call for a banding together of concerned people to create a counterforce and, presumably, a new and better world. This number is well constructed and skillfully performed. Its overall effect is not entertainment alone, but a strong statement about the condition of the world.

Organization

The tune opens with a tape of a protest outside the Democratic convention in Chicago in 1968. We hear a militant organizer exhorting the marchers to keep moving forward and then the chant, "The whole world is watching." Under the chant, the bass and drums enter, in time with the marchers' rhythm. Then the chant fades as guitar, piano, and horns enter and move into the introduction to the song.

The song itself consists of two verses of sixteen measures followed by an eight-measure chorus. The two verses have different lyrics but exactly the same melody. Each verse ends with the phrase, "Do you know what I mean?" After the first set of verses and refrain, there is another bit of the taped chant, then an instrumental interlude of eight measures, followed by another set of two verses and the refrain. The accompaniment patterns are exactly the same in the second set as in the first. The climax of the song comes in the second refrain, with an added double-time tambourine, when the lead singer moves to the extreme high end of his range. The second set of verses and refrain is followed by an instrumental coda, built on an ostinato begun by bass and drums and joined by the piano, guitar, and horns. The rhythm of this closing pattern is something like the Morse code sounds we associate with the beginnings of news broadcasts. Musically, the repeating bass pattern is part of a whole-tone scale.

The total effect of the number is strong and urgent, and illustrates the power of music to give voice to political ideas and feelings. The listener can sense how rock music of this sort was important to the counterculture. Figure 49-5 outlines the structure of the number.

FIGURE 49-5. LISTENING GUIDE

LISTENING GUIDE, "PROLOGUE" AND "SOMEDAY," BY CHICAGO

Tape of Chanting Pickets
Instrumental Introduction
Tempo Change (faster)
A (Verse): 16 Measures
A' (Verse, Same Melody, New Text): 16 Measures
B (Refrain): 8 Measures
   Tempo change (slower)
   Chanting Pickets
   8-Measure Instrumental Interlude
   Tempo Change (faster)
A'' (Verse): 16 Measures
A''' (Verse): 16 Measures
B (Refrain): 8 Measures
(Tambourine Added)
Coda: Ostinato, Crescendo

CONCLUSION

This chapter has provided a very sketchy survey of the complex and fascinating worlds of jazz and popular music. Many important stylistic trends and developments have been mentioned only briefly, or not at all. Scores of important jazz and popular artists have been omitted. Within this very brief survey, however, a few examples have been provided to illustrate how serious listening and analysis can be applied to music from these worlds. These types of music are built out of the same elements as any other type of music, and careful listening helps us understand their art and appeal. Critical listening adds to the enjoyment of any style of music; it focuses our attention on the actual music and helps us to develop informed tastes.

Popular music and jazz will obviously continue. It is easy to predict that new styles will evolve, that the strengths of earlier styles will be combined in new ways, and that new stars will arise, some of whom will last and some of whom will disappear as quickly as they arose. But great talent and creativity will always exist in the world of popular music and deserve our serious attention.

Glossary

absolute music   Music having no specific literary or pictorial reference: also called abstract music.

abstract music   See *absolute music*.

accent   A note or rhythmic pulse that is given special prominence, usually by being played more loudly.

acoustic guitar   A guitar whose sound is amplified by the soundbox, without the aid of electric amplification.

adagio   1. A tempo term, designating a slow tempo; 2. a movement or piece in this tempo, e.g. Barber's *Adagio for Strings*.

aleatoric music   See *chance music*.

allegro   A tempo term, indicating a fast tempo, or a movement in this tempo.

alto   The lower of the two female voices of a chorus, or the second highest instrument of a particular family.

alto clarinet   A larger size of clarinet, lower than the standard B flat or A clarinet, used in bands.

alto flute   A larger and lower size of flute.

anacrusis   See *upbeat*.

andante   A tempo term, indicating a moderately slow tempo, or a movement or piece in this tempo.

appoggiatura   A rhythmically strong dissonant note which then resolves to the expected consonant note.

aria   An operatic number for solo voice and orchestra; the term implies a complete musical form, which can be performed as a separate number in another context.

arpeggio   A series of pitches that outline a chord.

atonality   A musical system which has no tonal center; see Chapter 43.

back beat   A rhythmic style common in some styles of popular music, in which the second and fourth beats of each measure are strongly accented.

banjo   A string instrument used in some styles of folk and popular music.

ballett   A strongly rhythmic choral piece popular in Elizabethan England, related to dance music; see Chapter 10.

bar   Synonym for *measure* or metrical unit.

baritone   A type of male voice, between *tenor* and *bass*.

baryton   An instrument of the *viol* family, for which Haydn wrote some music.

bass   1. The lowest male voice, or bottom voice of a standard chorus; 2. the lowest instrument or line in any *ensemble* or instrumental family.

bass clarinet   A large, low clarinet, used in the expanded Romantic orchestra.

bass drum   A large drum of indefinite pitch, used in orchestras and bands.

basset horn   An obsolete alto version of the clarinet.

bass flute   The lowest instrument of the flute family.

bass guitar   A misnomer for the *electric bass* used in popular music.

basso buffo   Italian for "comic bass," a type of low male voice called for in many operas.

basso continuo   A Baroque bass line, usually played by a bass string instrument and a keyboard instrument to fill in the chords.

bassoon   The bass instrument of the double-reed group of the woodwind family.

beat   A rhythmic pulse.

bebop   A type of jazz characterized by involved melodic lines and complex rhythms.

blues   A type of American popular music, vocal and instrumental, marked by a twelve-bar structure and unusual notes not found in the standard diatonic scale.

bolero A complex Latin compound meter.

boogie-woogie A style of jazz piano playing; see Chapter 49.

brass A collective term for the family of orchestral instruments that have cup-shaped mouthpieces, including the trumpet, French horn, trombone, and tuba.

bridge 1. The piece of wood that supports the strings on a string instrument, and transmits their vibrations to the soundbox; 2. the middle or contrasting section of a popular song, the B in an AABA structure.

bugle A valveless member of the trumpet family, used to play standard military signals.

cadence A momentary or final conclusion at the end of a section or movement; cadences may be melodic, rhythmic, harmonic, or all three.

cadenza A section near the end of a concerto movement, when the orchestra rests, allowing the soloist opportunity for virtuoso display; see Chapter 24.

cantata A vocal form of the Baroque period, usually consisting of several movements, intended for religious use; see Chapter 14.

cantus firmus A preexisting melody, appearing usually in long notes in the tenor of a Renaissance Mass; by extension, use of a preexisting melody in long notes in other types of compositions.

cassation A generic term for light instrumental music of the Classical period.

castanets A percussion instrument consisting of two pieces of wood which are clapped together; they are used by Spanish dancers, and usually are used in orchestral music to create a Spanish flavor.

castrati Adult male sopranos and altos, traditionally used in leading roles in Italian Baroque opera.

cello The tenor instrument of the string family.

chamber music Music written for small *ensembles*, usually one player (or singer) to a part; see Chapter 21.

chance music Music in which the composer leaves some elements to the choice of the performer, e.g., by specifying melodic ideas but leaving their order and tempo to the players.

chanson A French Renaissance vocal piece, usually marked by strong rhythm and repeating sections.

chant A generic term for the monophonic repertory of medieval sacred music, or a piece in that style.

chapel The group of singers and instrumentalists employed by a Renaissance court or church.

choir 1. A vocal ensemble; 2. a family of instruments, used as a unit, for example, a brass choir.

chorale A German Protestant hymn tune.

chord A combination of notes, heard as a simultaneous unit.

chorus A vocal ensemble, or a piece written for a vocal ensemble.

chromatic Containing sharps and flats, as well as the notes of the diatonic scale.

clarinet A single-reed instrument of the woodwind family.

clavier A generic Baroque term for keyboard instruments.

clavichord A Baroque keyboard instrument, having strings which are struck rather than plucked.

coda In musical structure, a concluding section, outside the basic structure, which serves to add to the sense of finality.

codetta Diminutive of *coda*; a shorter concluding section.

composer control A characteristic of Western art music, meaning that the composer rather than the performer determines all elements of a musical work.

compound meter A subdivided, multi-level meter.

concertino The small group of soloists in a *concerto grosso*.

concertmaster The first chair violinist in

an orchestra.

concerto   A multimovement work for soloist and orchestra; see Chapter 24.

concerto grosso   A Baroque instrumental form for a small group of soloists and a string orchestra; see Chapter 15.

concert overture   A type of Romantic program music for orchestra.

consonance   That quality of chords that makes them sound restful or free of tension: opposite of *dissonance*.

consort   A set of like instruments in different sizes, such as a recorder consort.

continuo   Short for *basso continuo*.

contrabass clarinet   The largest size of clarinet, larger than the bass clarinet, used in bands.

contrabassoon   The largest and lowest double-reed instrument; the lowest instrument in the orchestra.

contrapuntal   The adjective form of *counterpoint*.

cornet   A smaller version of the trumpet, used mostly in military bands.

cornetto   An early brass instrument with a cup-shaped mouthpiece, but with a wooden tube.

counter-melody   A melodic idea that serves as background or counterpoint to the main melody.

counterpoint   Music consisting of two or more melodic lines, as opposed to a single melody and accompaniment.

countersubject   The continuation of the subject of a fugue in one voice, designed to work well with the entry of the subject in another voice.

crescendo   A gradual increase in volume.

cycle   A group of *Lieder* written and performed as a unit, consisting of settings of related poems.

cymbals   A percussion instrument consisting of two metal plates which are struck together, or struck with drumsticks.

da capo   "From the beginning"; indication that the first section is to be repeated, usually in an ABA form.

decrescendo   A gradual decrease in volume.

development   1. The process of manipu-

lating earlier thematic material; 2. the section of a sonata-allegro structure that comes after the exposition.

diatonic   Containing only the seven notes of the standard Western scale, without sharps or flats.

diminuendo   Synonym for *descrescendo*.

dissonance   The non-restful quality of some chords that demands resolution.

distortion   A recording effect caused by amplification at so loud a level that the musical sound is no longer true in pitch and tone quality.

divertimento   A generic term for court entertainment music of the Classic period; see Chapter 23.

dominant   In standard harmony, the fifth note of the diatonic scale, or the triad formed on that note; see Chapter 4.

dominant pedal   A sustained sounding of the dominant in the bass, which often occurs immediately before the recapitulation in sonata-allegro form.

double bass   The largest instrument of the string family, which functions as the bass voice of the string section.

double exposition   A modification of sonata-allegro structure common in the concerto, consisting of an orchestral exposition, followed by a second exposition played by the soloist; see Chapter 24.

double reeds   A category of woodwind instruments, in which the column of air is set in motion by the vibration of two exposed reeds.

double-stops   A technique of string bowing, in which two or more strings are bowed at once.

downbeat   The first or major pulse in a metrical unit or measure.

dramma giocosa   A term used by Mozart to designate opera that is neither comic nor serious in the usual sense; see Chapter 25.

dulcian   A Renaissance double-reed instrument, related to the later bassoon.

duple meter   Meter in which metrical units are divided into two pulses, or into multiples of two.

duration   An acoustic term for the length of time a musical note continues to sound.

dynamics Volume level, and changes in that level.

electric bass An amplified version of the double-bass, having a much smaller soundbox.

electric guitar An amplified version of the guitar, the primary instrument of rock music.

electric piano An amplified version of the piano.

electronic organ A version of the organ in which the various sounds are produced electronically rather than by pipes.

electronic music Music in which some of the sounds are produced by electronic means: see Chapter 46.

embouchure The proper position of the lips and muscles around the mouth for playing a wind instrument.

English horn The alto version of the oboe.

ensemble A performing group, vocal or instrumental.

episode A section of a fugue which contrasts with the exposition sections in texture and melodic material.

ethnomusicology A branch of the study of music which studies musics of other cultures.

étude A piece designed to help a student of an instrument develop proficiency in some specific technical area.

evaded cadence A cadence which sets up expectations that it will resolve in a particular way, and then resolves in a different way.

exposition 1. The first section of a sonata-allegro structure, consisting of two sections, one in the tonic, and the second in a related key, 2. a section of a fugue, consisting of successive entries of the subject.

expressionism An artistic movement of the twentieth century, concerned with depicting subjective reactions to outward reality, rather than the reality itself.

fantasia A piece marked by its improvisatory and free character, as opposed to symmetrical structure.

false recapitulation A deliberately deceptive reference to the first theme before the recapitulation actually begins in sonata-allegro form.

figured bass A Baroque bass line, containing numbers and symbols indicating the chord pattern.

final The main note of one of the church modes, roughly analogous to the tonic in tonal music.

finale The last movement of a multi-movement large work, such as a symphony.

fingerboard A long strip of wood on string instruments, against which the strings are pressed to change their pitch.

flugelhorn An alto version of the trumpet, used mostly in marching bands and popular music.

flutes One of the classes of woodwind instruments, in which the air column is set in motion by a carefully directed stream of air.

folk music 1. The traditional music of an ethnic group, passed on by oral tradition; 2. a type of popular music, marked by poetic lyrics, simple, folk-like melodies, and relatively simple accompaniment patterns.

form A synonym for *structure*; see Chapter 1.

forte A dynamic indication meaning "loud."

fortepiano A name for the early version of the piano, so named because, unlike the harpsichord, it was capable of some dynamic range and could play both loud (*forte*) and soft (*piano*).

fortissimo A dynamic indication meaning "very loud."

four-four time A common duple meter in Western art music.

four-voice imitation A polyphonic texture in which all the voices sing the same material.

French horn A brass instrument having a coiled body and a widely flaring bell.

frequency An acoustic term denoting the number of cycles per second of a particular note.

frottola A generic term for Italian vocal

pieces of the sixteenth century, in homophonic texture, with repeating sections.

fugato A section in fugal style within a composition that is not written in this style.

fugue A highly developed imitative counterpoint form, common during the Baroque era; see Chapter 13.

galliard A lively dance of the Renaissance period, usually in 6/8 meter.

gamba Short for *viola da gamba*.

gigue ("jig") A Baroque dance form in lively 6/8 meter, often used as the final movement of a sonata or Concerto.

glissando Sliding from one note to another, for example on the violin or trombone.

gongs A percussion instrument, consisting of a large metal disc.

Gregorian chant Synonym for *chant*; see Chapter 8.

half step Synonym for *semitone*; in the Western scale system, the distance between any note and the nearest possible note.

harmonic cadence A cadence in which the harmony moves from dissonant chords to consonant ones.

harmonic series An acoustic term for the several upper partials or overtones which are components of any musical sound.

harmony The chord progressions underlying a composition, or the study of chord progressions.

harp A large triangular plucked string instrument.

harpsichord A keyboard stringed instrument, whose strings are plucked rather than struck.

homophony A texture with one prominent melody, supported by accompaniment parts in other voices.

hymn A religious song with several stanzas sung to the same melody, intended for congregational singing.

horn Synonym for *French horn*.

idiom The concept of the appropriateness of music written for a particular instrument or voice, because of the particular abilities and strengths of that voice.

imitation The repetition in close succession of a melodic idea in different voices.

Impressionism A twentieth-century musical style marked by streams of non-functional chords and delicate instrumental colors; see Chapter 40.

improvisation The art of performing music spontaneously and freely, much more common in folk and popular music than in Western art music.

instrumental color A synonym for *timbre*; see Chapter 3.

internal cadences Temporary or partial resting places within a musical work, providing a pause without bringing the work to a complete end.

interval The distance between any two musical notes.

inversion Changing ascending intervals into descending ones and vice versa, so that a melody is presented upside down.

Janizary music Synonym for *Turkish music*.

jazz A type of American music of the twentieth century, marked by strong rhythm and improvisation; see Chapter 49.

key The main note or tonal center of a composition written in the standard Western harmonic system.

keyboard instruments Any instrument equipped with a series of keys played by the fingers; important keyboard instruments include the harpsichord, piano, organ, and synthesizer.

kinesthetic sense The sense of movement, which is involved in our perception and enjoyment of music.

krummhorn A Renaissance wind instrument, having a capped double reed.

largo A tempo term, meaning "very slow."

legato To be played without any separation between notes; opposite of *staccato*.

leitmotif A melodic idea associated with a particular idea, character, or event; see Chapter 37.

lento A tempo term, meaning "slow."

libretto The text of an opera or other vocal composition, usually written by a different person than the composer.

Lied (pl. *Lieder*) A German song, usually referring to the song literature of the Romantic period; see Chapters 34, 35.

lute A Renaissance plucked string instrument, similar to the guitar in tuning and playing technique.

madrigal The major secular vocal form of the Renaissance, especially popular in Italy.

maestro di capella The Italian term for the music director and composer of a major court or church.

major scale A diatonic scale with a half-step between the third and fourth notes, and whole steps between all other notes.

major triad A triad consisting of a major third and a fifth above the bottom note.

mandolin A plucked string instrument used chiefly in folk and country music.

marimba A percussion instrument of definite pitch, related to the xylophone.

Mass 1. The main liturgical ceremony of the Catholic church; 2. a polyphonic setting for chorus of the Ordinary parts of the Mass—Kyrie, Gloria, Sanctus, and Agnus Dei.

measure A metrical unit, marked off by bar lines; synonym of *bar*.

melisma A group of notes sung on one syllable.

melismatic chant A chant marked by the presence of many melismas.

melodic cadence A cadence in which the melodic line comes to rest.

melodic curve The contour of a melody.

melody A series of pitches, heard as a coherent unit.

meter A fixed pattern of time units or beats.

metronome A mechanical device used to mark tempos accurately.

mezzo-forte A dynamic indication meaning "somewhat loud."

mezzo-piano A dynamic indication meaning "somewhat soft."

mezzo-soprano A type of female voice, halfway in range between soprano and alto.

minor scale A diatonic scale with a half-step between the second and third notes; there are three varieties of minor scale in use in Western music.

minstrel shows A type of entertainment popular early in the twentieth century; see Chapter 49.

minuet A stylized dance form of the Classic period, commonly used for the third movement of a symphony.

mode One of the eight scale patterns in use in music of the Middle Ages and Renaissance, before the emergence of tonality and major and minor modes.

moderato A tempo indication meaning somewhere between *andante* and *allegro*.

monophony Music consisting of a single unaccompanied melodic line.

monothematic Having one theme.

motet An important type of Renaissance sacred polyphony, generally based on four-voice imitation of phrases of preexisting chant.

motet style Four-voice imitation in a piece other than a motet.

motive A short recognizable figure that recurs throughout a composition; the shortest identifiable melodic unit.

mouthpiece A fitting on a wind instrument to facilitate blowing into it.

movement A complete musical piece that forms one of the independent sections of a larger work, such as a symphony, concerto, or suite.

Musique Concrète A school of electronic composition which uses sound material from various sources as its basic material.

mute A device attached to or inserted in an instrument to lower its volume or change its color.

nationalism The use of musical ideas associated with a particular country or region, an important aim of Romantic music.

neoclassicism The use in twentieth-century music of ideas, styles, or forms from Baroque or Classic music, or the school of composers who championed these ideas.

neume In chant notation, a figure that signifies a cluster of notes.

note A single musical sound.

notation A system for writing musical ideas down on paper.

oboe The soprano instrument of the double-reed class.

octave The interval between any note and its duplicate eight notes away.

opera A dramatic presentation in which music is the main element, written for soloists, chorus, and orchestra; see Chapters 25, 36, 37, 44.

opera buffa A type of Baroque and Classical comic opera, with everyday characters, stock comic characters, spoken dialogue, and happy endings.

opera seria A type of Baroque and Classical opera with mythological plots, opportunities for virtuoso singing, and no spoken dialogue.

operetta A musical dramatic presentation of light and sentimental character.

oratorio A large concert piece for soloists, chorus, and orchestra, usually with a Biblical plot; see Chapter 16.

orchestration The art of arranging music for a specific instrumental group.

organ A large keyboard instrument, consisting of several sets of pipes activated by the player's hands or feet, or producing its sounds electronically.

ostinato A clearly defined musical unit persistently repeated.

orchestra A standard instrumental group, consisting of strings, woodwinds, brasses, and percussion.

overdubbing A recording technique which combines tracks recorded at different times into a combined finished product.

overlapped cadence A cadence in which three voices come to rest while a fourth begins a new idea, a common technique in Renaissance polyphony.

overtone One of the upper partials which are components of any musical sound.

overture An instrumental composition written as an introduction to an opera or similar work.

paired imitation A Renaissance technique of varying a four-voice choral texture by using the voices in pairs.

pan-diatonicism The use of the diatonic scale without its traditional harmonic implications.

pan-tonality The potential use of any note of the chromatic scale as a temporary tonal center; sometimes used as a synonym for atonality.

paraphrase style A synonym for *motet style*.

passacaglia A Baroque form based on continuous variation over an ostinato bass.

passion An oratorio-like setting of one of the Gospel accounts of the suffering and death of Christ.

pavane A Renaissance dance form in moderate 4/4 meter.

pedal A long-held note, usually in the bass; see *dominant pedal*.

percussion instruments One of the families of orchestral instruments, consisting of instruments that are struck rather than bowed or blown into, such as drums, cymbals, etc.

phrase A division of a musical idea, analogous to a clause in prose.

pianissimo A dynamic indication meaning "very soft."

piano 1. The well-known keyboard instrument; 2. a dynamic indication meaning "soft."

pianoforte 1. An older term for the *piano*; 2. another name for the *fortepiano*.

Picardy third A major third used in the last chord of a piece in a minor key.

piccolo The smallest instrument of the flute family.

pickup See *upbeat*.

pipe organ A keyboard instrument which produces sound by routing air through specific ranks of pipes.

pitch The quality of highness or lowness of a musical sound.

pizzicato A term indicating that string

players are to pluck the strings rather than bowing them, or the resulting effect.

polyphony Music having several simultaneous independent voices, in contrast to *monophony* and *homophony*.

polytonality A system of composing using two or more simultaneous tonal centers.

prelude 1. A piece written to precede some other event; 2. in Baroque music, a free, improvisatory piece, often paired with a more regular structure, such as a *fugue*.

première The first performance, or first performance in a particular area, of a musical work.

presto A tempo indication, meaning "extremely fast."

program music Music that intentionally refers to a story, picture, mood, or idea.

program symphony A multimovement work of orchestral program music, such as the "Faust" Symphony of Liszt.

quartet 1. Any piece of music intended for four players or singers; 2. sometimes used as a short form of *string quartet*.

quintet 1. Any piece of music intended for five players or singers; 2. in chamber music, a piece for a string quartet plus an additional instrument, such as a piano or woodwind.

ragtime A type of early jazz; see Chapter 49.

range 1. The span of pitches possible to perform on a particular instrument (or voice); 2. the span of pitches utilized by a composer in a particular work.

recapitulation The final section in a sonata-allegro form, when the material from the exposition returns, now entirely in the tonic key.

recitative A section of music for voice or instrumental solo, without regular meter.

recorder A Renaissance and Baroque instrument, related to the flute, but with a mouthpiece and held straight in front of the player.

reed A piece of cane or other material used to activate the column of air inside some woodwind instruments.

refrain In vocal music, a recurring section with the same text and music, which is sung between sections of new text.

resolution The passage from dissonance to consonance; dissonant chords are said to "resolve" in certain ways at cadences.

rest A silence of specified duration in the course of a musical line, or the notation sign which indicates such a pause.

retrograde A technique of manipulating a melody in such a way that it appears backwards.

retrograde inversion Manipulation of a melody combining inversion and retrograde, so that the melody is presented upside down and backwards; retrograde and retrograde inversion are two of the possible forms of the row or series in twelve-tone composition.

rhythm A general term for all the temporal events in music—that is, their arrangement in time.

rhythm section In jazz, the supporting chordal and rhythm instruments (such as piano, bass, and drums) that keep the rhythm and chord patterns going under the solo melodic contributions of the other players.

rhythmic cadence A cadence formed by slowing down the rhythmic motion.

ricercar A Renaissance instrumental piece in four-voice imitation or motet style, the forerunner of the *fugue*.

ritornello In Baroque music, a recurring instrumental section that returns between solo sections.

ritornello form The characteristic form of *concerto grosso* first movements; see Chapter 15.

rondo A standard form, consisting of alternation between one section which repeats and a series of contrasting sections.

row The arrangement of all twelve

pitches chosen as the basis for a twelve-tone composition; see Chapters 39, 43.

rubato A flexible approach to tempo and rhythmic details, necessary in some styles.

sackbut A Renaissance brass instrument related to the later trombone.

saxophone A single reed instrument, used mostly in bands and popular music.

scale An arrangement of usable pitches.

scat singing A type of singing in jazz, marked by imitation of virtuoso solo instruments and nonsense syllables.

scherzo A rollicking type of music in ternary meter; Romantic composers often substituted a scherzo for the Classical *minuet* and trio as the third movement of a symphony.

score Complete notation of large ensemble music, containing the parts for all instruments.

semitone Synonym for *half-step*.

sequence Repetition of a short melodic unit at a different pitch.

serenade A type of light instrumental music written during the Classical period; see Chapter 23.

serialism Synonym for twelve-tone composition, or later extensions into other elements besides pitch; see Chapters 39 and 43.

shawm A Renaissance wind instrument, having a double reed.

siciliano A Baroque dance form, marked by moderate tempo, 6/8 meter, and a lyrical melody with dotted rhythms.

single reeds One of the classes of woodwind instruments, which use one reed attached to a mouthpiece as the means for setting the air column in motion; included in this category are the clarinet and saxophone.

Singspiel A German comic opera with spoken dialogue between musical numbers.

six-eight time A common compound meter, in which the measure is divided into two major units, each of which is subdivided into three smaller parts.

snare drum A small drum used in the orchestra, bands, and popular music.

sonata A multimovement form for solo piano or for another instrument with piano accompaniment.

sonata-allegro form The standard form for the first movement of Classical and Romantic symphonies, concertos, and sonatas; see Chapter 19.

sonata da camera A type of Baroque sonata, consisting of several binary dance movements.

sonata da chiesa A type of Baroque sonata, consisting of four movements (slow-fast-slow-fast).

song cycle See *cycle*.

soprano The highest female voice; the highest voice in a standard chorus.

sound box The large wooden portion of a string instrument, whose function is to amplify the sound.

sousaphone A type of tuba, constructed so that the tubing coils around the player and the bell faces forward, used in marching bands.

split four The common meter of rock music, consisting of four pulses, each divided into two even divisions.

Sprechstimme ("speech-song") A type of voice production halfway between song and speech used by composers of the Expressionistic school.

staccato An instruction to players to play a melody in detached fashion; opposite of *legato*.

stanza In songs, one poetic unit; all the stanzas are usually set to similar music.

step The interval between most notes of the diatonic scale; a step is the sum of two half-steps.

stops The mechanisms by which an organist controls which ranks of pipes will be used.

stretto In fugal writing, imitation of the subject in close succession, usually near the end of the fugue.

strings The family of instruments whose sound is produced by the vibration of bowed or plucked strings.

string quartet A very common chamber music group, consisting of two violins, a viola, and a cello.

strophic Used of songs, meaning that each verse of the poetry is set to the same music; opposite of *through-composed*.

structure Synonym for *form*; the element of music that deals with the organization and logic of the arrangement of the musical materials.

style The identifying characteristics of music of a particular time, place, and genre, resulting from the decisions about how each of the elements will be treated; see Chapter 5.

subject The main melodic idea which keeps recurring in a fugue.

suite 1. Light orchestral music consisting of a number of binary dance movements; 2. an arrangement for orchestra of important tunes from an opera, ballet, etc.

swing A type of big band jazz and popular music of the thirties and forties; see Chapter 49.

symphonic poem A type of Romantic program music for orchestra in one movement.

symphony A large work for orchestra; one of the major forms of the Classical and Romantic periods.

synthesizer An electronic instrument equipped with a keyboard.

tempo The speed of a composition or a section.

tenor The highest male voice; in a chorus, the second line from the bottom.

ternary form Another name for ABA form; see Chapter 4.

texture A term used to classify music on the basis of the way the voices relate to one another.

thematic transformation A technique of varying recurring material so that it has a different significance because of the different musical context; a favorite technique of Liszt; see Chapter 32.

theme A musical idea that is the basis for a composition.

theme and variations A musical structure which consists of the basic material presented first in straightforward

fashion and then subjected to various changes.

through-composed Made up not of repeating sections, but of a continuous series of new musical ideas; used of a song, the opposite of *strophic*.

timbre The distinct quality of a particular musical sound, separate from pitch, duration, and volume, resulting from the acoustic properties of that sound.

toccata A Baroque term for a free, improvisatory piece, often paired with a fugue.

tonal center Another term for the tonic or main note in tonal harmony.

tonality Another name for the harmonic system in use in Western art music from about 1700 until about 1900.

tonic The first or key note of the diatonic scale, or the chord constructed on that note.

transition Material within a musical structure that functions not as thematic material, but rather as connective material between major sections.

transverse flute A Baroque term for a flute held sideways to the player, as opposed to the related recorder.

tremolo A Romantic string effect, consisting of very rapid bow strokes on the same note.

triad A basic harmonic unit in Western music, consisting of the bottom note, a third above it, and a fifth above it.

triangle A percussion instrument consisting of a small metal bar bent into a triangle shape, struck by another piece of metal.

trill Rapid alternation of two neighboring notes, often used in a cadential pattern.

trio 1. A musical piece written for three players; 2. the contrasting middle section of a minuet movement or a march.

trio sonata A standard Baroque form, written for two violins and *basso continuo*.

triple meter A metrical pattern in which the pulses or beats are arranged in sets of three.

trombone A tenor brass instrument equipped with a slide for changing the pitch, used in both orchestras and bands.

trumpet The highest of the brass instruments, used in both orchestra and bands.

tuba The bass instrument of the brass section.

Turkish music A type of Classical period music associated with Turkish subjects, using unusual percussion.

twelve-tone method A system of composing music without relying on tonal harmony, developed by Schoenberg; see Chapters 39, 43.

tympani Synonym for kettledrums, hemispherical drums of definite pitch which are an important percussion instrument of the orchestra.

unison The simultaneous playing of the same note or melody by several instruments, either at the same pitch or the distance of an octave.

upbeat The beat immediately before the first or major pulsation of a measure; synonym for *anacrusis* and *pickup*.

variation A restatement of musical material that keeps some elements of the first appearance and changes others.

valves On brass instruments, devices that reroute the air stream through extra tubing, thus changing the pitch of the instrument.

vibraphone A percussion instrument of definite pitch, similar to the *marimba* but with greater sustaining quality.

villancico A Spanish poetic and musical form of the Renaissance, marked by strong rhythms and repeating sections.

viol A family of string instruments in use from the sixteenth to the eighteenth century, with a darker, less brilliant sound than the violin family.

viola The alto member of the violin family, tuned a fifth lower than the violin.

viola da gamba A generic term for one class of *viols*, held between the player's knees.

violin The highest member of the string family.

violoncello The older, formal name for the *cello*.

violino piccolo An obsolete, slightly smaller version of the violin, sometimes called for in compositions by Bach.

virginals A small, table-top version of the harpsichord, popular as a home instrument in Elizabethan England.

voice 1. The mechanism for producing singing; 2. one of the lines in a contrapuntal texture, whether sung or played by instruments.

waltz A dance form in 3/4 meter.

whole step Synonym for the interval of a *tone*.

whole-tone scale A scale consisting entirely of whole tones, therefore having no implication of a tonal center, used by Impressionistic composers to blur the sense of harmonic direction; see Chapter 40.

woodwinds A major family of orchestral instruments, including the flute, oboe, clarinet, and bassoon.

word-painting The expression through musical means of the ideas of the text of vocal music.

xylophone A percussion instrument of definite pitch, consisting of tuned wooden bars which are struck with mallets.

Index

Strouse), 414
Byrd, William, 106
Byron, Lord, 252

Cabaret (Kander and Ebb), 403,
    408, 413
Cadence, 55–56
    evaded, 56
    final, 55
    internal, 55
    overlapped, 100
Cadenza, 153, 190, 225–226
Cage, John, 397
Call Me Madam (Berlin), 412
Camelot (Lerner and Loewe),
    405, 413
Campbell, Glen, 440
Campion, Thomas, 106
Cantata, 126, 131
    Bach's, 139
Cantata No. 140, "Wachet auf,
    uns ruft die Stimme,"
    140–147
Canticum Sacrum
    (Stravinsky), 362
Cantor, Eddie, 428
Cantus firmus style, 101, 141
Capitol building, 178
Captain and Tenille, 441
Caravaggio, 122, 178
Carissimi, Giaccomo, 157
Carlos, Walter, 130
Carmichael, Hoagy, 431
Carnival (Schumann), 316
Carousel (Rodgers and
    Hammerstein), 413
Carpenters, The, 441
Carter Family, 432
Cash, Johnny, 436
Cassation, 216
Castanets, 36, 254
Castrati, 126, 130, 192
Cathedrals, as cultural centers
    in Middle Ages, 73
Cello, 34
Cervantes, Miguel de, 121
Chabrier, Emanuel
    Espana, 254
Chamber music
    in Baroque period, 131
    in Classical period, 190–191,
        200, 202
    in Romantic period, 257
Chamber orchestra, 184
Champion, Gower, 404
Chance music, 349–350
Chandos Anthems (Handel), 157
Change, as characteristic of
    popular music, 422–423
Channing, Carol, 406, 408
Chanson, 86, 104

Chants, 49, 59, 79, 82–83, 93–98
    as major Western monophonic
        art music, 93
    composition of, 93–94
    early rhythmic practice of,
        94–95
    forms of, 94
Chapels, in Renaissance courts,
    76
Charles, Ray, 440
Chaucer, Geoffrey, 73
Chávez, Carlos, 388
    Sinfonia India, 388
Chiaroscuro, 122
Chicago, 451–452
Chinese scales, 254
Chopin, Frédéric, 262, 303–307
    life of, 303–304
    music of, 304–305
    Polonaise in A-Flat, 306–307
Choral music, 85–87
Chorale preludes, 139
Chords, 52
Chorus
    "For Unto Us A Child Is Born,"
        as example of, 160–163
    in cantata, 147
Chorus Line, 351
Chromaticism, 373, 374
Church instruments, 110
Church music
    in Middle Ages, 74
    performers of, in Baroque
        period, 125–126
"Ci darem la mano, La," 234
Cinderella stories, as theme in
    musical theater, 407–408
Claire de Lune (Debussy), 356
Clarinet, 27, 183
Clark, Dick, 434
Classical music, 13–14
Classical orchestra, 183–184
Classical period, 176–192
    aesthetic of, 178–180
    architecture, 178
    definition of, 176
    formation of USA in, 176–178
    literature of, 178
    music of, 180–192
    politics during, 176
    romantic influences during,
        179
    style of music of, 185–187
    visual arts of, 178
Clavier, 137
Clemenza di Tito, La (Mozart),
    192, 232
Cliburn, Van, 257
Clooney, Rosemary, 434
Cocteau, Jean, 360
Coda, 132, 189

Codetta, 132
Cohan, George M., 411, 412,
    428–429
Cole, Nat "King," 434
Coleman, Cy, 448
Coleridge, Samuel Taylor, 253
Collaborative effort, of musical
    theater productions,
    404–405
Collins, Judy, 12, 439
Color, 24–25
    impressionist, 355
    in Baroque style, 127
    in *Composition for
        Synthesizer*, 396, 397
    in "Let it be," 63
    in *Tristan und Isolde*, 65
Coltrane, John, 440
Columbia-Princeton Electronic
    Music Center, 396
Comden, Betty, 413
Coming Home, 341
Commercials, 18
Community, and music, 6
Como, Perry, 434
Company (Sondheim), 408,
    415, 419
Composer control, 14
Composers
    Baroque, 124
    Classical, 180, 187
    Elizabethan, 106
    in Middle Ages, 79
    Renaissance, 80, 110
    twentieth century, 350, 352
Composer's music, 10, 14
Composition for Synthesizer
    (Babbitt), 396
Concertino, 150
Concertmaster, 150
Concerto for Orchestra (Bartók),
    369–371
Concerto in E-flat Major
    (Liszt), 297
Concertos, 165, 189–190, 260,
    262, 350
    Mozart's piano, 223–228
Concerto grosso, 127, 131, 166
    Brandenburg Concertos as
        example of, 149–150
Concord Sonata (Ives), 387
Conductors, 184
Connecticut Yankee, A (Rodgers
    and Hart), 413
Consonance, 56, 347
Consorts, 89
Constitution, 176
Consul, The (Menotti), 388
Contrabass clarinet, 27
Contrabassoon, 29
Contrapuntal technique, 137,

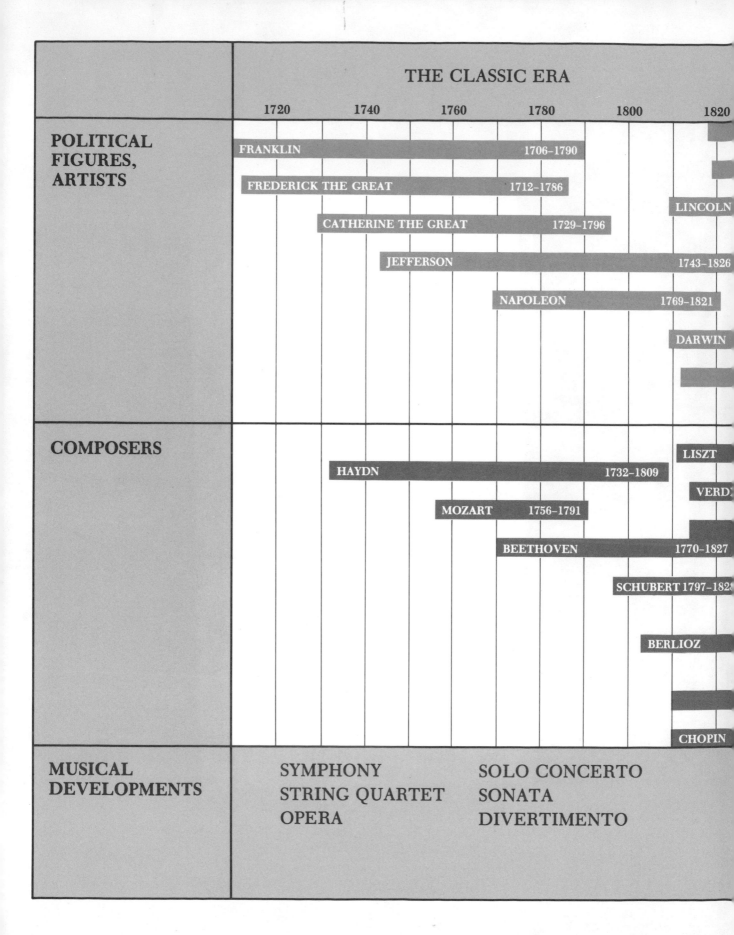

THE CLASSIC ERA

	1720	1740	1760	1780	1800	1820

POLITICAL FIGURES, ARTISTS

FRANKLIN 1706–1790

FREDERICK THE GREAT 1712–1786

CATHERINE THE GREAT 1729–1796

JEFFERSON 1743–1826

NAPOLEON 1769–1821

LINCOLN

DARWIN

COMPOSERS

HAYDN 1732–1809

MOZART 1756–1791

BEETHOVEN 1770–1827

SCHUBERT 1797–1828

LISZT

VERDI

BERLIOZ

CHOPIN

MUSICAL DEVELOPMENTS

SYMPHONY   SOLO CONCERTO
STRING QUARTET SONATA
OPERA   DIVERTIMENTO